CAMPER'S
digest

First Edition

CECIL COFFEY
Author

BILL WALLACE
Editor

Associate Editor
Sheldon Factor

Art Editor
Art McGuire

Editorial Assistant
Patricia Wallace

FOLLETT PUBLISHING COMPANY — CHICAGO/NEW YORK

Library of Congress catalog card number 73-102640   ISBN 0 695-80092-2

Printed in U.S.A.

Cecil Coffey, author of CAMPER'S DIGEST

Born and reared in Western North Carolina (Leicester, near Asheville) in the shadow of the Great Smokies and Pisgah National Forest. Adventure in the outdoors has been second nature since childhood.

Background to CAMPER'S DIGEST

"During the past five years I have camped or closely observed camping from Newfoundland to the deserts of the Southwest. This includes all of the provinces of Canada and 48 states (plus Hawaii at an earlier date). Some of the camping has been under "plush" conditions. Much has not. For example, my 12-year-old son and I camped two years ago in remote areas of national forests in Montana and New Mexico largely by "improvising" — just to see how we might manage. We survived and enjoyed it."

"Although I love the outdoors and have pursued outdoor interests in an avocation sense, I researched and wrote CAMPER'S DIGEST as a journalist. Unlike most camping books which show one man's preferences, CAMPER'S DIGEST is what the name implies — a digest of diverse techniques and camping approaches. In addition to my own observations and experiences, the book reflects information and assistance from more than 600 helpful sources."

Other related activities include a five-year stint as chief book editor, Southern Publishing Association, Nashville, Tenn.; public relations counsel to hospitals and related agencies; co-founder of *Outdoor World* magazine (published in Atlanta) and its first editorial director. Presently devoting full time to free lance writing, mostly books, much of it in the outdoor field. CAMPER'S DIGEST is his sixth book. Two more are in production.

Bill Wallace, editor of CAMPER'S DIGEST

Bill Wallace, editor of Camper's Digest, has had many years' experience in the outdoor field. Has camped, fished and hunted throughout the U.S., Canada and Mexico. As a free lance outdoor writer has contributed articles to outdoor publications and is currently Consulting Editor of Fishing & Hunting Guide Magazine. In addition he works as a design consultant for outdoor products used in camping, boating, fishing and hunting activities. He lives in Chicago, but also owns a ranch in the Stillwater Valley in Montana.

Table of Contents

One day . . .

One day the wind changes.

It's a little warmer, not blowing as fast, there are only a few gusts, but they are gentle. It carries with it the scent of open water, of fallow fields, of earth-rich woodlands.

Then you notice.

The crocus, the hyacinth are breaking open the soil near the house and in the garden plot. The ice spots have vanished.

Somewhere in the distance, from the next block or from across the tracks drifts a faint, familiar chortle, repeated, then silence.

Soon the leaden gray skies will thin out, lift and vanish.

Then the good, vital feeling will return to men. The call will come quietly at first . . . but in a few days it will be as strong and compelling as the life drive of which it is a part.

People everywhere throughout our still luxuriously beautiful land will awaken and respond.

It's time...

Camping is good for man.

Each year thousands more are discovering the benefits of living for awhile, close to forests, rivers, lakes, mountains; of hiking, exploring, cooking, sleeping in the open, of walking in sunshine, breathing clean, clear air.

Camping is growing at a fabulous rate for several reasons. First it is a type of vacation that appeals to all members of young and growing families, to to people of all ages, single or married. And second, it is economical.

It is estimated that a family of two adults and two children would need about $30 per day for all expenses on the average camping trip staying at public campgrounds. The same family would need $60 to $80 per day if they stayed at hotels, motels or resorts and ate in restaurants.

These are probably the two main reasons, but there are others. The governing officials of large cities across the U.S. continually boast of the beauty and greatness of their massive urban complexes. Somehow the citizens are not in agreement.

If you would like to see an expression of this disagreement, park or stand near a main road leading into a state or U.S. highway on a summer Friday afternoon or Saturday morning. Autos with trailers, boats, car top carriers; station wagons, motor homes will be lined up bumper to bumper straining to get away. You would think the city was on fire.

This exodus takes place because the city is polluted. The atmosphere is filled with smoke, the streets and sidewalks are covered with trash and litter and the air is filled with shreiking sirens, screams, racing motors and motorcycles, howling masses of people tormented by other people, and their own inability to cope with a hostile environment.

There is no relief in the public municipal parks and beaches because they are polluted and overcrowded too. By noon each day of any given weekend the parks are a mess, strewn with partly eaten hot dog buns, papers, ice cream sticks, bottles and newspapers . . . a crowd of pushed, harassed and unhappy people.

Those who have discovered camping have the answer.

They run . . .

. . . as far from the city as they can. To the hills, to the backwoods, isolated lakes . . . to peace, to the stillness that makes them whole and human again. They look out from a mountain top and know once more that the world *is* good and that there *is* meaning to life.

Camper's Digest has been researched, written and produced to encourage camping in general, and to make camping a pleasure for everyone involved, beginners and veterans alike.

Any digest on camping today must include both the old and the new. Experienced campers, rugged individualists still enjoy roughing it, but welcome new innovations in equipment and food, information about new wilderness areas and other mountains to conquer. They will find this in Camper's Digest.

Beginners or those who would like to start, need information about the various types of camping, the basics about food, clothing, shelter and safety, about the right equipment, costs, where to go, and when. All this is included in Camper's Digest.

The author and editor welcome you to these pages and wish you happy camping days and peaceful nights around a crackling campfire.

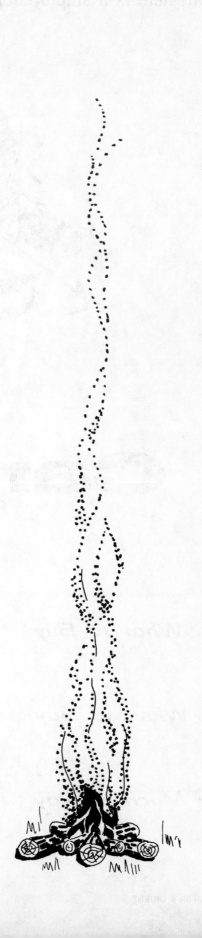

For those who haven't camped before and/or haven't purchased any gear, here is a step-by-step guide to the practical side of camping.

Camp Gear

What to Buy

When to Buy

How Much to Pay

Planning the trip

Once you decide to go camping, the first step is to begin planning. Planning begins with budget. How much can you spend? This will determine how far you can go, how long you can stay and what mode of camping you can undertake. These three factors may be juggled a bit; for example, you can go in better style and can stay longer if your travel distance is cut.

In most cases, a short camping trip, both in distance and in time, is best for a first experience. It is a kind of shakedown cruise. It helps you to adapt to camping, reveals flaws in your plans and procedures and provides the experience you need for longer and more complicated trips.

In arriving at a logical and practical budget, many factors must be considered. The total anticipated cost will vary with each family and in each locality, as well as with the kind of camping contemplated. On the average, a camping trip will cost about one-third of the amount necessary to travel via the motel-restaurant route.

Study areas

Planning the camping trip should begin with a study of the areas you would like to visit. A postcard to the headquarters office of a national forest or a national park will bring to you camping information, illustrated brochures and maps of these areas. The same holds for state parks. It is wise to write for this information one or two months in advance of your projected camping trip.

Study the materials, note the descriptions of the various camping sites and determine which would be the most attractive to your family. Pay particular attention to the convenience and comfort facilities provided so that you will not have to take any unnecessary equipment and supplies.

It also is well to study popular camping directories which list information about campgrounds. Such publications should be taken along in the event the campground you have chosen has a "Full" sign hanging out and you have to make a quick adjustment to another site.

Better to rent

Meanwhile, visit retail establishments that sell camping gear and supplies and learn if any of these rent equipment. An easy way to enter your first camping experience is to rent a tent trailer or a travel trailer. Usually these will come supplied with most housekeeping facilities and all you will have to provide are such items as food, clothes, linens, first aid materials and entertainment items.

Naturally this is costlier than the more rugged types of camping, but it may be worth it.

By renting the basic equipment, you can determine exactly what this major budget item will cost. Because most of the large items are self-contained in the trailer, your car will have more room for the other items. This will enable you to take along all of the foods your family most enjoys. In a sense, you will feel that you have merely transported your home to the outdoors.

To sum up, planning the trip includes the following steps: determining the amount you can spend, selecting the campsite location, settling on the dates of departure and return, renting or buying the basic camping equipment, listing the kinds of foods and quantities you wish to take and listing other items which might come in handy. When you feel your planning is complete and the big day approaches, follow your plans to the letter and then head for sure adventure.

Renting equipment

It can't be too strongly recommended that new campers beg, borrow or rent camping equipment. The wide variety of attractive equipment offered in retail showrooms will tempt any camper—novice or veteran—to buy something on the spot. But you as a beginner should resist that temptation, unless there is no other way to acquire what you need.

For one thing, you may discover that much of the equipment used on your first camping trip is not suitable for your family. This borders on disaster if you have shelled out hundreds or thousands of dollars for something entirely undesirable.

When deciding on equipment, you must take into account the kind of camping experience anticipated, the size of your family, the ages of the children, the financial outlay, convenience factors, and available storage space.

Try a "dry run" camp

If you are totally unfamiliar with camping equipment, take a dry run by setting up a camp in the back yard or in a local park, and by reading all the instruction sheets accompanying the equipment.

It may be that a camping club in your community or an organization such as the YMCA conducts classes in camping techniques. By all means attend such a class if you can. These will introduce you to outdoor cooking considerably beyond that which you do on the back patio, and will give you understanding of the outdoors environment. Incidentally, such courses and also the trial runs not only will save you headaches when you camp, but will enable you to leave a lot of unnecessary items behind.

What to take

You need a shelter. It can be a tent, a tent trailer, a travel trailer, a pickup camper or a motor home. Each has its advantages and you may wish to experiment with more than one.

If you are renting or buying a tent, look for these features when making your selection:

1. Roominess. Be sure the tent will accommodate the entire family comfortably. If there is a question, choose one that is larger than you really need. Extra room can always be used, but

These traveling families find modern conveniences of the travel trailer and coach camper to their liking as they stop for a time in the Grand Tetons.

inadequate space can ruin a good camping trip.

Probably the three most popular tent designs are wall tents, cabin tents (a variation of the wall tent) and umbrella tents. Those with outside aluminum frames are the easiest to erect. Most highwall tents and cabin tents will accommodate large families, and umbrella tents usually are adequate for four to six persons.

2. Quality. Inspect the fabric. The best tents are made of specially treated, lightweight fabrics such as Palina cloth or poplin, or heavier army duck. Drill is popular, though not as durable for frequent year-after-year use. Better tents have double stitched seams.

Door openings should have zippers that will completely close the opening (do not buy a tent that doesn't have a zipper across the bottom threshold). Window flaps should have inside zippers. Insist on a raised threshold, the higher the better. This makes the tent more waterproof.

Many new campers prefer sleeping off the ground, as this family is doing in its tent trailer at Lake Glendale Campground, Shawnee National Forest, Illinois.

3. Other features. Most good quality tents preferred by family campers have outside frame suspensions with no inside poles to obstruct the interior. A minimum of guy ropes are used on the outside. The best frames are made of annodized aluminum. These won't rust or corrode. A wellmade tent not only will feature double seams but these seams, folded before sewing, are also strengthened at corners and other points of strain by extra sewing or by grommets.

4. Costs. The quality of the tent almost always can be measured by the price tag. A family-size tent made to last for many years will cost $100 or more.

The camper trailer

The camper trailer—sometimes called tent camper or popup convertible—is simply a plush tenting arrangement. It offers all the thrills of tent camping, but with off-the-ground comfort. It takes only a matter of minutes to set up, with the beds ready for sleeping.

Most any kind of terrain is suitable for the camper trailer—if you can drive there. The popular models will sleep as many as eight and some have provision for tent or screened room attachments. When buying or renting a camper trailer, consider these features:

1. It is a vehicle as well as a camping home. Its construction, type of suspension and other automotive features are just as important to the camper as are the desired quality features in a tent. It must meet legal and operative standards on the highway.

2. The camper trailer is versatile. It can be left at a campsite while you drive to some nearby or distant attraction. It allows a full rear view of the road when driving and is easy to tow with the family car. In addition to these features, it offers many home conveniences in a camping setting.

3. It is the least expensive of the recreational vehicles. Prices generally range from $400 to $2,000, depending on size, equipment and construction extras.

The truck camper

As the name implies, this is a truck on which has been mounted—temporarily or permanently—a living unit that may have all the features of a modest-size travel trailer or motor home. Many campers prefer these for weekend excursions, for hunting and fishing trips and for general cross-country travel.

There is slight inconvenience if the family is large and some have to ride in the back. Also, it is neccessary to transport the whole camping package anytime the vehicle moves. The two most important features

to look for in selecting a truck camper are the construction qualities and the inside arrangements.

The travel trailer

The travel trailer may be anything from a small unit to a large self-contained trailer home. It meets the legal requirements for towing by automobile and it has the general construction features of a mobile home. Again, the main features to look for are construction qualities and inside arrangements.

The motor home

The motor home is the latest recreational vehicle to become popular. It is a mobile home facility built onto the frame of a truck or bus. It is quite plush and may cost as much as $25,000 or more. The minimotor home is an economy version which meets the needs of many camping families.

Camping menus

Simplicity is the key word in preparing successful meals in camp. This doesn't mean you have to eat out of a can or have half-cooked or greasy food. To the contrary, by proper planning you can come up with some of the most tempting dishes your family has ever enjoyed.

The dishes should not only be simple but the menus as well. You can always elaborate a bit if there is enough time or if you feel like it. For the most part, you can provide the same basic foods you provide at home.

You may wish to try some of the many "dry" dishes available at your camping supply dealer. But remember that the family has been out of doors, has been quite active. You will be surprised to see them eating two or three times as much as they normally do at home, particularly at breakfast.

1. Breakfast. This meal can be quickly prepared. Instant dry or hot cereals, pancake mixes, fruit juices, eggs and potatoes are easy to prepare at campsite. So is toast, in a simple camp oven or on top of the stove in French style.

2. Lunch. There is nothing wrong with sandwiches and soup for lunch. Canned items such as baked beans,

Any good home cook can perform as well while camping with a kitchen unit such as this one designed by American Plywood Association. Plans are available free from American Plywood Association, 1119 A Street, Tacoma, Washington 98401.

chili, spaghetti or stew may be quickly prepared. There is so much activity going on, the family will appreciate a quick and simple lunch, particularly if the evening meal offers more.

3. Supper. The evening meal should be eaten early and chances are your family will be ready for it by 5 o'clock. This can be the most delightful meal of the day. Even a potluck stew goes well in the evening. Some canned vegetables may be added to the menu, but how nice it is if you bring along fresh sweet corn on the cob and some lettuce or other leafy vegetables.

Instant mashed or hash brown potatoes go well with such a meal, but your family will never forget potatoes baked directly in the hot coals of a campfire or wrapped in foil. If you possibly can, prepare the family's favorite main dish. By a little improvising, you can broil, fry, bake, stew or steam.

Remember to take along enough food of all kinds for two or three days, if you plan to stay that long. If you plan to stay longer, you will need to locate a store where you can purchase fresh milk and other perishables.

In packing food items at home, use plastic as much as possible. Avoid taking glass to camp. Covered plastic containers, plastic bags, aluminum foil, wax paper all come in handy at the camp kitchen. Take along paper and plastic items: plates, cups and forks, knives and spoons. Do as little dishwashing as possible. Cups designed for hot drinks may be used for soup as well.

Cooking, dining conveniences

In camp you must have something to cook on, utensils to cook with and eat with, containers for food and beverages. Here are some recommended items:

1. Camp stoves. The two basic types of camp stoves are those that burn white gas and those equipped with propane cylinders. Propane stoves are becoming more popular because they light instantly and need no pumping or priming. They are safe and clean, not unlike cooking at home. They are a little more costly to operate. Gas stoves burn inexpensive white gas. Both types of stoves usually have two or more burners, the more popular family style having three. The stoves fold up like suitcases for easy carrying. Accessories include folding camp

ovens, toasters and griddles.

2. Cooking sets. Many family campers have come to prefer the no-scour, no-stick convenience of Teflon-coated pots and pans. These include frying pans, various size pots and plastic cups and dishes—all nesting into one bucket.

For the first camping experience, however, an old frying pan, a couple of buckets and two or three pots will indicate to you whether you need more and different utensils, which is good to know before purchasing an expensive set.

3. Coolers. Ice chests and insulated jugs are necessary for the average family campout. Foam-insulated ice chests are considered "musts" by many campers. Insulated jugs will keep beverages hot or cold up to 72 hours.

Ice sometimes will last for 48 hours or longer. It is a good idea to take along additional plastic water jugs or bags, especially when you are not certain of an adequate or clean water supply.

4. Chairs and tables. Campers do not have to dine uncomfortably. Most improved campsites provide tables and benches. But what if the family wishes to stop enroute for an outdoor meal? Whether in camp or on the way, it is a good idea to have handy one or more folding tables and enough camp stools for the entire group. Some folding tables seat up to ten persons. The better ones are made of aluminum which won't rust or corrode. Incidentally, they may also be used at home or on a picnic at a nearby park.

Sleeping gear

If you camp in a tent, your sleeping gear likely will be a suitable sleeping bag placed on a folding cot or an air mattress. Camper vehicles contain the basic sleeping gear and all you have to add are sheets and blankets.

In selecting a sleeping bag it is important to consider weather conditions in the area you plan to camp. The warmest sleeping bags are made of goose down and running a close second are those made of duck down or multi-layers of bonded polyester

fiberfill. Do not purchase a sleeping bag that does not have a tag clearly indicating the kind of fill. Here are some features to look for in sleeping bags:

1. Insulation. Insulation materials should be adequate for the climate you anticipate. If you are planning all kinds of camping under all weather conditions at all seasons of the year, naturally you will wish to buy the best insulated bag. There are ways of ventilating it if the weather is hot.

2. Construction. The zipper should be strong and durable and should have enough material overlapping so that it will not let in cold air. Gasket-type weather stripping inserted on both sides of the zipper will seal out cold drafts and will prevent the zipper from coming in direct contact with the sleeping camper.

3. Size. There are different sizes of sleeping bags to fit people of various proportions. The king-size sleeping bag will normally measure 85 by 40 inches, the next size 80 by 34, the next, 75 by 34, and a fourth size, 67 by 34. The sleeping bag shouldn't be too large, but obviously it must not be too small. When in doubt, get the larger size.

4. Cots and air mattresses. Modern camp cots are made of strong, lightweight aluminum frames and stretch canvas or duck covers. These may be stacked double-decker style and will provide comfort similar to the bed at home.

Army cots made of canvas and wood are still popular, though heavier than those made of aluminum. Additional insulation between the canvas and the sleeper will keep the cold from creeping through, particularly if he is not using a sleeping bag.

A good air mattress, of course, is important to the camper whether he sleeps on a cot or on the tent floor. It should be large enough for comfort and it should have separate valves for inflating the body part and the pillow part. The outer edges are larger than the center sections to provide comfort and reduce "roll off." The strongest and most durable material for these is rubberized

nylon.

Some are made of rubberized cotton or rayon and these are adequate for the occasional camper. Foam pads are becoming increasing popular for use as mattresses, and before making a purchase you should investigate these as well.

Other accessories

In addition to the basics already discussed, campers need to have plenty of lighting. Favored are lanterns which burn propane, gas or kerosene (coal oil). Propane lanterns instantly deliver light power equal to a 100-watt or even a 200-watt bulb. Gas lanterns will burn eight to 12 hours on two pints of economical white gasoline. Carrying cases and lantern hangers are available.

It is very important that each camper be equipped with a flashlight (preferably waterproofed) and that an extra supply of batteries be taken along.

Tent campers and tent-trailer campers appreciate the modern tent heater which provides safe, flameless heat for as much as 18 to 20 hours without refilling. These are called catalytic heaters. Various sizes are available that deliver up to 8,000 BTU's. Other types of heaters are less expensive and generally satisfactory.

Other items to be taken along may include portable sinks, portable toilets and, of course, camping tools. Camping tools are always handy and the basic ones are shovels, axes and knives.

Finally, there are the miscellaneous needs such as a first aid kit, insecticides, a compass, backpacks if you plan to hike, at least one complete change of clothing for each member of the family and such luxuries as you can crowd in.

_____ Tent
_____ Camping (tent) trailer
_____ Pickup camper
_____ Travel trailer
_____ Motor home
    SLEEPING GEAR
_____ Sleeping bags
_____ Camp cots
_____ Air mattresses or foam-rubber pads
_____ Extra blankets
_____ Sheets or sleeping bag liners
_____ Pillows

Modern sleeping bags provide clean, warm and comfortable bedding for first-time campers.

DINING NEEDS
- ____ Camp stoves
- ____ Extra fuel
- ____ Portable oven
- ____ Cookwear (including frying pan)
- ____ Ice chest
- ____ Insulated jugs
- ____ Portable sink or large dishwashing pan
- ____ Folding table
- ____ Folding chairs
- ____ Plates, knives, forks, spoons, cups, etc.
- ____ Serving knives, forks, etc.
- ____ Measuring cups and spoons
- ____ Napkins, paper towels
- ____ Tablecloth
- ____ Dish towels, sponge, dishcloth
- ____ Can and bottle opener
- ____ Scouring pads
- ____ Soap
- ____ Detergent
- ____ Aluminum foil
- ____ Wax paper
- ____ Plastic bags
- ____ Pot holders or asbestos gloves

FOOD
- ____ Basics for three meals per day (mostly from your home pantry and refrigerator)
- ____ Spices and seasonings
- ____ One extra (surprise) item for each day

Note: List (itemize) simple foods most enjoyed by your family. Then follow list in packing.

CLOTHING
- ____ Two or more complete changes—pants, shirts, underwear, shoes, socks—for each camper
- ____ Extra socks
- ____ Handkerchiefs
- ____ Sweaters
- ____ Jackets
- ____ Waterproof footgear
- ____ Ponchos or raincoats
- ____ Adequate headgear
- ____ Extra shoe laces

TOOLS
- ____ Ax
- ____ Knife
- ____ Shovel
- ____ File and whetstone
- ____ Nails
- ____ Stout cord
- ____ Soft wire
- ____ Pliers
- ____ Screwdrivers
- ____ Sewing kit
- ____ Camp saw

OTHER ESSENTIALS
- ____ Lantern
- ____ Bath towels
- ____ Face cloths
- ____ Metal mirror
- ____ Small washbasin
- ____ Plastic water bucket
- ____ Personal toilet articles
- ____ Flashlights (one for each camper), extra batteries and bulbs
- ____ Matches (in waterproof container)
- ____ Clothesline and clothespins
- ____ Time piece
- ____ Toilet tissue
- ____ First aid kit and Red Cross First Aid manual
- ____ Insect repellent
- ____ Tarpaulins
- ____ Large sheets of plastic or other waterproof sheets for various uses
- ____ Snakebite kit (may be part of first aid kit)

OPTIONAL ITEMS
- ____ Folding toilet seat
- ____ Small broom
- ____ Lighter and lighter fuel
- ____ Oilcloth for camp table (washable and durable)
- ____ Portable radio, TV
- ____ Compass and maps
- ____ Books
- ____ Games and recreation gear
- ____ Toys
- ____ Dining canopy (screened if desired)
- ____ Fire starters (dry tinder, etc.)
- ____ Pre-cut firewood
- ____ Cameras and film
- ____ Swimwear
- ____ Packsack for hiking

You won't take all items listed, of course, and there may be others that you will wish to add to the list.

Have fun
Generally, camping and the activities associated with it will provide about all the amusement a family will need. But there are times when something "extra" will add to the enjoyment of camping. For certain, every member of the family will appreciate having something interesting to do if bad weather sets in.

Children will find fun quickly. They will run and jump and get dirty, and they should be permitted to do this within the confines of certain regulations and if they avoid disturbing other campers. If hiking or swimming are part of the camping schedule, don't be concerned about finding more fun for the members of the party, regardless of their ages. After a day of such activity, they will be ready to settle down quietly—and rest.

Games, crafts
But for the quiet times, which every camping family must have, take along some crafts for the youngsters, a variety of books that fit the reading preferences of all members of the family and some simple games that can be played indoors. Many campers enjoy napping while listening to good music on the radio. Others like to read. Some might even enjoy keeping a camp diary. Generally, any quiet-time activity that is popular at home will be popular at camp.

Games of identification are popular, both enroute and at camp. Challenging the campers to keep a list of the animals or trees or flowers seen in the vicinity can bring a lot of fun. The small fry may enjoy drawing pictures of what they observe about camp. And, of course, they always appreciate a good story.

For $1, you can purchase from the Rand Manufacturing Company, 3323 South Dye Road, Flint Michigan 48507, a helpful book called **Travel and Camping Fun Book.** It will keep the kids busy for hours and provide some fun for Mom and Dad as well.

Whatever you do when you camp, have fun. Don't permit the weather, the inconveniences, the new sounds to bug you. Determine to have fun, and you will.

Tent Camping – Comfortable Economical Peaceful

To the confirmed tenter, a simple canvas shelter is symbolic of a pioneer past. Further, a tent is economical. A good one will last a lifetime if it is properly cared for. And a camper, fed up with noise and overcrowded conditions sometimes prevalent at popular camping spots, may quickly and easily transport his tent shelter to a more secluded area of his own choosing. This is one reason many motor campers keep a reliable tent handy.

Tents are the oldest form of man-made shelters. Skins of animals, cloth, canvas and bark and boughs of trees have been used as tent materials. The word, "tent," comes from the French word, *tente*, which in turn comes from the Latin *tentus*. It literally means canvas stretched.

Many types

At least 200 styles of tents are in use, and more are being designed

Tents set-up just about anywhere, provide headquarters for family activities . . . give highly adequate shelter, yet fit in with natural surroundings.

every year. New materials appear on the market from time to time. Nylon, for example, has become an important fabric in the manufacture of better quality tents. New methods of construction and new accessory gear have contributed greatly to tent improvement in recent years.

But several of the older fabrics and design features continue in popularity and serviceability. Duck, drill and poplin are among the older fabrics still widely used. And the wall tent,

frequently in modified form, is more popular than ever. There is not much chance that these older, proven and tested fabrics and styles will become obsolete.

Tents vary in size, shape and price. Price nearly always determines the quality. If in doubt, compare prices of tents offered in the size and style you prefer. Five or ten dollars won't make much difference, if any, but beware of a $39.95 "bargain" if the same size and style of tent is also offered for

$79.50. This is not to say that the $39.95 tent is worthless, but it won't provide the longlasting service and economy that you can expect from the more expensive tent.

Advance knowledge

Fortunately, the people who sell and service the better camping gear are, for the most part, knowledgeable and reputable. They will explain clearly the poor, good and best features to look for in a tent. You should, however, be knowledgeable to some degree before you go shopping for your camping shelter. Some protection is offered through a government requirement that all tents carry an attached label identifying the kind of fabric used in their manufacture.

But there is more to selecting the proper tent for your needs than to recognize quality in fabrics and manufacturing methods, important though these be. The first consideration should be given to style.

Which type?

Style or design is determined largely by the kind of camping you intend to do. If it is a family vacation at an improved campground, your tent selection will be one of several designed for semipermanent camping; if you plan to backpack into a wilderness area, your tent will be entirely different.

When you shop for your tent, you will quickly discover that tastes vary, and if you seek advice from other tent campers, you will get a variety of recommendations. Outfitters and sales people in sporting goods stores will offer varying advice. There is nothing wrong with this; it actually gives you better opportunity to exercise your own wise and independent judgment.

After all, *your* kind of camping will be different because the combination of factors affecting your decisions are different. It is just as important to shop carefully for a tent as it is to shop for the right suit of clothes.

Most popular

Here are descriptions of the more popular and most useful tent styles for all camping occasions:

The wall tent. When you mention wall tent in some circles, you will get a quick assertion that this tent has just about disappeared, that it is no longer popular. Veteran campers will disagree and will quickly tell you of their undying love for the the wall tent. And they will point to its continued usefulness in many camping situations, particularly in semipermanent wilderness camps.

It is true that the standard wall tent—the one minus a sewed-in floor and designed for rigging with nature's materials found at the campsite—is not often chosen for family use, but its modern variations are. The old-fashioned wall tent more likely will

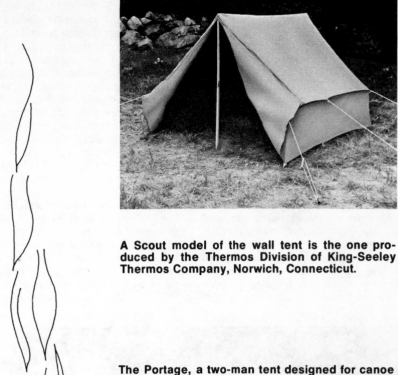

A Scout model of the wall tent is the one produced by the Thermos Division of King-Seeley Thermos Company, Norwich, Connecticut.

The Portage, a two-man tent designed for canoe trips. By Hirsch-Weis.

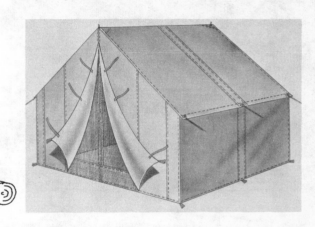

The H. Wenzel Tent and Duck Company of St. Louis, Missouri, makes this standard two-man Forester wall tent.

be seen in use where permanent wood floors and sometimes sides are provided for its annual use on the same spot. Youth camps make use of this arrangement. Forest workers still use wall tents, and so do many military units.

Size choice

The wall-tent style comes in a wide variety of sizes. Its best housekeeping feature is its usable space—both floor space and headroom. It is heavy and bulky to transport, but this is hardly a problem if the camping gear is moved by car, boat or pack train. The wall tent is favored by pack train operators and others who transport equipment and supplies into primitive areas for groups of campers.

Wall tents are easy to heat in cold weather, and the better ones are adequately ventilated for hot weather comfort. Camp furniture may be con-

by sewing a doubled strip of tent material to the outside ridge of the tent, then sewing or riveting special tapes or rope ties to the doubled ridge. These are tied to an outside ridgepole, thereby eliminating the necessity of the ridgepole running inside the tent from end to end. Either way, there is a good deal of work involved. But there is satisfaction, too.

Standard rigging

Basically, a standard wall tent is best rigged by first lashing together two poles a foot or two from the top, then separating them at the bottom just enough so when stood upright, they follow the roof line to an anchor point on the ground. A set of two poles so rigged is placed at either end of the tent. The ridgepole, holding the crest of the roof either from the inside or by outside ties, is rested in the top "V's" of the crossed support poles.

framework provides for the suspension of the tent from outside supports.

Look first

By all means, don't run to your nearest wall tent dealer in a sudden urge to camp like the pioneers or weathered outdoorsmen until you have observed the basic wall tent firsthand. One of the best examples, incidentally, is the wall tent used by the military services.

Regardless of the reservations you likely hold now, sooner or later as you become a seasoned camper, you will seriously consider acquiring or improvising a wall tent for certain semi-permanent camping. Even on your first tent purchase, you may select a more modern adaptation of the old standby wall tent. You may, for example, settle for a cottage tent.

The cottage tent. The sign or the advertisement may call them bunga-

The Thunderbird Patio Camper by Wenzel is a shelter made to order for vacation camping of several days to several weeks duration.

veniently arranged inside, indeed not unlike a room arrangement at home. A clothes hanger may be suspended from the ridgepole near the rear, and a lantern may be hung near the center. Sleeping gear, cots or sleeping bags may be placed along the sides, and other furnishings may be arranged to provide plenty of walking room.

As you may have guessed, the standard wall tent is not easy to erect and therefore is not ideal for an overnight stop. Some suspension methods make the task less difficult, but many professionals still prefer to follow the original methods of cutting ridgepoles, side poles and front and rear cross-poles.

The favorite trick is to use what is called a tape ridge rigging. This is made

The ridgepole is lashed to the support poles at this point and the rigging is made steady by the use of strong guy ropes. Sometimes additional poles are lashed to the shears, as the crossed poles are called, and the tent eaves (where the roof ends and the walls begin) are tied to these. This eliminates the need for eave-anchoring guy ropes.

Chances are that any wall tent camping which you do will not require all of this. Ropes may be substituted for poles, but seldom is this procedure as satisfactory. It is possible to purchase an aluminum framework for wall tents which calls for the tent to be draped over the framework after it is assembled and erected. Another type of

lows, cabin tents or a term associated with a specific brand name. There are numerous styles of cottage tents, and most have one feature in common: they are large. This is why the cottage tent is preferred by larger families and by groups. The popular models have sewed-in floors, the walls are high and are well ventilated and, if desired, can be purchased with provision for side rooms or an enclosed, screened canopy attached to the entrance area.

Needless to say, cabin tents for families or groups are heavy and bulky. But this is not a problem when there are two or more persons knowledgeable in setting them up. Erecting a cottage tent is not done in a hurry,

but two persons can do an adequate job in 15 or 20 minutes.

It is important that enough guy ropes and stakes be used and that these be firmly anchored or tied in case of storm. Don't hesitate to add guy lines if you doubt the tent's stability. A large tent naturally is more susceptible to high winds. It pays to remember this.

Today's modern cottage tent may have two or three rooms, a screened "porch," an under-roof cooking area with bugproof netting and other desirable features. For a family outing of a week or more, it comes close to the ideal in most respects.

The umbrella tent. This tent is the most popular tent style, mainly for two very basic reasons: it is easy to transport, and it is easy to erect. It also provides good headroom and walk-around room. The most popular models are those with inside or outside suspension frames. These eliminate the center pole which for years was the main support for the umbrella tent. The inside-frame, poleless model is somewhat heavier and is more costly.

The outside umbrella frames have some convenience advantages, but you must go outside to loosen guy ropes during a storm.

Some campers feel that the older, center-pole model is still best because it is easy to erect, may be adjusted more satisfactorily during a rain and serves another useful purpose by being a divider for interior arrangements.

Further, it is a good place for a clothes hanger, a small table unit or nails for hanging cameras or other gear carried by straps. Anything that gets gear and supplies off the floor is always helpful in a crowded tent situation, particularly during spells of inclement weather when you have to stay inside.

Add rooms

Umbrella tents may also have attached rooms, screened canopies and such. Some have rear openings and extra material to form a hood that fits snugly over the rear door of a station wagon. This is like adding an extra room off the ground. All-in-all, the

A modification of the wall tent is the cottage tent or cabin tent. This one by Thermos sleeps six.

umbrella is a popular tent, and some families like it so well that they take along two tents for lengthy outings — one for sleeping and one for daytime living-dining activities.

Trail tents. These tents are often called pack tents, mountain tents, backpacking tents and the like. They are lightweight, compact and durable and come in a variety of sizes and shapes. For the most part, the trail tent is low slung and is ideal for the backpacker, the mountain climber, hunters and fishermen.

A variation of the trail tent is the better known pup tent, which is more attractive in price than it is in use. It makes a good play tent for youngsters and may be used effectively as an "extra" tent at a semipermanent camp.

The better models, with sewed-in floors and zippered netting at each end, will suffice on short trail trips in good weather. But for longer trips and extremes in temperature, this is not the best tent. A good many former infantrymen will verify this. Some larger, more elaborate models negate the bad features of the standard pup tents.

Two models of the popular umbrella tent style, the standard size offered by Hirsch-Weis below, and the expanded size by Thermos above, show the attractive physical features of these tents. Umbrella tents are also economical.

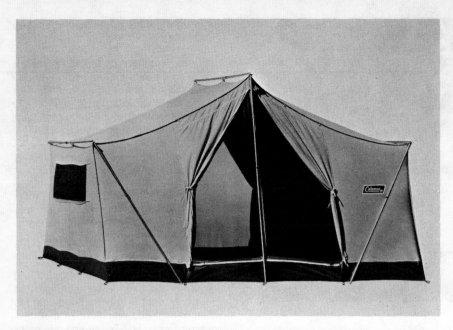

Coleman's Vagabond Deluxe is large enough for six adults or a large family.

Explorer

The explorer tent may be used as a stand-up trail tent, and the more popular size is designed for two or three persons. It is easy to erect and can withstand very high winds.

Other styles. Except for a few recent innovations in tent design most modern tents are adaptations of the wall tent, the cottage tent (actually a modified wall tent), the umbrella tent and the trail tent. Manufacturers give these different names, and some of the basic styles are never mentioned by name in their literature. The accompanying pictures indicate the variations in design, as well as names.

The pop tent is relatively new and is different. It is shaped like an igloo. It gets its name from the way it is erected: it pops up like an umbrella. It is light, sets up in minutes, has sewed-in floor, is well ventilated and roomy. You may be told that it requires no stakes or guy ropes, and it doesn't—if the wind isn't blowing.

Obviously, it does need some anchoring, though the weight of people and gear inside will take care of this under normal circumstances. It makes a good tent for family camping on a semipermanent basis. The reason you don't see more of these, perhaps, is due to the price, usually about double that of the same size tent in a more conventional style.

Wing tent

The wing tent is not exactly a new

idea, but it is relatively new on the commercial market. It, too, is expensive. It is practical for normal family camping. Basically a square tent, it gets its name from a wing-like fly extended beyond each corner—high at two corners, low at the other two. Its vertical walls and mostly high ceiling allow for full use of the interior space.

Tent Prices

As with most camping items made primarily of fabric, a tent gives you serviceability and long-wearing features according to the price you pay. This is as sure a guideline as you can go by, though it is not the only one.

Adequate family-size tents designed and manufactured for much use cost about $100. You may be able to find an 8-by-10 footer for under $50, but its usefulness will be limited.

Umbrella tents among the family group give you the most floor space for the money. A good 9 by 9 will cost $50 to $75; a 10 by 10, up to $100; a 9 by 15, about $125.

Cottage tents cost more and are worth more. A 9 by 12 may be purchased for $100 to $140; a 10-by-18 footer for $150 to $225.

Backpacker models

The professional tents designed for backpackers, mountain climbers and wilderness explorers are somewhat more costly for the size tent you get. The "Fortnight Four-man Gerry Rainvent Tent," for example, sells for $180. The size is 8' by 9' by 6' high, but it weighs only 9 pounds, 11 ounces—including tent, fly, poles, stringers and skewers. The catalog description of this tent reveals why the price is roughly twice that of a comparable-sized, top-quality standard tent:

"Coated nylon sewn-in floor comes up sidewalls to protect sleeping bags . . . breathable nylon fabrics won't condense moisture . . . coated nylon rain fly keeps inside dry . . . full ventilation at both ends of tent, closed by nylon mosquito netting and nylon zippered window and door . . . exterior poles of sectional aluminum take down to 14" . . . aluminum cross-ridge for more headroom . . . sleeps four adults . . . double wall (tent and fly) makes tent cooler in summer, warmer in winter." Smaller models range in price from $90 to $125.

Tent Fabrics

By law, tentmakers are required to identify the fabric used in a tent. You will find this information on an attached tag. It is a helpful guide to tent selection.

It is easy to become confused by the dozen or more kinds of fabric used in tentmaking. Compounding this are the many kinds of fabric treatment, weaves and such that are touted as

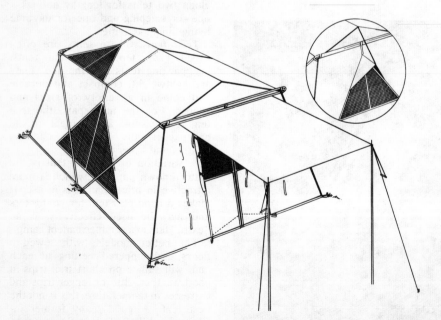

The Star Lite by Camel Manufacturing Company, Knoxville, Tennessee. not only offers a view of the stars to sleeping campers; the roof opening gives additional ventilation.

LIGHTWEIGHTS

ideal for backpacking into high country

One of three pup tents offered by Hirsch-Weis Company.

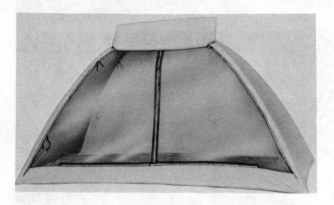

Mountain tents are preferred by many backpackers. This is the Hi-Lo model produced by Hirsch-Weis Company. The tent is high enough in front so you can sit up inside.

In recent years the pup tent has been improved to the point that it is not as uncomfortable as some GIs may remember. This model by Coleman features sewed-in floor and zippered nylon opening.

This has been dubbed Pocket Camper by Thermos. The name fits. It is a useful tent for Scout outings, father-son trips and canoe jaunts.

The Explorer is considered by many campers as the perfect tent for two or three people who like a shelter that will erect rapidly, will roll up compactly, is not too heavy and requires a minimum of frame. This model is by Hirsch-Weis.

The Camponaire by Gerry is a lightweight backpacking tent that can accommodate three adults or two adults and two children.

assets to the product.

What are the facts?

First, the fabrics most used today are duck, drill, poplin, nylon, sheeting, plastic, combinations of two or more and special materials patented and sold under brand names.

Fabrics may be designated by weight or thread count or both. Weight is indicated in ounces per square yard—before treatment for waterproofing, which adds some weight to the fabric.

Waterproofing is recommended by most camping authorities despite the fact that such treatment reduces the "breathing" effectiveness of the material. But ventilation may be achieved by window and entrance openings. Waterproofing reduces shrinkage and mildew and causes a tent to dry more quickly.

Tents are made stronger by good seams. Therefore, wide stretches of even good fabric cause a tent to be weaker at stress points than if the seams come about every 24 to 30 inches. Beckets at the tent's base should be attached on the seams, not between. Otherwise, the driving of stakes will strain these too much, likely causing them to pull off.

More threads

Sometimes the fabric is described in terms of the number of threads in a square inch. The higher the count for a given fabric, the better the material. If the threads are counted crosswise, this is called warp; if lengthwise, it is called filled. Frequently, the description will list both (ex. 120 x 240).

Pay little attention to claims of sizing (a process of adding starch to facilitate weaving, but also done sometimes to fake strength and quality in an inferior fabric) and other processes puffed up by superlatives. Your interest is in what the fabric will do and how it will wear, which the advertising should clearly indicate and guarantee.

Here are descriptions of popular fabrics used in tentmaking:

Army duck. This is still the best material for larger tents and those meeting rough use. Available in weights of 8, 10 and 12 ounces per square yard, this is perhaps the most durable of all tent fabrics. Most commercial tents of building size are made of army duck. So are many professional outdoorsmen's tents.

Duck. Similar to army duck fabric, this material is also referred to as single fill duck—meaning that the fill is not doubled as it is in the weave of army duck. Coarser threads are often used, making this fabric as heavy—sometimes heavier—as army duck. But it makes a good tent and comes in weights per square yard of 8, 10, 12 and 14 ounces.

Nylon. Nylon is used with other fabrics as a strengthening factor, but

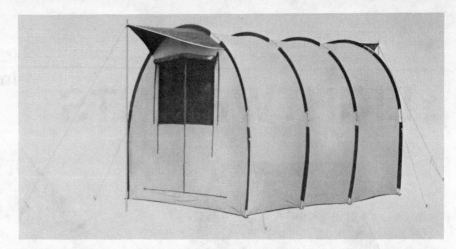

Another family-type tent that is somewhat different is Thermos' Prairie Schooner, which comes in two sizes.

A screened patio is very useful at family campouts. This model is manufactured by Hirsch-Weis.

Pop tents often are more costly, but because of their versatility and ease of handling many campers are finding them to their liking.

Maintaining unique design features is this mountain tent which is adaptable also to the weekend hiker or the canoeist.

some excellent tents are made from nylon itself. Nylon is not a waterproof material and must be vinyl-coated to make it so. This also cuts off fabric "breathing," causing moisture to collect on the inside.

A way around this is not to waterproof the nylon and to use a plastic fly as an outer roof. Some of the best backpacking tents are made with this provision. Nylon is lightweight, which makes it ideal for backpacking.

Drill. This fabric is called sail drill, boat drill, forest drill and various brand names. It has a close weave, is of medium weight and makes good tent material for average use. Probably most of the colorful tents seen at improved campgrounds are made primarily of drill. It is not recommended for rough wear.

Poplin. Because of its tight weave and style of weave, poplin is excellent for use in the wind. It is a good all-round material for camping that does not demand too much stress and wear. It is comparatively light in weight.

Other materials used in today's tents include palina cloth (found in some better quality tents), suma cloth (lightweight, combed cotton fabric of very tight weave, and excellent for backpacking), nylon-pima (a combination of nylon and cotton woven so tightly that very little waterproofing is needed) and sheeting (actually similar to bed sheeting and to be avoided except in play tents).

Workmanship

The best fabric and the most attractive designs do not guarantee a good tent. The difference is in the workmanship. How can you make sure the manufacturing quality is there?

First, look at the seams. These should all be tight. The edges should all be double hemmed, through four layers of fabric by interlocking the folded cut edges. The best seams do not lie flat, though for normal wear these may do.

Next, examine the zippers and other closure attachments. Window and entrance openings should have strong, well-attached, inside-outside zippers.

The netting should be made of nylon and securely sewn to the tent fabric and zipper connectors. Check the floor carefully. A good floor is made of vinyl-coated material, usually nylon. The vinyl coating keeps out ground moisture and discourages mildew. The better tents are made with the waterproofed floor reaching six or eight inches up the tent wall on all sides.

Strain points

Observe closely the strain points— where the most roof weight is placed, where guy ropes and stakes are attached and any point where grommets or beckets are attached. These points must be reinforced with double layers of fabric and extra stitching if they are to hold up.

Don't be too concerned if the stakes that come with your tent prove to be less than adequate. Unfortunately, many good tents come supplied with foot-long stakes. These should be 18 inches. Even longer stakes may be needed in certain terrain for certain tents, but you'll likely have to make these yourself. The newer aluminum stakes are lightweight and are quite useful in rocky or otherwise hard ground.

Tents never seem to have enough rope. A length of 50 to 100 feet of quarter-inch manila rope and an equal length of nylon cord are handy items to have around when pitching a tent, erecting a fly or doing any one of a dozen camp chores. Therefore, it is not necessary to severely question the rope lengths when purchasing a tent — if other manufacturing qualities are good.

Summary

In shopping for a tent, don't expect to find everything you are looking for in a single tent. But buy the best you can afford, and build your inventory of camping gear from there. Your preferences will change as you become a more experienced camper. Your tent, however, can make all of your camping experiences a delight if you buy one large enough — light enough if backpacking — that is well made of good materials and that fits your kind of camping.

Even though more costly, versatility and ease of handling of pop tents make them desirable by many campers.

The Steelheader has numerous supplementary uses to the camper. It is excellent for stream fishing when the weather is bad. By Hirsch-Weis.

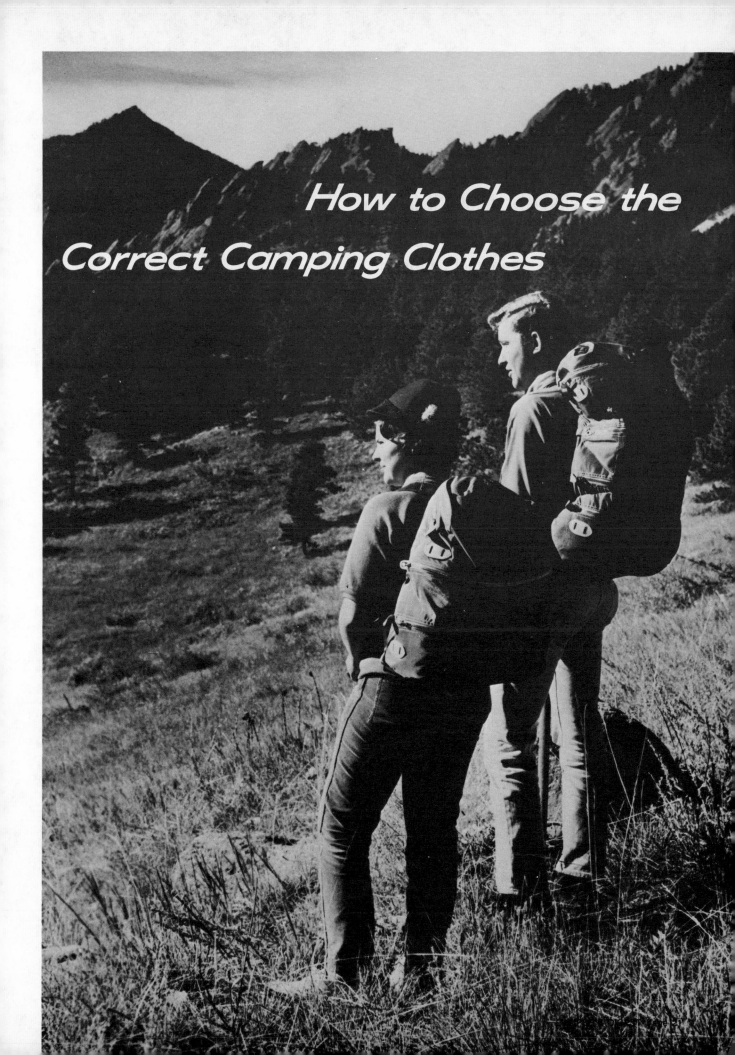

How to Choose the Correct Camping Clothes

Dressing appropriately and comfortably when camping is relatively simple. It is also necessary if you want to thoroughly enjoy camping with the freedom to function in all weather and over any terrain.

What to Wear - When

People who really enjoy outdoor activities such as camping get the feel of a planned outing when they start wardrobe selections. Just as there is excitement in selecting an outfit for any important occasion, so there is excitement in selecting clothing for camping.

For one thing, there is a great deal of variety in the camper's clothing line. This adds interest to the process of selection, but more importantly it enables a camper to fit his wardrobe to the specific camping situation. Obviously, clothing must fit the season, the terrain and the type of camping contemplated.

The clothing you select may be a potpourri of items already hanging in your wardrobe or stashed away in a dresser drawer. As a matter of fact, a first camping excursion that is not too long is best made without the purchase of special clothing, except possibly footwear.

This gives the new camper opportunity to learn what is comfortable and what is not, what is practical and what is not. Further, it enables him to observe what the "well-dressed" camper is wearing this season. Likely, it is last season's outfit.

Comfort all-important

Most people like to be appropriately dressed on all occasions, and this is true of campers. But the appearance of outdoor clothing is not of first importance. The one all-important criterion is comfort.

The experienced camper keeps his wardrobe simple. He chooses wearing apparel that is light in weight, shows little dirt, is washable and resists snags and tears. The complete outfit is designed to keep him comfortable and dry in all weather conditions that he is likely to encounter.

If you want to have "window shopping" fun in your living room on a cold winter's evening, write for some of the catalogs available from manufacturers and outfitters listed in the "Camping Outfitters" section.

These catalogs beautifully picture and describe the finest in outdoor clothing and gear. Equally important, every description is loaded with valuable information on maintaining comfort in all kinds of outdoor situations. For example, the Alaska Sleeping Bag Company of Beaverton, Oregon, gives this pertinent information about its famous Klondike Shirt:

"The Alaska 'Klondike' Shirt is made of heavy 20-oz. diagonal weave 100 percent pure virgin wool. The 'Klondike' has been demanded by Alaska lumberjacks, sourdoughs, fishermen and professional hunters for many years. The heavy weight and weave of the fabric keep out dampness and chilling winds. The natural oils in the wool act as a water-repellent, yet allow this shirt to breathe so that the wearer is never damp with perspiration. The 'Klondike' is cut full and will not bind when worn as a shirt or over-clothing as a jacket."

Heat factory

Gerry Cunningham, whose Colorado Outdoor Sports Corporation designs and manufactures top quality camping clothing and equipment, says: "Your body is, in reality, a heat and moisture factory. It burns food to produce from 2,400 to 4,500 calories of heat each day, plus about two pints of water in the form of perspiration. To keep warm, heat must be conserved and water vapor carried off without passing into the clothing layers."

This bit of information is vital to the camper heading for high altitudes at any season, or one who plans to pitch camp in the winter snow. Understanding this problem and knowing how to cope with it could, in severe cold, mean the difference between life and death.

Even summer campers at lower elevations, including those in the desert or at the seashore, quickly learn that the cooler night air really feels cold if the clothing is damp from perspiration.

The answer to the problem, says Mr. Cunningham, is ventilation. "Successful ventilation," he says, "requires two conditions: 1) there must be a space next to your skin for air circulation; and 2) air must be free to enter your clothing, usually at the wrist and pants cuffs and waist, and to leave, usually at the neck.

Net underwear

"Experienced campers and other outdoorsmen understand this and generally agree that a basic answer is net underwear coupled with conventional outdoor trousers and shirt, under average circumstances, and insulated wind-proof and water-repellent outer garments as determined by the weather conditions."

In his helpful booklet, **Wilderness Traveler,** Mr. Cunningham lists these simple rules for the camper with little or no previous experience:

"1) Ventilating net underwear is an advantage if you can get it. Otherwise, use your regular underwear.

"2) Shirts should be wool if the weather is cool and/or damp. Anything light will do in summer.

"3) Pants can be wool whipcord for cool and damp weather. Dungarees will do in summer. Shorts are good on the trail but you may miss the long legs at night in northern climates.

"4) A wool sweater for cool nights.

"5) A light, wind-proof jacket.

"For rainy weather a good poncho is best, but a sheet of plastic could serve almost as well. The important thing is that it be lightweight because, hopefully, you will be carrying it most of the time, not wearing it."

Footwear

Like other items in the clothing category, the selection of footwear is determined by the weather, the terrain and the activities associated with the camping program. There is a tendency for inexperienced campers to go to one of two extremes: tightly laced knee-high leather boots or canvas sneakers. Both have their places in camping, the high boots for hiking through snake-infested country and sneakers for comfort in camp. But for normal out-

door use these are not favored.

Many campers, even backpackers, carry an extra pair of shoes. The camper who packs his gear into the campsite by motor vehicle may take two or three kinds of shoes if there is probability that each pair will be needed.

Without doubt, the shoe is the most important single item in the clothing category if the camping activity amounts to anything more than pitching camp and sitting down. A good many outdoor vacations have turned into torture trips because the footwear was either ill chosen or poorly fitted or both. The camper who backpacks or

Obviously, clothing must fit the season, the terrain and the type of camping contemplated.

takes to woods and fields on any kind of lengthy trip should very carefully select his footwear.

First, he will not, under any circumstances, purchase the same shoe size he wears at the office. If he does, he will do well enough around camp and perhaps for a short hike. But if he tries any climbing or hikes eight or ten miles at a stretch, he'll soon know that his shoes are too small. He will end up with blisters and abrasions. When he takes his shoes off to cool his hot feet, he'll discover that his feet have swollen. Very likely it will take some soaking in cold water for them to once again fit his shoes.

A hiker's feet don't become swollen simply because shoes are too small; the swelling comes from the varying pressures of walking which stimulate the circulation system and cause more blood to be pumped into the feet. This is normal and is not cause for alarm if the footwear is appropriate.

Proper shoe size

Shoes for hiking should be one full size longer and one full size wider than the size you ordinarily buy for city wear. If you prefer to wear heavy socks, you won't go wrong by purchasing shoes one and one-half sizes larger than normal. Hiking shoes should fit snugly at the heels and be loose enough in front for the toes to move freely.

Of course, for driving or casual wear around camp your sneakers or moccasin-type loafers may be the same size that you ordinarily wear. In fact, these just as well could come from your home wardrobe.

But if you are camping in rough country and you want to get out of camp into the woods or along a high mountain trail, probably the best footwear is the six-inch or eight-inch moccasin-type shoe. This shoe has a comfortably low cut, with the uppers reaching just above the ankle bone. It is suitable for all members of the family.

Campers agree more on the kind of footwear needed on the trail than they do on that worn about camp. In camp the atmosphere is somewhat homelike, and a person prefers to wear what is most comfortable to him.

Shop for quality

Good outdoor shoes are made of quality leather with soles made of rubber or thick composition. Flexibleness is important. Avoid leather soles because these polish very quickly and are slippery. Some campers buy quality leather-soled boots, then have an additional sole of rubber or composition added. The important criterion in shopping for the right footwear is quality.

Treat your boots with neatsfoot oil to preserve the leather and also to make them more waterproof. Standard shoe laces of good materials are best, and a couple of spare pairs should be taken along.

New shoes should always be broken in by wearing them for short periods before undertaking a lengthy hike. Some campers wear them in the house, while working in the yard or on short walks to a corner drugstore or through a city park. It is a good idea to apply a liberal amount of neatsfoot oil **before** wearing your new shoes. Some hikers break in new shoes by standing in

Like other items in the clothing category, the selection of footwear is determined by the weather, the terrain and the activities associated with the camping program. These Gerry Trail Shoes are safe, light and comfortable for canoeing and light trail use. Such shoes are especially favored by women.

water for 10 to 15 minutes and then hiking until the shoes dry on their feet.

When camping involves transportation by canoe and very little hiking, except for portaging, lightweight moccasins are the most ideal footwear. If the portages are long and you have a great deal to carry, you will need the six-inch shoes. In this case, wear the light shoes in the canoe and change to the boots when you portage. If the weather is mild, some canoe campers wear only the heavier boots for use when portaging, and remove them when paddling the canoe.

Hiking shoes

Good hiking shoes are lightweight, but are tough and durable. The best

weight for adult shoes is two to four pounds per pair, but some people get along very well in boots weighing up to six pounds. As mentioned before, the shoes should be large enough for freedom of movement inside, especially for the toes and the ball of the foot. Leather is the best material for hiking shoes, although many hunters select a boot that is made of rubber at the bottom and leather at the top.

Pac boots

Eddie Bauer, expedition outfitter of Seattle, Washington, offers several styles of these Pac Boots ranging in price from $17.50 to $24.50. The

The Gerry Mountaineer Boot is a type of shoe capable of meeting most any terrain challenge.

Alaska Sleeping Bag Company offers the Canadian Sub-Zero Pac, a leather-topped rubber boot for both men and women, $18.95 and $16.95 respectively. Provision is made for extra liners, at $4.95 per pair, which assures comfort in extreme cold and in wet-cold weather.

Following are descriptions of several top-quality boots and shoes for camp and trail and available at better camping outfitters or by mail order.

1. Gerry Mountaineer Boot. Designed for rough wear, this boot features notch-top for better ankle support and less dirt catching down the top, and also a special gusset overlap which keeps dirt out. The tongue is padded and a sole counter protects the boots against rock cuts. The soles are made of Vibram, which assures extra-long wear. The color is rough tan, weight, five pounds and the price, $33.95.

2. Gerry Camper Boot. This boot features the leather rough out for better scuff resistance. The soft, pliable leather and the deep lug soles add to the dependability and comfort of these boots on the trail and around camp. The weight is four pounds and the price is $24.95.

Ladies' choice

3. Gerry Trail Shoe. This is a favorite with women, and here is why: the shoe is light and comfortable and may be used both for canoeing and for trail use, except in extremely rough terrain. The outer leather is suede, the ankles are padded and the construction is seamless. The lug sole assures a good grip. The weight is 2¼ pounds and the price is $18.95.

4. Eddie Bauer K-99 8-inch Boots. Advertised as "the finest boots ever made for mountain men," these boots live up to their billing. Comfortable, safe, long wearing, they are used by professional outdoorsmen the world over.

Handmade, the K-99 features Swiss Vibram lug soles and heels, molded as one single unit. Each boot is fitted with a chrome steel shank, and every stress point is reinforced exceedingly well. Price, $37.50.

5. Eddie Bauer K-6 Trail Boots. Designed for backpacking, hiking, climbing and general outdoor vacation wear, these boots feature fully padded uppers for maximum comfort and protection on the trail, flap-over closure and snug-fitting top to keep out dirt and pebbles and Vibram one-piece soles and heels. Price, $24.50.

6. Eddie Bauer K-2 6-inch Field Boots. Like the other K series, this boot features Vibram one-piece soles and heels, cleated for positive traction on rock, snow, ice and mud. A popular style trail boot, the K-2 is ideal for most outdoor activities. Price, $25.00.

The Packer, an 8-inch boot, is a proven favorite with many hunters, fishermen, hikers and mountaineers.

The right socks

Oversize shoes and heavy socks of neat fit are considered the best combination for comfortable walking. The experienced hiker wears only wool socks, for these are the most suitable in heat or cold, whether dry or wet.

Some of the professional models are reinforced at the toes and heels with nylon. A good rule when purchasing socks is to select the best ones, which means also that the length will reach well above the boot top.

If you are one of the few individuals whose feet are allergic to wool, wear a thin pair of cotton socks next to the skin. Many hikers who are not allergic

Eddie Bauer, expedition outfitter, says the K-2 6-inch Field Boot is that firm's most popular trail boot.

to wool wear the extra cotton socks for comfort. If your feet are tender, or if they perspire, dust both your feet and socks with foot powder and give your feet alcohol baths morning and evening the first couple of days on the trail.

Change socks

It is important that you wash your feet at least once a day, preferably at night, and change your socks daily. It doesn't do any harm to pause at a cool, mountain stream and bathe your feet. Hikers frequently change then to a clean, dry pair of socks.

It's a good feeling and is restful to the feet. If the weather is hot and you perspire freely, you may wish to change socks several times on the

trail. This is why it is important to carry one or more spare pairs Hang the damp socks on the outside of your pack, and they will dry for further use later in the day.

A convenience reason for purchasing only good woolen socks is because they are easy to wash. Apply soap and wash them in lukewarm water, rinse at least twice, squeeze— don't wring—until they are as free of excess water as you can make them. Stretch the socks back into shape, hang them over a line to dry in the breeze or lay them flat on a surface such as a rock exposed to the sun or to the campfire. Drying should be slow.

Underwear

Underwear commonly worn at home and on the job may be perfectly all right for camping. The only way to know for sure is to experiment. Leisure-type camping in average good weather doesn't demand much extra in clothing items such as shirts and underwear. But on the trail or in extreme climates, ordinary underwear can be the cause of a great deal of discomfort.

Some types of underwear absorb perspiration, which can be disastrous in cold weather. Most ordinary underwear tends to chafe in hot weather, and frequent changes may be necessary.

Ventilating net underwear is ideal for all seasons. This provides ventilating space next to the skin. Gerry Cunningham says net underwear is most effective, both in cold weather and in hot weather, when the holes are larger than one-fourth inch. The wide mesh patterns create hundreds of small airways which in reality make air barriers between body and outer clothing.

This allows perspiration to vaporize instead of dampening clothing. This type of underwear has long been used by Scandinavian fishermen, which certainly says something for it. Many outdoorsmen remove their outer shirt on hot summer days and wear only the net shirt, which helps to cool the skin.

Two-piece

Other types of effective outdoor underwear for colder climates are two-piece suits made of two layers, the inside next-to-skin layer being absorbent cotton and the outer layer of a wool blend. These are so constructed that a layer of insulating air is trapped between the two layers of cloth. Some high-grade underwear for outdoor use is made of 15 percent cashmere, 75 percent wool worsted and 10 percent nylon. It is innerlined with soft, white mercerized cotton. The cost of good outdoor underwear ranges from $7 to $15 per set.

Trousers

Around most popular campgrounds

the men wear work pants or jeans and women wear slacks or jeans. In warm weather shorts and pedal pushers are frequently worn by women, shorts by men. These are not very practical, however, if any hiking is done through brushy country or in tall grass where chiggers or red bugs are prevalent. Denim is a good fabric for general camping, but tight fitting western styles are not the most comfortable for camping. Slacks or pants with cuffs are not suitable for hiking.

Dungarees make good camping and hiking trousers in summer, but probably the best for cool and damp weather are trousers made of wool whipcord. The Colorado Outdoor Sports Corporation manufactures trail pants made of tough Burlington 90-10 Orlon whipcord that is as warm as wool, but stronger. These pants feature a heavy duty waistband, strong belt loops and deep pockets. The hip pockets have flaps. The price is $25 and well worth it.

The Alaska Sleeping Bag Company features a similarly designed whipcord trouser made of 100 percent pure virgin wool. It sells for $18.95. A model for the big, big man costs $1 more.

Other trousers ideal for many camping activities are the stay-press trousers made of cotton-Dacron. Most outfitters carry stocks of rain pants, wind pants, pants insulated with northern goose down and other special trousers for special camping circumstances.

For average camping, wear something you already own, but come next season, you may seek more rugged adventure. In that case, shop carefully for type, fit and quality.

Shirts

The formula for selecting the right shirt is simple: if you are heading for higher elevations or the weather is likely to be cool and/or damp, wear a wool shirt. In summer, something lighter will do. Where the climate is likely to change from day to day or from day to night, take along two of each.

A favorite shirt among professional outdoorsmen, particularly in the West, is a 100 percent virgin wool shirt manufactured by Pendleton Mills in Pendleton, Oregon. These cost about $15 each. When buying a woolen shirt for outdoor use, buy only the best for complete satisfaction and long use.

Many experienced campers take along at least one shirt that is of jacket weight. The buffalo plaid shirt is probably the most popular of this type.

In lightweight camping, of course, you may wear most any kind of lightweight shirt, the drip drys or the wash-and-wears, if you prefer.

If you want to appear a little more rugged than you do when on the golf

The experienced camper keeps his wardrobe simple. He chooses wearing apparel that is light in weight, shows little dirt, is washable and resists snags and tears. Meeting these criteria is this Gerry Chapparral Jacket.

course and if you expect to come in contact with a little dirt on your outing, you will be pleased by the feel and wearability of light denim shirts. Likely, you will come to prefer them for summer wear. These are made for both men and women and come in both long-sleeve and short-sleeve models.

Cotton flannel

If the weather turns cooler or if the nights get cool but not cold, cotton flannel shirts are entirely adequate. In some areas, it may be necessary to add a sweater or windbreaker in the evening, or to exchange the cotton shirt for a wool shirt.

When traveling to your campsite by motor vehicle, you can easily take a variety of shirts for all occasions. But if you plan to backpack or follow a canoe trail for several days, determine accurately what extremes the weather may reach and select shirts accordingly. When traveling under your own steam, you may wish to carry only one extra shirt. It should be the right one.

Outer garments

Outer garments considered basic for most camping excursions are jackets, sweaters and rainwear. For colder weather insulated jackets, vests and sometimes entire outer suits may be necessary. Again, the rule is to fit the clothing to the occasion.

Jackets

Jackets for the outdoorsman come in many styles and colors. One that is light, windproof and water-repellent is the most versatile and the most basic. A lightweight poplin jacket is frequently carried by backpackers and other campers to be slipped on when the weather gets chilly. This jacket worn over a sweater often is all that is needed for cool, summer nights in the open.

For higher elevations and cooler climates, many campers take along heavy Mackinaw Cruisers. Made somewhat like a shirt-style jacket, these colorful outer garments are remarkably warm and water-repellent. Seven outside pockets are standard.

Another cruiser which has matching pants is made of 100 percent virgin wool forestry cloth, the same material U.S. Forest Service uniforms are made of. Good cruisers cost from $25 to $50.

Camping in sub-freezing weather calls for insulated jackets. Among the several wellmade insulated jackets for campers is the Gerry Camper. Selling for $36, made of nylon fabrics with prime duck-down insulation, this jacket is easy to pack, weighs only 1 pound, 6 ounces, yet is quite warm. The hand warmer pockets are down-insulated. An accessory Alpine hood is available for $7.

Down-fill

Other down-filled jackets range in price from $45 to $85. These are available in all sizes for men, women and children. If you really want to get fancy and plan to spend a good deal of time in the polar regions or in extreme cold weather near home, you may wish to purchase a fur parka—of muskrat, seal, wolf, take your choice—for $385 to $595. Most campers will pass by these bargains, but will give a second look to the catalog descriptions and illustrations.

Rainwear

The best all-round rainwear is a poncho. The poncho has additional uses such as a temporary shelter, a ground cloth and protective wrapping of goods in camp that must be kept dry.

The poncho is a simple, flat sheet of waterproof material with a slit in the center for slipping over the head. The sides may be closed under the arms by snaps. The usual materials are rubber, oiled cotton, vinyl-coated nylon, rubberized cotton or nylon and plastic. The plastic type works very well under normal circumstances, but most models will not hold up under hard wear.

A poncho is not adequate unless it reaches to the knees. There are a variety of sizes, and men, women or children should have no trouble finding the right size. Some models incorporate hoods and some come equipped with nylon zipper fronts to allow ventilation.

The better models also are made with double layers of material over the shoulders, chest, back and hood center. This reduces condensation. The best ponchos cost less than $25.

Other good rainwear designed for long and hard use include rain parkas, rain pants and rain chaps (for pulling on over regular pants).

Rain hats and rain caps come in various styles and colors and these are necessary unless you wear a poncho with a hood.

Headgear

Every camper should be equipped with a hat or cap. It will not be necessary to wear one at all times, of course, but a cap or hat is nice to have when bugs and flies swarm around the head, when the sun beats down or when the rains come. Adequate head protection is absolutely necessary in cold weather.

In addition to the headgear for rainy weather described in the preceding section, a camper should consider a 3-inch brim hat made of felt. Most professional outdoorsmen wear this type of hat the year around. It gives

protection from extremes of weather in all seasons. In the summer many campers wear cotton caps resembling a baseball cap, but such headgear is totally inadequate in driving rain.

Felt hat best

The best all-round hats for men, women and children are the felt hats already mentioned. These come in many models. One model is extremely lightweight and can be rolled up and packed into a duffle bag without damage. It can be shaped to suit the occasion, brim turned up for sunny weather and turned down for rainy weather.

Other styles of rain headgear are the Alaska style cap and a similar cap with a strong, waterproof bill. These are also insulated to withstand extremely cold weather.

Some campers prefer hunting caps and fishing-style hats. Camping in the desert calls for a hat with a high crown similar to that worn by western Indians. The head is kept cool by the insulating space between the head and the crown. This type of hat is very practical, but is little used probably because it makes the wearer feel self-conscious.

The best all-round rainwear is a poncho. This one with attached hood is made of lightweight, plastic-coated nylon woven in a rip-stop fabric. Such garments are adaptable as improvised tents or other waterproof covering.

The water-repellent, cotton poplin hat worn by many golfers also makes a good hat for summer camping. It sells for around $5. Parkas and hoods round out the hat selection generally worn by campers.

Gloves and mittens

It is taken for granted that gloves or mittens are necessary in the winter season. But a pair of lightweight work gloves will find frequent use around a camp at any season. Gloves worn when chopping or digging will prevent blisters. Likewise, the hands are protected from scratches and abrasions if gloves are worn by a hiker who is following a narrow trail through brush and briars.

Satisfactory work gloves range in price from about 50 cents for cotton gloves to about $2 for reinforced, longer wearing models.

For extremely cold temperatures, the best handwear is a pair of goose-down insulated mits. These will cost from $10 to $20.

Sleepwear

For average camping you can sleep

The Gerry Mountaineer MK II Jacket is made of all-nylon, is thickly insulated and is generally the type of outer garment preferred by high country backpackers and mountaineers.

in the same nighttime garment you wear at home. Some backpackers sleep in their underwear or in their clothing, depending on the circumstances.

But there are special sleeping suits designed for outdoor use. One model sold by Eddie Bauer is a flannel, two-piece sleeping bag suit with built-in feet. This suit may be worn around camp, and if you want to take a short walk before dressing in the morning, you simply have to slip on a pair of shoes. These suits come in colors of firehouse red and beige and sell for $7.50 to $8.50.

In high altitude camping or outdoor activity calling for insulated underwear (preferably worn over ventilating net underwear), these same garments may double as sleepwear and often do.

Other clothing items

Always take along a good supply of bandanas or large-size handerchiefs. If there is likelihood that you will want to drive to a nearby restaurant on occasion, take along some casual sportswear or more formal wear if the restaurant of your choice requires coat and tie.

Warm and pliable camp slippers are nice to have along. So is a bathing suit or swimming trunks. And don't forget a second belt if one of a different width and style is needed.

To sum up: always take enough of the right kind of clothing, but not **too much**. Two shirts will usually suffice; so will two sets of underwear. You must have at least two pairs of socks; a third may come in handy. One pair of good trail pants may be sufficient, although you will appreciate the convenience of changing into shorts or lightweight trousers at the end of the day.

A wool sweater is standard wear when the temperature drops below 50°, which it frequently does at night. A light, windproof jacket, a poncho, adequate headgear and good trail shoes round out the essentials. Any other items add to comfort and convenience, but are not essential. Your clothing selection should meet your own needs and preferences, and certainly to your pocketbook.

On keeping warm

Since camping has mushroomed into a year-round outdoor activity for millions, a great deal of study has been given to the problem of keeping warm. Some of this has been dictated by the necessities of the military.

Gerry Cunningham, who has done considerable research and design in this field, maintains that the most effective insulation is in special layer-type construction of outdoor garments. This begins with a ventilating layer of net underwear worn next to the skin and conventional clothing—the wool shirt, heavy trousers—composing the next layer. Then comes the outer garment which Mr. Cunningham says, must be so constructed that it will trap dead air inside.

"The most important fact to remember about insulation," he says, "is *thickness*." Down, therefore, becomes the best insulator because it gives the greater thickness in ratio to weight than any other material, and it is more compressible. Mr. Cunningham cites this U. S. Army Quartermaster

Temperature	Sleeping	Light Work	Heavy Work
40F	1.5"	.8"	.20"
20F	2.0"	1.0"	.27"
0F	2.5"	1.3"	.35"
−20F	3.0"	1.6"	.40"
−40F	3.5"	1.9"	.48"
−60F	4.0"	2.1"	.52"

data as a guide for insulating values.

Obviously a garment designed for lower temperatures requires more thickness, and if it is to be worn in warmer temperatures, it should be so designed that air may circulate in through the cuffs and out at the neck to provide necessary added ventilation.

The outer shell of this down-insulated garment may be made windproof or water-repellent. It is better, however, if an outer windbreaker jacket or parka is worn over the insulating jacket. The same insulating principles, incidentally, go into the manufacture of insulated pants, headgear and mittens.

How to Assure Sleeping Comfort

When it comes to sleeping under the stars, "roughing it" doesn't have to be synonymous with "discomfort."

The Grand Teton, a Wenzel bag, features attached hood, double mattress pocket, weather-stripped zipper and provision for zipping another bag to it.

Sleeping gear is to a camper what shoes are to a hiker—his most important comfort equipment. After all, one-third of camping time is spent sleeping—or should be. Adequate comfort, which means adequate warmth more than anything else, is the one criterion of assuring adequate rest. No matter how rough a camper's day, he is rested and refreshed and raring to go come morning—if he has had a comfortable bed down.

Comfort sometimes is elusive. It may mean one thing to you and something entirely different to another camper. Some campers still prefer to bed down directly on the ground with only a ground cloth on which to lie. Others are uncomfortable, psychologically at least, unless they sleep off the ground—if only a few inches. Fortunately, there is great variety in bedding for the camper, and you can be assured of as much comfort, or more, than you get at home.

Staying warm

More campers complain about sleepless nights because they can't stay warm, than about all the other sleep disrupters combined. The reasons for this vary, but the basic cause is due to the fact that more heat is lost than is produced. To enjoy a heat balance requires that the heat production be increased to offset the heat loss, or the heat loss must be reduced to equalize the heat production.

Heat production comes basically from two sources, one internal and one external. The body's burning of food produces heat. This may be supplemented by radiant heat which comes from the sun, a reflector fire or other outside source. Obviously, the production of heat varies with the time of day, the intensity of the outside source, the size of the individual, his metabolic rate and the amount and kinds of food he has consumed.

Heat sleeping bag

Some widely used ways of increasing heat production and decreasing heat loss are such simple procedures as preheating the sleeping bag by holding it near a fire just before retiring, covering head, feet and hands warmly and snugly and by setting up a windscreen to ward off any winds.

It is a law of physics that heat goes from a hot area to a cold area, and from a low area to a high area. When there is a wide temperature difference between the two areas the heat flow will be faster. When the outside temperature changes drastically downward, a sleeping camper will quickly feel a chill unless he has an adequate barrier to prevent body heat from flowing outward. The sleeping bag is designed to provide this barrier.

A sleeping bag, properly constructed, will prevent body heat from escaping, within the range of the sleeping bag rating, but at the same time it will permit moisture given off by the body to evaporate. Dampness is a factor that will quickly upset the heat balance, and this is why the better sleeping bags are designed to keep the body both warm and dry.

Good insulating materials that go into sleeping bags, and certain types of outdoor clothing for that matter, do not of themselves assure warmth. The best insulation is air, and materials that can trap air and hold it in place are the best for good insulation. Sleeping bags contain a layer of air-filled insulation near the body, thus halting or retarding heat escape.

It has been demonstrated that the closer the air barrier is to the body, the more warmth is retained. If the insulation qualities of bedding are poor, you will not stay warm on a cold night. The thickness of properly contained insulation—assuring enough trapped air—constitutes the factor that determines at what temperatures you can stay warm and comfortable.

In general, here are the basic rules to keep in mind for staying warm:

1. Eat well. This is no time to diet.

2. Try to avoid sweating, but if you do, make certain that there is adequate ventilation to carry away excess moisture.

3. Protect your sleeping area from wind and rain.

4. Cover all extremities well. It may sound silly, but a good head-covering will actually help to keep the feet warm.

5. Thickness of insulation is all-important. Several layers of materials work better than a single piece. For example, three light blankets are much more effective than one heavy blanket equaling the same weight as the three.

Choosing sleeping gear

The most popular types of sleeping gear are sleeping bags and cots—except for those campers using home-like beds in camping vehicles. Considered here will be the various types of bedding used mainly by tent campers and backpackers.

The sleeping bag. This is the choice bedding of most outdoorsmen. Experienced campers know that selecting the sleeping bag is so critical that it can make or break a camping trip.

There is a wide choice of sleeping bags—various grades of covering, lining and insulation—and there are several styles. Casual shopping will reveal that some sleeping bags may be purchased for less than $10; others can cost well over $100. Basically, you should look for the sleeping bag that will keep you warm at the lowest temperature anticipated. This is the first requisite.

Unfortunately, it is difficult to tell at first glance if a sleeping bag actually will give you the comfort you seek. The insulating values on sleeping bags are stated on the manufacturers' attached labels, and in some states the accuracy of this labeling is controlled by strict laws. A federal law requires that the labels be attached.

But this does not always guarantee satisfactory warmth. The outer covering, the insulation materials used, the inner lining and the method of opening and closing the bag enter the picture. More on this later.

Warmth variations

Obviously, the bag with greatest warming capacity is one you would expect to use in the coldest climate. Conversely, a bag with minimum insulation is adequate, from a warmth standpoint, at a low altitude camping site in midsummer.

There is much controversy about which sleeping bag is right for what, among even the most experienced outdoorsmen. One reputable authority will write emphatically that expensive sleeping bags designed to provide adequate warmth at 50 degrees below zero are totally unsatisfactory at 50 or 60 degrees above zero.

Another will take strong exception to attachable canopies used to keep rain and dew off the sleeper's face, claiming that most campers don't sleep out in the open in this fashion. Still other well known and widely quoted "authorities" will argue against mummy bags, slots for air mattresses, separate inner linings and the like.

What this all boils down to is that selecting the right sleeping bag for the individual is indeed an individual choice. Even the lowest priced, shoddiest manufactured ones can provide a great deal of fun for the youngsters. And the most elaborate down-filled bags, designed to last a lifetime, are worthless to the person who definitely is against "roughing it."

What to look for

The sleeping bag shopper needs to know what to look for in the light of his camping purposes and the contents of his pocketbook. If camping is a regular thing with you and you expect to be doing a good deal of it in years to come, by all means don't economize in the selection of a sleeping bag.

The efficiency of a sleeping bag is in

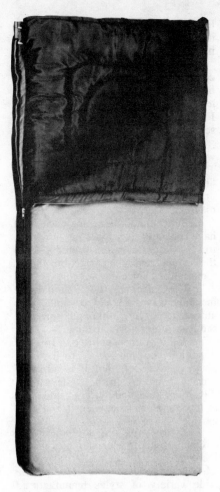

This model by Coleman is filled with three pounds of Dacron 88, its cover is of water repellent 8.1 oz. drill tent fabric and it is lined in insulated Milium material. Other features are a trouble-free zipper, air mattress pockets and headflap carrying case.

direct proportion to the quality of materials and workmanship. Good insulation materials will not provide the warmth factors they are capable of if design and workmanship are inferior. For example, unshielded zippers, coarse stitching and inadequate covering material will let in cold air, no matter how much insulation nor what kind. Obviously, these factors also contribute to the shortening of the sleeping bag's useful life.

Many a camper has discovered after two or three uses that he has been sold a bill of goods. Actually, he has sold himself a bill of goods by hasty buying or by ignorance of what makes a good sleeping bag. Fortunately, those who buy sleeping bags in the upper price range can be reasonably sure that price is a good indication of quality.

If you are thinking of spending a good deal of money for a sleeping bag that will last for years, and you are not sure of your preference, you should first rent or borrow such bedding—perhaps for three or four outings—before buying your own. This will

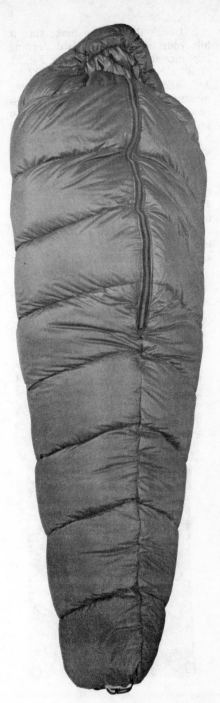

The Trailwise mummy bag by Ski Hut has been designed specifically for the mountaineer or backpacker. Filled with goose down and carefully constructed, it will keep the camper warm in very cold weather.

enable you to judge the relative merits of the various styles, brands and materials.

When you go shopping for your own sleeping bag, look for these features:

1. A manufacturer's label stating what kind of material is used for the cover, lining and insulation. The label has added significance if it reads, "Do not remove under penalty of law." The do-not-remove warning is aimed at those who sell sleeping bags, not at the ultimate users.

2. Check the size to make sure it fills your needs. A standard sleeping bag measures about 75" by 34", a "tall" sleeping bag measures 80" by 34" and a king-size sleeping bag measures 85" by 34". When in doubt, buy the larger size. There is more space to heat, but there is also more room to move about in. These are measurements for rectangular shaped bags; mummy bag measurements will generally be the same, except for the tapered areas. Incidentally, there are special sleeping bags for youngsters measuring about 67" by 34".

3. Check how well the sleeping bag is sewed together and how well the zippers work. The zippers should have

insulated flaps covering them to eliminate the possibility of "cold spots" next to the zipper.

4. The filling is the most important component. The price is largely based on this. Most expensive is goose down; least expensive is cotton. Dacron Fiberfill is a good middle-ground selection.

5. The outside covering should be water repellent, but not waterproof. Those with rubberized bottoms are fine—if you never take them to the dry cleaners. A separate ground cloth may be better.

6. Better quality sleeping bags often have pockets for inserting air mattresses. Some campers prefer to keep the air mattresses separate, but that is a matter of choice.

7. The sleeping bag should be machine washable and dryable in an automatic dryer, although some of the best require dry cleaning.

To keep your sleeping bag in good condition you should see to it that it always stays dry, that it is aired by turning inside out in the sunlight each day, if possible, and that a ground cloth is always placed between it and bare earth.

Sleeping bag styles

One reputable sleeping bag manufacturer makes more than 100 styles. This will give you some idea of the wide variety of styles manufactured and sold. The reason for this is a combination of personal preferences and the many different camping needs.

But there are only two basic styles—the rectangular bag and the mummy bag. Other styles are adaptations designed to meet specific camping criteria.

The most popular style is the square cut or rectangular sleeping bag. It is roomy and comfortable. The better rectangular bags open fully, which gives them added uses (robe or comforter) and makes them easy to clean

and air. Usually two can be zipped together for sleeping two or more persons. Some come with attachable head shelters and hoods.

The mummy bag is popular with many and is considered the best type of sleeping bag for backpackers. This tapered bag is trim, snug fitting and gives maximum warmth for minimum weight. It fits so well that you don't turn over inside it; you turn bag and all.

Combination sleeping bags such as the Hirsch-Weis "Four Seasons" model are becoming quite popular with campers who may expect any kind and all kinds of weather conditions. This particular model is two bags in one, which makes it adaptable to cool, medium or warm temperature conditions—plus convertibility to a double bag.

For station wagons

Another popular style is the sleeping bag made to fit the floors of station wagons and pickup trucks, as well as bunks and other prebuilt frames.

Gerry Cunningham has designed a sleeping bag which combines the best features of the rectangular bag and the mummy bag. Its shape and dimensions are somewhere in between. It holds heat well, yet is engineered to zip to another bag for double sleeping.

The sleeping bag has joined the slumber party. Many mothers have stocked specially designed, indoor sleeping bags for that expected unexpected—the day Johnny brings home a dozen college buddies for the weekend. These, of course, may have other uses, even serving as "extras" on a family campout.

Materials and construction

Frequently a sleeping bag will be described in terms of weight, which means the weight of the insulation material only. A two-pound bag has two pounds of insulation material. Total weight may be five pounds or more.

Two pounds of insulation materials do not guarantee the same warmth in every bag. Obviously, the material would be spread thinner in a very large bag than in an average size bag.

Coleman has patented this new all-season Twin Tri-Temp design. It provides three choices of warmth—one layer, two layers or three layers may be used as cover.

MODERATELY COOL (50° to 65°)
Sleep under one layer.

COLD (Above 32° F)
Sleep under two layers.

EXTREME COLD (Below 32° F)
Sleep under three layers.

TRI-TEMP opens to double bag
for station wagon sleeping.

And the kind of material also has a bearing on warmth.

Whatever is said about styles of sleeping bags and the materials of which they are made, the most important part is the insulation. Insulation has two purposes, the primary one being the prevention of body heat from escaping into cold air outside the bag. Insulation creates a space of "dead air" between the sleeper and the outside. The more of this space there is between the sleeping bag's inner lining and the outside cover, the more body heat will be retained.

The other purpose of insulation is to properly dispose of moisture naturally given off by the body. Particularly in freezing temperatures it is absolutely necessary that the sleeper stay dry as well as warm. As a matter of fact, let moisture build up, and cold will follow. Because of this problem, sleeping bags are never made with waterproof material. Water repellent, yes, but not waterproof. The sleeping bag must breathe in order for moisture to be properly dissipated.

Therefore, it stands to reason that given the right amount and kind of insulation material, a person will stay comfortable in a well constructed sleeping bag. The durability of the sleeping bag is determined to a large degree by the quality of outside cover material and inside liner material—plus such essentials as zippers and thread and how effectively these are used.

Goosedown best

Of the insulation materials used today in sleeping bags and outdoor clothing, prime northern goose down is the best for both warmth and dissipation of body moisture. Carefully processed duck down is second best. Down provides the most warmth for the least weight, an important factor in backpacking, and it has the ability to instantly spring back to its original loft (thickness or depth) after being compressed. It is also the most expensive initially, but it is good for a lifetime.

Dacron fiberfill is popular because it meets the needs of most family campers at less cost. It retains its bounce, is not affected by moisture and gives good warmth without too much weight. Most good bags in the medium-price range use Dacron fiberfill.

The least expensive sleeping bags depend on kapok or cotton batting for insulation. But don't count on these being effective if there is a sudden change in the weather. And don't count on them lasting for very long. At the same time, don't count them out. You can get substantial satisfaction out of the cheaper bags for a season or two, or at least until you know exactly what kind of sleeping bag is for you permanently. Besides, if your pocketbook says economize, by all means economize. Don't let a better sleeping bag stand between you and outdoor fun.

Popular prices

Most popularly priced bags contain cotton flannel linings. These come in a myriad of designs and colors. Some campers, however, like to get the same feel that their sheets at home give. This calls for sleeping bag lining made of percale. Most down-filled bags come with nylon lining, in some models with down-proof cotton. If you prefer, you also can find bags with linings made of satin and rayon.

A separate sheet liner helps to keep the sleeping bag clean, and it offers

The Gerry Shortie Foam Pad, made by Colorado Outdoor Sports Corporation, is preferred by many backpackers. It snaps to pillow-stuffed sacks and also may be attached to another pad for full length comfort.

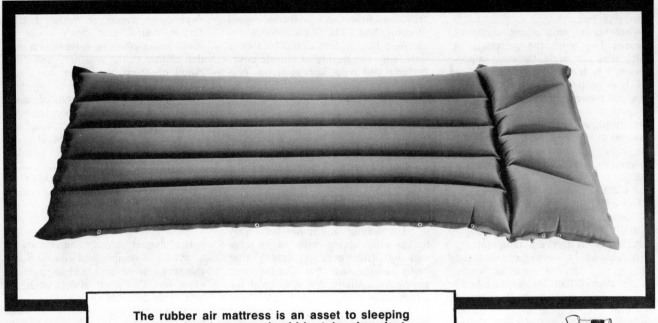

The rubber air mattress is an asset to sleeping bag comfort, but care should be taken in selecting one of quality. This model by Hirsch-Weis offers such desirable features as cloth outside, double rubbercoated inside, metal valve with cap and snaps for joining two together.

a certain freshness to the sleeper because it can be laundered every day, if necessary. Some bags come with built-in tie loops to accommodate sheet liners.

The outer cover of the sleeping bag should be determined by the kind of camping you will do most often. It's mainly a matter of weight. Army duck, the heavier the better, is excellent cover material if weight is not the main criterion. For backpackers, nylon is the answer. In between are some perfectly good cover materials—oxford cloth, army twill, poplin and cotton balloon cloth. Some covers are waterproofed on the bottom side. But a ground cloth serves the same purpose.

Zippers

Every person using a sleeping bag needs to know two or three facts about zippers. On a cold night you'll be glad you took the time to learn. The quality of materials and construction must be very high. You want a zipper that will work instantly, effectively and that will not jam. It should be just as easy to zip from the inside as from the outside.

If you anticipate moderately cold to very cold weather, insist on a heavy-duty zipper. And make certain that an insulating flap covers the zipper the full length, so that no part of the metal touches your body while sleeping. This eliminates any possibility of a zipper cold spot.

Finally, in judging materials and construction, observe the quilting. This is the process which binds the components together. Effective quilting

holds the insulation in place, voiding "cold spots," but not so much that the material is overly compressed. This process is not necessary in bags using down. Down insulation eliminates possible cold spots by filling the entire space allotted to it. A wrap-around, baffle-type construction is used with the better, down-filled bags.

Costs and description

Perhaps the best way to show what you can get for your money is to take a look at some good sleeping bags in various price ranges. A variety is shown in the accompanying photos. A wider variety is awaiting you at your favorite sporting goods store, camping supply center or camper's catalog.

Blankets, mattresses and cots

Some campers still prefer blankets to sleeping bags. In fact, some make their own sleeping bags from blankets. The procedure is simple: fold two blankets in half, lengthwise; slide one inside the other; fold up and fasten the bottom with large, 6-inch safety pins. Note: the blanket should be made of fluffy wool.

Cots are favorites with many campers, the only exception being backpackers who must keep weight down. Canvas and wood cots, used widely since the days of World War I, are available today. Some campers wouldn't use anything else.

A relatively new type is a cot made of canvas and framed aluminum or lightweight steel. Some are insulated on the bottom side. Because these cots are lower, they fit closer to the tent walls and thereby provide more

inside space. They are lighter in weight, and more costly.

All cots need blankets or pads for insulation and other comfort purposes. A pillow is a welcome luxury, as are sheets.

Air mattresses and foam pads are widely used by campers, often in conjunction with sleeping bags. Some sleeping bags have slots into which the air mattress fits. Backpackers do very well with a "shorty" foam pad that reaches from the shoulders to just below the hips.

Air mattresses

The best air mattresses are made of rubberized cloth. Most come in tubular shape. These are modestly priced. The best ones have a quilted contour. These are expensive. The cheapies are made of plastic. It pays to buy the best for camping purposes.

The width dimension of an air mattress when inflated is somewhat smaller than when deflated. Remember this when buying. And don't inflate any more than just enough to raise your shoulders and hips an inch or two off the ground.

Some air mattresses come equipped with foot-operated pumps; others with a hand-operated, rubber-bulb pump. The cheapies require lung power for inflation. Always inflate a new air mattress, or an old one for that matter, before you take it on a trip. Leave it inflated a day or so to check for leaks. One final note: beware of plastic valves. Metal is preferable.

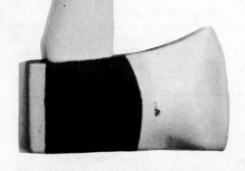

Camp Tools

The right tools, used correctly, and taken care of, will make camping more pleasurable, safer and less of a chore.

How to Use Them

YOU'RE THE SOLUTION TO WATER POLLUTION

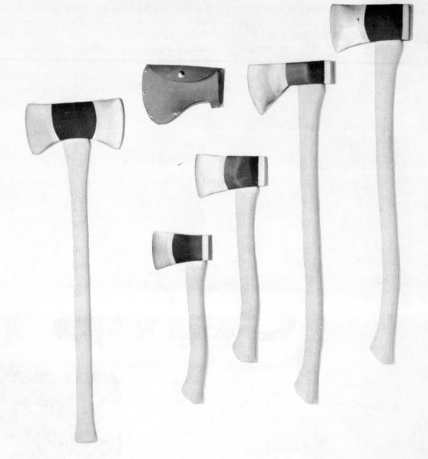

It may be true, as the oldtimer outdoorsman said, that the only tools you need in the woods are a good ax and a good knife. But even he would agree that a few others might be useful. A camper should not skimp on any tools he can use and can conveniently carry.

Times were when the ax and the knife were considered the only essential tools to the outdoorsman. But today's camper often takes along some that are more sophisticated.

A camper's tool selection begins with his ax and knife, but to his list he may quickly add a hammer and saw and a dozen other helpful items which serve as tools.

He likely will need a shovel, some rope and/or wire, an assortment of nails, pliers, a screw-driver set, scissors and sewing kit, a digging tool such as a mattock and a file or whetstone with which to sharpen blades.

As he considers other items, he may take along a rake, a broom, a repair kit for canvas and other fabrics used in the manufacture of his gear, an air mattress repair kit, a block and tackle, a metal wedge for splitting firewood and a swing blade for cutting tall grass and weeds at the campsite.

Many tools

Naturally, most of these will be eliminated by the backpacker, but the automobile camper may easily take tools of all kinds. Experience teaches what is always necessary, what probably will be necessary, what might be necessary, and what would be nice to have along in case of the unexpected. Packing room, the type of camping and the length of the trip dictate how much will be taken.

The ax

The camper should give first attention to his ax and knife. With them he can provide fuel, build a shelter, build all kinds of camp furnishings and, if necessary, defend himself.

There is no reason for not buying an ax made of the finest steel, with a handle made of knot-free hickory cut from second growth trees. Price will spell the difference, though not by much, between an inferior product and one that is totally satisfactory. Not only should the blade and handle

Professional axes, left to right, Timber Cruiser, double-bitted King of the Woods (but not for most campers); pack ax, precision-built personal ax for campers, hikers, hunters and canoe voyageurs; belt ax, heavyduty ax that will take on all routine trail and camp jobs from splitting kindling to felling saplings; Hudson Bay ax, the favorite of guides, trappers and woodsmen in the northern wilderness areas; and camper ax, all-purpose design to do every job from felling trees to splitting kindling and chunking stove lengths.

be made of the best materials, but the workmanship should be of the highest quality.

The ax should come with a good cutting edge, neither razor sharp nor too dull. The edge should be smooth, which it will be if the ax is new, and it should be kept that way. The handle likewise should be smooth and mounted into the ax so that the blade is in direct line with the bottom of the handle.

The selection of an ax is easier than the selection of a knife. This is true mainly because most ax manufacturers make high-grade tools. Sometimes axes made of low-grade steel are imported and sold through discount houses.

This inferior quality usually will be revealed through the price tag. The purchase of an ax at a reputable sporting goods store or a hardware store almost always assures your getting a good quality product.

Safety factor

Good axes often come sheathed in leather, or a leather sheath may be purchased separately. This is a worth-

while safety factor and affords good protection of the blade when the ax is not in use. Examine the leather closely. It should be heavy enough to bear the weight of the ax and to withstand other strains. It may be equipped with belt loops or slots wide enough for outdoor belts.

This may be a convenience feature, although many veteran campers prefer to pack an ax in some fashion apart from the belt loop. The leather should be oil-tanned, and if it does not come that way, you can do the job yourself by applying warm neatsfoot oil. This oil is available at hardware and sporting goods stores.

A camping ax should be of medium weight for average use, heavy enough to chop the timber with which a camper will be concerned, yet light enough to transport comfortably. The most useful axes for general purposes weigh up to four pounds and not less than three pounds. Routine cutting chores may be done with a two-pounder.

Long handle

Experienced campers prefer axes

with long handles, although there are numerous good uses for the short-handle ax such as the ones used by Boy Scouts. Where several persons are camping together, both models may be conveniently added to the gear.

The small ax is good for splitting kindling and similar uses around camp, but the long-handle ax is definitely the only one which makes chopping a sizable log or tree something less than drudgery.

Before deciding on which ax is for you, try out different ones. If you are not used to swinging an ax, or prefer not to do any heavy chopping, possibly the short-handle, two-pounder will do.

Kinds of axes

Probably the most popular ax among wilderness campers is the Hudson

it often is used to good advantage by many outdoorsmen in blazing a trail, chopping and splitting wood for small campfires and for smoothing poles. Boy Scouts and other youth groups are trained in the skillful use of these small axes. A hatchet usually weighs about one pound and is attached to a 12-inch handle.

The double-bitted ax is not the ax for campers. It is dangerous, is unweildy in the hands of the inexperienced and cannot be used to hammer or drive nails and stakes. Professional woodcutters are the main users of this ax.

The best ax for general camping, including canoe trips requiring portaging, is the standard poleax. This ax had a long handle of about 30

into a log and the chips will fly. That is, the chips will fly if you aim the blade at a 45-degree angle and hit what you aim toward. To sharpen, check for nicks along the blade's edge and use a file or grindstone (if one is available) to take out the worst nicks.

A handstone with fine grit on one side and coarse grit on the other should be used to finish the sharpening. The fine-grit side, kept moist while in use, will give a smooth, sharp edge. If only a knife stone or whetstone is available, this may be used to edge the blade after filing.

Clear area

When you are ready to use the ax, first make sure that all obstructions have been cleared from the swinging area. These may be limbs above or

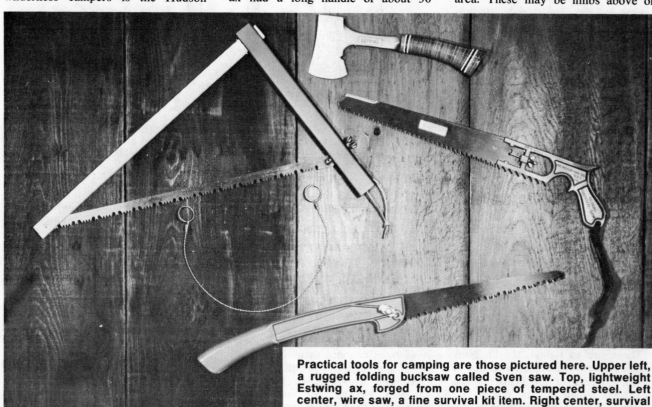

Practical tools for camping are those pictured here. Upper left, a rugged folding bucksaw called Sven saw. Top, lightweight Estwing ax, forged from one piece of tempered steel. Left center, wire saw, a fine survival kit item. Right center, survival saw, a unique design feature including reversible handle of hardened aluminum alloy. Bottom, Swedish folding saw, featuring a fast-cutting 11″ blade.

Bay ax. This ax weighs two pounds and comes with a 26-inch handle, making it a handy tool on the trail. It is not, however, the ideal ax for heavy work. But for average use in splitting kindling and firewood from cut lengths and for trimming of small limbs, the Hudson Bay is made to order. Many campers will have little need of more.

Of less use, and much more dangerous, is the hatchet. Some will debate this, but in the hands of the unskilled who attempt too much with it, the hatchet can be a frustrating tool. Because of its short handle, the cutting edge is always closer to the body.

A missed stroke can end up in a leg or hand if great care isn't taken. Yet,

inches—sometimes as much as 36 inches—and weighs three pounds. Properly maintained, it will fell a large tree and go through a log with a minimum of time and effort.

Axmanship

As with any tool, there are right ways and wrong ways to handle an ax. You begin by treating it with respect. It will do the job for you, but it can also become a dangerous weapon. If you are inexperienced or if you are not sure that you handle an ax correctly, by all means take the time to learn and practice until you can use it well—and safely.

Your ax should be sharp, not razor sharp, but sharp. A sharp ax will bite

scrub brush on the ground. Clear more than the chopping area as a safety precaution.

The rule is to be careful. Even so, sometimes your ax will glance off a knot or a limb, and you should be prepared for this by always maintaining the right stance and distance from the tree or log. Some dangers can be avoided by a little forethought. One is that of flying sticks caused by leaning a limb against a log or chopping block and attempting to break it after it is only partly cut in two.

A precaution for the care of the cutting edge is to avoid plunging the ax into the ground. If it hits a stone, it will be nicked and require sharpening. An expert axman will seldom drive his ax into the ground.

The handle of the ax is quite important to what you can do with this tool. As mentioned, the best handles are made from second-growth hickory. This wood is tough, yet has enough give in it to withstand and absorb shocks that most woods cannot take. Satisfactory ax handles may be made from maple and oak, but take care that the wood is of the same basic coloration all the way through.

Straight handle

Some handles curve down rather sharply. These are not the best and will cause more jolt and strain to the wrists and hands than will the better, straight handles. The straight handles are made with a slightly enlarged, sometimes slightly curved end.

Do not buy an ax with a handle that has been painted or lacquered; neither should you apply such solutions yourself. You can apply permanent protection, if you wish, by rubbing on linseed oil—preferably boiled and applied while still warm.

One very serious danger is that of the ax head coming loose from the handle in the middle of a chopping procedure. A three-pound head of steel, sharp on one edge, can cause severe damage or injury when it flies through the air.

The answer to this danger is to inspect the fit of the head and handle several times a day, always before each use if the ax has been idle for a period of time. You may have observed one or more wedges that have been driven into the head end of the handle.

These are to tighten the fit. New handles come with provision for a wooden wedge in the center of the head end. When for any reason you detect a slipping or loosening of the handle, hammer a small wooden wedge into the area where the handle ends in the ax opening. If problems continue, possibly a new handle is called for.

Pay no attention to advice that the handle will be more secure if you soak the ax head and that end of the handle in water for a few hours. There may be a temporary tightening, but it won't last. And more damage to the ax and handle will be done than the temporary tightening effect is worth.

Felling a tree

Before felling a tree, make certain that you have good reason for doing so. A tree takes a long time to grow, and you don't want to destroy its usefulness for the mere pleasure of chopping it down. When you need

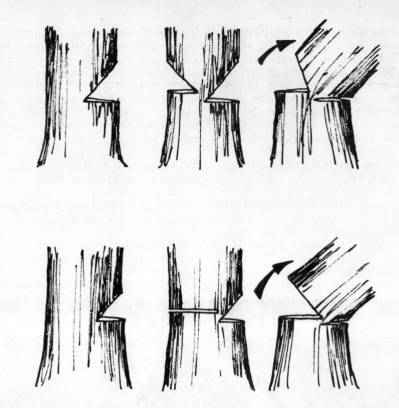

In felling a tree, whether by ax (above) or by saw (below), cut a wide notch on the side of the tree facing its fall direction. Then cut a second notch on the opposite side and through to a point an inch or so above the first notch.

firewood in camp and there is no other source, look for a tree that is dead.

This makes the best firewood, and the felling of a dead tree does little permanent damage to the forest. Of course, you don't cut into any tree without permission from the owner or, in the case of national forests, from the proper authorities.

Unless your ax weighs at least three pounds and has a long handle, avoid trees of more than six or eight inches in diameter. You will know you have been working, even with this size tree, by the time you have it chopped up into wood for the campfire.

Examine the tree to see which way it is leaning and if it appears to be perfectly perpendicular, notice which side has the heaviest limbs. The tree will tend to fall in the direction of its lean side or heaviest side. The wind may be a factor, and it is best to avoid felling trees entirely when the wind is high.

When you have determined which way the tree will fall, examine its path of descent. Will it destroy too much young timber? Will it fall into your campsite? Will it endanger the home of a squirrel or a bird? Will it block a roadway?

Cut into trunk

After these questions have been answered to your satisfaction, begin by cutting into the trunk of the tree on the side of its fall direction. For easiest cutting, make your 45° angle just above the stump area. With smaller trees, you should cut approximately halfway through on this side. About one-third of the way is enough for larger trees.

Then move to the other side of the tree and make a similar cut about one or two inches higher than the first cut. This is important. If the second cut is at the same level or lower than the first cut, you will have little control over the way the tree might fall.

You will hear creakings and groanings from the tree before you have cut all the way through in the second notch. The tree may sway back and forth a bit, and then very slowly start to lean in the direction of your prescribed falling pattern. Don't attempt to help it along by pushing it or by giving it some extra chops. Move to one side— never directly to the rear—and permit the tree to fall of its own momentum.

Do not hurry, for if you fall and the tree bounces back or to one side, it could crush you. The reason for staying away from the rear of the falling tree trunk is that it might kick back, which often happens when the trunk splits. A green tree with numerous limbs sometimes will jump back in a springing action when the limbs hit the ground. Incidentally, when felling a dead tree, make certain that you are not endangered by large limbs which might break off.

Limb it

When your tree is down, the next step is to limb it. Starting at the lowest limb on the tree trunk, cut the limbs from the underside at an angle that will separate them smoothly and flush with the trunk. As a safety precaution, stand on the side of the trunk opposite from the limbs being cut.

Continue to cut off the limbs, working your way toward the top of the tree, until the trunk itself is no larger than a limb. Cut the top off at this point. As you cut the limbs, take care to remove each one from the swinging area of the ax. And don't leave them scattered in a haphazard fashion; pile them in one spot where they will not interfere with other forest growth and will not look unsightly.

A saw is best for cutting a large log in two, but you may have to use your ax for this. This is another reason for not felling a tree larger than you can handle all the way. The procedures for chopping a log in two are simple: make a notch at a 45° angle that will come to a point within an inch of the other side of the log. If the log is small enough to roll over, the notch may come to a point halfway through and then a similar notch may be made on the opposite side.

In all cutting and chopping, stand with legs wide apart approximately an ax handle's distance from the log or tree. When the tree has been cut into firewood lengths, the ax may be used for splitting the larger pieces. If the lengths have been chopped in two, the most convenient way to split these is to lean them at an angle against a chopping block or, preferably, against the fork of a large limb or log, so that the ax blade may enter the length at one end and in direct line with the grain.

If the lengths have been sawed, they should be stood on end and the ax should strike directly in line with the grain on the side next to the axman. If the ax is driven directly into the center, it likely will get stuck there and be very difficult to remove. To assist in the splitting of larger pieces, a metal wedge may be used. Wooden wedges may be made on the spot to help spread open a log that has been partially split by the ax.

The best way to good axmanship is to watch an expert at work. If you camp in the national forests or in an area where forestry products are being harvested, ask permission to observe some of the men at work. They'll answer your questions and you can quickly see that they have learned the procedures of axmanship to near perfection.

Knives for camping

The knife is the second most essential tool for the camper; some outdoorsmen will say it is the first

with them. There is no question that it is a primary tool and one that should be carefully selected.

Selecting the right ax is elementary compared to selecting the right knife. For one thing, a knife can be made to look good even if it is worthless. If you are not a good judge of steel and craftsmanship that goes into the making of a knife, by all means rely upon the advice of a reputable dealer. Or on the reputation of a well-known brand. Good quality knives often are advertised or recommended in camping magazines.

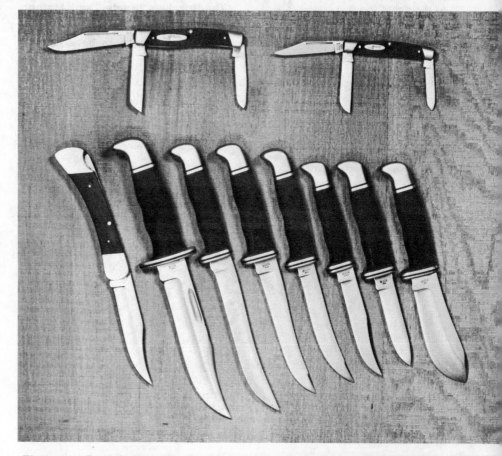

These are Buck knives. The blades are hand forged from a special high-carbon steel, semi-hollow ground, then finished and honed by hand. Buck knives are entirely handmade. Those shown here will supply every knife need in camp.

Choose good brand

Surplus knives, particularly those said to have been manufactured for foreign military units, are not necessarily good knives. By all means, beware of ordering these through advertisements placed by unknown companies. If such surplus knives are advertized in catalogs of reputable firms, you can be relatively sure of getting your money's worth.

In shopping for a knife, beware of beginners' faults: 1) the wrong kind of knife, 2) the wrong size or 3) cheap materials and cheap construction. A good buyer's rule is to purchase the best knife you can afford and one

that is convenient in size.

It is easy to be attracted to a large, sheathed knife. But the best size for general camping purposes is one with a blade of four to six inches in length. A sheath should always be purchased with such a knife, which may be worn on the belt.

The camper should be forewarned that even bad knives can be made to look good. The first thing to beware of is a knife with a fancy handle or blade, or one with trick blades. The best knives are made of heat treated high-carbon steel. These can be kept

razor-sharp by proper use and by keeping them honed on a good oilstone, which a knowledgeable hardware merchant can recommend.

Pocket knife

Along with the larger knife may be a second, a good-quality pocket knife such as the Swiss Army knife or the Boy Scout model. A combination-type pocket knife—with such features as an awl, a spike, a bottle opener and a screw driver—may be useful to the camper, but the only good ones are expensive.

A visit to a hardware store will reveal many kinds and styles of knives.

You may prefer a size and style that most campers would not choose. The important thing to remember is to buy the knife that best suits your needs and tastes. If you make a wrong purchase, you will soon know it. A little experience will enable you to be a wiser purchaser the next time.

The blade should be kept quite sharp, the fineness of the edge being determined by the uses to which it will be put. Some outdoorsmen have been known to so sharpen their knives that they could shave with them. The handle should be easy to grip and should be part of the balance necessary to the right "feel."

The Henckels "Hunter" with leather belt sheath is rugged enough to take on any camp or trail task, yet is handsome enough to be a collector's item.

Three Sports Handyman sharpening stones come in a plastic kit that can be carried in the pocket. Top stone is for knives and ice augers, the round stone is for sharpening axes and hatchets and the bottom stone puts a point on fish hooks. From Worth Tackle Co., Stevens Point, Wisconsin.

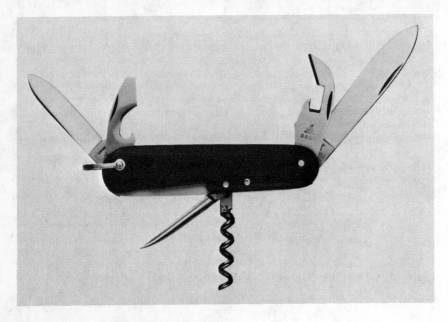

The Henckels "Sportsman" is a type of pocket-knife that every camper should possess. In effect, it is the equivalent of seven precision tools.

One of the best all around knives made. It is a Case Cheyenne Model 400. It is entirely hand made, has a 5″ blade made of special steel that will not rust. Holds an edge sharp enough to shave with. This would be the one knife which would be ideal for hunting, fishing and camping. Comes with a heavy leather sheath that completely encloses the knife and is riveted to keep the knife from cutting through.

The camp saw

Many novice campers readily see a useful purpose in taking along an ax and a knife, but never give a thought to a saw. Modern outdoorsmen, particularly those who work and camp in forest areas, have learned that a saw may be more useful at times than an ax. For example, with the proper saw you can gather firewood more easily and more quickly than with an ax.

Probably the best one-man saw devised to date is the bucksaw. Basically this is a three-piece wooden frame onto which a saw is fastened near the bottom and a turnbuckle near the top. Today's models are not nearly as good as those used 30 or 40 years ago. However, by some improvising the bucksaw can be an ex-cellent saw easily carried. The weight shouldn't be more than three or four pounds.

Another good saw to take to camp is one mounted to a bowed steel frame. One end of the frame becomes the handle and the top of the frame is held with one hand to guide the saw as it cuts.

Various types of blades are manufactured, including the straight V-tooth blade. This probably is the best blade for beginners and for average cutting chores around camp. Your supplier or hardware merchant can show you samples of blade types and advise you on their usefulness.

Keep sharp

Keeping a saw blade sharp and "set" is just as important, if not more so, as keeping an ax blade sharp and smooth. One reason for buying the V-tooth blade is the comparative ease with which it can be serviced.

This type of blade will come properly filed and "set" and very likely will stay that way for an entire camping season. Before heading for the wilds the following spring, a camper would be well advised to take his saw to a commercial saw maintenance shop. The "setting" of a saw—that is, lining the teeth up straight—is best done by a person trained to do the job.

When using a one-man camp saw, do not bear down with much weight on the saw. Neither a bucksaw nor a steel frame saw will work best when the sawer is bearing down. The saw will curve away from the line of cut and eventually become very difficult to move back and forth.

A little pressure is necessary, of course. Use even strokes that pull and push the blade distances of its entire length. With little or no pressure, depending on the kind of wood being cut, you will soon have a stack of firewood to last for hours or even days.

Shoveling and digging

Necessary to most types of camping is a shovel. Many campers prefer a tool that may be used for digging in the way of a mattock and also perform as a shovel. Soldiers in World War II carried a combination shovel and mattock tool for digging foxholes and trenches. This has been adapted for campers. Some of the military versions are still available in surplus stores.

You may prefer to carry a standard shovel. The most convenient model comes with a short handle. Separate digging tools, including picks, may be purchased with short handles similar to those used in the carpenter's hammer.

One thing is certain: a shovel is useful in numerous ways. It is used in camp to scoop up mounds of earth where the tent is to stand. It may be used likewise to level any area. It is useful when the car gets stuck in the mud or sand. It can be used to fill in a latrine or garbage pit when you break camp. And it is most useful, perhaps, in constructing drainage ditches around the tent or entire campsite. In short, you'd better take one along.

Tips on tool care

• Keep sharp the tools that require sharpening.

• Protect metal tools from water. Dry them off after using them in streams or rain.

• Wedge blade of ax in a log when not in use. This is a safety procedure and protects the blade from rain and sun damage. A better precaution is to encase the ax in its sheath and store it in a dry place.

• Wash your knife after using it to cut food. Dry it carefully. Do not clean it by running the blade into the ground. Don't jam it into a log.

• Use the right tool for the job. Do not attempt too much with a knife—such as chopping and splitting heavy wood. Don't use your ax as a wedge which must be hammered on the head.

• Tools are for work, not for play. Don't play cowboys-and-indians by throwing your ax and knife. Use your tools for what they are intended, nothing more.

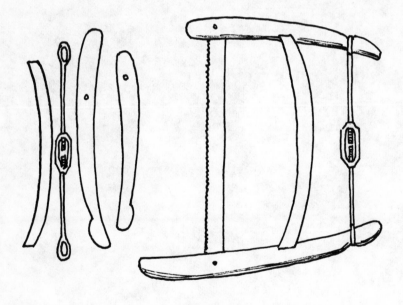

The old-fashioned three-piece bucksaw, sometimes hard to get, but still very useful in the woods.

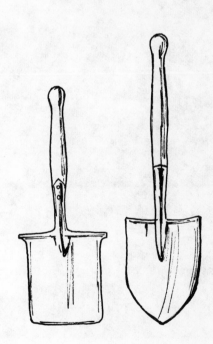

Two types of short handled shovels that find many uses in camp.

The Secrets of

Successful
Camp Cookery

To produce a good camp meal requires this: enough of the foods you like, that provide a balanced diet, and are tastefully prepared. This is the one big secret of cooking in camp, which, as it turns out, is no real secret; what you like to eat at home is what you also like in the outdoors. A surprisingly large number of novice campers fail to grasp this fact, however.

Obviously, some adaptations have to be made, particularly in backpacking and certain primitive camping. But even the hardy wilderness adventurers don't have to subsist on food they don't like. Today's lightweight dehydrated and freeze-dry foods are both tasty and nourishing—and very easy to prepare.

Heavyweight campers—those who have room to take about everything up to the kitchen sink—can select any variety of food items from the home refrigerator and pantry shelves.

All of which points up the fact that there is little danger of going hungry in camp or of becoming dissatisfied with the menu. This also exposes published campers' menus for what they are: valuable guides and nothing more. Your outdoor menu for a day, a week or a month is *your* decision and should reflect *your* tastes and the preferences of your family or the camping party. Two or three campouts will give you enough experience and training to handle this important chore for all the camping seasons to come.

First meal

Whatever you do, don't give in to the suggestion that camping and indigestion go together—not even if your first camp meal is a total flop. Your first meal will not be a total flop, of course, for it is a fact that the average camper will eat conglomerations in camp that he wouldn't touch at home and wouldn't pay for in a restaurant. For some reason, many persons actually expect to suffer gastronomically while camping. This, they believe, will demonstrate how rugged they are. Ridiculous!

Planning takes priority

The saddest camper is one who discovers too late that a vital food ingredient is missing, left at home. This happens all too often, sometimes miles from the nearest store. But not to the camper who carefully plans and prepares in advance.

The only logical time to plan camp meals is at home before the trip begins. The only logical way to plan is to begin with a list. The list should be made up according to categories, broken down into specifics for meals. Don't be concerned with quantities until your list is complete.

Your list begins with basics. The basics are such items as flour, seasonings, sugar, shortening or cooking oil—

The secrets of successful camp cookery are simple and basic, but the techniques are many. Get better meals, economically—ones that will cater to taste of every family member.

in short, those items that will be necessary in the preparation of numerous dishes.

Standard foods

The second part of your list should consist of standard food kinds—vegetables, fruits, proteins, deserts and such—that your family enjoys at home.

Add to this favorite supplements—peanut butter, jams and jellies, soups, cereals and beverages.

Finally, list some extras that delight your family. Popcorn, potato chips, marshmallows and exotic items would fall into this category.

Don't become concerned at this point that you might be listing too many items. You can start eliminating later as you plan individual meals. At the same time you can determine how much packing space you'll have for

food. Where you will be camping, how close you will be to a food market or other food sources, how long you will be camping and similar factors will determine the amount and, to some degree, the varieties of food taken. Incidentally, your best assistance for

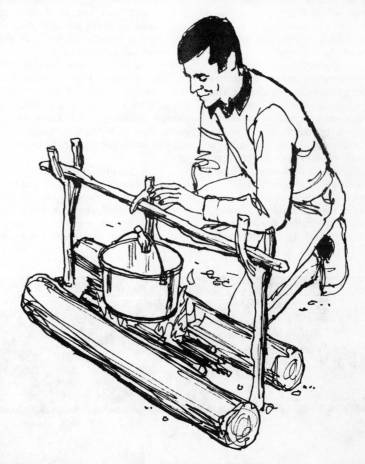

The hunter's fire is a favorite of many campers. Simply place two logs close together and lay the fire between them. Cooking utensils may be placed on the logs or hung from a crane as shown here.

planning the camping menus will be your own pantry and refrigerator. Also helpful are the numerous campers' cookbooks sold by most bookstores and larger newsstands.

Plan by meal

The next logical step is to plan the menu meal by meal. Instead of planning the meals for a given day, unless you are on a one-day trip, plan all of the breakfasts together, all of the lunches together and all of the dinners together.

Now you come to the critical point

in planning. This is the list that requires an entry for every item that goes into every dish. It also is the list that you should keep with you during the entire campout.

If you are on a five-day trip which calls for four breakfasts, list these 1, 2, 3, 4. Under the heading, "Breakfast No. 1," list every dish and every ingredient that will be necessary in the preparation of each dish. This may seem superfluous, but as you enter the third or fourth day you will be glad that you can check this list against remaining supplies.

It also is useful for double checking your basic supply list as you pack for the trip. Further, with this kind of detailed planning, you can serve breakfast No. 4 on the second day, if you wish. And nobody will suffer.

Repeat this procedure for all the breakfasts, then for all the lunches and, finally, for all the dinners.

Quantities

When your menus are completed in detail, you can quickly determine the quantity of each item. Usually the quantity becomes a critical measurement only when weight and bulk are factors. Ordinarily, you can take a little more than you need of each item. In fact, you should take more. Campers' appetites are notoriously big.

The procedure for making up your market list is simple: total the number of times eggs are called for—both on the plate and in cooking—add the number of eggs called for each day, and then add the daily totals to arrive at the grand total. Do the same for potatoes, apples and such. Adapt these procedures for foods that require volume measurements in addition to numbers.

Some campers prefer to add all of the items on each day's menu, and you may find this more satisfactory. By all means, plan your menus the way that is most convenient to you. The important word is *plan*. This is a critical priority.

Simple foods techniques

Before you finalize on that food list, consider simplifying it. There is no need for elaborate, Full-course meals in camp.

The convenience of transporting and preserving food for camping—thanks to modern coolers, packaging and the like—could lead one to believe that camp cooking is not unlike home cooking. This is mostly correct, but there are some subtle differences.

You can prepare just about anything in camp that you prepare at home, but the techniques are different. Further, to carry on a full home schedule in the camp's culinary department may be more than you wish to tackle. After all, you are camping for the enjoyment of it.

Camp facilities

The cooking facilities in camp are not quite equal to those in the home kitchen, although they are surprisingly efficient. If the menus are simple, cooking is no drudgery—even on a two-burner or over an open fire.

Most foods for camp should require a short cooking time and a short time in preparation for the skillet or pot. Occasionally, a surprise dish is in order. Fresh strawberries from a nearby farm will bring an enthusiastic response, no matter which meal features this "surprise."

Food prepared in camp should be wholesome and easy to digest. To make certain of this, take an ample supply of fruits and vegetables and avoid using the skillet more than is necessary, particularly in preparing the evening meal.

Some quick-energy foods are helpful for snacks, for example during a rest stop on a morning hike. But too many snacks can spoil the regular meals—and can upset the best of digestive systems.

Simple menus are not hard to prepare. Breakfast doesn't change much, lunch for most campers requires only three or four simple items. The dinner menu is the most complicated.

Hot breakfast

Except in emergencies, don't settle for a cold breakfast. Warm, nourishing food and plenty of it makes breakfast the substantial meal that it ought to be. Camping demands a good deal of physical activity, and it is the wise camper who is properly fortified for such activity.

These are the main items around which breakfast may be planned: fruit (fresh, if possible) or fruit juice; eggs (sometimes cooked with meat); bread (pancakes, toast, biscuits) and/or cereal (preferably hot); beverage preferably hot).

Lunch can be built around a good, filling sandwich, sometimes served with soup. Add to this a liberal amount of fresh or dried fruits and a candy bar. A slice of carrot or a celery stalk, chilled in the ice box, goes well with a camper's lunch. Nuts are excellent for energy and bulk. The beverage may be hot or cold, depending on the weather and the activity engaged in.

Dinner can be kept quite simple by building the entire menu around a single main dish. This is an added convenience in that it requires only a single, large pot for cooking. Camper's stew made of favorite ingredients is more welcome camping than at home. Add to this main dish a salad and a desert, and you have a fine dinner.

Freeze-dry, dehydrated foods

By far the greatest food born to campers has been the introduction of revolutionary new freeze-dry foods. Some are precooked and some are frozen raw. Vegetables and fruits are exceptionally tasty and nutritious when preserved in this manner.

Freeze-dry means that foods are extremely low temperatures. The ice

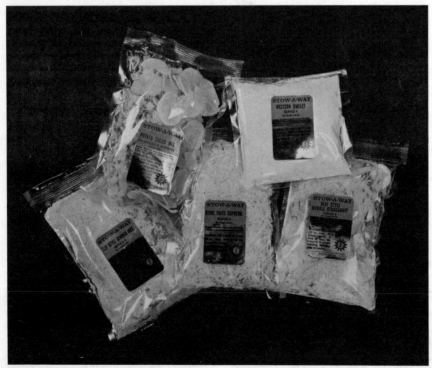

Prepackaged lightweight camp meals made by Stow-A-Way Products of Cohasset, Massachusetts, are sold in clear, sealed bags for easy identification.

crystals around them are then evaporated rapidly. There is no loss of nutrition or flavor and no shrinkage. The great loss is in weight, a welcome feature for any camper. These foods require no refrigeration and are returned to their original, fresh appearance after being soaked a few minutes in water. Meats, fish and poultry are preserved in similar fashion, and the lack of weight is fantastic.

Other convenience foods for campers are preserved by dehydration. Often the bulk is reduced as well as the weight. Water also is used to reconstitute these. Add instant beverages, instant puddings and other instant food types, and the preparation of any outdoor meal is made easy and simple.

Probably the easiest way to cook in camp is to use the prepackaged "cookout" foods, freeze-dry and dehydrated, especially manufactured and packed for campers. You can purchase these in complete units containing a day's food requirements for as many as eight people. You can also purchase individual lunches and individual suppers. Or, you can purchase individual items.

Bernard Food Industries, Inc., one of several reputable food manufacturers catering to campers, produces some 90 food items in the Kamp Pack Foods line. These foods are nonperishable, come packed in waterproof, airtight containers and preserve the taste to an amazing degree. All you have to do is add water and cook.

Typical menu

Here is a typical day's menu, packaged in quantities to serve four adults:

Breakfast
  Zoom instant cereal with milk and sugar
  Egg omelette
  Corn bread mix
  Whole milk

Lunch
  Spaghetti tomato dinner
  Hot biscuit mix
  Instant vanilla pudding
  Orangeade

Dinner
  Chicken noodle soup mix
  Chili con carne with beans
  Hot biscuit mix
  Raspberry applesauce mix
  Chocolate milk shake mix

These are menus selected from many combinations available for individual meals. Total cost for four persons is $11.65, or less than $3 per day per person.

An eight-person pack containing 24 full meals sells for $16.50. Broken down, the cost is less than 70 cents per meal. Notice what one pack contains:

Breakfast
  Instant Zoom cereal with milk, sugar and apricot pearls
  Sweet cream buttermilk pancakes with "golden clear no stick" (re-

places shortening) for cooking
  Maple flavored syrup
  Hot chocolate

Lunch (choice of hot or cold)
  Hot lunch includes spanish rice
  Pilot biscuits
  Fruit sauce mix
  Fruit punch
  Cold lunch includes beef jerky
  Cheese and crackers
  Candy
  Fruit punch

Dinner
  Minestrone soup
  Beef vegetable stew
  Hot biscuits
  Instant vanilla pudding
  Strawberry milk shake

If you prefer—and many do—you can make up your own menu by buying individual items. For example, you can buy a four-person pack of applesauce

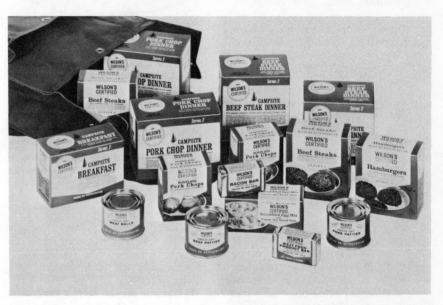

Wilson and Company, Inc., has developed an entire line of freeze-dry "Campsite" meat products.

mix for 78 cents. Freeze-dry beef vegetable stew for serving four persons costs $2.16.

Interestingly enough, the applesauce mix mentioned above weighs only four ounces; the stew weighs eight ounces.

Unless you get the idea that the servings of these lightweight foods are skimpy, be informed that the servings are "heaping." And the taste is all there, thanks to some great new improvements in seasoning.

The food value and the freshness are retained, thanks to improved processing and packaging. If you once ate dehydrated and concentrated field rations during World War II and the Korean War, don't be influenced by the memory. You are in for a surprise when you taste such foods today.

Cooking prepared foods

Water is all you add to the contents of prepared freeze-dry and dehydrated foods for campers. But there are some

simple steps in doing the job right.

For one thing, these foods require no hard boiling. A low bed of coals or a low flame on a stove provides about the right amount of heat. Those items requiring simmering should be brought to the bubbling point very slowly, and the heat should be barely enough to keep the bubbles coming up.

Replace water as it boils down. This is particularly important at high altitudes where water evaporates rapidly. Stir the cooking ingredients frequently enough to keep them from sticking. Keep cooking pans covered. For added zest and flavor, reduce the heat and cook longer. To shorten the cooking time, allow the ingredients to soak longer than the directions call for. In short, suit the cooking procedure to the occasion and your personal preferences.

Some of these foods require that a paste be made of the package contents before cooking. A pan or mixing bowl and some cold water meet this requirement. In fact, most of the mixing can be done right in the food container. Stir in enough water to form a paste, break up all lumps and slowly add the rest of the water called for until the ingredients are ready for cooking.

Instant foods needed

Even if you take most of your camp larder from the home kitchen, it's a good idea to have some of the instant foods on hand. A sudden storm, the failure of your camp stove (may be out of fuel) and any number of "emergencies" may make a simple food package quite attractive to the whole family. Many campers make it a point to utilize the freeze-dry and dehydrated foods for one or two meals each day. This enables the cook to concentrate on the third meal more with an outdoor gourmet's approach.

Of course, backpackers eat very well on the trail when they depend mainly on the lightweight, prepackaged foods. For one thing, they can carry more meals and more variety.

Before another phase of camp cookery is introduced, it should be pointed out that the supermarket shelves feature scores of standard lightweight foods—from soups to nuts—that you should consider for any kind of camping. Some of these may need additional wrapping or packaging to withstand outdoor elements, but this is no problem.

Popular camp cooking equipment

Given the right kind of open fire, the right utensils and the right weather, you can prepare the best tasting meals you've ever eaten—that is, if you cook your favorite foods. For details on making the kinds of fires most suitable, see "Fires for All Occasions." Meanwhile, consider the most popular and most useful items of cooking equipment used by today's campers.

Camp stoves. The most popular camp stoves for years have been the one-, two- or three-burner models that burn white (unleaded) gasoline. These stoves fold up luggage-style and are easy to pack and carry.

The fuel is economical, and two gallons will supply the average family for a week's campout. Maintenance is relatively simple, and such stoves will operate efficiently through many years of camping pleasure.

Appearing on the scene in recent years are stoves fueled with bottled gas or liquid petroleum. These stoves are similar to the gasoline models, the main differences being disposable fuel cylinders, no generator and no air pumping. Operating expense is considerably more than for the standard gasoline burners.

The camp oven more and more is becoming a common sight at family campouts. Definitely a great help in preparing better outdoor meals.

Hardly bigger than a soup can, this SVEA gasoline stove by Primus is ideal for backpackers and useful to all campers.

Backpackers usually prefer small one-burner stoves—many imported from Europe—that are fueled by alcohol, white gas, naphtha or benzene. These weigh less than two pounds and consume very small quantities of fuel.

Some campers in the more permanent camps still prefer wood-burning stoves. Even backpackers and others improvise these from cans, buckets and metal drums. Some suppliers carry the fixtures for converting empty oil drums into first-rate stoves which provide heat for both cooking and shelter warmth.

The Dutch oven. The real outdoorsmen agree: the Dutch oven is the best single piece of cooking gear. And it is conspicuously missing from most suppliers' shelves—the real Dutch oven, that is. Aluminum models can be purchased most anywhere, and these are

Typical Dutch Oven

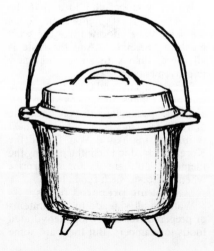

satisfactory for cooking on a gas stove. But the old-fashioned model made of cast iron is the only one for an open fire. It, or something like it, was used by your great grandmother in all likelihood. And she did a pretty good job with it.

The Dutch oven is heavy and certainly not for the backpacker. But this disadvantage is far overshadowed by what the oven can do. You can use it for practically every type of cooking. Broiling might be a little difficult, but not much else is.

The Dutch oven should have a rim on the cover, and it should rest on short legs. Hot coals under the oven and hot coals on the lid (this is where the rim plays an important role) guarantee satisfactory baking of any bake recipe.

Used primarily for baking, the Dutch oven also makes a good kettle for boiling, simmering and just about any cooking process that you wish to transfer from the home kitchen to your campsite.

Season oven

When the Dutch oven is new, the inside should be rubbed with vegetable oil and set in a warm place (a low oven is okay) for a few hours. Wipe off the excess oil and repeat the process several times. This seasons the oven and keeps foods from sticking in the future. The same procedure works well on any cast-iron cooking utensil.

One of the best old-fashioned Dutch ovens is manufactured by Lodge Manufacturing Company, South Pittsburg, Tennessee.

Reflector oven. This is a favorite with many campers. Commercial models are available, although you can make one from a square or rectangular metal can—such as a five-gallon cooking-oil can.

The reflector oven is used primarily for baking and roasting. The best results are realized when the heat comes from a reflector-type fire. The operation is simple: the baking shelf receives reflected heat from the oven's slanted upper and lower sides, which in turn receive heat from the flames of a fire.

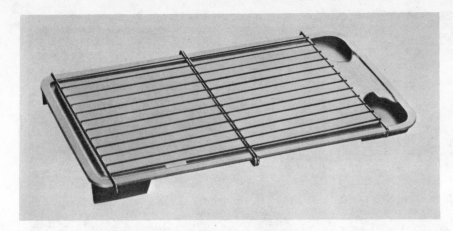

Broiler, griddle, toaster—you name it—and this type of unit will fit the need.

One of the new cooking-lighting combinations is this one by Coleman. The lantern and camp stove operate off the filled propane bottle.

The "Tepee" toaster is a favorite with veteran campers.

More heat is directed to the oven when the fire is built against a large rock, log or stack of logs. Care must be taken to prevent burning of the food on the bottom side. Properly utilized, this oven will bake biscuits that are just as tasty as those coming from the kitchen oven at home.

Good reflector ovens manufactured commercially sell for $5 to $12, depending on the size. Most are collapsible for easy carrying and storing.

Nested cookers. These are cooking sets, usually made of aluminum, low in weight and long on convenience. The largest pot houses all the others. When buying such a set, select one with the large kettle having enough capacity for your largest single need. The others, diminishing in size to a small one about right for boiling two or three eggs, will suit your in-between needs.

Many experienced campers avoid buying a pre-arranged kit, preferring to make up their own by individual selection. You should think twice before buying an aluminum set containing drinking cups, plates and frypan. The frypans of stainless steel or cast-iron are best. And if you have ever burned your lips on an aluminum cup, you know why some other material is better for drinking cups.

Grills and griddles. Various types of grills are used by campers on both wood fires and camp stoves. These may be purchased at camping supply stores or they may be improvised.

Griddles, too, are very convenient, particularly at breakfast time. Flapjacks, eggs over or sunny-side up, French toast and other tempting dishes are easily and efficiently prepared on a griddle. The griddle, incidentally, can substitute for a stove top on which you can set your kettles. A fire built between two logs on which the griddle rests will enable you to fry and boil foods to your heart's content.

The Primus Compact Camp Kitchen is a combination lantern-and-stove, propane-fueled unit.

For the camper who wants to make sure that he has both cooking and eating facilities readily available, Camp 'Otel Corporation has produced this camp table-stove combo. Made mostly of aluminum and weighing less than 30 pounds, the unit carries all cooking utensils, plates, cups, eating silver and all kitchen supplies, with plenty of space left for food.

Porta-Trace, an affiliate of Gagne Associates, Inc., Binghamton, New York, offers this Porta-Galley.

Aluminum foil. It shouldn't come as any surprise to the home cook that aluminum foil has about as many uses in the outdoor kitchen. Potatoes wrapped in foil and buried in hot coals will be perfectly baked in an hour or so. Or fresh corn-on-the-cob, seasoned with butter and salt, will come out of the ashes with more goodness and taste than you can imagine. The foil is perfect for keeping out dirt and ashes. Foil is indispensable to today's camp cook, whether in a modern campground or on the trail.

Other items. A visit to a camping supply store or a few minutes spent leafing through a supplier's catalog will quickly reveal many kinds of kettles, pans, broilers, toasters and even pressure cookers available to the camper. These are not gadgets or needless cooking aids.

Since every cook does things his own way, each may prefer cooking gear that others wouldn't use. The variety offered today is a real benefit to every type of camp cook. A word of caution, however: don't buy everything that strikes your fancy. Don't buy any item until you know it will be useful.

Preservation of camp foods

Fresh food will not last long unless it is kept cool, preferably by ice refrigeration. There is no problem of early spoilage of most dry items, although these must be protected from moisture and insects. All foods should be kept in protective containers for purposes of cleanliness, freshness, convenience and security from raiding animals and insects.

A camp cooler is considered necessary to stationary camping. Most campers use insulated ice chests, although many wheel campers plug in small refrigerators where electricity is available.

A cold spring or stream does a good job of preserving perishables. A water box, made of wood or mesh wire, may be loaded with food items (protected with plastic or other waterproof material from direct contact with the water, of course) and anchored in the spring or running water. Canned foods can be cooled by placing them in a burlap bag or net, attached to a rope or wire and tied to a tree or bush alongside the stream. Before doing this, however, you should identify the contents on each can lid. Paper labels will fade and sometimes come off, and the name written on the lid will keep you from guessing what's inside. Use a grease pencil or wax crayon to write the identifying names.

Many books have been written on the subject of outdoor cookery. One or two would be useful in your camping library. Beware of the variety dealing with backyard culinary arts. You need something different for camping. One of the best is Bradford Angier's **Wilderness Cookery,** published by The Stackpole Company of Harrisburg, Pennsylvania.

As with most other outdoor skills, campers are great improvisers when it comes to cooking. You, too, will develop your own methods and techniques, will settle on a select list of favorite camp foods and will come to prefer certain utensils and other cooking gear. And then you will have achieved the independence and self-confidence of the best camp cooks.

Food coolers, usually ice chests, are considered necessary for most family camping. The two models shown here are popular with today's campers.

This is Campers Kitchen, a product of Campers Kitchen Company, San Antonio, Texas. Units are designed to give maximum work space, yet to fold into compact containers that are easy to pack in station wagon or trunk.

How to Select

This is about as close to an ideal campsite as you can find. Woods, water, mountains provide beautiful scenery, the terrain slopes gently away from the campsite to provide drainage, and the location is adequately sheltered from wind.

a Good Campsite

A good campsite accommodates the camper's shelter, offers certain terrain advantages and is convenient to such basics as water. But there are other important considerations, too . . .

You are traveling along Interstate 40 on the last lap of a hard, 500-mile day's journey when you spot the cloverleaf sign for which you've been looking.

"Great Smoky Mountains National Park."

You glance at your watch. Six o'clock. About an hour to go. You leave the interstate and follow U. S. 441 south through Knoxville, Tennessee's dogwood city. You notice the flags and other decorations commemorating Independence Day. Tomorrow is July 4.

The traffic seems to be quite heavy, and it is. Others have thought of a holiday in the mountains. You notice license plates from many states. You tell yourself that most of these will stop at Gatlinburg, the colorful little city nestled at the base of the Smokies. You tell your tired family that for once they don't have to worry about "No Vacancy" signs sure to be lighted at every motel. No sir! You're going to tow that handsome new travel trailer straight to The Chimneys or possibly to Heintooga Overlook, two of the most popular campgrounds in the entire national park system.

Forget it. You'll never make it. Every improved campsite in the Smokies has long since been taken. Those who know, get there early. And "early" in many national park campgrounds may mean several days. This is particularly true on weekends and holidays.

It's too bad you'll miss The Chimneys or Heintooga. But don't fret. Watch for privately owned campground signs. Possibly there will be a vacancy. Or, if worse comes to worse, head back to town for a hotel. And take comfort in the knowledge that you've learned two basic facts about camping: it is as popular as they say, and the wise camper gets to his campsite early.

The Early Camper Gets the Choice Site

It can be said without dispute that the early camper gets the choice site. And this can make all the difference in camping enjoyment and satisfaction. The rule holds whether you are heading for a popular national park campground or a remote and seldom visited sopt in the middle of a forest wilderness.

In the case of much-used campgrounds, the main reason for arriving early is to make certain that you'll get a campsite—any campsite, but

Early campers are the ones who get the choice sites. By the looks of things, campers should arrive early at Dugway Campground, White Mountain National Forest, New Hampshire.

hopefully one that will meet the comfort and privacy standard you've set for yourself. There are other important reasons for arriving early, not the least of which is to have ample time to properly set up camp. You will wish to check the wood supply and the fire regulations. And to locate the water tap. Where are the bathrooms? Uphill or downhill? Do these include showers? What about hot water?

And do you want to set up camp conveniently close to these facilities, or do you prefer to be some distance away so as to avoid the pedestrian traffic? The number of children in your family and their ages will have a bearing on your campsite selection.

Time for swim

By arriving early, you may have time for a short hike or a swim. After being cramped up in a car all day, most camping families appreciate the opportunity to unlimber before bedtime. Some of this is realized through the various chores assigned to each member of the family, including the youngest toddlers. But a hike, a swim or the tossing of a ball offer an additional enjoyment touch.

The early camper also has time to prepare the evening meal, unhurriedly, and it can be more than soup and sandwiches. Then to what many campers consider the high point of any camping experience—the campfire. Songs and stories, discussion of tomorrow's

plans, gentle breezes and the pungent but pleasant odor of burning cedar or birch soon combine to bring on that disturbingly relaxed feeling you'd almost forgotten.

If you are a backpacker or if your choice of camping sites is off the beaten path, you still should plan to reach your destination early. This is where you will put to good use your knowledge of basic campcraft.

Here you won't find many campsite improvements, if any. You will need plenty of time for scouting about to select the best campsite. Firewood

must be gathered. A water supply must be found. And sanitary facilities such as a latrine must be provided. In short, you will have to provide all conveniences not brought with you.

Advance Planning Is Always Helpful

Some novice campers never advance to the experienced stage simply because they don't plan in advance for likely contingencies. They have a romantic notion that the ideal, uncrowded spot is just waiting for them, that all they have to do is get there. They see themselves camped on a grassy spot under a tall pine or fir, overlooking a hidden lake softly reflecting a golden moon. It's a whole world, all theirs.

Unfortunately, things don't always work out that way—though they could. It takes some planning and a good deal of work to locate the ideal site and to get comfortably settled there. But achieving this is not necessarily difficult. There is help.

The secret to finding the ideal site, particularly during the seasons when it seems the whole country has headed for the outdoors, is to talk to the right people. The right people are rangers, fire wardens, local citizens or chambers of commerce in nearby towns. The rangers in particular are usually delighted to tell you about secluded camping sites, away from the crowded, better known campgrounds.

Fire wardens often know the backroads, the fire trails, along which are spots for camping seldom discovered by any but backpackers or forest

Acquiring a suitable campsite in a setting such as this poses no problem. Diamond Lake, situated in the scenic Oregon Cascades, has become one of the state's most popular recreational areas.

workers. And local citizens, from the chamber of commerce information specialists to gas station attendants, frequently have favorite spots in mind—and they may tell you about these if you take the time to inquire.

Study maps

By careful study of brochures, maps and by proper inquiry, you can find the kind of campsite you are looking for. These are in the national forests, the national parks, state and city operated parks and on private lands. Good advance planning is always helpful.

The Ideal Campsite on Improved Campgrounds

Improved campgrounds are ready for instant camping, or should be. A convenient parking space is provided. There is a reasonably flat, well drained spot for tent or trailer. There may be a water hookup, sometimes electrical outlets and occasionally sewer connections. Tables and fireplaces, or fireboxes, are standard.

A wood supply is provided or may be purchased nearby. Sometimes a camp store is operated by a conces-

This campsite is several feet above the water level and is situated on a point of land jutting out into Baker Lake, Baker National Forest. It has a view, quick access to water recreation and appears to offer ample privacy.

sionaire. Here you can purchase grocery staples, fuel, ice, insect repellent. Flush toilets and showers may be part of the layout. Sometimes horses, boats or bicycles are offered for rent. And frequently, guided nature walks and evening programs of films and lectures are offered the campers.

If you arrive early and find numerous campsites vacant, you can take the time to inspect each one. When you have narrowed the number of possibles to two or three, take a closer look at these. Your best site will be on a high level, particularly if you are camping near water. Low ground near water creates a damp chill during the night and is more apt to harbor mosquitoes and other biting insects. Your site should have some shade, but not too much. Preferably, it will be open to the morning sun, shaded from the afternoon sun. It should be well drained in case of rain.

Before unloading your gear, examine the table and cooking facility. The table may be wobbly and the cooking unit may be broken. Report these to the campground attendant and choose another site.

Check the nearness of water, latrine, garbage container and other con-

veniences. Also observe the distance to your camping neighbors and the amount of screening between your site and theirs. Are you far enough away from traffic, both vehicular and pedestrian? Is there room for the children to play? In short, does the layout satisfy you? If so, unload and make camp at once. You've passed the first major hurdle.

The Ideal Campsite in Primitive Areas

For the purposes of this discussion, primitive areas are those offering camping attractions but with few or no campsite improvements. A surprisingly large number of campers switch to this type of camping after a few trips to

improved campgrounds.

They want more privacy, more challenge to their pioneer prowess and new adventure. Such areas often are reached only by hiking, by pack horse or by canoe. But many can be reached by car. Take most any national forest backroad and you'll find all kinds of primitive campsites. You may need directions from the authorities. And you will want to tell somebody where you are going.

When you arrive at the part of the forest or desert where you'd like to pitch camp, your search for the best campsite will follow these general rules:

1. Look for high ground that slopes just enough to assure adequate drain-

age. If it also has a view, you have a bonus.

2. Don't pitch camp too close to dead or leaning trees. These might topple in a heavy wind. Watch for dead limbs on any trees shading the camping area.

3. Avoid any wash or draw, even if vegetation is growing there and the place seems to be well drained. A sudden cloudburst miles away may result in a flash flood through your campsite.

4. The higher you are above a lake or stream (15 to 20 feet at least) the less likelihood there is of your campsite being flooded by early morning mist.

5. Take advantage of prevailing winds. If these are gentle but steady, they will help to keep the camp dry, will ventilate the tent or other shelter, will dispel insects and fog.

6. Avoid pitching camp where you will be directly exposed to buffeting winds. If there is no choice, a windbreak may be necessary. Usually this problem is encountered more often in the desert or at the seashore.

7. The camp should be exposed to the sun part of the day, preferably in the morning. The sun helps to dry out things quickly and offers health and sanitation benefits.

8. Water and firewood should be reasonably close.

9. Helpful, but not necessary, is close location to the recreational

Obviously, these camping fishermen have found a campsite completely suitable to their tastes. They are preparing their catch of Rainbow trout.

pursuits that appeal to your family. These may be swimming, hiking, boating, nature study, camera subjects or simply the enjoyment of a good view.

10. Finally, determine how much work is involved in "improving" the site to your satisfaction. Such work may be fun and physically rewarding, but you don't want to spend the entire first day clearing brush and digging trenches.

The ideal campsite may vary from place to place and from season to season. Sometimes it is varied for special protection from weather extremes. A sheltered site is necessary to comfortable camping both in the high, cold country and in the hot, desert country, one to assure warmth and the other to assure coolness. Other variations are necessary in other terrains. For example, the Ontario Department of Lands and Forests offers these suggestions in **The Ontario Outdoorsman's Manual:**

"Previously occupied campsites are common on well-travelled routes. In selecting one or locating a new site, consider the following factors: —

"A point of land or an island offers the best protection from insects and reduces the risk of starting a bush fire. In cold weather, a more sheltered site will be preferred (prevailing winds in Ontario are from the west).

"The purpose of the trip (hunting, fishing, swimming, photographing, etc.) may influence the choice of a site.

"Water supply and sanitation.

"Choose a level site, sufficiently elevated to permit a quick run-off of rainwater.

"The shoreline must be suitable for landing a boat or canoe.

"Stay clear of large or dead trees that might come down in a windstorm.

"Select a site that is free of underbrush, or one that can be cleared without a great deal of work."

A basic requirement for the campsite

is safety. Never camp where there is a likelihood or even the possibility of a rock slide or snow slide. Do not camp in low places that could be flooded in a downpour. This holds for the desert as well as a rain forest.

If water is found only in an occasional water hole, don't camp near one. These draw animals, including snakes. In any locale known to include numerous animals it is wise to camp away from an animal path that leads to a watering site. For the most part, you won't be bothered by animals. This is particularly true if you camp in an area traversed by few humans. The wilderness area animals will travel a wide circle around you. (See "Safety First and First Aid.")

When you spot a likely looking clearing for a possible campsite, you may be surprised that someone else has been there before. If it appears that several parties have stopped there, you can be reasonably sure that it is a good site.

In fact, it may be so good that you'll discover campers there ahead of you. After a few seasons of wilderness camping, you too will have a list of favorite campsites and you will find yourself going back to some of these as opportunities afford.

Site seldom ideal

To avoid disappointment, be prepared to accept a campsite that is something less than ideal. Many veteran campers will tell you that the ideal site is seldom found, and if it is, the weather may turn bad.

On the other hand, it is not difficult to find a campsite close to ideal. And by a little woodsman ingenuity, you can turn it into a comfortable outdoor homestead, one that will be enjoyed by the entire family. The more you camp, the more you will be willing to accept the challenge of improving the campsite to meet your tastes. And you'll find yourself enjoying it.

Special Factors
In Site Selections

Some of the factors influencing the choice of a campsite in wooded country are these: a space that is level and is free from rain or snow drainage, access to a suitable water supply, wood for fire and construction of needed camp facilities and reasonable freedom from mosquitos and other insects.

If you like camping alongside a lake or stream, look for a point of land that juts out into the water and is several feet above the water level. This has several advantages. It has a view in at least two directions, it is more apt to catch a breeze and thereby eliminate most of the insect problem. Water is available a few steps away, drainage is good and fire hazards are minimized.

In desert camping, it is unlikely that you will be looking for a water supply since these are few and far between. You will be carrying your own water supply even if you know of a water source in the vicinity of your camping site.

If you wish to have a fire, and most campers do, your campsite should be near a fuel source. You may need materials for a windbreak and you will also look for a spot free of spined vegetation.

Sometimes a good campsite can be located in the desert on high gravel bars, but care should be taken to see that these are high enough above likely waterlines in the event of a sudden storm. Spring floods often pile up driftwood in such areas and this can be used for firewood.

In high, mountain country, look for a campsite on the edge of a thick growth of timber, if you are below the timberline, and preferably near water. A lush growth of foliage in a ravine or at the head of a valley often is an indication of water. If you're camping in snow, the timer provides a good windbreak and wood for fuel.

Camping in swampland can be interesting, but usually presents more difficulties than other camping situations. Obviously you look for the possible elevation, usually between bodies of water. Ground dampness can be partially eliminated by piling grass, leaves or tree boughs on which to place the sleeping gear.

Another way to dry out the ground is to build a fire over it and let the fire burn for several hours before scraping away the fire remains and replacing these with a layer of fresh soil. A padding of grass or some similar material readies the spot for the bed. If a tent is used, the same procedures may be followed in preparing the tent site.

Camping Experience
is the Best Teacher

Campsite selection will become easier as you gain camping experience. The outdoors is a great teacher and camping experience is part of this educational process. A sense of humor, a frame of mind to adapt and a determination to learn will be invaluable as you select a campsite at the start of your outdoor adventure.

If you prefer, you can find a campsite near gold. Panning for gold is a family pastime at Resurrection Creek Campground in the Chugach National Forest, Alaska. Note: they find gold, too, but not enough to start another gold rush.

This campsite in Oregon's Wallowa Lake State Park offers plenty of space, is well laid out and is equipped with the basics. It is also easy to keep clean.

The Orderly Way to Set Up Camp

The ideal camp layout is carefully arranged in zones and each camper is assigned daily responsibilities.

Like any type of construction, the setting up of your camp requires design and orderliness. And it requires a foreman. Somebody has to be in charge. Otherwise, the entire outing gets off to a very poor start.

The first job, of course, is to unload. This is a sizable chore if you've packed it all into your car or station wagon. If you are backpacking or traveling by canoe, organizing the procedures may be less detailed. The same holds if you camp in a recreational vehicle. In any case, there must be a planned layout, and the person in charge will give this his attention and direction.

Camp layout

Setting up a suitable camp requires a plan, a layout. From the Coleman Company is, **Outdoor Holiday Fun Guide:**

"After hunting up a suitable campsite, the family chores first begin. No two families follow the same routine for setting up, but work must be systematized if it is to be done efficiently."

"The work is better accomplished if every member of the family is assigned specific tasks. While the tent is going up, someone can be designated to clear the ground for uncluttered space in the cooking and dining area. Set up your folding chairs and table (if a picnic table is not available) and then, if you have them, relaxing sling chairs and a hammock—all in shady places.

Designate a 'wash-up' area, and furnish it with basin, canvas water bag, a mirror, and personal hygiene items. Set up the camp folding stands and place the insulated jug in a handy spot. Meanwhile, mother or daughter can spread a bright tablecloth and set the table for a meal in the outdoors!"

These campers in an Alabama national forest are giving priority to their shelter. Note that the gear has been carefully unloaded for easy distribution once the tent is erected.

"Hang the lantern in about the center of your camp, get out the transistor radio—or a guitar, if you play one, rig a tarpaulin windbreak—or any other niceties you prefer—and your wilderness campsite is ready for a real outdoor holiday."

On a camp layout in Ontario backwoods and along remote waterways, the Department of Lands and Forests recommends these basic items:

1. Shelter, in the form of a tent, a tent fly or a balsam bough or a covered lean-to.

2. Stone fireplace.

3. A pit latrine 200 feet from the campsite and downstream from the water supply.

4. A garbage pit halfway between camp and latrine.

Camps in Ontario that are to be used for an extended period, or repeatedly, should also have the following:

1. Pole table with seats or benches.

2. Washbasin stand.

3. Hooks or rack for storing utensils.

4. Clothesline.

5. Dock (if traveled to by boat or canoe).

6. Sheltered woodpile.

Generally speaking, the camp layout on any terrain should have these distinct features and divisions: sleeping area, cooking-dining area, bathroom area, latrine (at least 100 feet away from camp), loafing or fun area.

Making camp

The first step in making camp is the assignment of duties. Every member of the party, including the youngest members if they are old enough to walk and follow directions, should be given specific assignments. The order for setting up camp is of one's own choosing, but experience has shown that if the cooks get the first assignment, others will work better in the knowledge that a hot meal will be waiting when the chores are done. It is best to construct the cooking facility where prevailing winds will drive the smoke away from the tent site, rather than toward it.

A simultaneous step is the pitching of the tent. This may or may not take substantial time and effort, depending on the size and kind of tent and the number available to work on this assignment.

Other assignments include responsibilities for wood supply, water supply, the setting up of the bathing area, providing seating and eating facilities, the digging of a garbage pit and a latrine and the distribution of gear and supplies. Drainage ditches may be called for and a loafing-fun area (which may be done later, with all pitching in).

Pitching the tent

Most campers make tent erection the first duty in making camp, although the assurance of a hot meal when work is done causes many family campers to give first attention to the cooking area. But if the weather decides it for you, particularly in locales where sudden showers threaten, by all means pitch the tent as the first order of business.

A first step in tent pitching is ground preparation. It should be level, or nearly so, and this means the removal of **every** twig or pebble from the spot and a complete smoothing of the soil on which the tent floor will rest. A waterproof ground cloth (may be a tarp, a sheet of plastic, etc.) should go down first.

If the ground is apt to be cold or damp during the course of your stay, several layers of insulating materials should be placed between the ground cloth and the tent floor. These, too, must be smooth and flat. Folds of newspapers are sometimes used for this.

Some campers dig down four to six inches in a space roughly the dimensions of the tent floor, remove the dirt and fill the cavity with pine needles or leaves. This lifts the tent floor off the ground, makes it better for sleeping bags (particularly if air mattresses or pads are not used), offers good insulation, provides extra drainage and eliminates all danger of dampness. This is an excellent technique, especially in a camp set up for a week or longer.

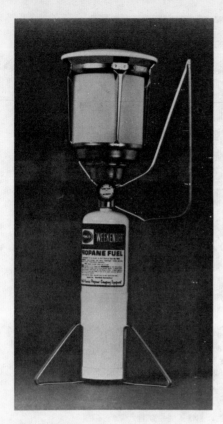

This Primus light unit operates from disposable propane fuel cylinders. Furnished with stand.

Bathroom area

When you camp in unimproved or semi-improved areas, an important part of the camp layout is the bathroom area. This is separate from the latrine area by at least 100 feet, unless pit toilets are already provided. The bathroom area may be anything from a place for a simple toilet articles and a washbasin to an elaborate layout with an improvised shower. If you are camping for more than a day, you will need clothesline strung between trees or posts, a place for the medicine chest and/or first aid kit. Hang the washbasin and some netting for the soap on nails driven into tree limbs or a post.

A stump or log may serve as a washstand. Or you can build one by lashing together some three-foot poles for the top, then resting this on two sets of crossed poles stood upright for legs. A few nails, a saw and a hammer will enable you to construct an even more professional model.

The water supply, if it has to be carried from a distant point, may be hoisted several feet off the ground and attached to a tepee framework. A lister bag with a bottom faucet may be used as a container. If the supply is nearby and can be replenished at will, simply keep available containers filled.

Stall shower

A shower stall may be built by framing four six-foot poles with the inside dimensions desired, then wrapping a tarp or other water-repellent material around the framework. Any number of containers may be devised to sprinkle or shower the water from the top of the framework. A few can be bought commercially. Of course, a rushing stream, a waterfall or a lake may eliminate the need for such bathing facilities.

One picture you frequently get of campers is of the unkempt, unshaven variety. This may be what you want, and that's fine if you and those around you can live with it. But there's something to be said for maintaining a regular bathing and shaving routine, even in a wilderness situation. Just remind yourself what it would be like to live in the wilderness all the time.

Cooking-dining area

The problem of a cooking facility is automatically settled if you take along a suitable portable unit, and many campers do. Your only fire will be the campfire, over which you may do a little cooking for the novelty of it.

However, there is a certain satisfaction in constructing one's own primitive cooking unit. This may be a fireplace or one of a number of woodsman's fires. In any case, this is a necessary first chore when you have to improvise. The spot should be sheltered from the wind, enough at least to keep smoke and fire under control.

One section of this area holds the food supplies and cooking gear. Another is set aside for dining, and still another for wood and water. The food preparation section ideally is in the center of things.

Garbage disposal

Sanitation in a wilderness camp is important to cleanliness and health, and necessary for good campkeeping.

The proper disposal of garbage is just as important here as it is back home. Burnables should be burned. Metal cans should be flattened and buried deep—after being burned to clear clinging food remains. If empty glass containers can't be carried out when you break camp, these too should be buried.

Food waste should never be dumped out in the expectation that some animal will come along and devour it. Neither should it be dumped into a stream or lake. If you do either, you probably are breaking a law. National parks and national forests, among others, have stringent rules regarding such actions.

In a totally unimproved campsite area it will be necessary for you to

Heat should be given early attention in the setting up of camp. This is a highly efficient heater with a capacity of 5 to 8,000 BTU.

dig a garbage pit 50 to 100 feet from your tent and cooking areas. Ideally, this will be downgrade from your water supply and in the general direction of the latrine. The garbage pit should be deep enough to handle all refuse for the duration of your stay.

Upon breaking camp, the pit should be filled with dirt and covered with boulders or logs if these are convenient. This lessens the possibility of animals digging up the refuse. Odor can be virtually eliminated if all disposable food is dumped first into plastic bags and these are securely closed before being taken to the garbage pit. Some campers burn food scraps, but this is not always possible.

The latrine

As mentioned before, the latrine is ideally placed at least 100 feet from the campsite and is always downgrade from the water supply. It should be in a small clearing that is screened by boulders, bushes or other terrain features. A tarpaulan may be used as a screen, or a fort-like structure of poles may be built.

The immediate area should be cleared of all underbrush, loose boulders and high grass. The pathway leading to the latrine should likewise be cleared.

The latrine itself is simply a ditch a foot or two deep and several feet long. Sandy soil is more ideal, but a mixture of rocks and loose dirt in the bottom are nearly as effective. Depending on how long and how much the latrine will be used, it may be only the simple ditch or it may be a network of ditches providing for more elaborate drainage.

A pile of loose dirt and a shovel adjacent to the latrine enable the

Every good camp layout will have a loafing area. If you can get someone to act as a waiter, you've got it made. That's living!

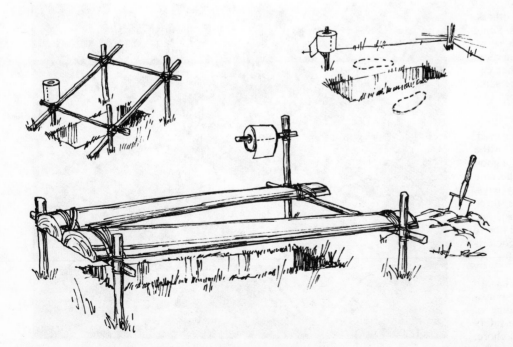

Sanitation is important in camp. A latrine—basically a narrow ditch—is called for when toilet facilities are not already provided. A straddle latrine (upper right) is satisfactory for overnight camping. Something more elaborate from the comfort angle is desirable for a longer stay.

campers to keep the bottom covered as the facility is used. A handful of lime after each use is even better. Portable toilet seats may be brought to camp for use at the latrine, or some poles from the woods may be used to improvise.

Loafing-fun area

This area may be considered superfluous by some hardy campers who claim all the fun you need is realized in the act of camping itself. But it is mostly those bent on catching a record-size trout at daybreak or tracking down an elusive grizzly who fail to see the value of loafing and playing while camping.

The average camper who does it unhurriedly and avoids programming every minute receives an added benefit from his fun and loafing area. Here is the place for hammock or canvas chaise chair. Perhaps some log seats will be placed around the campfire. On one side will be the horseshoe court, and on the other side the badminton. The flat side of a round log will hold the checkerboard.

Activity games for the children may be organized for this area. It should be large enough for movement such as running and jumping. A game of touch football or catch or dodge ball may be just the thing for after-dinner exercise—an hour or so after dinner to give the food time to digest. Most improved campgrounds permit such group sports only on playgrounds or areas set aside for such purposes.

Daily assignments

When the camp is completely set up to your satisfaction, take a little time to relax. But not long. There is one further important step to assure a comfortable and pleasant stay. This is the assignment of daily chores.

Some chores are easier than others. Some are more fun than others. Some can be done best by men, others by women. Children take delight in most anything they can do or think they can do. But they tire quickly of the same thing. So do grownups, for that matter.

Two cooks

Daily assignments should be varied. If there are two or more cooks in the group (Isn't every adult camper a good cook, or shouldn't he be?), alternate cooking chores by meals or by days. Perhaps the ideal is to have three cooks—one to prepare breakfast, one to be responsible for lunch and one to concentrate on dinner. The cook is responsible for menus and for replenishing the larder as needed.

Another camping specialty has to do with fires. The fireman is responsible for fuel supplies, the building of cooking fires and campfires, fire safety and care of tools needed in this chore.

He should be a teacher of fire methods and fire safety, particularly if youngsters are around. Small fry can help while they learn.

Maintaining the water supply is another important chore. Water for drinking and cooking should be pure, and the "water boy" may have to boil or chemically treat the water before use. He is also charged with maintaining water supplies for bathing and other uses. He will replenish the ice chest and maintain the coolers.

Nobody likes to wash dishes, but this has to be done. The use of disposable paper or plastic plates eliminates much of this chore. But such items as pots and pans must be washed after use. The dishwasher washes and rinses dishes and pots and pans, disposes of all garbage and maintains cooking and eating ware.

Maid's duties

Then there is the work of the "maid." Ever think of taking a maid to camp? Well, you don't have to. Every camper has the privilege of being maid. When assigned to this duty, the "maid" airs the bedding, does the laundry and keeps the premises clean.

Mother will agree that this is one of the best reasons for family camping as she watches the duty rotate from dad to the offspring. Incidentally, the more often dad and the children do this, the more likelihood there is of mother being the first to suggest another camping trip.

Finally, there is the delightful daily chore of planning the fun schedule. The final decision should be a group decision, but one person each day should be responsible for a list of recommendations. The "fun superintendent" checks the schedule at

campground headquarters, consults maps for interesting spots to hike to, plans some games for both indoors and outdoors and in general comes up with a variety of possibilities.

All chores cease to be chores, in the normal meaning of the term, when approached with a light spirit. After all, these too are part of the fun of camping.

Breaking camp

The fun is almost over and you have to go home. This is a difficult time, for a certain reluctance sets in—particularly if you've had a totally pleasant stay.

But it must be done and again there must be direction. Breaking camp does not take long. It begins by emptying the tent. The bedding is rolled up or folded, the clothing is packed, personal and loose items are gathered and packed. The cooking and dining equipment is cleaned and stowed away. The tent is swept out and taken down. It is carefully folded. Everything, except the water bucket and shovel, is packed into the car. The water bucket's contents are used to douse the fire, the shovel to fill in the garbage pit and the latrine. The campsite is inspected and is left in better shape than it was in when you arrived. A place is found in the car for the bucket and shovel.

As you drive away, you notice a strange silence in the car. Everybody suddenly has that feeling peculiar to those leaving home for the first time.

If you leave your public campsite looking like this, one day you may have to pay an exhorbitant maintenance fee. Or you may not be allowed to camp in public areas at all.

A hike is more than a walk. It is fun. Very practical and extremely healthful for campers.

You'll Get More

Out of Camping

if you Hike!

A surprisingly large number of people camp for the hiking opportunities this affords. Hiking is the most basic of outdoor pleasures. And those fortunate enough to become addicted to it early in life have gained something for which there is no substitute. Youngsters living near deep woods have found it a place of mystery and adventure, and a good place to escape from a world dominated by grownups.

And what grownup who has had this experience as a boy or girl doesn't relive those pleasant days when he gets opportunity to tramp through the woods, along a mountain trail or any place not cluttered with the "refinements" of civilization?

About walking, former President Harry S. Truman once wrote that ". . . it is necessary that you walk as if you

Mountain hiking, winter or summer, is a favorite recreation of the Wanderbirds Hiking Club of Washington, D. C.

are going some place." Mr. Truman has been a regular walker since his military service before and during World War I. His favorite routine, even as president, was to walk a mile and a half, at 120 steps a minute, in the morning between 6:30 and 7.

The former President has long maintained that walking is by far the best exercise for anyone more than 50 years old. Many medical experts believe that walking is the best exercise for any person able to walk at any age. It is an exercise with the whole outdoors a gymnasium.

Long walk

Hiking may be defined as a longer, more taxing walk done with purpose and destination in mind. It may make your muscles sore the first day or two. It will make you tired. It will make you sweat. But it offers therapy to body and mind, solace to the soul.

It is a tonic not contained in bottles nor bought by prescription. It is a

tranquilizer beyond description, and if you become addicted, all that walking can do to you will be beneficial.

Hiking is for anyone, old or young, who enjoys reasonably good health and can walk. Whether it is a stroll along a nature trail or a fast clip along a rugged mountain path requiring great stamina, hiking is fun.

Where to hike

Hiking may be enjoyed most anywhere. Obviously, the outdoor enthusiast prefers to enjoy this recreational pursuit away from concrete sidewalks and busy city streets. He may find some good hiking trails in the larger city parks. If he lives in a smaller city, he doesn't have far to travel to find open country through which he may blaze his own trail.

But for most hikers, the best rewards and satisfaction come from hiking along trails in state parks, national forests and national parks. Excellent hiking trails for all types of hiking are

provided in the national parks, in most of the national forests and in many state parks as well.

Hiking trails

Special trails catering to hikers are on the increase. Many such trails likewise offer various camping opportunities. Sparking current attention given to the need for additional hiking trails are groups of hiking and camping enthusiasts who advocate a national system of trails.

Congress began a series of actions dealing with this proposal when in 1967 it received the National Trails Bill from President Johnson. The bill was based on a 155-page report prepared jointly by the Departments of Agriculture and Interior. The report proposed that a system of great trails be established throughout the nation so that any citizen would be in easy proximity to outstanding hiking opportunities.

Two trails already in use are being upgraded by federal, state and private organizations. These are the Appalachian Trail and the Pacific Crest Trail. The government report recommended that several great historic trails be reclaimed as hiking trails. Some of these are the Lewis and Clark Trail, a route stretching some 4,600 miles from St. Louis, Missouri, to the coast of Oregon; the Potomac Heritage Trail, 825 miles of beauty and history from the beginning of the Potomac River to where it empties into the sea; and the Chisholm Trail which runs between San Antonio, Texas, and Abilene, Kansas.

Coast to coast

Other trails would connect with some of these, making it possible for a hiker to follow a trail from coast to coast or from border to border. Plans are even afoot to extend certain north-south trails virtually from pole to pole.

The great trails already established, and those proposed, pass through existing national forests, national parks and other government lands where improved campgrounds and backpacking trails abound. Naturally, trails appeal to the backpacker. But the camping family in improved campgrounds likewise utilizes trail facilities by making its camp a base camp for trail adventure and enjoyment.

As camping in the popular scenic areas of easy access becomes more crowded, the value of a good trail system will become more pronounced. Serious campers would do well to support the addition of more hiking and packhorse trails.

Appalachian trail

The most famous and the most used of all the great trails is the Appalachian Trail. This trail stretches 2,000 miles from Springer Mountain, Georgia, to Mount Katahdin, Maine. It touches on

13 states, traverses eight national forests, two national parks and several state parks. A good many miles cross private lands. Ownership of the trail is divided as follows:

Federal . . . . 682 miles
State . . . . .452 miles
Private . . . . .866 miles

Hikers on this trail are big users of national park and national forest facilities along the way. Many people have walked the entire length, but much of the trail's use comes from those on a day's outing or extended overnight trips. The trail winds and climbs through the Great Smoky Mountains National Park and along the Blue Ridge into Shenandoah National Park.

For the most part, it is a mountain and hill trail, working northward to the Poconos of Pennsylvania, on into the foothills of the Catskills, through the Berkshires and, finally, on into the Green and White Mountains.

Volunteer maintenance

Most of the Appalachian Trail is maintained by volunteer individuals and groups, although portions are kept clear by the Forest Service and National Park Service. Coordinating all of this is the Appalachian Trail Conference, Washington, D. C. By agreements with the Forest Service, the National Park Service and 12 of the 13 states through which the trail passes, the Appalachian Trail Conference is able to protect the trail against incompatible developments within a mile on either side.

One program of special interest to campers, backpackers in particular, is a string of three-sided shelters along the trail. The Forest Service and the National Park Service have constructed dozens of these, primarily along the southern sections of the trail. Those in the Great Smoky Mountains National Park and adjacent national forest areas are quite crowded in the summer months (first-come, first-served basis) and enjoy considerable use throughout the year.

Ultimately, this shelter chain will become part of the entire 2,000-mile trail, being interrupted only where larger campgrounds are established at points where the trail touches major outdoor attractions reached by vehicles also. Along some sections of the trail local clubs maintain huts and cabins, some of which provide food as well as lodging.

In the White Mountain National Forest, for example, the Appalachian Mountain Club maintains a chain of huts where hikers, for a reasonable charge, can obtain food and lodging. In Virginia, Maryland and Pennsylvania, locked cabins are available on reserved basis from the Potomac Appalachian Trail Club.

More information

Guidebooks, maps and other information about the Appalachian Trail are available from two main sources: The Appalachian Trail Conference, 1916 Sunderland Place, N. W., Washington, D. C., and the Appalachian Mountain Club, 5 Joy Street, Boston, Mass. The latter has the most comprehensive information materials on the White Mountains portion of the trail. The Forest Service issues a folder entitled **The Appalachian Trail,** Miscellaneous Publication No. 951, which is available for five cents from the Superintendent of Documents, U. S. Government Printing Office, Washington, D. C. 20402.

Hikers and campers are apt to en-

counter a wide variety of weather along the Appalachian Trail. The U. S. Forest Service has issued this statement relative to weather and other factors affecting safety and comfort:

"In the South, sections of the Appalachian Trail may become overgrown with summer brush and hard to follow. In New England a hot summer afternoon can turn into a cold rainy nightmare in a matter of minutes. Wear or carry clothes which can protect you against sudden cold, rain, briars, and poison ivy. Wear comfortable sturdy shoes. Take along basic first aid supplies.

Don't travel alone

"Some of the Trail traverses extremely rough terrain and exposed mountain tops, so hikers are urged not to travel alone.

"Parents should make sure that young people are with experienced leaders familiar with the territory and the idiosyncrasies of the weather. New england mountains may not seem high, but in winter they can be treacherous. Inexperienced hikers should stay at low elevations in winter.

"Time your hike so you arrive at your destination before dark. If you are not an experienced mountaineer, or with one, be careful about hand-over-hand climbing on ledges; getting down is always harder. Build up to

strenuous trips. Sudden overexertion may be permanently damaging."

The example of individuals, private organizations and private landowners working compatably with federal and state government agencies to maintain the popular Appalachian Trail is a good omen for the future of other great trails.

Pacific Crest trail

The Pacific Crest Trail is the western counterpart to the Appalachian Trail in the east. This trail, needing restoring and improving in some stretches, runs 2,156 miles from Canada to Mexico. It touches on or comes near to five national parks — Mount Rainier, Crater Lake, Lassen Volcanic, Yosemite and Kings Canyon.

Except for a few miles through privately owned lands and through the national parks mentioned, this trail stays within the bounds of national forest areas. Information may be obtained from Pacific Crest Trail System Conference, Hotel Green, Pasadena, California.

Rules of hiking

A casual stroll through a city park or along a short nature trail in a national park requires no special rules. But a hike to a point several miles from camp and other people calls for important preparation steps and certain rules along the trail. Here are some tips on

safe and rewarding hiking:

1. Know where you are going. Don't hike off at random in unknown territory.

2. Take at least one person with you. In case you become lost or have an accident, you will be glad you have company. Perhaps the ideal hiking group is a party of four. One can stay with an injured or ill hiker while the others go for help — or the three can carry the injured person to safety.

This rule is more important if you hike away from the well traveled trails where you are not likely to meet many other hikers.

3. Someone in camp should know where you have gone. A neighbor camper or a member of the family or party who has stayed behind may be the person or persons you tell. A ranger or campground attendant may be informed of your plans. Some trails in national parks and national forests are open only to those hikers who first register and indicate their destinations.

4. Be reasonable in distance and time. If you are not accustomed to strenuous, long-distance hiking, by all means toughen up by going on several shorter hikes, increasing the distance a little each day. Allow for plenty of time to reach your destination or to return to camp by the deadline you have set.

5. Wear suitable clothing. This particularly applies to shoes. It is very foolish to begin a lengthy hike wearing the wrong kind of shoes or new shoes. Hiking shoes should be well broken in and should be completely comfortable. Other clothing worn should be determined by the

Hiking may be defined as a longer, more taxing walk that is done with purpose and destination in mind. Here, members of the Wasatch Mountain Club have reached a vantage point in Little Cottonwood Canyon, Wasatch National Forest.

time of year, the terrain features and weather extremes likely to be encountered.

6. Take some sort of pack with you, even if your hike is only for a few hours. A compact first aid kit, the food you will need, your camera and other essential or helpful items may be comfortably carried this way. Avoid overloading.

7. Never rush. Set a pace and schedule rest stops to fit the needs of the slowest member of the party, who likely will be the one who tires first and more often.

8. Observe signs and landmarks along the way to facilitate easy and

quick return, if you return by the same route.

9. Stay on the trail. Avoid shortcuts which could get you lost, injured or both.

10. In ascending steep slopes set a pace that will not get you out of breath, even if you have to stop after every step or two. Traveling a steep trail toward the top of a ridge or mountain can be more rewarding physically and esthetically if you pause frequently to look back and down. There is a new dimension every 10 or 20 steps as you climb upward.

11. Always carry a canteen of safe water. If your trip is long, some water purifying tablets will be helpful. Water may be purified by boiling, of course, if you have a container for that. Getting water to boil at high altitudes is difficult.

12. Always be courteous and helpful to other hikers and give the right-of-way to pack and saddle stock at all times.

Safe place for fires

13. Build fires only in safe places and within the regulations and laws governing fires in the area where you hike.

14. Don't leave the trail to explore unless someone is with you and one of you understands directions. A compass is almost a must under such circumstances.

15. Keep an eye on the weather. If a storm is brewing, look for the best shelter. If the sun is beaming down, wear a hat and take other precautionary steps to avoid sunburn. Sunburn is easy to get in high altitudes, even when the air is cool.

16. If you detect chafing where clothing rubs against the skin, stop immediately and apply some preventive first aid. Chafed spots on the feet may be stopped from becoming blisters by applying adhesive tape. If other clothing rubs too much, sometimes adjustment will help. But it is good to have along a small plastic can of talc, preferably medicated.

17. Always maintain a positive frame of mind. Enjoy your hike.

Hiker's clothing

Tight-fitting clothing has no place on the trail. Clothing should be loose, permitting free perspiration, and with the help of a windbreaker or poncho, should be adequate to meet changing weather conditions. Of course, special clothing is required for extremes of weather and this is discussed in the articles on desert and beach camping and the chapter on winter camping. Basic information on clothing is given in another chapter.

The most important clothing worn on a hike are shoes and socks. Loafers, sandals and light canvas shoes are

totally inadequate on real hikes over rugged terrain. Your feet are your means of transportation and they deserve the best. Here are some facts and suggestions gathered from experienced outdoorsmen who know:

It is normal for your feet to change their size as you hike. Sometimes your feet will swell to fill shoes one to two sizes larger than you usually wear. For this reason, and because they prefer heavy socks, many hikers purchase hiking shoes in sizes larger than they are accustomed to. A well made hiking shoe or boot, properly fitted, can take care of foot expansion during long trips over rough terrain.

The ideal footgear should allow ample room for wiggling the toes, and should fit snugly enough to prevent chafing and the forming of blisters at the heels. New boots should always be broken in thoroughly on short hikes near home before any lengthy hike is undertaken.

In addition to fitting properly, good hiking shoes should have strong but pliable soles, and the uppers should be strong and flexible. Leather is the best base material, with cleated rubber or strong composition material being best for the soles.

Above ankle

Hiking shoes or boots should come above the ankle, but not too high unless you are hiking through snake infested country where the trail is not properly cleared. Most hikers prefer the six- to eight-inch boots. Women's hiking boots are similar to men's.

Blisters may be caused by wrong socks or wet feet, as well as by poorly fitted shoes. The best socks are made of thick wool, preferably white, and with a little loose fit in the foot. Buy them a size larger than you normally wear and the slight shrinkage caused by perspiration and washing will still leave them large enough. Always take a second pair with you, even on short hikes. Damp socks contribute to tender feet and to blisters.

Many hikers prefer to wear two pairs of socks made of lightweight wool. Some prefer to wear a cotton pair next to the skin. The wearing of two pairs of socks lessens the danger of irritation, fills the space better for oversized shoes and insulates in colder weather.

Socks should be washed frequently and a clean, dry pair should be put on when you remove those you have hiked in.

Experienced hikers wash their feet well the night before a hike, often soaking them alternately in hot and cold water, one minute each for ten minutes. Salt added to the water helps to toughen the feet. Of course, all toe nails should be trimmed squarely.

Hiker's equipment

The hiker takes as little equipment as possible. If he is backpacking and plans to be out one or more nights, obviously he carries with him all the necessary clothing, gear and food for living on the trail. Modern frames and packs, bedding and dried foods are light in weight. This enables today's hiker to carry all the necessities without being overloaded.

The equipment you take on a hike will depend on the kind of hike and such variables as the weather. Some useful items for most any hike are short pieces of string or rope, some matches, a first aid kit, a pocket knife, a compass, maps, cooking gear — if you plan to be on the trail for more than two meals — sunglasses and insect repellent.

Always keep your hands empty. This is the relaxing way to hike and you may need them for emergencies. Small items of equipment may be carried in your pockets, the rest in a light packsack, a heavier and larger one if the hike is lengthy and involves several days.

Hiker's food

A short hike requires only a sandwich lunch which can be tucked nicely into your packsack. Any hike burns up a good deal of energy, and many experienced hikers carry some dried fruits, such as raisins, or candy bars to munch on every three or four miles.

For longer hikes, perhaps on a backpacking trip of several days, carefully selected dehydrated foods should form the basic menu. Sometimes wild foods may be used to supplement those you carry. But don't count on this. The fish may not be biting and the berries may not be ripe.

Small stoves and one-person cook kits, available at camping supply stores, are quite adequate for the hiker's cooking needs.

Some final tips

• There is an old rule for hikers and campers which is more pertinent today than ever. It says, "Take nothing but pictures, leave nothing but footprints." Some hikers take this so much to heart that they keep a knapsack pocket reserved for bits of paper — chewing gum and candy wrappers, empty cigarette packages, etc. — which others have thrown carelessly along the trail.

• For more fun take along a field guide on birds, trees, mammals or some other nature subject in which you are interested.

Mountain climbing may be considered a form of hiking, certainly the most strenuous form.

Backpacking is the most rugged form of camping, and it can be the most rewarding. Confirmed backpackers claim that real campers sooner or later will turn to backpacking for the ultimate thrill of going it alone, against the elements, under one's own power. A backpacker is the closest thing to a pioneer that the average man or woman can become in the modern world.

On the trail, in a remote wilderness area, the backpacker may actually see something or do something that will be a first—that is, be the first human being to have that particular experience. On the north american continent are vast areas of mountains and forests, lands on which very few human beings have set foot.

There is still much to be discovered, perhaps a hidden lake or a water hole, perhaps a new flower or a tree in a habitat heretofore considered foreign to it. But the most probable first-time experiences for the backpacker are these: a one-time view of a brilliant

---

Backpackers pride themselves on being the "real campers." They carry the basics on their backs and travel by walking. And what trips they take!

Backpacking the Wilderness Trails

These backpackers, carrying "Gerry" Vagabond Packs mounted to K frames, pause to view the scenery in the Indian Peaks area of Colorado.

sunset, an unusual shadow cast by fleecy white clouds, the day and night reflections in a cool, mountain lake.

Solitude

Perhaps the ever changing vistas of natural beauty and the opportunity to be alone—really alone—are the lures that draw the backpacker to the wilderness trails again and again. On the trail he may pause to admire a stand of virgin spruce, or poplar, or oak. On flushing a deer or a grouse, he will suddenly feel akin to these creatures of the wild. Though he may be frightened by the fury of a summer storm, he will also see in it beauty beyond description.

This is because he finds himself a part of it, living out in it, and he feels it. At another time of year he may notice the quiet settling down of the forest and its creatures as the cold breath of winter slips down through the mountain passes. And he may be caught in a sudden shower of snow flakes, great white fluffs so large and so close together and so many that they fall as a sheet.

And he may come to the sudden realization that this will not let up, that tons of it will fall in a few hours, covering the trees and the bushes and everything that doesn't keep moving. And he is a part of it, enjoying it, thrilling to the dangerous challenges it holds out to him.

And so the backpacker has his experiences, his **alone,** and they stay with him. They affect his thinking, his attitudes, his innermost soul. He is secretly satisfied that he has been able to meet them with hardly more than the bare necessities for comfort and safety, and that he has carried these necessities on his back. He is glad that the sophistications of civilization are not crutches to him.

He knows that he has really lived, the pioneer way. He knows that for periods of time he can sweep behind him the ills of civilization. He always has a memory reminder ready to activate him to answer the call of the wild. And he will be glad to go, at every opportunity. And he will take his kids, and they will come to love it and someday take their kids.

True heritage

A confirmed backpacker knows that he has promulgated a true heritage that must be passed on from generation to generation. It is almost a religion with him.

Backpacking may be practiced anywhere, even on a city street. Those going out for the first time, or those going out for the first time in several months, should take some shakedown hikes. Even if it is only for a mile or two in a city park, the procedure is a good one and helps to make the larger adventure more pleasurable when it is undertaken.

The wilderness

Backpacking basically is that type of camping which the average camper can follow when his choice of sites is beyond where he can drive and is some distance removed from any larger base camp. It is enjoyed to the fullest when the camping is done in a wilderness area. Wilderness has always been an integral part of the American heritage. Without the wilderness, North America would not be the great advanced civilized land that it is.

From the wilderness came both the land and the materials necessary for the building of a nation. So much dependence was placed upon wilderness resources that their very existence was threatened. Thus came into being the national parks, the national forests and other public land agencies.

Since times of the Bible, going into the wilderness for the purpose of refreshing the spirit and restoring physical balance to the body has been a recognized boon to mankind. The population explosion and the knowledge explosion have combined to draw most of the people into the confines of urban life.

This has brought about a recognition that something is missing, and **that** something is what the wilderness areas can offer. Man generally does not recognize the values of such things until he is separated from them. Then he comes to appreciate them even more.

Probably the American pioneer had little regard for his environment in the sense that we view the wilderness today. He saw it as a land to be conquered and put to domestic or commercial use. He saw himself confined by it. True, he saw the beauty of its forests and he appreciated the solitude it offered and the freedom, but these appreciations were somewhat blunted. There was such an abundance of forests and wildlife and untamed lands. Now, in this century, with man confined by a highly complex civilization, has developed a deeper appreciation of wilderness.

Just traveling

For most, enough thrill and satisfaction is found in just traveling in the primitive areas, camping where they are when night falls and enjoying the full satisfaction of completely escaping from the pressures of daily living. For the first timer, the wilderness experience will be unlike anything he has ever known, and his reactions—emotional, physical and spiritual—will be completely, uniquely his.

What to take

In backpacking you take only what you need and no more. The secret to enjoyable backpacking is to be comfortable at all times. The more careful you are in selecting what goes into the pack, as well as the clothes you wear, the more comfortable you will be at all times, on the trail and during periods in camp.

Obviously the pack should be geared to your size, your physical capacities, the distance to be traveled, the time to be on the trail and the number of people going with you. Don't be surprised if everything doesn't go exactly as you would like it to on your first trip. It may take several backpacking trips to settle down to just the right gear and procedures for you.

The amount of weight that can be packed comfortably depends on the backpacker's age, health and physical condition. For a typical trip of two days or more in mountain country, the load limit should be within 35 pounds for a man, 25 pounds for a woman. New gear and new lightweight foods have enabled many backpackers to bring these figures to 20 pounds or less.

Gerry Cunningham, in his booklet, **"How to Enjoy Backpacking"** (Colorado Outdoor Sports Corporation, Denver, Colorado), says this about pack weights: "An ounce of technique is worth a pound of equipment. If you keep thinking, 'How can I do without?' your pack will be light."

This makes sense. Every item, no matter how small, should meet this test before it is placed in the pack. This applies to food, clothing, shelter, sleeping gear and most certainly for any luxury items.

What, specifically, should you take on a backpacking trip? This will vary,

Packs come in numerous styles and sizes. Notice that the pack on the left is designed to carry the sleeping bag below the main sack. The sack has two main compartments, one accessible from the top and the other accessible through a zippered opening. The side pockets and a map pocket give added capacity.

but one of the best suggestion lists is that published by the Forest Service, U. S. Department of Agriculture, in its **"Backpacking in the National Forest Wilderness."** Here are the Forest Service recommendations:

Pack
Tent or tarp for roof overhead
Sleeping bag
Air mattress
Cooking utensils
Dishes — plates, cups, cutlery
Food: 1½ pounds per person per day
Clothing: slacks or jeans — 2 pair; long-sleeved cotton shirt — at least 2; wool shirt or sweater; parka or windbreaker; wool socks — 2 changes; underwear; camp shoes and socks; rain gear (rain shirt, poncho, or plastic raincoat); handkerchiefs
Flashlight with extra batteries and bulb

First aid kit — make your own: band-aids, compresses, 4-inch Ace bandage, triangular bandage, antiseptic, aspirin, eye wash, adhesive tape
Bug repellent
Maps and map case
Suntan lotion
Dark glasses
Rope (nylon cord)
Toilet tissue
Trowel
Knife
Ax or hatchet
Small pliers
Matches
Soap and towel
Needle and thread
Safety pins

This recently developed K frame weighs but 2 pounds, 5 ounces, yet has no load weight limit.

As you study this list, you may see two or three items that you might do without. Or you may have some substitutes in mind. This is all right. You must suit yourself. The important point to remember is to keep the weight down. Obviously, the weight will come down a little each day as you use up your food.

Count camera

In figuring weight don't forget to count the camera you're carrying, the binoculars, the light meter, the bird guidebook in your pocket. Even with these, you can keep the weight of your load under 30 pounds. About 50 pounds is considered maximum for a man, 40 for a woman. But a lot of experts will question the necessity of going beyond 30 pounds for either, unless the trip is for a week or longer. Under 20 pounds is more ideal.

Gerry Cunningham has put together several suggested outfits with weight totals considerably below the norm. His "one man weekend outfit" weighs 13 pounds, 2 ounces; the "father and son weekend outfit" weighs 15 pounds, 2 ounces, for the father, and 8 pounds, 13 ounces, for the son; the "his and hers weekend outfit" weighs 18 pounds, 7 ounces, for him, and 9 pounds, 5 ounces, for her; the "his and hers 7 day outfit" weighs 37 pounds for him, and 18 pounds, 5 ounces, for her. It should be emphasized that these weights are beginning-of-trip weights. The "his and hers 7 day outfit," for example, includes 28 pounds of food. This reduces by four pounds each day.

The following sections show how to select equipment and supplies to meet all your backpacking needs while staying within reasonable weight limitation.

Clothing for backpackers

Footwear is the backpacker's most important clothing selection. The

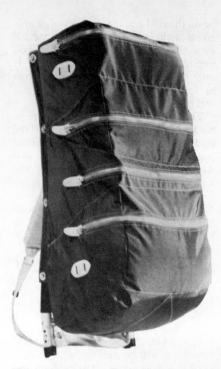

This pack is called the Traveler Sack. A comfortable rig for long trips, it is designed for those who must carry considerable gear. Notice that each compartment is entered separately by wide zippered openings.

selection is not easy because so many have their own preferences. There are certain guidelines, however, which will help you to select the right boot for the occasion. Many good boots in numerous styles and cuts are readily available today. They all have good points, but for average backpacking you will prefer certain types.

The general rule is to select boots that will fit well over two pairs of socks, one thin and one thick. Good hiking boots protect the ankles while providing strong support of the foot. The height of the boot above the ankle is determined usually by user preferences and the kind of hiking anticipated.

Leather is the most popular shoe material, but the soles should be made of rubber, synthetic or cord. Many hikers buy shoes with leather soles and have rubber lug soles added then and there.

Other essential clothing items include good socks, a change of underwear, a sweater for evening, a raincoat or poncho in case of rain, jeans (not tight-legged, western style) or strong whipcord trousers, short-sleeved cotton workshirt or a loose fitting, drip-dry shirt, a hat or cap and a heavier long-sleeved shirt for weather or terrain conditions requiring added protection.

Foods and cooking

The secret of satisfying cooking on a backpacking trip lies in the word,

An innovation in packs is this Expansi-Pak, shown in normal size at left and in expanded size at right. The inset shows how the pack attaches to the pack frame by metal-to-metal "T" keys.

dehydration. Almost any kind of food may now be purchased in dehydrated form and many of these make nourishing and appetizing meals on the trail.

Dehydration is not exactly new. Many years ago the Indians parched corn by drying it in the ashes of their campfires. They sometimes would grind the kernels into a kind of powder which they would put into a sack. At mealtime they would simply put the dry powder into their mouths and swallow it with the help of the water.

It would swell slowly in their stomachs and give them a full feeling and considerable energy. They supplemented this with the wild food they found in the wilderness. A small sack of parched corn could last for months. Daniel Boone discovered this early and never set off on the trail without a sack of parched corn.

Not too much

The temptation is to take too much food. There are exact amounts which will provide the basics. It is not wise to take much more than is necessary. In season various types of wild food are available for the taking. In the early summer there will be berries, water cress, among others; in the autumn there will be nuts, seeds from the trees and plants. And in many wilderness areas the fishing is good.

Although weight limitations must selected, this is not the most important consideration. Of first importance is nutrition. A few days on the trail will soon reveal results of poorly chosen menus. A balanced diet is extremely important if the hiker is to maintain his strength and good health.

Diet imbalance should not be a great problem today, what with the many varieties of dehydrated foods available in any supermarket and the wonderful new freeze-dry foods stocked by most camping suppliers and sporting goods stores. (See "The Secrets of Successful Camp Cookery.")

Lightweight foods

Many lightweight foods popular with backpackers are found on the pantry shelves of most homes. Some of these are dry beans, peas, lentils, potatoes, corn meal, flour, macaroni, dried fruits, dry skim milk, peanuts, peanut butter, milk chocolate and oatmeal.

How to pack food items sometimes creates more of a problem than selecting the items. Many backpackers solve this by preparing every meal before

The rule in backpacking is to take only what you need and no more. These outfits for two persons adhere to that rule. The Wilderness Traveler Master Backpacker Outfit (total weight, 15½ pounds) includes two- or three-man tent with rainfly and poles, sleeping bag, foam pad, pack and aluminum pack frame, mess kit and food. The Wilderness Traveler Companion Backpacker Outfit (total weight, 8 pounds) includes sleeping bag, foam pad, pack and frame and mess kit.

leaving home. That is, everything is done except the act of cooking. Amounts of sugar, oatmeal and anything else that must be measured before using are carefully measured in advance and placed in separate poly bags.

All the small poly bags are sealed, labeled and placed in larger poly bags designated for specific meals. Most packs will have room for one more poly bag, this one filled with special goodies such as small boxes of raisins, hard candy, dried fruit. There are times on the trail when a little extra energy is needed.

Cooking gear must be simple and also light. A two-quart pot with lid, perhaps a smaller one and a lightweight coffeepot for hot water are more than ample. A small frying pan may be added, as well as other gear.

But remember the problems of weight and bulk.

Backpacking families often use a nesting set of pots with covers, frying pan, coffeepot, cups and plates. If you are in doubt about fuel availability at your destination, take along a small gasoline or butane stove. This will add about 1½ pounds to your load.

A waterbag is helpful. There are many types, the lightest being the plastic version of the goatskin. This will hang from a tree.

Sleeping gear

Naturally you want your bed to be comfortable, but it also must be light. It is important that you carry a very light sleeping bag. Whether to carry an air mattress, a cotton tick or some other pad for your sleeping bag will be determined by your preferences, the weight of your pack and by the amount of rugged terrain which you will traverse.

Fortunately for those who prefer something more than hard earth under the sleeping bag, there are many good air mattresses and comfortable foam pads on the market. Foam pads are preferred by a growing number, but air mattresses are easier to pack and carry and are satisfactory to most users. Air mattresses and pads come in different lengths, and it is not unusual to find one considerably shorter than the sleeping bag. A mattress reaching from the shoulders to just below the hips is quite adequate, although a poncho or other fabric item

final decision is yours, of course, but you won't find it easy to make. Here, however, are some facts and tips which may be helpful:

Weight and warmth are the prime considerations. The lightest bags for the warmth provided are down-filled bags. These roll up into a compact package and are easy to carry. They are the most expensive. Simple blanket bags are often used by summer campers, but these are heavier, more bulky and are not as warm. They are much less costly. Kapok bags, once more popular than at present, are warm but bulky. Dacron is popular because it does the job and is modestly priced.

Determine how much warmth you

Choosing a pack

When shopping for a pack you will see a wide variety offered. But there are only two basic kinds used primarily for backpacking. These are the rucksack and the packboard. Modern backpackers swear by two modified types, the frame rucksack and the packframe.

A modern version of the packboard is a lightweight aluminum packframe, angled to fit the contours of the body. Only nylon bands rest against the back. These packboards come in sizes to fit persons of different sizes and shapes. The weight of this pack is placed on the hips by means of a waist strap com-

Packs carried here are lightweight. Minimum capacity intended only for a day's needs.

should be placed under the leg and feet portion of the sleeping bag for added warmth.

Beginning backpackers often blow up the air mattress too much. This makes it uncomfortable. A good test is to sit on the mattress. If you sink barely to the ground, the inflation is just right. Deflate the mattress in the morning by taking out the plug or valve while your body weight can help force out the air.

Sleeping bags are conversation subjects around many a campfire. Leaf through a half-dozen supplier catalogs and you'll discover the debate continues among the experts. The

will need, then find the sleeping bag meeting that criterion. But don't buy the first one you see. Examine the stitching and other manufacturing features. Stitching should be such that the filling cannot bunch, but the stitching should not go clear through the inner and outer cloth of the bag.

The best bags have zippers going all the way down one side and across the foot end. Many backpackers prefer mummy bags, named that because of their shape. These often are used in colder weather or higher elevations.

No matter what sleeping bag you choose, air it out just after each use.

ing out from the lower part of the frame.

The packframe may be bought with pack attached or without a pack. If you have no pack and you prefer the packframe, by all means consider buying the whole package at one time. The ideal pack for this packframe comes with compartments and outside pockets.

Rucksack

The rucksack is best used for light loads and short trips. When it is mounted on a light aluminum frame, as is often the case these days, it is easy to carry and convenient to use while on the trail. It is ideal for the youngsters who are not expected to carry adult loads.

The packboard literally got its name from using a board as the basic strong and ridged piece supporting the pack. The modern aluminum packframe has become a popular adaptation of the packboard principle, but the older packboard is still preferred by many outdoorsmen.

For example, the Alaskan packboard is quite satisfactory and it is used in many areas. The army used a similar packboard during World War II and some of these are available today as surplus. A commercial model of the Alaska packboard is called Trapper Nelson Pack Board.

The Alaska packboard is constructed around a 15" by 30" wooden frame. Strong canvas is wrapped around the frame and is tightly laced for rigidity. The space between the two layers of canvas gives good ventilation. With a little experimenting, those handy with tools can make their own packboards of this type.

Basket type

Another type of pack is the pack basket, an old favorite with the Indians. It is made of woven materials such as tree bark. Used largely in the north woods, they are best for canoe camping and for short hikes to campsites. They are used sometimes to carry bulky items such as canned goods.

You will wish to examine several different kinds of packs before choosing the one for you. You will want one that is strong, light, waterproof and large enough to carry what you need. Watch for such quality features as wide straps made of leather with padding on the bottom side where the straps cross the shoulder. Don't buy a pack with straps that must cross on the chest. This hampers breathing. The pack should fit. It should rest high on your back, touching only the shoulders and on the hips.

The size of your pack will be determined by several factors: your build and general health, how many persons you normally expect to backpack with, the types of terrain over which you will be hiking and the duration of the trip.

For an all-day hike, a simple knapsack or frame-mounted rucksack will hold the essentials—lunch, personal incidentals, perhaps a camera or nature guidebook and a first aid kit. The Boy Scout model knapsack is about right for one-day trips.

The rucksack with aluminum frame can be perfectly satisfactory on easy, weekend jaunts which require little weight and only a modest amount of strenuous effort.

Most knapsacks and rucksacks average 14 or 15 inches in width, 5 inches depth in outside-to-inside dimensions and 15 to 17 inches in height.

Versatile packboard

The packboard mentioned before is the most versatile device for carrying a variety of loads. The packboard types, including the modern packframe made of aluminum and nylon webbing, have been designed to enable

Two medium size backpacks provide enough carrying space to include necessary gear for two, plus a few luxuries.

the carrier to walk upright with the center of gravity held to a relatively constant position. The frame and its cargo become part of the person's body in relationship to movement.

For a person hiking over relatively level terrain the packboard should be such that the load is carried high on the back, about even with the shoulders. This avoids interference with leg movement.

But the mountain climber or the hiker on consistently steep trails needs a packboard which will permit the weight to be concentrated lower, possibly at the small of the back. This enables him to maintain balance while using his hands to help pull himself up over rough terrain.

The person who needs to have completely free movement of both arms and legs—perhaps the photographer—in various kinds of terrain will distribute his load more or less evenly from his shoulders to the small of his back. Method of packing and packboard design determine this.

In all cases, the weight should be in as close to the back as possible. This offers definite mechanical advantages.

There is on the market today a modified packboard which enables the backpacker to adjust his load to fit the terrain and activity anticipated. With a little experimenting, you can adapt most any standard frame and sack to suit the weight center—center of gravity, some call it—to your personal preferences.

Tumpline. A tumpline is designed for giving rest to weary shoulders. It is a simple band about 3 inches wide and about 18 inches long that fits around the front of the head at about

the natural hairline. It can be made out of most anything soft—a folded handkerchief, a sock or a belt. Or you can buy those commercially made. The tumpline is fastened to the bottom corners of the pack, and when the head is pressed forward, much of the weight is taken from the shoulders. When the shoulders are sore, the tumpline may be shortened and thereby cause more weight of the pack to shift to the head. When the head grows weary, the tumpline may be lengthened, causing the weight to return to the shoulders.

There is a safety factor in using the tumpline, and this is seen when crossing on a log or stepping stones over a stream, or when walking down a steep hill. By putting all the weight of the pack on the tumpline, you may take your arms out of the shoulder straps. Thus if you lose your balance and fall, a quick jerk of your head will release the pack and perhaps save you from serious injury.

How to load your pack

The key word in good packing is organization. This means that you will departmentalize your equipment, preferably in plastic bags so that you will have many bags within a bag. One bag is the mess bag in which will go your cup, plate, fork and spoon. The mending bag will include needle and thread and other items which may be needed. If you carry a second pair of shoes, which is a good idea, or perhaps some light moccosins for camp, these go into the shoe bag. Extra socks may also go into this bag. Your toilet bag will include toothbrush, toothpaste and the like.

If you can get plastic bags in a variety of colors, by all means do so as colors can identify the contents.

Properly equipped backpackers can camp comfortably in any kind of terrain or weather conditions.

Otherwise, each bag should be labeled so that you don't have to take every bag out to find what you are looking for each time you open your pack.

When all the items are in the small bags, place them into the packsack. Blankets or bedrolls, if packed inside, should be placed on the side of the pack that rests against your back. Place at the bottom of the pack the items you probably will not need until the end of day or when you make camp. (Bedrolls packed on the bottom form a kind of shelf on which to build the content arrangement.) Anything that has to do with emergency—first aid kit, poncho, flashlight—should be placed on top. Packing you will discover, is the key to comfort and convenience.

You can pack efficiently if you have only a packboard and no pack. The pack is formed from a tarp. To assembly, you simply arrange the gear and supplies on one corner of a folded tarp. The tarp becomes the wrapper, and you simply wrap and fold as you would a gift package. The pack "package" has about the same outside dimensions as the packboard. The wrapped pack, everything inside except the ax, then is lashed firmly to the packboard. The bedroll may be lashed to the top, and the ax may be shoved up through the pack lashings.

Backpacker's shelter

Some backpackers, perhaps to prove their manliness or to emphasize their youth, head for the wilderness trails without a shelter. This is foolish in most areas since there are so many lightweight tent shelters available. Several types of shelters may be improvised with the use of a tarpaulin,

This is a popular tent for backpackers. Notice the side windows for ventilation, even during rain.

poncho or even a sheet of plastic.

Except for the ax, a tarp or some sort of tough waterproof sheet probably is the most useful item in the backpacker's gear. The tarp should be about 8 feet by 8 feet, with grommets sewed in about 18 inches apart along all sides. The standard tarp used is made of waterproof, 8-ounce canvas. It is strong, wears well and will last a long time. But it is not as light as many backpackers prefer today.

In recent years a good deal of experimenting has been done with nylon and plastic. Unfortunately, nylon itself is not waterproof and when waterproofing is applied, air circulation is cut off. There is nothing wrong with such fabric for the usual tarp uses, but a tent must breathe.

But great improvements of nylon with a coating of vinyl plastic on either side have made this a near ideal tarp for backpackers. It may be used as a tent fly or as the outer roof of a two-roof tent.

Trail shelter

In some places the backpacker may not need a tent if he can secure space in three-sided trail shelters provided in some of the national forests and national parks. The Forest Service describes these as following "a general pattern. A slightly raised platform in back is to sleep on and can accommodate from eight to a dozen people. In front is a firepit usually with a large back rock to reflect the heat of the fire into the shelter. There is some type of sanitary facility nearby and drinkable water.

Designed for through hikers, shelters are occupied on a first-come, first-served basis. Latecomers rig up a shelter outside.

Adequate shelter

To be sure of an adequate shelter in any kind of weather, the wise backpacker carries a lightweight tent. The best ones have a sewed-in floor, a zippered netting across the front and one or more additional net-covered openings for cross ventilation. These are insectproof, animalproof, snakeproof and waterproof. Stakes the size of a large nail and lightweight telescopic aluminum poles are carried wrapped in the tent.

Lightweight materials for backpacking tents present the same problems that lightweight nylon-plastic tarps do when these are used as shelters. In a small, watertight nylon tent, even the breath will condense and cause serious dampness. Waterproofed cotton, on the other hand, doesn't stay waterproof too long. The answer is to use both, the cotton as the inner tent and waterproofed nylon as the outer tent. Some good two-roof tents are made of nylon inside and plastic outside.

Making camp

Sleeping out under the stars near

Backpacking is enjoyed to the fullest when the camping is done in a wilderness area. A wilderness ranger is shown here giving directions to backpackers in Desolation Valley, a part of California's Eldorado National Forest.

rushing stream or a placid lake is great fun. But fun can quickly turn into trouble, even disaster, if care isn't taken in picking the campsite. Sometimes the choice will be made for you by the caretakers of public lands. In that case, don't be too concerned. But when you have to make the choice, remember these simple but important rules:

1. Look for drinking water and fuel wood.

2. Look for a level site, high and dry and with a view—even a short-range one.

3. Determine if you can easily clear enough of the site for a safe fire.

4. Pitch your tent and otherwise face your camp toward a lake or up a canyon if you wish to take advantage of prevailing winds at night, the reverse if you don't.

5. Avoid camping under dead trees or limbs or in the path of potential rock slides.

Sources of information

The national forests and national parks all offer backpacking opportunities. Many of these are in wilderness areas. The national forests alone contain 85 huge wilderness areas. These areas are true wildernesses into which you may not drive for the simple reason that they are not traversed by roads and highways.

Write to any agency in charge of public lands where you may wish to backpack, and you will receive a courteous reply along with information and maps. Two Forest Service booklets will be especially helpful. These are **Wilderness** and **Camping**.

The following organizations publish books, booklets, magazines, brochures and maps on subjects pertinent to the wilderness backpacker (see "Where To Write for More Information" for addresses): Adirondack Mountain Club, Appalachian Mountain Club, Appalachian Trail Conference, Green Mountain Club, Mazamas, The Sierra Club, Federation of Western Outdoor Clubs, Wilderness Society.

Then there are trail systems which may take in some of those mentioned and others privately owned. Among the better known trail systems are these:

The Appalachian Trail, more than 2,000 miles, Maine to Georgia; The Baker Trail, 110 miles in Pennsylvania; The Bruce Trail, 480 miles along the Niagara Escarpment in Ontario.

Canoe Camping Provides
New Experiences, Covers
More Territory

Camps set up by canoe campers when they land utilize, for the most part, the same kinds of gear carried by back country packers—whether they arrive at their destinations by foot, horse or vehicle.

Some campers who travel by water sleep aboard their anchored boats, but most don't call this camping. Campers do, however, travel to their selected campsites via all types of vessels from a simple outboard fishing boat to a high speed cabin cruiser. But others prefer to travel by their own labor via canoe into areas where motorized boats may not or cannot intrude.

Canoe camping has become exceedingly popular in recent years, although it is not new by any means. Modern camping gear and the establishment of canoe trails by governmental and private agencies have added to the popularity.

Some canoeists prefer the more placid waters of lakes connected by portage trails or streams; others enjoy traveling down a white river and making camp each evening along its banks.

All will agree that canoeing is an exciting and rewarding sport. It offers an added dimension to camping and is apt to become a habit to any outdoor enthusiast who is properly introduced to it.

The canoe

The canoe is a beautiful craft. Few can refrain from gazing approvingly at its distinctive profile on a placid lake, spotlighted by the setting sun or a full moon.

Those who are unfamiliar with the canoe often regard it as an unstable, dangerous craft. This simply is not true. Any craft can be dangerous if you don't know how to operate it. The same applies to motor vehicles. As a matter of fact, the canoe is easier to handle than most any other water conveyance and it is just as safe as the simple, flat bottom row boat.

Probably the best, all-round canoe for two or three persons is one about 18 feet long, 3 feet wide at the center and 14 inches deep. This canoe will remain stable in rough weather while supporting two men and 800 pounds of equipment or three men and 600 pounds of equipment. Flat-bottomed construction is preferred.

Canoes vary in size, shape and in materials used in their construction. For light loads and relatively easy paddling, a pointed-stern canoe is best. A square-stern canoe will take heavy loads and an outboard motor. The lake canoe is best designed for both speed and holding a straight course in the wind. It has a regular keel, a rounded bottom and good width. The ends are low. The type preferred for river travel (appropriately called the river canoe) has little or no keel a flat bottom (draws less water and provides stability) and slim ends.

Many guides in New England, Canada and elsewhere still prefer the traditional canvas-covered wooden canoe. This is an excellent craft, and to those who spend a great deal of their time in water wilderness areas it offers psychological comfort and security. It must be painted on the outside every year and the inside must be varnished just as often.

The canvas-covered canoe requires careful handling and maintenance, but in the hands of an experienced or thoroughly trained canoeist it is com-

The 17' "Princess" and the 13' "Brave" are Fiberglas canoes manufactured by Rivers & Gilman Moulded Products, Inc.

There is a whole new world of camping adventure when you travel by boat or canoe—or maybe raft. Travel further, see more, enjoy solitude. No motor boats allowed.

pletely dependable and long lasting. It has some other distinct advantages:

1. You can make better time with it against the wind.

2. It is somewhat easier to handle in wind and white caps.

3. It is an extremely quiet craft, enabling the careful paddler to move in close to wildlife on shore without being heard.

4. It comes in a wide variety of sizes and types.

Following is a table of canoe dimensions and weights suggested by Ontario's Department of Lands and Forests (weights for canvas-covered wood canoes; aluminum craft are a little lighter):

Length ft.	Width in.	Depth in.	Weight lbs.	Capacity lbs.	persons
14	32	12	60	500	1-2
15	33	12	65	500	1-2
16	34	13	70-75	600	2-3
17	35-37	14½	75-85	650-950	3-4
18*	46	18	135	1600	4-5

*Weight and capacity for freight handling

There are some problems, however, in using and maintaining this canoe, which cause novices and the more inexperienced to shy away from purchasing them. One such negative factor is the necessity to repaint frequently and to refinish the interior. Another is the likelihood of frequent repairs of cut or punctured canvas. And the canoe must be stored carefully in the winter. Northwoods professionals seem to welcome these chores.

The most popular all-round canoe is one made of aluminum alloy. Perhaps the main reasons for such popularity are these:

This canoe does not have to be painted; and if it hits a sharp object, usually the only damage is a dent. This can be pounded back into its original shape.

Campers especially like this canoe because it can be used as a reflector by the campfire and it is lightweight. Most models will flip themselves right side up if they are accidentally overturned, and air pockets plus floatation materials make them unsinkable.

No paint needed

Although the aluminum canoe does not have to be painted, some campers do apply a coat of soft green paint to subdue the glare in strong sunlight. Many of the old timers feel that too much noise is made by the slapping of tiny waves against the canoe's side. The average canoeist hardly notices this.

Aluminum canoes ride rather high in the water when empty and this can cause trouble in high winds. But this is hardly a problem to the camper who will keep the canoe weighted down with gear during most times of use.

Any disadvantages of this canoe certainly are offset by its light weight, its tough construction and its minimum maintenance needs. Incidentally, some of the sounds made while paddling can be virtually eliminated by applying rubber gunwale guards for both stern and bow paddlers.

The safest aluminum canoe for campers is one equipped with Styrofoam floatation chambers in addition to the customary air pockets at either end. Other safety factors are supplied by the human cargo.

Fiberglass

A comparative newcomer to the canoe field is one made of molded fiberglass. These are very durable, easy to maintain and easy to repair. Most models are heavier and therefore are not as popular to canoeists who plan to portage.

On the other hand, fiberglass canoes have some distinct advantages. They can be left out of doors all the time, don't have to be repainted each year and it is practically impossible to puncture or split them. A fiberglass canoe is good for a night fire reflector, but it does not conduct heat and cold to the extremes that an aluminum canoe does.

Paddling techniques

Experts agree that the best paddles are made of maple, with ash running a close second. Probably the most popular paddles are made of spruce. These are light and for that reason are frequently chosen by beginners. But the wood is more apt to break, and this is something you don't want to happen when you are racing a sudden rain squall to shore. Besides, the maple and ash paddles are not *that* heavy, and once you get used to them, you will hardly notice the difference.

In following a canoe trail for a week or more, there are distinct advantages in having two or three persons occupying each canoe. Two persons are necessary to making good time in an 18- or 20-footer loaded with several hundred pounds of gear. The bow paddler uses a paddle which reaches to his chin when he stands, and the stern paddler uses one which reaches about to his natural hairline.

These measurements are general guides, and you will have to choose the exact length that works best for you. Some paddlers prefer to use paddles that are longer than they are tall; others like them shorter than the average. But a paddle that is too short makes it awkward and difficult to

This 17' canoe weighs 69 pounds, one of several features attractive to backpackers who take to the water.

submerge the entire blade for a full, smooth stroke.

The best paddling position is from a kneeling position. This can cause you to tire quickly unless you sit on the thwart or a seat occasionally for resting. The object of kneeling is to give more stability to the canoe by keeping the weight low and also to be able to put more power into the strokes. The amount of water turbulence and the direction of flow have a bearing on how a canoeist positions himself and applies his efforts.

Steering-pace setting

The sternman and the bowman have two distinct responsibilities: the sternman steers and the bowman sets the pace. Each has basic strokes, the bow stroke being most commonly used by the bowman to move the canoe forward and the J stroke used by the sternman to both move the canoe forward and to keep it on a straight course.

The bow stroke calls for one hand to grasp the grip of the paddle and the other to hold the shaft two or three inches above the blade. The hands should be separated by about the width of the paddler's shoulders. The lower arm is kept straight while the upper arm pushes forward across the paddler's body as the lower arm pulls.

(Note: Upper arm and lower arm referred to here are the relative positions of both arms, not separate parts of the same arm.)

The upper arm at the end of the stroke is fully extended over the water, and the lower hand stops about even with the hip. The paddler should immediately relax his arms, turn the paddle to a flat position and move it forward low over the water to the proper position for another stroke. The blade is dipped in smoothly and the stroke is repeated.

"J" stroke

At the other end of the canoe, meanwhile, the sternman is making the J stroke. To make the J stroke, the sternman starts ahead and pulls back in a similar manner to the bowman making the bowstroke, except as the paddle nears a position parallel to the body, it is turned into an outward hook in the general shape of the letter J. This twist keeps the canoe on a straight course. If both paddlers use the bowstroke, the canoe will veer off course.

The backwater stroke is another basic stroke. This is used to both stop the canoe and to make it move backward. In this stroke the paddle is held behind the paddler, is pushed forward with the lower arm and pulled back with the upper arm until it is at a point slightly ahead of the paddler.

The paddle is quickly twisted so that the blade comes smoothly out of the

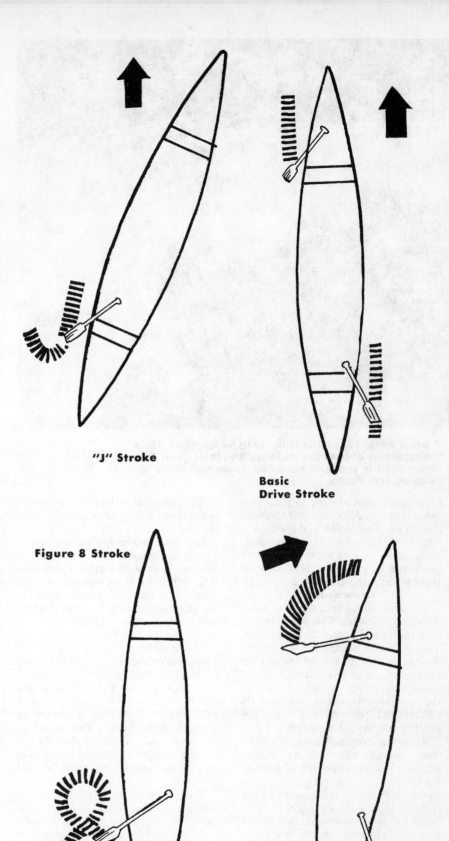

"J" Stroke

Basic Drive Stroke

Figure 8 Stroke

Sweep Stroke

A white water canoe trip is never to be forgotten. Note the positions of both the paddlers and their gear. This canoe load is properly balanced. Grumman Allied Industries, Inc. Photo

water and is moved close to the water behind the paddler again to repeat the stroke. This stroke is the same for both bowman and sternman, although the J stroke may be necessary to hold the canoe in position, particularly in slight water turbulences.

Draw sroke

The draw stroke is designed to move the canoe sideways. This stroke begins with the paddle abeam of the paddler. The stroke is sompleted by pulling the paddle straight toward the paddler to within about six inches of the canoe. Repeating is done by lifting the paddle just above the water's surface and positioning it again for another pull toward the paddler.

It can't be overemphasized that both arms should relax during paddle recovery in connection with all strokes. Remember that the buoyancy of the water helps to lift the paddles to the surface, and it isn't necessary to make this a strenuous movement. If you find yourself straining while paddling, very likely you are stroking incorrectly. Practice will enable you to stroke properly and to relax properly.

Turning the canoe calls for the sculling draw stroke. This stroke is used by both the bowman and the sternman, and on both sides of the canoe. The stroke is made in the form of a figure 8. The paddle starts back of the paddler close to the canoe, is brought forward and out, then toward the canoe in a flat position. It then is

headed down at a slant to the bottom of the figure 8 and flat once again to the starting point.

The canoe moves toward the side on which the paddlers are working, if they are both working from the same side. When they are working on the opposite sides, the canoe turns to the right or to the left, depending on which side each is paddling.

Sculling

The sculling stroke is very helpful when sudden moves are necessary and when navigating white water streams. Sometimes it must be worked so fast that it is necessary for the bowman to call signals and the sternman to respond immediately. The bowman, of course, can see all the obstructions coming up, but the ultimate decision relative to course is made by the sternman.

The pushover is a stroke that is opposite to the draw stroke. Some canoeists call this an "out-draw."

Another important stroke which is used to swing the bow or the stern from side to side is the quarter sweep stroke. This stroke may be made by either the bowman or the sternman. The bowman places the paddle flat against the side of the canoe and forward, then sweeps it outward until the paddle is at right angles with the canoe. The sternman places the paddle behind his position and sweeps it out until it is at right angles with the canoe. By thus working on both sides

of the canoe, the craft is turned quickly.

Sweep stroke

When canoeing alone, the full sweep stroke is perhaps best for making a quick turn. The paddler usually sits slightly back of amidship, and he places the paddle ahead of him and parallel to the canoe. He then pulls it back in an arc until the paddle is again parallel. This stroke causes the canoe to move away from the side on which the paddler is working.

The stroke most used for a person canoeing alone is the pitch stroke. Again the paddle is placed ahead of him at right angles to the canoe and is pulled back with the inside of the blade turning toward the stern as the paddle is moved. This turning continues until the blade is parallel to the canoe's side and is still in the water.

Numerous other strokes are used by experienced canoeists, but those cited here will suffice for the average canoe camper. As more experience is gained, other strokes may be added for variety and usefulness.

Gear and supplies

It is necessary, for successful canoe camping, to pack most gear and supplies in waterproof carrying bags or boxes. Anything that may be damaged or destroyed by water should be packed in these containers. Many canoe campers use sturdy plastic bags, often placed within duffel or laundry bags, into which they pack food, clothing and sleeping bags.

Military surplus stores sell such waterproof containers as ammo boxes, which some campers find useful when traveling by canoe. There is not a great variety of waterproof containers for this type of camping, but most outfitters and leading sporting goods stores usually carry items that will suffice. Some campers use their own ingenuity.

Most waterproof containers will float free in case of a canoe upset and certainly are much more easily retrieved when floating than when resting on the bottom of a lake or stream.

Other gear preferred by canoe campers includes a tent. Sometimes tarps and fly sheets are used in combination with the canoe itself to provide shelter. A typical list of other gear and supply items might include the following:

Lightweight sleeping bag, air mattress, small gasoline stove, cook kit, ax or hatchet, water container, foam plastic ice chest, bucket for heating water, a grill, a gasoline lantern, a folding stove, waterproof, floatable box for camera equipment, folding stools, life jackets, necessary clothing and food. Personal items such as radio, books and the like may be brought along, but it must be remembered that if portaging is part of the trip, these will all have to be carried overland.

Canvas pack

The most popular form of pack used by canoe campers who portage a great deal is one made of canvas that measures about 25 inches long and 15 to 20 inches wide, and opens at the top. Simple shoulder straps are attached at the top center and run to the bottom corners. This is popularly called the Duluth. It goes by other names such as Woods, Northwestern and Maine.

The better Duluth bags carried by most outfitters are made of waterproofed duck in the form of a reinforced boxlike bag. Sometimes pockets are sewed on the outside for smaller items. Buckles and rings may be placed at strategic points for attaching an optional tump line or for tying on such items as ponchos.

It is important that the shoulder straps be broad where they fit over the shoulders. Further, it is helpful if these are padded with fleece-attached sheepskin.

Food items often are carried in a pack basket which protects them from being jammed together and affords easy carrying on the back. This basket may be swung from a tree limb in camp or may be placed on the ground in an upright position. Access to the food is convenient. This is a favorite in the northeastern United States and sections of Canada.

A growing number of canoe campers are utilizing the packboard, the same one used on backpacking trips. Most any type of pack that is suitable for backpacking will likewise be suitable for canoe camping. It is important that extra measures be taken to assure waterproofing, the simplest way being to place the packsack into a waterproof plastic bag, described earlier.

Loading a canoe

A canoe should be afloat when it is loaded. The basic rule to follow is to keep the weight as centered and low as possible. If the weight is properly distributed, the paddlers or occupants, when they step in, will cause the canoe to ride with the bow slightly higher than the stern. This makes it easier to steer. However, if the canoe sinks evenly to the waterline, with neither bow nor stern higher, it will move through the water more smoothly and is a little easier to paddle. It is absolutely necessary to trim the cargo, that is, to so position it that the weight is on dead center. This brings side-to-side balance and improves stability.

A rugged portage calls for a durable lightweight canoe. The gear and supplies also should be lightweight. Old Town Canoe Company Photo

Many canoe campers place some light wooden slats or poles in the bottom before loading so that if any water gets in, the cargo will not become soaked. When there is rain or the water surface is rough, it is the duty of the stern paddler to bail out the water from time to time. When the gear is securely wrapped in waterproof containers, it will not be damaged by excess water in the canoe.

Do not lash, tie or otherwise attach your cargo bundles to the craft itself. If the canoe should tip over, which is not too likely, the gear then will fall out and float on the water. Empty, the canoe will be much easier to upright.

Spare paddle

Some "necessity" items should ride by themselves separate from your pack and gear. The canoe should carry a spare paddle and a life preserver for each occupant. A repair kit is essential, particularly if the canoe is a canvas-covered model. Some canoe campers lash a small ax to the gunwale with the blade under the thwart and between the ribs.

A rope should be attached to the bow. Keep a waterproof flashlight handy at all times. Check the batteries frequently. For such small items, a canoe box is available for attachment or may be fitted to a new canoe at the factory.

When packing the canoe for a day's trip, it is the better part of wisdom to leave easily accessible those items that you likely will use along the way. For example, a quick stop for a meal calls for the necessary food and eating utensils to be packed separately, or at least convenient to reach without shifting the major cargo. The same holds for cameras, fishing tackle, jackets and such.

Experienced canoeists attempt to pack their gear and supplies in not more than three packs, each within weight limits for convenient carrying. This means that two canoeists having only three packs can make a portage in two trips. On the first trip each takes a pack; on the second, one handles the canoe while the other carries the remaining pack. Along the way they can help each other as circumstances require.

Every canoe camper ultimately adopts his own system. As he gains experience, he develops his own methods of packing and limits the items he carries to his individual tastes and requirements.

Portaging

Some campers hesitate to follow the beautiful canoe trails because they assume that portaging will be too difficult for them. Properly done, this part of the trip is not difficult at

The "Totebox Pack," a relatively new product, is designed specifically for portaging.

all. In fact, it comes as a welcome change, offers a different kind of exercise and a different kind of scenery.

The experienced canoeist uses his paddles to form the carrying yoke when he portages the canoe. He begins by lashing these with a heavy line between the front seat and the center thwart, with the handles pointed toward the front seat. The upper portion of the blade at a point where it is about three inches wide is positioned slightly in front of the thwart. The distance between the blades is adjusted

so that they will fit comfortably on the shoulders.

The canoe should balance at about the center thwart, perhaps with a slight tug towards the stern. When buying a canoe or renting one, it might be wise to test the balance first.

When the canoeist's head and shoulders are in place, he reaches ahead and takes hold of each gunwale and pulls down to achieve the desired balance. This causes the bow to ride some six feet above the ground. Then he simply walks to the next launching point.

Balance

Getting the canoe up to the shoulders and properly balanced is not quite as simple as it sounds. If you have never done this, by all means get an experienced canoeman to show you how. It will take only a few minutes and will save you a lot of extra effort and strain.

The experienced canoeman will first tell you to turn the canoe over, then he will ask your companion to raise the bow as far above his head as his arms will reach. At this point he will invite you to step under, place your head and shoulders in the right position and lift.

If you are not toughened to this procedure and some of your portages require walking 200 feet or more, you may wish to wear an extra jacket or to otherwise pad the shoulders at the spots where the canoe will rest. Sometimes a tumpline is helpful. This consists of a broad band of soft leather, which fits around your forehead at about the normal hairline and which is

Canoe campers eye a likely campsite on an island in the Basswood River, Minnesota-Canada Boundary Waters.

attached to the canoe in such a way that your head can assume some of the weight. This is similar to the method used by backpackers to disburse the weight of heavy packs.

Canoe handling tips

In boarding a canoe, the most experienced member of the party should be the last one in. He should hold the canoe in place until he is certain the others are in "balanced" positions. In landing, the best rule is "last in, first out."

If there is an abrupt rise in the wind on a lake, or you see a thunderstorm approaching, head for shore at once. Meet large waves head-on or permit them to catch up at right angles to the stern. Never try a dangerous rapids run unless you have had considerable experience.

Pointed poles sometimes are better for ascending a shallow, swift section of a river. Tracking (pulling the canoe with attached rope while walking on land) may save a strenuous portage. Tracking and poling combined (one canoeist pulling on land while the other stays with the canoe and poles) can be quite effective.

Two canoes placed side by side and joined by horizontal poles lashed to the thwarts make a thoroughly stable craft for crossing a choppy lake. A small outboard motor may be attached to the rear crosspole.

Some safety rules

For a more detailed description of safety rules, see "Safety First and First Aid." But here are some key rules to keep in mind when canoeing:

1. Don't attempt any new water maneuvers until your experience warrants it.

2. Choose the right canoe for the water conditions, the load, the distance and the experience of each passenger.

3. Know where you are going and know that each day's travel is reasonable.

4. Don't overload the canoe.

5. Distribute the weight evenly.

6. Never stand up in a moving canoe.

7. If the canoe flips over, stay with it. Do not try to swim to shore.

8. Do not wear heavy boots while canoeing.

9. Do not go out if the wind is too strong and the waves are high.

10. Unless you are really expert and have experts with you, portage around white water rapids.

Canoeing is an excellent sport. Opportunities to learn the techniques are available almost everywhere. It's a family activity. And thousands of families have taken their canoeing knowhow, along with their camping knowhow, to some of the best outdoor adventure imaginable. In two's or in groups, campers can go a long way toward their camping goals by heading down a river or across a lake to beauty spots only they can reach.

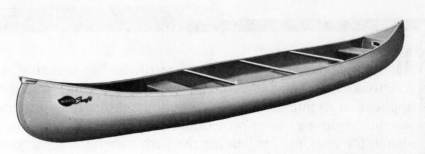

MirroCraft by Mirro Aluminum Company. Excellent type for travel by river.

A 15' model produced by AeroCraft. Has fairly low profile and ends, suitable for medium size lakes.

Delcraft Model 17DE by Delhi Corporation. Has ample space for packing supplies. Good design for all around use.

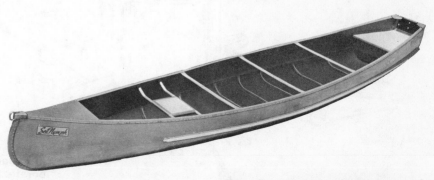

The Sea Nymph 16' square end. This is a fine type for long trips over big, open waters. For use with small horsepower outboard motors. Easy to paddle when motor can't be used.

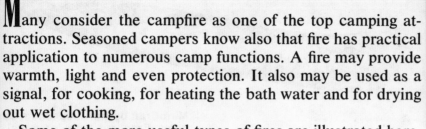

FIRES FOR ALL OCCASIONS

Many consider the campfire as one of the top camping attractions. Seasoned campers know also that fire has practical application to numerous camp functions. A fire may provide warmth, light and even protection. It also may be used as a signal, for cooking, for heating the bath water and for drying out wet clothing.

Some of the more useful types of fires are illustrated here.

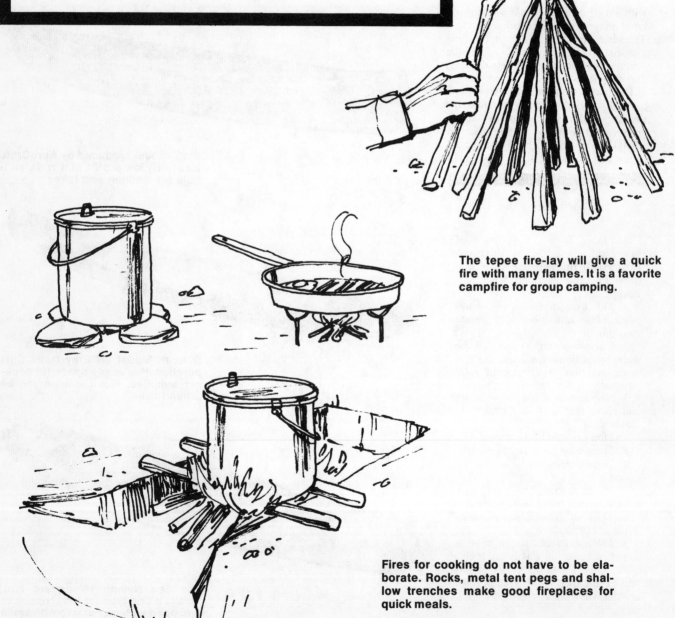

The tepee fire-lay will give a quick fire with many flames. It is a favorite campfire for group camping.

Fires for cooking do not have to be elaborate. Rocks, metal tent pegs and shallow trenches make good fireplaces for quick meals.

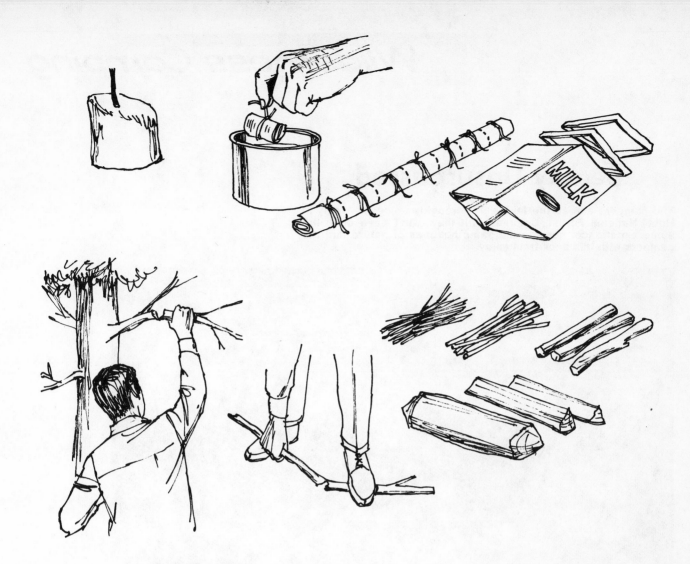

No matter what kind of fire is used in camp, it does its job more quickly if good fire starters are used. Many seasoned campers carry a candle stub for fire lighting during wet weather. Other campers take along newspaper sheets which they roll up, tie and cut into short sections for dipping into melted paraffin. Milk cartons may be flattened and cut into narrow strips for use as fire starters. A good source of quick-burning fuel, some of it suitable for starting fires, is a dead branch on a tree. Often small dead branches will be within reach and can be broken off, then broken up for fire starting use.

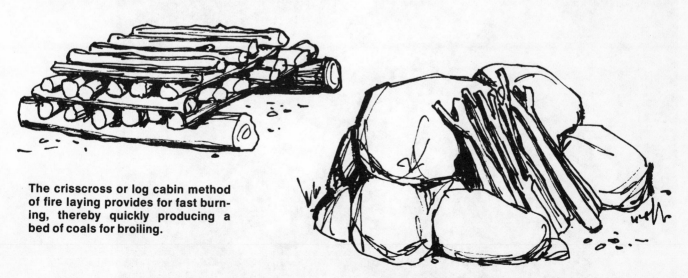

The crisscross or log cabin method of fire laying provides for fast burning, thereby quickly producing a bed of coals for broiling.

A reflector fire is just what the name implies. It reflects heat to warm the camp and it also reflects heat for baking in a reflector oven (See Camp Cookery section).

Beauty Unsurpassed

The campers across the lake will thoroughly enjoy their stay in Routt National Forest, Colorado, but they won't have quite the same experience, nor see the same beauties of nature that the campers with this pack train enjoy.

with Pack Animals

Much of the public land in both the United States and Canada is untouched wilderness. Out of 14,000,000 acres within the boundaries of 33 American national parks, only about 700,000 acres have been developed for recreational purposes. This includes campsites, visitor centers, roads and other facilities. In the national forests are 58 wilderness areas, lands practically untouched by man. No roads run through them, only trails and waterways. No commercial enterprises—lumbering, mining, etc.—are permitted. Nothing with wheels may enter these areas.

These vast areas are exceedingly attractive to back country campers. Hikers, canoeists and campers riding or walking with pack animals are about the only people—other than government employees—who ever see these vast areas of natural beauty.

The pack horse trip is rapidly becoming the most popular wilderness experience, particularly among those who prefer to have outfitters make all the arrangements for such excursions. Many others who have once experienced a pack-horse trip into wilderness country have come to make this kind of camping a regular habit.

The Forest Service and the National Park Service have issued a joint description of wilderness traveling and camping and some regulations which apply to wilderness areas in both national parks and national forests. Three types of stock trips are described:

Walking with pack animals. With this arrangement, you do your own packing and are responsible for the welfare of the animals. The packer from whom you rent the animals will help you get started. Then you are on your own.

The recommended load limit on burros is about 75 pounds, and about 150 pounds for a mule. The lighter your equipment and the more you use dehydrated and freeze-dry foods, the fewer animals will you need for a trip.

Gerry Cunningham in his valuable booklet, **Wilderness Trips You Can Enjoy,** makes this observation about lightening the load on pack trips: "... the usual pack horse outfitter uses very cumbersome and heavy equipment, requiring a string of pack horses at the ratio of one pack horse for each rider. Such quantities of stock pose serious grazing problems and the forest service has found it necessary to close some areas to the use of pack animals. If the philosophy of light but comfortable equipment is applied to horseback trips, a man and his wife could spend a week on the trail carrying only 25 pounds each

Wranglers lead saddle horses and pack animals into the high country where a group of wilderness campers awaits.

in saddle bags on their regular riding horses." Because of weight problems and more strict regulations in some areas, many packers are using lighter weight gear and supplies.

Spot trips. This type of traveling with stock is favored by many because it eliminates the problems of caring for the animals while at camp, and it takes the entire burden of transportation and supply maintenance off the camper. You are packed into a base camp and your packer returns for you at the end of your stay.

The conservationists are satisfied, for animals are not left to graze in meadows or to trample flowers and bushes around the camp. You can either ride with the packer to your base camp, or hike in and have your food and equipment packed in. A modification of this is a type of family backpacking that is popular in the Sierra Nevada mountains. A burro is rented and enough lightweight supplies and equipment are packed on his back (up to 75 pounds) to maintain up to four people for almost a week. The campers hike to their permanent campsite as they lead the burro.

Touring trips. On this type of trip,

New lightweight fabrics, lightweight foods and lighter gear have combined to drastically reduce the pack weight carried by horses on the trail. The outfits shown here are the Wilderness Traveler Master Trailrider Outfit (with the tent), 13 pounds, and the Companion, 7½ pounds. The only necessary additional weight would be from food for extended travel.

the packer and stock are with you for the entire journey. The American Forestry Association, the Sierra Club, the Wilderness Society and similar organizations schedule and sponsor such trips each year.

If you are planning a stock trip, write to the headquarters of the national park or national forest you will be visiting. Request a list of the pack stations authorized to pack and rent walking stock, and also a copy of the grazing regulations. Select a packer and deal directly with him to reserve the services you desire.

Wilderness travelers are responsible for obeying the general regulations issued by the authority covering each wilderness area. In addition, these regulations have been issued by both the national parks and national forests to apply specifically to wilderness travel (not necessarily to other national forest and national park areas):

1. Motorcycles, or other motor vehicles, bicycles, boats or portable motors such as power plants and chain saws, are not permitted in national park or national forest wilderness.

2. Destruction, defacement or removal or disturbance of the property or any natural features or objects in any manner is prohibited. This includes:

    a. Cutting, blazing, marking, driving nails into or otherwise damaging growing trees or standing snags (dead trees). No pine boughs or ferns for beds!

    b. Writing, carving or painting of names or other inscriptions anywhere.

    c. Destruction, defacement or moving signs.

3. Specimens of plants, minerals, animal life or other natural or historical objects may only be collected for scientific study. Written authorization must be obtained in advance from the park superintendent or forest supervisor. Permits are not issued for personal collections.

4. Clean your camp before you leave. Tin cans, foil, glass, worn-out or useless gear and other unburnables must be carried out of the mountains with you.

5. Campfire permits are required for all back country travel. Obtain them at any ranger station. Please comply with conditions stated on the permit.

6. Smoking while traveling is not permitted. If you have to smoke, stop and do it in a safe place.

7. Do not use soap directly in springs, streams or lakes. Keep wash water, fish entrails, garbage and trash out of these waters.

8. Loose herding of pack and saddle animals on trails is allowed only on designated, hazardous trails. If you are bringing your own stock into the forests or parks, write for a copy of the local grazing and loose herding regulations.

9. Avoid taking short cuts on switchbacks. Keeping to the trail is safer, easier and saves trail maintenance costs.

In these areas, state regulations on hunting and fishing (particularly in the issuance of licenses) apply to wilderness area travelers.

In the national parks guns, loaded or unloaded, are prohibited in areas specified as "wilderness." Dogs or cats are not permitted in any of the back country of the parks, not even on a leash. Fishing is allowed. Shooting or molesting any bird or animal is prohibited.

For a descriptive folder, send 15 cents to Superintendent of Documents, Government Printing Office, Washington, D. C., and ask for **National Forest Wilderness and Primitive Areas.** The headquarters office of Yosemite National Park, Yosemite, California 95389, will send a copy of **To the Wilderness Traveler.**

Top. The most reluctant campers to leave a favored campsite are the wilderness campers who have found a setting such as this.

Bottom. These are not Indians waiting to attack the settlement at daybreak. They are wilderness campers getting ready to bed down for the night.

Knots That Every Camper Should Know

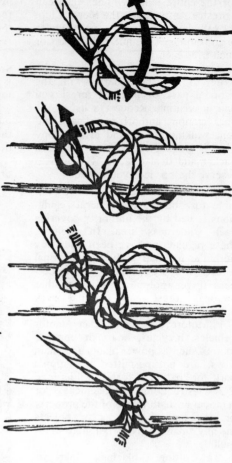

If you wish to become a knot expert, see the bibliography for books on the subject. It has been estimated that more than 8,000 different knots are possible. Campers do not have to become proficient in tying thousands of knots or even hundreds. But there are a few that every camper should be able to put to practical use. These are the square knot, the sheet bend, the clove hitch, the tautline hitch, the bowline and two half hitches.

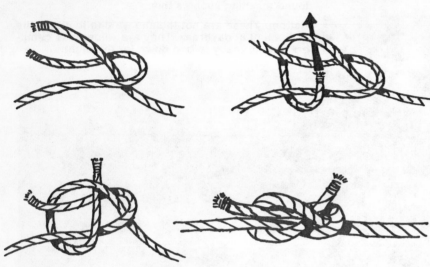

Two half hitches may be used in meeting such needs as clotheslines and windbreak supports.

The sheet bend, the best knot for tying two ropes together.

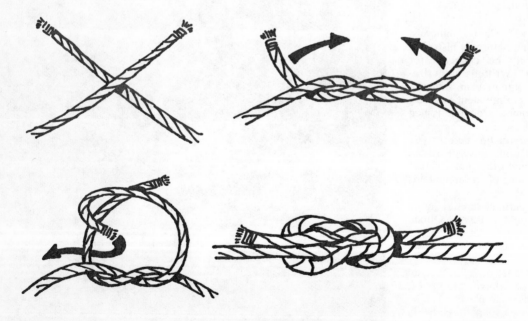

The square knot, useful for first aid work and for tying bundles.

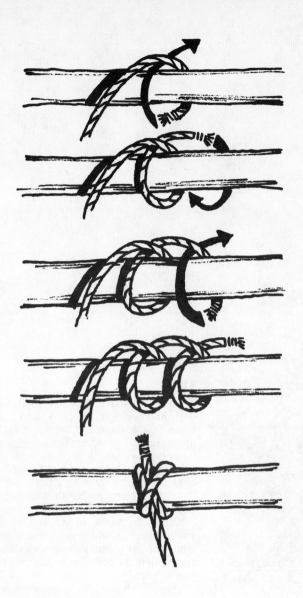

The clove hitch is useful in making camp structures and in tying a rope to a tree or well anchored post.

The tautline hitch is best known among campers for its use in tying tent lines to pegs or other anchors.

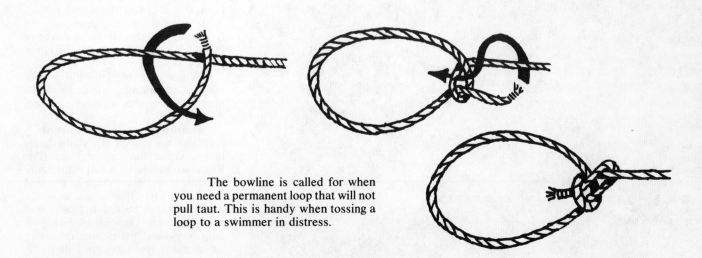

The bowline is called for when you need a permanent loop that will not pull taut. This is handy when tossing a loop to a swimmer in distress.

The Rockies offer to the camper some of North America's most scenic grandeur. This horsepacking scene is at Geneva Lake and Snowmass Mountain near Aspen, Colorado.

When you have to keep wipin' at the shadows that fill up a cove . . . when you have to lie down and look up to see out . . . when the morn gloam busts over a hogback so bright it plumb pains you . . . when a quietus settles over the land a little 'fore dark, well, stranger, you're in North Carolina's high country.

"You can swear to it. And when you get back to where you came from, you'll be so journey proud you just cain't quit talking 'bout the sights you've seen."

This is the way the state of North Carolina introduces its Land of the Sky in one of the state's publications sent to those requesting information about the Old North State.

The language, you will immediately recognize, is different. It is different because it is mountain talk, a part of the heritage the mountain people brought from Scotland and England. And, as a writer has described, "it is part of the character and flavor of North Carolina's Blue Ridge and Great Smoky Mountains."

It is one of many delightful provincial features awaiting the camper who likes to camp high in these southern mountains.

Mountain camping different

Just as the speech of the old-timers in the Great Smokies and the Blue Ridge is different, so is mountain camping. Every mountain range in the land has its own mysterious character which lures thousands back to the same spot year after year. Camping in the mountains anywhere makes one feel above the world, beyond reach of daily demands. At every turn of the trail through the gorges and over the ridges and along the rivers and lakes, a new wonder beckons, a new vista unfolds.

In the southern mountains, for example, flame azalea, wild orchids and rhododendron are among the hundreds of wild flowers which grow in profusion. The blooming season begins in early spring at the lower elevations and gradually creeps to the tops of the highest peaks, enveloping the mountains in sloping gardens of ephemeral beauty. The evergreens are always there, and in the autumn these form a perfect background for the russet, orange and scarlet vistas that the leaves of other trees make.

Fortunately, most of the national parks and many of the national forests encompass some of the wildest and most beautiful mountain country in the world. Good roads make it comparatively easy for the average family camper to reach excellent spots for camping, and various government agencies have seen to it that these spots have been properly equipped and well laid out. Some well graded and paved roads follow the crest of ridges and wind around the mountainsides, thus making the coming and going a most pleasant and rewarding experience.

Blue ridge

The Blue Ridge Parkway of the Blue Ridge and the Great Smoky Mountains is one of the most outstanding roads in the United States. It has been called "a balcony from which you can enjoy an uninterrupted view of the vastness of the Blue Ridge and Great Smoky Mountains." No commercial vehicles are permitted on this road and neither are commercial enterprises.

It is designed for leisurely enjoyment of the scenic wonders along the way. It begins at Roanoke, Virginia, and rides the crest to the Great Smoky Mountains National Park. Soon it will be extended to a point near Atlanta, Georgia. At the north end it is joined to the Skyline Drive which follows the mountaincrest of the Shenandoah National Park to its northern border.

Excellent camping and picnicking facilities are located at intervals along the way. And within a short distance

The Appeal of High Altitude Camping

No matter the season, mountain camping calls for heavier clothing and bedding than is required at lower elevations. Shown here is famous Mt. Washington, White Mountain National Forest, New Hampshire. This is great country for backpack camping. U. S. Forest Service Photo

> There is something about camping in the high mountains that makes one feel above the world, beyond reach of its daily demands. It promotes the sense of security that results from isolation.

of the parkway are hundreds of private, state and federal campgrounds and other recreational facilities. In short, it is an ideal route for a variety of experiences in mountain camping.

The enjoyment of climbing

The enjoyment of mountain camping begins as you start upgrade. Suddenly there is a valley below, then a gorge which ends at a waterfall tumbling down from a plateau in high country. The road twists and winds and climbs. You notice more guardrails and here and there an overlook. You stop and drink in the view. The world below seems small and far away. You are up high where things are big.

Then you look up and realize that the ribbon you see winding back and forth until it reaches a mountain pass is the very road on which you are traveling. You start your motor and continue upward. You notice the gears shifting down as the grade becomes steeper in places. There is a popping sound in your ears. This is nothing to become alarmed about, for it is merely an indication that you have changed altitudes.

Finally, you come to a turnoff and a sign which reads, "Mountain Campground." You drive a half-mile along this road and, suddenly, there in an alpine setting is the spot you have chosen for a mountain campout. It sits just above a jewel-like lake fed by cold, mountain springs, or possibly the melting water from a glacier. The campground is an improved one, and you quickly settle down to the easiest and most popular form of mountain camping. What you do next is your choice to make.

Prepare for high camping

No matter the season, mountain camping calls for heavier clothing and bedding than is required at lower elevations. Sweaters and blankets are necessary for summer camping, even in the southern mountains. The days may be warm, but the nights are always cool.

When traveling by car to a mountain camping site, you should always toss in a bundle of protective clothing items. Of course, in winter you go prepared for the extremes of temperatures anticipated in a given area. The same holds for camping near or above the treeline in the very high mountains.

But on a casual trip in midsummer when you expect to swim during the warmer part of the day, you still may need a variety of clothing for changing weather conditions. A wool shirt, a sweater and even a heavier jacket are recommended. A lined denim jacket is an excellent coat for all occasions. It's a good work coat, does not soil easily, is somewhat rain repellent and is warm. A pair of winter trousers and winter pajamas feel good on a summer's evening in the mountains.

Sleeping bags or other bedding should be sufficiently insulated to keep you warm at a 40° temperature, unless the nighttime temperatures at your camping location frequently go below that. An excellent sleeping bag for elevations under 7,000 feet is the "Appalachian Sleeper" manufactured by the Colorado Outdoor Sports Corporation. This bag is a single, thick quilt of nylon amply filled with duck down. It is made to order for camping in the Great Smokies and is a favorite with the summer backpackers of that area.

Extra blanket

Both children and old folk enjoy mountain camping, but both need special attention in keeping warm. An extra blanket or a heavier sleeping bag usually will suffice. Some satisfactory children's sleeping bags are available for $25 to $40.

Most campers who take to the high country also plan to hike, or to do some mountain climbing. This calls for special attention to footwear. A medium weight boot with lug soles is favored. Unless the climbing is going to be strenuous, the best boot is one that is rugged enough for relatively easy climbs, but light enough for trail

Most of the national parks and many of the national forests encompass some of the wildest and most beautiful country in the world. USDA Photo

hiking. An added comfort around camp in the evenings is a pair of moccasins slipped on over wool kneesocks.

Good rainwear is essential in most mountain country, particularly in the summer when showers and thunderstorms come frequently and sometimes unexpectedly. A rain hat that breathes may also be useful in the bright sun by day and in the damp cold by night. Apparel accessories such as bandanas, scarfs, sunglasses and cotton work-type gloves often prove useful in mountain camping.

Physical dangers high altitudes

Going from sea level to an altitude of only 3,000 or 4,000 feet requires a certain amount of acclimatization. The air is thinner and a little practice is in order before any strenuous hiking is performed. Higher elevations may require several days of acclimatization. Older people and persons with heart or lung problems should camp and hike in the higher mountains only with permission of a physician.

A few individuals suffer from what is commonly known as altitude sickness. Others are fearful of heights, and probably should avoid any excursions that will take them to high precipices.

Nosebleed may occur at higher altitudes, in which case first aid should be applied. Sunburn and windburn come surprisingly fast at higher altitudes, and necessary precautions should be taken.

It is not uncommon for heat exhaustion and even sunstroke to overtake those who enter too ambitiously into mountain activities without proper preparation.

Some possible dangers common to mountain campers are rock slides, flash floods, thunderstorms and such. But common sense preparation alleviates most of these. You should be prepared for the physiological dangers previously cited.

Mountain types in North America

Mountains lure many campers because most of the highest and grandest are within national and state parks and forests. In the United States and Canada are 24 peaks exceeding 14,000 feet above sea level. The highest is Mount McKinley in Alaska with an altitude of 20,320 feet.

Hundreds of other peaks exceed 10,000 feet in elevation, and many more than that easily qualify as mountains. The mountains of New England and eastern Canada are beautiful beyond description and offer a wide variety of camping pleasures.

In the southern United States, large ranges of mountains extend to a little more than a hundred miles from the

A day's drive will take most anyone —no matter where he lives—to a mountain campsite such as this one.

Gulf of Mexico. Reaching their greatest altitude in western North Carolina and eastern Tennessee, these mountains include many tree-covered peaks of 6,000 feet or more.

Highest peak east of the Mississippi is Mount Mitchell (6,684 feet), part of a state park near Asheville, North Carolina. Almost as high is Clingman's Dome in the Great Smoky Mountains National Park.

Southern Ozarks

Mountains and lakes and beautiful rivers make the Ozarks of Arkansas and southern Missouri a mecca for campers and water enthusiasts.

Mountains of a different order are found in Texas, New Mexico and Arizona. Some of these are rocky desert types; others boast of beautiful

Mountain campers in the west frequently glimpse larger animals, such as big horn sheep. U. S. Forest Service Photo

forests, cold and clear lakes and rushing trout streams.

Farther north are the Rockies which encompass numerous national parks and national forests—including vast wilderness areas—and offer to the camper some of the nation's most scenic grandeur. The chain extends into Canada where thousands of campers enjoy that country's incomparable mountain parks.

Along the west coast of both the United States and Canada are mountains and mountain chains of every description, and these are visited by more campers, perhaps, than are the mountains of any other region.

In short, camping high is no problem in regard to access. A day's drive will take most anyone—no matter where he lives—to a mountain campsite.

You Shouldn't Get Lost,
But If You Do...
...Don't panic.
Stay where you are. Think.

Familiarize yourself with the
basic rules for locating camp,
and to make it easier for you
to be found.

There is no panic like the panic that comes from being lost. And there is no relief like the mental relief that comes when you realize that you can cope with this emergency. Even the seasoned outdoorsmen sometimes become lost, but not too often and not for long. You, too, may one day suddenly realize that you are lost. All kinds of strange feelings will sweep over you, and your imagination will run wild. You may see yourself lost and alone when night falls. You will become fearful of possible dangers from animals or the terrible ordeal of starvation. Take comfort in the thought that the worst part of the experience is in the beginning.

Wandering off the trail into a deep canyon or deep woods can get you lost. Only the experienced should do this, and only when properly equipped and accompanied by one or more other persons. U. S. Forest Service Photo

Here's what to do

There is only one thing to do: **stay where you are.** Be calm. And think. Try to reconstruct the route you followed to this point. Chances are, as the panic subsides and your mind clears, you will probably remember how you got lost and you will know how to get back. If you are sure of the correct route back, simply start walking. But if you are not sure, don't go anywhere. **Stay where you are.** There is no point in walking around in circles, wandering aimlessly, until your strength is gone.

Being lost is much easier to take if you have one or more companions with you. Also, there is considerable re-assurance in the knowledge that you have told a responsible person approximately where you intended to hike. You may have to wait a short while, but a search party is certain to come.

While you are waiting, you can climb a nearby hill, if there is one. From the top you may see a familiar landmark or other people. But don't guess. Unless you are certain that you can reach people or a familiar trail, stay where you are.

Any person who expects to enjoy the wilderness trails, particularly in areas where there is possibility of becoming lost, should by all means learn some basics before venturing far afield. He should become familiar with the compass, with maps and map reading, with nature's signs and with manmade signs and signals. With this kind of knowledge you probably won't get lost. And if you do, you will know what to do about it.

Carry map

Always carry a map if you are in a strange area. Know how to spot your position on the map at any time. To go from one point on the map to another may require the use of a compass or some other mechanical device.

The best kind of map is a topographical map. A map scale of two miles to the inch is suitable for canoe travel, but a larger scale map showing land contours is the best for hiking. In heavy bush country or anywhere out of sight of familiar landmarks, a compass is a must. Memory and instinct are not reliable guides.

Depending on the sun, unless you know exactly how, can also be unreliable. If your trip should be made cross-country, in which you do not follow established trails, you will need a protractor for measuring angles on the map to determine the courses to follow with your compass. Many models of compasses have built-in protractors.

Topographical maps

Roadmaps are useful for road travel, but have little value in the woods. Topographical maps are important here. These show the geographical features of the area covered by the map. The amount of detail depends on the scale of the map.

Bush travelers in Ontario are admonished by the Department of Lands and Forests to look for the following points in studying a topographical map:

(a) Locality covered; a general description is contained in the title at the bottom;

(b) Scale—e.g., 1 inch equals 2 miles;

(c) Magnetic declination—usually in a small diagram at the lower left corner;

(d) True North-South lines, parallel to the sides of the map. They may be added to the map by joining points of the same longitude noted on upper and lower margins;

(e) Legend—symbols for various topographical features, usually in lower border.

A map is no good unless you know how to use it. The first step in using a map is to "orient" it. This simply means that you position it so that north, which is at the top of the map, points north. This is best done with a compass, as will be explained later, but it also may be accomplished by lining up your position with a recognizable landmark that can be seen from where you stand and also is identified on the map.

Maps have a way of wearing out and of succumbing to dampness. Protect your maps by coating them with clear plastic spray or by carrying them in clear plastic envelopes. When using the envelopes, fold the maps so that sections in use are clearly visible.

What maps show

A topographic map will: include contour lines which indicate changes (in feet) in elevation (also the shape of mountains, valleys and any changing terrain); show nature's landmarks and manmade landmarks; indicate distances and other important features.

Many features may be included on a map. The more that are accurately pinpointed, the better the map. Among these features are—

Trails and roads, railroads, landing strips for aircraft, lakes, rivers, small streams, springs, wells, stream-fording points, swamps, safe and unsafe drinking water, waterfalls, islands, water craft landings, campsites, ranger stations, fire lookout towers, canyons, gorges, cliffs, caves, rockslide and flood danger areas, timber areas, grass areas, utility lines, bridges, tunnels, natural attractions, big game habitats and anything or any point bearing a proper name.

Maps with numerous features such as these usually will keep you from getting lost, if you do correct map reading; and, if you still get lost, such maps will help you to find your way out. Incidentally, if you return to the same area time after time, you will find yourself adding your own notes and points of interest to your map.

All good maps will have these references as a minimum: the date the map was issued, the scale, the contour interval and the declination.

Your best map, of course, is the latest one issued unless you yourself have kept an older map up to date. Sometimes stream courses are changed by man, occasionally by nature. A fire may burn out a large area or loggers may cut a large section. New structures for forest workers and new

Essential to wilderness travel are maps and a compass. A variety of compass styles is shown here. The instrument at the extreme right is not a compass, but a map measurer. Scale maps can be read simply by running the little wheel over the distance to be measured; mileage will appear directly on the dial.

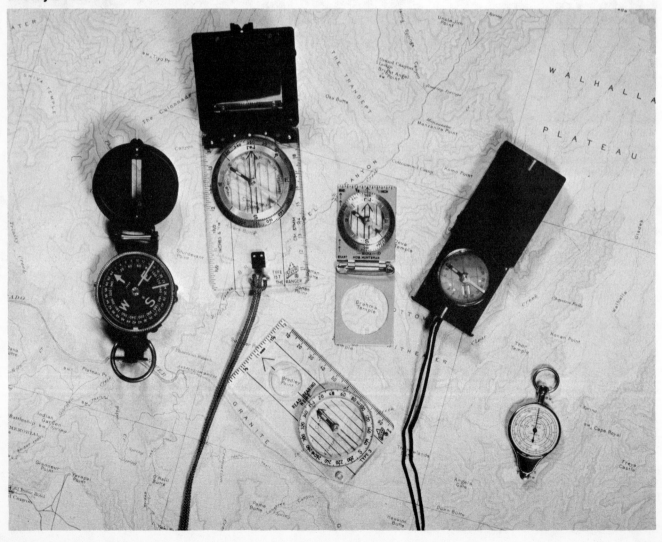

roads and trails call for map changes. For these and other reasons, maps are updated frequently.

Scaled map

The scale of a map refers to the miles represented by inches. The best scaled and marked maps for campers and wilderness hikers are those produced by the U.S. Geological Survey and the Canadian Department of Mines and Technical Surveys.

Geological survey maps come in sheets of approximately one foot by one-and-one-half feet. The number of miles represented by each inch varies according to the terrain covered. The more variations in terrain features and the more general features necessary to map accuracy, the less actual area is shown by the quadrangle sheets.

For example, the most used geological survey map is one showing slightly less (by a few feet) than one mile to the inch. But maps for some of the broad expanses of less used areas, particularly in the West, may be scaled at approximately one inch to two miles or one inch to approximately four miles. This can be done for such areas because there is less necessity for detailed symbols and explanation.

Even with such maps, it is next to impossible to measure exact distances for the simple reason that few trails, streams and land contours run in straight lines. There are instruments available to use on maps for minute measurements, but these are not necessary to the average hiker.

Magnetic north

Declination is important to the hiker only if he must use his compass and map frequently along the trail. Declination simply means the difference in direction between magnetic north and true north. Visualize, if you will, the North Pole as being true north. Magnetic north, the point to which the compass needle is always drawn, actually lies about 1,400 miles south of the North Pole at a point in Canada.

For this reason, in the eastern United States the compass needle will always point west of true north by approximately 14 degrees. A compass needle on the pacific coast of the United States will point to the east of true north by at least as many degrees.

This poses no problem on a typical hike, or for those following well-marked trails for long distances. But when traversing large areas where trails are scarce or poorly marked, declination becomes very important. Your map must be oriented. Good maps show declination symbols in the shape of a V, one side pointing to true north and one side to magnetic north. If the map covers certain critical

Backpackers should stop frequently on the trail to get their bearings. Many trails are well marked and require no special map or compass reading. Even so, it is wise to have these two items along on any extended trail trip.

areas, it may show the difference in degrees.

Map and compass

In orienting a map with a compass, the point of reference is magnetic north. In orienting by other methods, the point of reference is true north. It is important to keep this in mind if you have to change or wish to change from one to the other.

Contour lines, as mentioned, are important to accurate map reading. If you examine these closely, you will see that no two contour lines cross. The reason for this is that each line always remains at the same altitude above sea level. The curves and dips show the changing shapes and altitudes of terrain.

Each line represents a stated vertical distance from the line above or below it. A geological survey map scaled one inch to the mile usually shows contour intervals at every 20 feet of descent or climb.

On each map is a north-pointing arrow. If this is marked with N, or with a star, it indicates true north. MN indicates magnetic north. Geological survey maps and all better maps show both.

How to acquire maps

Maps are indexed. The indexes are not like those found in the back pages of books; rather, the indexes are maps themselves. Usually these are indexed by states. To purchase from the United States Geological Survey a quad-rangle map for a specific area requires first that you examine an index map of the state in which the area is located.

The index map is a map showing the main points of interest and topographic features, but not in minute detail. On the index map are named rectangles indicating that there is a detailed topographic map for that area.

Here is the procedure for ordering: write to the Geological Survey offices listed below for a free index map of each state you mention. This map will show the topographical maps which you may order for the states mentioned. Directions for ordering are printed on each index map.

Also listed on the backs of the "index to topographic maps" are names of commercial dealers who sell topographic maps. Prices generally range from about 25 cents for maps bought direct from the government to $1 or more for maps bought from commercial dealers.

To get your "index to topographic maps" for states east of the Mississippi River, write: Distribution Section, Geological Survey, 1200 South Eads Street, Arlington, Virginia 22202; for states west of the Mississippi River: Distribution Section, Geological Survey, Federal Center, Denver, Colorado 80225.

When writing, also ask for **"Popular Publications of the Geological Survey,"** a valuable reference tool in your map purchases. Two leaflets also will be valuable to you: **"United States Geological Survey"** and **"Topographic Maps."**

Using the compass

When you go shopping for a compass, you will immediately notice that all compass dials are not alike. Select one type, and familiarize yourself with it.

The marked end of the compass needle—sometimes pointed and sometimes painted—always points to the magnetic north. That is, it points to the magnetic north if no metal objects are nearby to attract it. It must be held level when being read.

Many persons do not know how to use a compass because they think it is difficult. Actually, the compass is a simple instrument. It consists of a free-swinging, magnetized steel needle that points to magnetic North. The needle swings freely only when the compass is in a horizontal position.

The force that directs the compass needle is the earth's magnetism, the earth itself being a huge magnet, with lines of force distributed between the north magnetic pole and the south magnetic pole. These are quite different from the geographic poles, as already explained, and only magnetic north is critical to compass readings in the northern hemisphere.

True north

Despite the fact that magnetic north is some 1,400 miles south of the geographic North Pole, at a point near Hudson's Bay, there are a few places where the compass actually points to the true north. These points are at zero declination, which is a line running irregularly from South Carolina to Lake Superior and north.

If you are on or near this line, you can be certain that your compass points to true North. The western Carolinas, eastern Tennessee, extreme southwest Virginia, eastern Kentucky, southwest Ohio, northeastern Indiana, southwestern Michigan and northeastern Minnesota lie on or near the zero declination line. By contrast, northern Maine and the pacific northwest lie some 20 degrees off the zero declination line—in opposite directions.

To get a compass bearing, requires first that the map be oriented. Start with the point on the map where you are standing, place the compass exactly over that point. Observing the direction symbols on the map, rotate the compass until its north reference is lined up with true North. Remember the declination factor.

Zero at north

Notice that your compass has a circular scale of degrees around its outer rim. The zero will be at the north

point and the degrees will be read in a clockwise direction.

Draw a line on the map from where you are to where you want to go. The pivotal point of the compass needle, when placed on the map, should be directly over the spot where you are. Turn the compass until the needle is parallel to the magnetic north indicator on the map.

Now focus your attention on the point where the line emerges from under the compass. Read the number of degrees indicated at this point on the compass circular degree scale. This is called the azimuth. (Incidentally, you should refer to cardinal points of the compass in this manner: East, azimuth 090 degrees; South, azimuth 180 degrees; West, azimuth 270 degrees; North, azimuth 360 degrees or 0 degrees.)

Aim for a landmark in line with your course, and take another azimuth reading when you reach the landmark. This is particularly important if you don't see beyond it or if you have to detour on the way to it.

Check azimuth

As you proceed, read the compass and map occasionally to make sure that you are still on course. As you stop for such readings, consider the azimuth for the return trip. It will always be the opposite at any given point to the one you are following. Your return heading will be your present azimuth plus 180 degrees.

The compass can do many things for you and when you buy one, study the manual carefully. Practice using map and compass before going too far into the wilds.

Other direction finders

By day, your watch can become a direction finder. Hold the watch flat in your hand, with the thumb and index finger of the other hand place a straw upright along the edge of the watch.

Turn the watch until the hour hand points toward the sun and falls into the shadow made by the straw. Draw an imaginary line from the center of the watch that exactly divides the small angle between the hour hand and 12 o'clock. The line points directly south if you perform this procedure between 6 a.m. and 6 p.m., standard time (a watch set to daylight saving time must be turned back one hour before figuring).

If you wish to find true South while the sun is shining before 6 a.m. and after 6 p.m., simply divide the large angle between the hour hand and 12 o'clock.

True north can automatically be determined by extending the imaginary line in the opposite direction.

A hiker who becomes lost may quickly get his bearings by climbing to the crest of a hill or ridge, from which point he can see any familiar landmarks.

U. S. Forest Service Photo

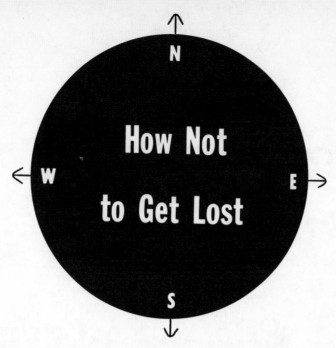

How Not to Get Lost

The Idaho Department of Game and Fish has issued a fine brochure on how not to get lost, and what to do if you do. Possibly the most significant part has to do with preventive measures. Among those recommended are these:

• Have plenty of dry matches, waxed or in a waterproof box.

• Be sure you have a compass, one that is reliable and that you can trust.

• Carry a map of your locality, even it it is only a sketch map.

• Discuss your plans with other members of your party. Do not change these plans when you are alone.

• Learn how to start a fire. A piece of candle inside your pack is always dry and makes an excellent fire starter.

• Watch where you are going. Do not hunt or wander aimlessly. Have a plan—and stick to it. Be doubly careful in stormy weather.

• Any hunter who is inexperienced should never be out alone.

• Be careful when crossing ridges. The slope on the other side may be in an entirely different watershed.

• Always try to get back to camp well before it gets dark.

Also important to the prevention of complications, should you get lost, are the equipment and supplies you carry with you. You should never enter a wilderness or thinly populated area without the essentials of food, adequate clothing and shelter. When you are lost, you may be forced to camp in undesirable spots. Properly equipped, you can turn these into suitable campsites.

Signal device

In addition to the standard gear and supplies carried by backpackers, you also should have some signaling devices and a survival kit. One excellent signal is a whistle similar to a policeman's whistle. A signal recognized everywhere is a series of threes—three sounds of the whistle spaced about five seconds apart, three shots from a gun, three visual devices that can be seen from the air, etc.

Searchers flying in aircraft will also respond to a large orange-colored handkerchief spread out in a clearing. This must be at least three feet by three feet. By day a mirror may be used to signal aircraft by reflecting light from the sun. Three fires by day or night constitute a distress signal. The flames can be seen at night and the smoke can be seen by day.

While you wait for rescue, make the best of the situation. Assess your gear and supplies to determine what you can do with each item and how long you can survive without adding to these. If you have no clear idea as to which way you should go, stay where you are. If you are sick or injured, by all means stay where you are.

Survival kit

You can make up your own survial kit or you can purchase one prepackaged from your camping supply dealer. Laacke and Joys of Milwaukee, Wisconsin, sells a handy trail kit for $3.98. The kit weighs only eight ounces, and everything is packaged in a heavy-duty, weather-tight, resealable vinyl bag. The contents include three fortified chocolate bars, 12″ by 18″ heavy-duty cooking foil, 20 matches, two all-weather fire starters, compass, insect repellent, soap tissues, first aid kit, ammonia inhalant, three antiseptic swabs, three adhesive compresses, 25′ of small game snare wire, 25′ of 15 lb. test nylon fishing line, 8 assorted hooks, 8 sinkers, razor blade, signal whistle, ground-to-air signal code and complete survival instructions. This has to be a bargain, should your life ever depend on it.

Wild edibles, enough to sustain life, are available throughout the north american wilderness. So are the materials for protection against the elements. Chances are, you will never face a situation requiring a knowledge of these. But if you think you might, by all means acquaint yourself with the techniques for living off the land. Entire books are devoted to this subject. Consult your outfitter for the titles of good books on survival camping.

Peace and Solitude
in the Desert

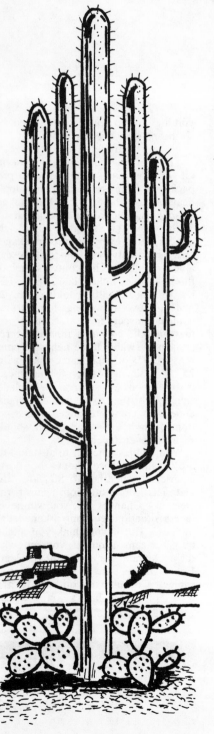

Mention the desert to those who have never seen this kind of country, or to those who have merely driven across it, and most people will retort that we just as well could do without it. They immediately conjur up the notion, fanned by western movies depicting the lost wagon train with water supplies gone or the old prospector crawling toward a dry water hole, that the desert is a place barren of anything worthwhile to a civilized man.

This is a generally erroneous concept. The desert is alive. It is beautiful. It has a lot to offer, as thousands of campers have discovered. To anyone who takes the time to study it, the desert becomes a place of strong attractions. It offers challenge and inspiration not found anywhere else.

Contrary to popular assumptions, it does rain in the desert. Sometimes in downpours. Often the rains cause floods, as campers nicely bedded down in a dry wash have discovered to their dismay.

Many flowers

Gentle rains usually come in the winter, but not every winter in the same place. Following bountiful rain in the winter, the desert in spring produces so many varieties of flowers in such great profusion that the mind tends to disbelieve what the eyes see. The desert will not bloom that way again until the following winter of rains.

At any time of the year the wise desert camper will constantly be looking for sharp contrasts. He won't be surprised when an angry thunderstorm suddenly sweeps across his campsite in the middle of summer.

Neither will he neglect to prepare for the inferno of the day and the chill that may come at night. He will resist the temptation to misjudge distances. He will respect the wide range of elevations, for most of the desert is not flat and sandy. Much of it is composed of mountains, some so high that snow rests on their crowns most of the year.

The desert encompasses much of western Arizona, southeastern California, Nevada and Utah. It also touches parts of Idaho, eastern Oregon, a small part of southwestern Colorado, a sizable portion of west Texas and most of southern and western New Mexico. Patches of desert appear elsewhere in the United States.

Clear air

One of the great attractions in desert camping is the clean air found there. This is particularly attractive to those whose day-to-day life is bound up in cities suffering from smog. Although many people camp in the desert, most of the desert campgrounds are relatively uncrowded. Thousands of acres are open to those who like the peace and solitude found in a hidden desert valley or a mountain canyon.

Many go to the desert to exchange cold and rain for warm sunshine. Not a few consider the desert near ideal for

The American deserts offer a constantly changing panorama of color, weather and temperatures. They are filled with exotic flowers, unusual wildlife and clean air.

hiking. Then there are the ghost towns and the abandoned mines. It is good country for horseback riding. In some places it is a bonanza for rock hounds. Its unique wildlife attracts many. And, of course, the clear air and the contrasting shadows make it a photographer's paradise.

Desert campsite

A camper can enjoy the desert if he is prepared for strong and sudden winds, the extremes of temperature and the danger of running out of food, water and fuel.

Special care must be taken in selecting a proper campsite. Wind direction, the view, the vegetation and terrain, as well as the availability of fuel and water, are very important considerations.

For satisfactory desert camping, select a level spot that is well drained and has a good view of the desert. Then follow these guide rules:

1. Endeavor to protect the campsite from direct exposure to prevailing winds. Since wind directions change frequently in the desert, some sort of wind screen is helpful.

2. Camp on high ground. Flash floods are frequent in summer and early fall, and the walls of water brought by these are surprisingly high. Such cloudbursts and resulting floods are rare in winter and spring, but don't take any chances.

3. Take into account the extremes of temperature. Nights are cold in the desert, particularly in the winter, but daytime is usually warm. Some campers prefer to locate their camp with an exposure to the southeast and some with an exposure to the southwest, depending on whether they prefer exposure to an early morning sun or a late afternoon sun. In spring and fall, a north exposure may be best for a

cooler daytime camp.

4. The campsite should be near vegetation. Some of this vegetation is good for campfires. Trees and shrubs attract more of the desert's wildlife, and birds and animals are fun to watch.

5. Don't expect to find water and fuel available. Take these with you. Site selection in the desert is not usually determined by proximity of water or fuel.

Shelter

It is said that the desert was the proving ground for camping trailers and certain other recreational vehicles. There is no doubt that the use of shelters mounted on wheels is extremely popular in desert country. But the tent remains the most used shelter. It can be transported to many places where the typical vehicle can't reach.

Veteran desert campers consider the best tent to be a wall tent with sewed-in

Some desert campsites are found amidst patches of bristlecone pines, said to be the world's oldest living things. U. S. Forest Service Photo

floor. A tent in the desert must be securely anchored with guy ropes and the edges well battened down. A wall tent meets these criteria. Umbrella tents blow down more easily. Some campers who use umbrella tents collapse them during the day when they are away from camp. Umbrella tents in the desert require more anchoring than the usual four corner stakes and center pole.

Desert camping is most popular in spring, fall and winter. During the hotter months white tents are preferred because they reflect heat. Any tent will be cooler if a second roof is used to provide an insulating air space between the two roofs. In winter the tent should be closed after sundown to keep in some of the day's warmth.

The tent is not enough. Some type of windbreak should be erected to protect as much of the campsite as possible, certainly the cooking and sitting areas. Desert winds frequently change directions as well as intensity, and it is practical to erect four-sided protection. A screen that is easy to move and anchor will suffice. Terrain features may protect in part.

Sometimes in the desert you will see canvas fences or canvas panels that can easily be moved, and at other times you will see simple windbreak tarps attached to the car at one end and to a bush or post at the other. You will soon discover what best suits you.

Clothing

It is necessary to pack clothing that will provide protection from the heat of the day and the cold of the night. Desert temperatures are often extremes. In almost any season of the year, depending on the elevation above sea level of the campsite, a camper may encounter extremely hot weather and quite cold weather.

Headgear is important and perhaps the best headgear to wear is the kind worn by the Navajo and some sheepherders. The tall hat provides an insulating space in the crown. It is true that most campers don't wear these hats, partly because they are not readily available. Probably the next best thing is the traditional cowboy stetson, preferably a straw with some ventilating holes.

Food and cooking

Most desert campers depend on canned and dried foods. Fresh foods do not keep well in the desert. Portable ice boxes, of course, preserve the food as long as the ice lasts. But if you plan to camp longer than a weekend, you must be near a supply center where ice is available.

Otherwise, food should be kept in a wood or metal box, tightly closed to keep out desert animals and insects, and the box should be placed in a cool, shady spot. Canned fruit juices, vegetables and fruit, dried beans and dried meats are seen on desert camp shelves. The various instant foods are quite popular.

A first experience in trying to cook over a campfire in the desert usually suffices, and the camper turns quickly from being a novice to one who is more practical minded. The desert winds make it very difficult to keep a fire going. Most campers use a gasoline stove. It is cooler, easier to control and easy to move inside the tent if a sandstorm comes up.

Campfires are built primarily for some nighttime warmth and for fireside relaxation. It is easier to bring fuel for the campfires from home than to spend long hours scrounging the desert for it.

Large pieces of wood or compressed wood logs are the best fuel to bring from home. Don't cut desert trees or bushes. They may look dead, but likely aren't.

Water in the desert

A very important necessity is water. Extra water should always be carried when motoring to the campsite. The water requirements are often greater in the desert than elsewhere. Several gallons per day per person should be taken along if practical. Otherwise, water rationing will be necessary.

The desert, of course, has occasional water holes. Numerous animal tracks frequently will indicate a water hole. If a number of animals have left signs around the water hole, likely the water is good to drink. One thing to be mindful of when approaching a desert water hole is to watch for snakes.

The sidewinder rattlesnake, in particular, buries itself in the sand at the edge of water holes and waits for small rodents. As a precaution, stir loose sand at the water's edge and examine the surrounding terrain carefully. This is especially important if you need to lie down to drink. Venom received in the head is far more dangerous than that received in the arm or leg.

If your water supply becomes exhausted, don't panic; this is a time to use the head and to look for signs of water. Sometimes you will find stretches of damp sand. Dig a hole in this and wait. Water may seep into it. If there is no damp sand, start digging down and dig a hole three to six feet deep. If the sand becomes damp as you dig, keep digging until you hit water.

Sometimes water may be found in dried stream beds. In arroyos you may see rock dams built naturally during flooding seasons. Dig on the upper side of these and you may find water. Another source of water may be found along the edge where the flow of floodwaters has curved. There is a tendency for running water to dig a little deeper here, leaving deposits of water after the main stream has receded.

Air Force researchers advise those looking for water in the desert to listen for the sound of birds chirping. If you hear birds chirping in brushy terrain, this means that water may be nearby. Watch for flocks of birds circling in the desert. They may be circling over a water hole.

Becoming acclimatized

Becoming acclimatized to the desert is not difficult, but it does take several days to get used to extremely hot and dry weather. To properly make this adaptation, enter the work or exercise phases of desert camping in a gradual way. The same applies to heat exposure to direct sunlight.

It is important to get plenty of rest at night and to rest frequently during the day. The heaviest work of the day

Thousands of campers have discovered that the desert and semidesert areas are beautiful and, contrary to popular opinion, alive.

should be done in the cooler hours of the morning or late afternoon. Temperatures of 100° or more are common in the desert, but these will not have as severe effect as would 85° in extremely humid areas. The low humidity and the desert breezes cause perspiration to evaporate quickly from the skin and this in turn helps the body to remain cool.

This, of course, requires that more water be consumed than is normal. It is not unusual for 10 to 12 quarts of drinking water to be consumed daily under severe desert or tropic heat. Sometimes more is necessary when heavy exercise is taken.

Drink frequently

If the water supply is inadequate under such circumstances, a person may quickly lose his efficiency, have his judgment impaired and suffer morale deterioration. If water is withheld for several hours, body temperatures rise and bring on heat exhaustion. Thirst quenchers such as chewing gum will not take the place of water.

Water should be drunk frequently and in small amounts each time. Actually, you may drink water when thirsty as often as is practical.

The intake of additional salt is helpful in desert camping. When there is a good deal of activity and considerable perspiring, two salt tablets should be taken with each quart of water drunk. Never take salt tablets immediately following a meal or with a hot drink. This will almost always bring on nausea. Take the salt tablets immediately *before* eating or drinking and the danger of nausea will be practically eliminated.

Heat exhaustion

Perhaps the worst malady to strike a desert camper is heat exhaustion. This is brought on by a loss of water and salt from the body. It often begins with too much perspiration, a headache or both. The skin will be pale and cold and dizziness, weakness and cramps will follow. The best immediate treatment is to find a shady spot in as much coolness as possible. The drinking of salted water brings some relief.

Heat stroke is brought on by too much exposure to high temperatures and often strikes persons before they are acclimatized. The symptoms of this are cessation of perspiration, a dry skin and collapse. Sometimes there is dizziness, fast pulse and vomiting.

This is sometimes called sun stroke, and quick treatment—emergency first aid—often is necessary to prevent death. Place the patient in the shade and remove as much clothing as possible. Sprinkle the body with water. If the patient can drink, give him cold water. Fan him and massage the skin. This increases circulation and speeds the cooling.

When the body is deficient in salt,

heat cramps in muscles of limbs and the stomach wall may occur. Drinking large amounts of salted water brings relief very quickly.

Other physical problems are prickly heat and the usual blisters and scratches. Clean, loose, dry clothing is important to the prevention of prickly heat. To treat prickly heat, take fewer baths and soap only as necessary. This prevents additional skin irritation. Sun tan increases resistance to prickly heat.

Sandstorm dangers

A dangerous aspect of desert camping is the sandstorm or, as some people call it, the "duster." A person experiencing a major sandstorm never forgets it. A little precaution will keep it from being dangerous in most cases. In many desert areas a sandstorm can be seen approaching 20 or 30 miles away. It often looks like a rainstorm, at a distance the clouds appearing dark. As it gets closer, however, its color changes to a dust tone.

About the only thing a camper can do if he is caught in a sudden sandstorm and cannot reach an adequate shelter is to cover his nose and mouth with any

cloth that may be available. This may be a bandana, a scarf or even a shirt or blouse. Your back should be turned to the wind. This is a partial protection of your eyes and your breathing.

There are no unusual hazards associated with the sand in a sandstorm. If the intensity is extremely severe, the sand will pit auto paint. Accompanying winds may blow down unsecured tents. Sometimes they will capsize trailers. But heavy winds may do this anywhere.

The main sandy areas of the southwest are in the Rio Grande Valley in southern New Mexico, the White Sands National Monument in New Mexico, the lower Colorado River valley separating Arizona and California, Monument Valley on the Arizona-Utah boundary, Southern California's Salton Sea and the Great Sand Dunes National Monument in Colorado. Those who have seen the brilliant photography of David Muench and others in *Arizona Highways* know

that on calm, clear days these areas are a delight.

Desert driving

In desert travel always maintain an adequate fuel supply. Keep the gas tank as full as possible, frequently refilling it wherever gasoline stations are found. This is important even on paved roads. There are vast distances between gasoline stations on unpaved roads. It is the wise camper who carries several gallons of fuel in spare cans.

It is important, also, to take along other motoring necessities, particularly basic tools, spare tires, fan belts, extra water for the radiator, tow rope, ax and shovel, tire chains and, of course, a jack. It is helpful to know how to repair punctured tires by the tube method. Some desert campers prefer to inflate their tires with tubes. They carry spare tubes, tire pumps and patching kits.

For exploring off the beaten path in a vehicle, it is wise to use four-wheel-drive vehicles. Pickups, jeeps and similar vehicles are available in four-wheel drive.

If you get stuck in the sand, immediately take your foot off the accelerator. The more the wheels spin, the deeper they dig. Before doing anything else, study the situation. If the wheels are not too deep, it may be possible to place brush, dead limbs from trees, bushes or stones in front of or in back of the stuck wheels so that when the vehicle is rocked back and forth it may be eased out. Once this step is accomplished, drive away quickly.

Always carry tire chains. These may be put on for increased traction in areas where there is danger of getting stuck in the sand. Some desert motorists carry with them large pieces of corrugated cardboard, wooden boards or aluminum matting similar to that used in the construction of temporary airfields.

It is claimed by some that to let part of the air pressure from the rear tires will assist in getting out of soft sand.

In severe cases it doesn't always add enough traction to the tires and if there is no way to inflate them again, even when a person does get out of the sand he may have to drive over such rugged terrain that the tires could be damaged because of the low inflation pressure. But it is better than not getting out at all.

The dangers from driving in soft sand are not always off the road. A severe and sudden windstorm may dump tons of sand in drifts on sections of a secondary or paved road, and it is just as easy to get stuck here as elsewhere. A good rule to follow when suddenly coming upon a stretch of sand is to stop the car, get out and walk across the stretch. You can determine its depth, its looseness and also the best route to take when driving. When going across sand, don't drive slowly. Put the car in the lowest gear (an automobile with standard gear shifts is best) and start it rolling, then gun it. Go as fast as possible.

By all means, avoid getting stuck in an arroyo, or dry wash. This is extremely dangerous, as you will quickly learn if you find yourself in the path of a sudden flood from a rainstorm—even if the rainstorm is miles away. Work doubly hard to get out of there and by all means don't rest or sleep in the car while it is stuck in such places.

Avoid cactus

The desert in some places tempts the driver to leave the road and strike off across grassy plains. But remember that the short grass also contains stickers from cactus and other plants. The wise driver avoids running over any kind of cactus of any size. Most of these will not puncture a tire, but when thousands of them stick into a tire, eventually some will push through.

The tumbleweed is another nuisance and can be a real problem if you pitch your tent or unroll the bedroll where the plant's sharp, pointed seeds have collected. To avoid this, sweep an area where the tent or bedroll is to be placed. The tumbleweed is not actually a species, but may be one of several globeshaped weeds. These roll and tumble to new locations in the wind after they die. Most common is the Russian thistle, a plant not native to the west. It was introduced there from other parts of the world.

Information sources

Several publications and organizations specialize in desert information. Among the most reliable of these are the following:

Arizona Highways magazine, 2039 E. Ellis Avenue, Phoenix, Arizona 85009.

Desert Magazine, Palm Desert, California 92260.

Westways, magazine of the Automobile Club of Southern California, 2601 South Figueroa, Los Angeles.

U. S. Forest Service offices at 517 Gold Avenue, S. W., Albuquerque, New Mexico 87101, and at 630 Sansome Street, San Francisco, California 94111.

American Automobile Association clubs of the desert area, publishers of excellent maps and guides.

Arizona Development Board, 1500 West Jefferson Street, Phoenix, Arizona 85007.

Chamber of Commerce offices and state outdoor departments.

HOW TO DISTILL WATER IN THE DESERT

Thanks to some basic research by the United States Department of Agriculture's Agricultural Research Service Water Conservation Laboratory, located at Tempe, Arizona, it now is relatively easy to acquire water in the desert. The end product of the research is a "solar still."

The "solar still" is made by digging a cone-shaped hole, at the bottom of which is placed a pan or other wide-mouthed container. A plain sheet of plastic is placed over the hole and weighted down with a rock at its center so that the plastic becomes cone-shaped with the bottom of the cone just above the pan.

The edge of the plastic is kept from slipping into the hole by dirt to weight it down. The plastic sheet does not touch the sides of the hole.

This arrangement causes moisture in the earth to condense on the under-side of the plastic and roll down into the container at the bottom—when the sun is shining, of course. The researchers suggest that a "wettable" plastic be used so that water will not drop off before running to the bottom of the cone.

To speed up the process, chunks of cactus or other fleshy plants may be placed to form a lining around the hole. A tube for drinking can be inserted into the container so that the still will not be disturbed when water is being withdrawn.

There are more efficient solar stills, some available commercially, but none as inexpensive or easy to construct as this one. The research was conducted by Doctors Ray D. Jackson and Cornelius H. M. van Bavel.

"The water's warm and flat," says Dr. Jackson, shown having a drink, "but it will keep you alive in an emergency."

Ideal tool for shaping a solar still is a long handled spade. If tools aren't available a sharp rock can be used to loosen dirt which can then be scooped out by hand. The hole being dug in the above photo will be cone shaped.

The upper right photo shows the next step—to place a wide mouth receptacle at the center in the bottom of the hole. To speed up the process and produce more water, large chunks of cactus are used to line the sides of the hole.

The last step, as shown in the photo at right, is to line the hole with plastic sheeting. Dirt and rocks are placed around the edges of the plastic to keep it from slipping into the hole. A rock is used to weight the center of the plastic to form an inverted cone. Center of cone does not touch the bottle or pan in the bottom. Moisture will now form on the underside of the plastic and drip into the pan. Demonstrator is drinking the water through a plastic tube which was placed in the container before covering.

WHAT YOU SHOULD KNOW ABOUT THE WEATHER

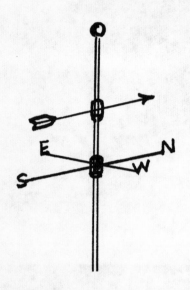

Deep in the recesses of the Great Smokies and surrounding mountain ranges the old-timers enjoy listening to the radio weatherman in the sure knowledge that they know more about the weather than he does. It's a fact that many mountaineers are good weather prophets.

They observe the signs of nature with the same intensity that a professional forecaster observes his thermometer and barometer. Some of the mountaineer's weather reading may appear to be based on superstition, but he is not often wrong.

The old-timer will tell you to get ready for a cold snap if the cat sits with her back to the fire. He says, too, that if a great number of spiders gather in the house in September and October, you can look for a severe winter. In the southern mountains he will point to the fur on animals. If the rabbit and the squirrel and the opossum wear a thick fur in fall, this is a sure sign that winter will be colder than usual.

A circle around the moon means rain, and a circle around the sun is an indication of fair weather. If the rain falls when the sun is shining, it will rain the same time the next day. When the rhododendron leaves droop in late fall, and then roll up tightly like a cigar, extremely cold winter weather is on its way.

Whether or not you accept such prognostications, it's a fact that weather is a primary concern to every camper. He is outside in it, not sheltered in a house built to withstand weather extremes. It isn't necessary to learn the superstitions and sayings about the weather, but it is helpful for a camper to take along a thermometer, a barometer and a transistor radio. Generally this will suffice for camp weather forecasting.

Barometer reading

When reading a barometer in camp, don't become alarmed by minor daily changes. Watch for sudden drops. These are the most significant and always mean a drastic change in the weather, such as heavy rains and/or moisture-laden winds.

Thermometers are important in areas where drastic variations in temperatures are likely to be encountered. This is particularly true where night-time temperatures may drop to freezing or lower. Dressed in warm clothing or sleeping in a warm bag tends to fool the camper as to what the real temperature is. An accurate thermometer reading will enable you to determine what steps must be taken to keep food and drink from freezing, and it will quickly tell you if you have provided for enough warmth during the colder hours of the night. The thermometer is very helpful in extremely hot weather. A desert breeze may persuade you that it is not so hot after all, but the thermometer may warn you that too much activity shouldn't be entered into at certain hours.

Radio forecasts give weather information for large areas and this, too, can be helpful. For example, scattered showers or thunderstorms may be predicted. These may not touch the place where you are camping, but knowing that such bad weather is in the offing will enable you to be prepared for it.

There are numerous signs to look for in weather conditions which are not based on superstition at all. Frequently, when there is going to be a change in the weather, there will be a change in the wind first. The winds bring the weather. The kind of weather they usually depends on where they come from.

Rain sign

On a warm day if the wind blows in from a large body of water, look for rain. If it blows from an area that is dry, there may be sand and dust, but likely no rain.

If you camp in the eastern part of the United States in summer, a south wind will be warm and probably wet; a north wind will bring cooler temperatures; a west wind will be warm and probably dry; and an east wind will be warm and wet. Variations of weather may come when two winds or weather fronts converge. In the winter when precipitation moves northward from the Gulf of Mexico and meets a cold front moving in from the Northwest, snow is certain.

When you get up in the morning and find heavy dew or frost on your tent, don't worry about the weather. It will be fair. If your tent is dry, there may be precipitation before the day is over.

When you see large, billowing clouds moving fast, look for weather changes. When you see two layers of clouds moving in different directions, look for real turbulence.

If your campfire smoke rises straight up, the weather likely will be fair for the next few hours. If the smoke flattens and spreads out close to the ground, look for foul weather.

Extremes of weather such as hurricanes and tornadoes are usually predicted by the weather bureau. Tornadoes can't be forecast quite as accurately as can hurricanes, but tornado watches are issued for areas where such storms are possibilities.

Here are some signs to look for that will help you to reasonably predict the weather:

Look for bad weather if—
The swallows chase insects near the surface of water.
Your bones ache or a bad tooth flares up.
Sounds of aircraft and trains seem near and loud.
The nights are warmer than usual.
The humidity seems unusually high.
Distant mountains seem closer than normal.
The barometer drops significantly.
A west wind shifts to south or east.
Look for good weather if—
the swallows fly high.
There is morning dew or frost.
Spiders spin webs in grass.
Morning fog breaks an hour or two before noon.
The preceding two or three days have been bad.
A significant break appears in the clouds to the west.
The barometer rises significantly.

Weather of all kinds will come, and there is nothing you can do to prevent it. But you can be prepared. Study the weather patterns for the area in which you are camping and prepare accordingly. You may have fun even in bad weather. A lot of campers do.

Safety First and First Aid

Safety procedures and first aid practices should be familiar to every camper.

With a little foreknowledge and preparation, camping is probably the safest outdoor activity you can engage in. Most of its hazards are the same you encounter anywhere. A bump or bruise or cut can be your lot at home or anywhere else. So can a splinter, a burn, a bee sting, an allergy.

There are a few hazards that can become dangerous when camping unless you are prepared for them.

Observe health and safety measures, the ones you already practice and the special ones that may be posted for your particular camping site.

Keep yourself and your family clean, and keep the campsite clean. Obey all sanitary regulations, both those that

Camping is a safe outdoor activity, but it does take some foreknowledge and preparation for the other recreational pursuits it affords. These canoe campers have taken preventive measures by wearing life jackets while paddling.
U. S. Forest Service Photo

are posted and the ones you know to be common sense.

Be careful with sharp-edged tools. If you don't know how to use these safely, don't begin by tackling a major camp chore with them. Understand fires and know how to control them.

Be careful what you swallow. This particularly applies to water, but it can also apply to wild foods that you might gather.

Always take to camp a Red Cross first aid manual or some other reputable first aid book. If you take camping seriously, first take a Red Cross-sponsored first aid course. Before pitching camp. make it a rule to learn as soon as possible the nearest sources of help.

Nature's spoilers

Some years ago, the big city newspapers seemed to take delight in reporting the woes suffered by individuals and families who dared to venture into the wilds. Some of the stories were meant to be humorous with fun being poked at persons who got into trouble in the outdoors through a lack of knowledge.

One account told of a typical city-dwelling, indoor family who purchased a camping outfit and headed for the woods. In a couple of days, mother was covered with poison ivy, daughter was having stomach cramps from eating wild greens, son was spotted with scores of chigger bites and father had dysentery as a result of drinking polluted water.

To top it off, when the family decided to get away from all this misery for a few hours and drove into a nearby town, a bear visited their camp while they were gone and tore their tent to shreds in order to get to some food that had been left open.

Don't let this story scare you off, for all of these hazards can be successfully thwarted by some simple precautionary steps.

Learn what poison ivy looks like and avoid it. Learn what to do to keep chiggers from biting. Learn to identify plants and fruits before cooking or eating them. If responsible authorities have not declared a water source to be safe, know what to do to make it safe. And any second-time camper in bear country knows, either from experience or observation, that food must be properly stored and kept out of reach of bears.

You will not come face to face with many truly wild animals. You may glimpse some at a distance, but such animals as wolves, coyotes, mountain lions and bobcats, for instance, will steer a wide circle around you. These animals are extremely shy.

Don't panic

Smaller animals that you likely will see are not dangerous, particularly if left alone. Don't become alarmed by

POISON IVY

POISON OAK

POISON SUMAC

The basic caution to take in identifying the above is to beware of any shrub, bush or vine with white berries. Poison Ivy has broad, pointed leaves, three to a cluster. It grows either as a climbing vine or as a bush. Poison Oak has a broad round tip leaf like an Oak leaf. Usually a shrub in form. Poison Sumac has long, narrow, pointed leaf and is in the form of a small tree or shrub.

the visit of a skunk, and certainly don't do anything to upset him. He knows you are there, and so long as you make no move to hamper his searchings for bits of food, he will not become a bother.

Bears are different

But bears are different. The real wild kind will not come near you, in most instances. But the "tramp" bears that hang around campgrounds have lost their fear of humans. No matter how tame they act, stay away from them. They are still animals of the wild, and their wild nature can burst forth at any time.

Bears are particularly bothersome in some of the more popular national parks. The National Park Service has issued this statement relative to bears:

"Like all animals in our National Parks, bears are wild animals. Because of their protected status they have lost their fear of man. While this may make them appear tame, actually in this state they are more dangerous.

"Troublesome bears are trapped and removed to remote areas of the park or, in extreme cases, must be destroyed. In order that visitors may continue to enjoy the sight of bears roaming freely in our National Parks, and to avoid personal injury, please follow these suggestions when camping:

"Keep a clean camp and use a minimum of odorous food. Seal surplus food in clean wrapping material or in airtight containers. Ice chests are generally not bearproof. A good deodorizer is effective in eliminating food odors from your camp.

"Food left on tables or stored in a tent in open boxes or food containers is a natural target for bears and an invitation for bear damage. Back country campers often suspend their supplies between two trees out of bear's reach.

Safe in trunk

"Food should not be stored in vehicles with convertible tops. Properly wrapped or sealed food is normally safe when stored in the trunk of a hard-top car provided all windows are closed.

"Burn all garbage and food containers. Do not bury food scraps and containers. In the back country pack out any noncumbustible litter to the nearest trash containers provided.

"Report any bear damage or personal injuries to a park ranger immediately."

Game animals of the hoof and horn variety are not dangerous, except during mating time. This is not the time when most people vacation, and even then these animals are not dangerous unless tracked down or surprised.

Poisonous plants

The three most common poisonous plants causing severe skin rash are poison ivy, poison oak and poison sumac. Poison ivy grows almost everywhere, except in California and Nevada. It is recognized by its clusters of three pointed leaves, green in spring and red and orange in the fall, and it generally grows along the ground or twists around trees and fenceposts. All parts of the plant are toxic. Even a dog, clothing, a camp tool or anything that has touched poison ivy can transfer the toxic substance to a person susceptible to its effects.

Fortunately, your physician can prescribe a shot or tablets which may give a degree of immunity. As an added precaution, scrub with rubbing alcohol or a strong laundry soap—the old-fashioned yellow Octagon soap is ideal—when you have contacted poison ivy or the other plants of that type.

Poison oak is similar in appearance and effect, except that it grows as a shrub or bush. Its leaves are somewhat different, not shining as are the leaves of poison ivy. They look more like oak leaves in shape. This plant is less common than poison ivy, except along the pacific coast. It is also found in the southeast and in some sections of the central states.

Poison sumac also grows as a bush or tree and sometimes reaches a height of 20 to 25 feet. It looks like ordinary sumac, except for its leaves and berries. Its leaves are smooth along the edges; plain sumac leaves are sawtoothed. Poison sumac berries are almost white with a greenish tint; plain sumac berries are red. Poison sumac is found mostly in swampy areas of coastal states in the east and south.

The pesky insects

It's the pesky insects that are the most bother to campers. Most campsites are bothered by insects, particularly so during rainy or humid weather. Camping too near a lake or pond also is inviting insects.

Most insects can be discouraged by spraying insecticide around the camp and by applying repellent to the skin and clothing. The best immediate treatment for fly and mosquito bites is alcohol or any of the new spray-can compounds prepared for this purpose.

For ticks and chiggers, prevention is the best cure. Sulfur sprinkled in the shoes or a mixture of sulfur and alcohol rubbed on exposed skin will discourage these insects from attaching themselves to you. Kerosene is also a good preventive.

Ticks are prevalent in many mountain areas during late spring and summer. Even if you use tick repellents, it is a good idea to examine yourself for ticks each day. Some of these insects carry Rocky Mountain spotted fever. If you intend to spend a great deal of time in areas where ticks are prevalent, ask your doctor to give you shots for Rocky Mountain spotted fever. If you find ticks partially embedded in your

There is little to fear from most creatures of the wild, for they will steer a wide course around you. But bears are different, especially the "tramp" kind that hang around campgrounds. These have lost their fear of humans, but they are still wild animals and unpredictable. The skilled treeclimber in this picture is a black bear of Superior National Forest.

U. S. Forest Service Photo

skin, hold a lighted match close to them. This often will cause them to withdraw.

In the south and southwest you may occasionally see a black widow spider. The female is deadly to children. Fortunately, she is not abundant and not aggressive. If you are bitten by one, or suspect that you have been bitten by one apply turpentine to the bite, and go to a doctor as soon as possible.

Scorpions are found in many places, particularly in the desert and in Florida, and these are highly toxic. Seek medical aid if you have been stung by a scorpion.

Bees, hornets and wasps are among several stinging insects. Their stings are painful, cause swelling that may last for several hours or even days, and their stings can be serious (sometimes fatal). Occasionally a person is highly allergic to the venom of bees. In such instances, first aid and a physician are the two immediate needs.

Most bees will not sting without some provocation, such as stepping on them or swatting at them. Disturbing their nests sometimes will bring attack.

Many persons are stung by honey bees, usually on the feet when they walk barefoot through clover blossoms. The honey bee can sting only once and its barbed stinger sometimes is left in the victim. This must be removed to stop the irritation.

Alcohol, a paste of baking soda and even mud will relieve the effects of bee stings.

Snakes and snake bite

Snake bite is the most feared camping hazard and probably the least likely to happen. But it can happen, and does occasionally. Some 2,400 persons are bitten by poisonous snakes each year in the United States. Fewer than one percent of the victims die. Most of these are considered poor health risks because of other health factors.

In the United States 19 of the 116 species of snakes are venomous. For the layman, these add up to four venomous types: rattlesnakes, the cottonmouth moccasin, the copperhead and the coral snake.

Every camper should know how to treat snake bite and, equally important, should know how to prevent it. An excellent publication on snakes and snake bite in handy pocket form is **Brief Guide to Snake Bite,** a supplement which was published recently in "Outdoor World" magazine, 1645 Tullie Circle, N. E., Atlanta, Georgia 30329. Send 30 cents to the magazine for a copy.

Most poisonous snake bites are on the arms, hands, legs or feet. Obviously, a person should wear proper boots in snake-infested country and always be aware of where he is placing his hands or feet.

A bite by a poisonous snake constitutes a medical emergency. First aid treatment should begin at once. All campers should carry snake bite kits designed for emergency, on-the-spot treatment.

The standard recommendations for treatment steps are these:

1. Keep the victim calm and relaxed. Assure him that he will be all right. Keep him completely inactive.

2. When the bite is on a limb of the body, apply a constricting band between the bite and the heart, close to the bite if this step is taken within a minute or two after the snake has struck. The tourniquet should be loosened for about two minutes out of every ten. Continue this for one hour, possibly a little longer, if necessary.

3. An incision about one-fourth inch deep should be made at each fang mark. A razor blade sterilized by a match or a blade provided in a snake bite kit will do the job. Otherwise, a knife blade or other sharp instrument may be used if nothing better is available. In making an incision, stab sharply one time to the required depth. This will hardly be felt, for the victim will already be feeling the effects of the bite.

4. Start suction immediately. A good snake bite kit will contain suction cups; otherwise, it will be necessary to suck out the venom with your mouth. Apply suction for at least the first hour. Don't become alarmed if the victim swells or seems to suffer more. You can't get all of the venom out, but you can remove enough to make the difference between life and death.

5. During the second hour, immerse the bite area in an ice bath, if ice is available. Cold applications may help. Do not keep the bite area, or bitten member, in the ice bath more than one hour.

The victim should be placed in the care of a physician as soon as possible. Possibly someone can call a physician quickly, or after initial first aid treatment the victim may be rushed to professional medical aid.

Proper antivenom is necessary, and this should be injected by a physician. When traveling in remote areas, however, antivenom should be carried with the first aid materials for possible use in the field. A physician can test your reaction to antivenom before you head for snake-infested areas.

Serious emergencies

The three most serious emergencies likely to be encountered are cessation of breathing, severe bleeding and unconscoiusness. These require immediate treatment, on the spot.

When breathing stops, as in drowning, the brain begins to die from lack of oxygen. The victim's mouth should

Cottonmouth moccasin

Coral Snake

Copperhead

Rattlesnake

be pulled open and the air passages cleared (sweep your fingers around to discover any obstructions). Artificial respiration should begin at once and should be kept up, for hours if necessary. The mouth-to-mouth method is the easiest to apply.

The **Official U. S. Coastguard Recreational Boating Guide** makes these recommendations for mouth-to-mouth artificial respiration:

1. Place the unconscious victim on his back, as you must be able to see his face.

2. Move an injured victim cautiously.

3. If there is foreign matter visible at the mouth, turn his head to the side, force his mouth open and quickly clean the mouth and throat with your fingers or a piece of cloth.

4. Place the victim's head in the "sniffing position," placing the head as far back as possible so that his neck is extended, and hold his lower jaw upward so that it "juts out." (It is most important that the jaw be held in this position).

5. Hold the jaw in this position in one hand, approach the victum's head from his left side.

6. Insert the thumb of your left hand between the victim's teeth and grasp his lower jaw at the midline.

7. Lift the lower jaw forcefully upward so that the lower teeth are higher than the upper teeth.

8. Hold the jaw in this position as long as the victim is unconscious.

9. Close the victim's nose with your right hand.

10. After taking a deep breath, place your mouth over the victim's mouth, *with airtight contact.* Do not hold the victim's mouth open widely, as you must take the entire mouth of the victim inside your lips.

11. Blow into the victim's mouth, forcefully if adult and gently if children.

12. While blowing, watch the victim's chest. When the chest rises, stop blowing and quickly remove your mouth from the victim's mouth.

13. Let the victim exhale passively by the elasticity of his lungs and chest.

14. When the chest does not rise, improve the support of the air passageway and blow more forcefully.

15. Repeat these inflations 12 to 20 times per minute.

Small children

When applying mouth-to-mouth artificial respiration to small children, tilt the head fully back and surround the mouth and nose completely with your mouth. Blow with only enough force to produce a visible rise with in the victim's chest and no more. This should be repeated every two seconds.

Continue direct artificial respiration until the victim breathes for himself, or until more expert help is obtained. There are other methods of artificial respiration, which may be learned in first aid courses.

To stop severe bleeding in an open wound, apply direct pressure on the wound itself. Use any clean material in applying this pressure.

Raise the wound area higher than the level of the heart, if possible, and keep the patient still. In some in-

stances, hand pressure applied to the artery above the wound may be better than direct pressure on the wound. If a restrictive bandage or tourniquet over an artery is necessary, which it frequently is when transporting a patient to a doctor, be sure to loosen it briefly every 15 minutes.

An unconscious victim may suffocate if left lying on his back. He should be turned on his side with his face toward the ground, so that his tongue will fall forward. This also causes any fluids to run out rather than down into the air passages.

The first aid kit

Various types of first aid kits are available to campers. You may wish to make up your own. Here is a list of minimums suggested by the Ontario Department of Lands and Forests:

Rolls of one-inch and two-inch gauze bandage
Sterile gauze dressings, three inches square
Absorbent cotton
Adhesive tape
Adhesive finger dressings
Tube of antiseptic ointment
Antiseptic
Aromatic spirits of ammonia
Tube of burn ointment
Headache tablets

Add to this a snake bite kit, if there is danger of poisonous snakes in your camping environment, and personal medicines. Chances are, you won't use your first aid materials very much. But if there is need, you'll be glad you took the kit along. Prevention and treatment know-how are the criteria for safety first and first aid.

How to Drownproof Yourself

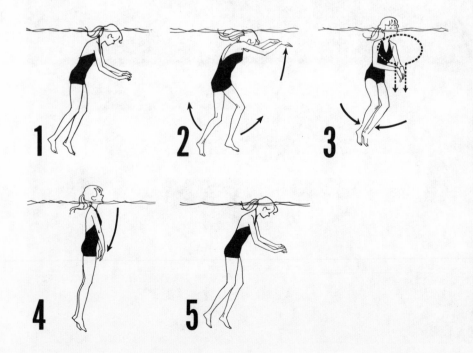

Waterbased recreation is growing in popularity and so is the importance of water safety. Over 5,000 persons drown each year, one-third of these between the ages of five and 15 years. Campers who swim do not always have readily available the latest rescue equipment. It is essential, therefore, that those who venture into the water have some knowledge of swimming.

Here are five basic steps (recommended by the U. S. Department of Agriculture) in drownproofing yourself. This method of floating will keep you alive in water even if you can't swim.

1. Take a deep breath, relax in the water with your arms and legs dangling.

2. When you want a breath, put your arms straight out in front of your shoulders. Spread your legs for a scissors kick, one forward and one back.

3. Raise your head until it is nearly vertical, push down with your hands in a keyhole pattern, bring your feet together. Exhale through your nose while you are surfacing.

4. When your chin is even with the surface, open your eyes wide and inhale through your mouth.

5. Relax and settle down into the water again. If you feel you are going to settle too deeply, give a slight downward push with your hands. Relax until you want another breath.

U. S. D. A. Photo

Outdoor enthusiasts have always enjoyed winter recreation, but until recently winter camping was not a favorite with many. Now, however, thanks to new insulation techniques, better clothing and gear, freeze-dry and dehydrated foods packaged for campers and more adequate shelters—plus some new methods of transportation—winter camping is challenging other forms in the ratings.

Many thousands who wouldn't venture out before are finding fun in the snow. Skiing, ice skating, ice fishing and all kinds of exploring expeditions are now part of the camping scene. The accompanying pictures show some of the reasons why.

WINTER CAMPING IS FUN

Backpacking is a common sight in the national forests during mid-winter. U. S. Forest Service Photo

The recently introduced Sno-Camper promises to further revolutionize winter camping.

Good for traveling over snow to a winter campout is this new all-terrain vehicle, The Stalker. Made by Ski-Tow Manufacturing Company, the vehicle is equally at home in sand dunes, swamplands, rivers and lakes—in fact, most anywhere.

The Forest service conducts a ski tour in the Mammoth Lakes area of Inyo National Forest. U. S. Forest Service Photo

The Popular New

"Give me comfort, convenience, and a bed off the ground," says the housewife, mother of two, "and I might enjoy camping." "Of course," says the recreational vehicle dealer. "Which would you prefer, a travel trailer, a truck camper, a camping trailer, or a motor home?"

Recreational Vehicles

This year more than two million recreational vehicle owners will set their courses along the highways into every part of the country. The passengers they take along, usually their families, will bring the total recreational vehicle users to more than eight million.

The rapidly expanding recreational vehicle industry is in the midst of a boom, increasing by some 285 percent during the seven years prior to 1969. Here are some figures showing the new importance of recreational vehicles among the travel-and outdoor-minded:

In 1956 manufacturers produced 15,370 travel trailer units—mostly in California. During 1964 some 90,370 travel trailers were manufactured. Production figures in 1967 showed a total of 132,540 units manufactured. By mid-1969, the estimate was for 180,000 units during the year.

These figures, released by the Recreational Vehicle Institute, guardian and promoter of the industry, also were coupled with the following projections for 1969: camping trailers, 95,000 units; truck campers, 165,000 units; and motor homes, 50,000 units. This means that during 1969 almost one-half million recreational vehicles were manufactured.

Some definitions

What are recreational vehicles? The industry itself has set forth some understandable definitions.

The Recreational Vehicle Institute in its booklet **Recreational Vehicle Facts and Trends** defines recreational vehicles as ". . . vehicular-type portable structures, primarily designed as temporary living accommodations for recreational, camping and travel use. There are four basic types of recreational vehicle products categories— travel trailers, truck campers, camping trailers and self-powered motor homes. They can either be towed, hauled or driven from one site to another. These products are designed, built, sold and serviced by a nationwide group of manufacturers, dealers and suppliers known as 'The Recreational Vehicle Industry'."

The RVI defines travel trailers as ". . . vehicular structures mounted on wheels," truck campers as ". . . portable structures to be loaded onto or affixed to the bed or chassis of a truck," camping trailers as ". . . structures mounted on wheels with collapsible side walls of fabric, plastic or other types of pliable materials" with tent-type or rigid tops, motor homes as ". . . fully self-contained luxury units . . . built directly on a truck or bus chassis."

Travel trailers

Production and sales figures show that travel trailers are the most popular type of recreational vehicle in use today. These are available in a wide range of sizes and styles, generally beginning with the compact 12-footer. The top luxury models are completely self-contained and reach lengths of about 35 feet.

The travel trailer was the first type of recreational vehicle to become popular as a means of temporary living accommodation for travel use. Naturally, campgrounds became attractive to those who wished to stop overnight enroute to some destination as well as to those who liked the idea of camping in a little less rugged fashion than usual.

The easy-to-tow travel trailer comes with many living innovations. The sleeping quarters are comfortable; a complete kitchen, with as many home-like conveniences as the purchaser

**FAN TRAVEL TRAILER
The Fan Coach Company, Inc., offers several styles and sizes.**

may wish to buy, makes cooking as easy as at home. Sanitary facilities are optional, and may include a bathroom as well furnished as the one at home, if not quite as large. Safe heating is standard in most, air conditioning is optional.

As the accompanying photos will show, purchasers of travel trailers have a wide selection of brand choices. There is also a wide range of prices, generally beginning at about $700 and topping out at about $10,000. Luxury options, of course, can make the price considerably higher.

Travel trailers are made with several types of construction. Some are framed by wood and covered with aluminum, some are all aluminum, both framing and covering. Others are constructed similarly to the framing and covering of aircraft, some are made of fiberglas-reinforced plastic and some are put together in a foam-core sandwich.

Unfortunately, there has been no national code setting construction standards, except for the plumbing, heating and electrical systems that are installed. It is to the credit of the industry that high standards have the industry that high standards have been maintained by most manufacturers.

Certain standards have been adopted by the Recreational Vehicle Institute, and these are subscribed to by the affiliated members. Presently the standards governing plumbing, heating and electrical systems are being revised to include all construction features.

Participating in this are the Recreational Vehicle Institute, National Fire Protection Association, Trailer Coach Association and a large group of technical experts in the fields of health and saftey. Final approval, expected to come in 1970, must come from the National Fire Protection Association and the United States of America Standards Institute.

These standards will apply to all recreational vehicles.

Truck campers

Truck campers first became popular among sportsmen because trucks can travel into remote areas better than cars. Today, truck campers are equally popular as family recreational vehicles. Some are elaborately furnished rivaling the luxury travel trailer and the motor home in convenience and facilities.

Manufacturers, including some of the large manufacturers of automobiles and trucks, have given a great deal of attention not only to the construction and features of the camper unit, but also to the added requirements of the vehicle itself.

There is general agreement among the manufacturers that suspension should be heavier than normal, oversize tires and wheels should be used in most instances, the electrical components should be heavy-duty and for heavier units or those designed for rugged use, a larger radiator is recommended.

The smaller camper units, 6 to 11 feet, are usually purchased by those who use their one-half ton pickups for other purposes. The camper itself simply slides onto the bed of the truck, and when it is not in use it is removed with the aid of jacks. Larger models, of course, may also be taken on and off of truck beds. These range from 11 to 18 feet; many are self-contained. Trucks larger than one-half ton are required for larger camper units. Weight and size determine the size truck.

Some campers are chassis-mounted, that is, are permanently attached directly to the truck frame. Such vehicles are used strictly for recreational and travel purposes, not for hauling.

Many of today's truck campers feature power steering, power brakes and automatic transmission, and handle as easily as a family car. They are geared to maintain top highway speeds. The trend definitely is to make them fully self-contained and more spacious.

Retail prices for the campers (less the vehicle) start under $1,000 and range up to $4,000. Much more can be paid for added luxuries and equipment.

Camping trailers

Many manufacturers call these tent trailers or tent campers. Whatever they are called, it is a fact that they are easily towed by any size or type of 4-wheel motor vehicle. They are economical to buy and to maintain. They offer the same appeal as tent camping, except with more convenience and time-saving features in packing and in setting up. Most feature built-ins such as water tanks, ice boxes or refrigerators and a cooking unit. Options include wardrobes, toilets and such.

Most units are equipped with raising and lowering systems that open and close with very little effort. The units are compact when being towed, but open out for use into large tent-top structures that sleep four to eight people. Attachable awnings and screened rooms provide for a lot of living space at the campsite.

Camping trailers are relatively inexpensive, some selling for about $300 and the top lines for as much as $2,000. The average cost is under $1,000. These are particularly popular with outdoor enthusiasts and families with young children. Some experienced campers who turn to the camping trailer purchase the unit barren of most fixtures and equipment. They follow their own preferences in outfitting, just as they would if tent camping. The novice probably should purchase a unit with the basics already installed.

Motor homes

This ultimate in recreational vehicles has been described as a "practical luxury." The motor home market is

THE AIRSTREAM
Fourteen models are available from Airstream, Inc.

booming, with the addition of new manufacturers every month or so. It is the type of unit that the man handy with construction tools can build himself—if he has the time and can afford it.

Motor homes are fully self-contained units built directly on a truck or bus chassis and measure up to 30 feet in length—sometimes more for custom jobs. Most feature the power equipment and conveniences of fine automobiles: power steering, power brakes, air conditioning, radio and stereo. Prices range from $5,000 to more than $40,000, occasionally going as high as $60,000 for custom workmanship and luxury equipment.

Some automobile and bus body companies build motor homes, others are manufactured by a rapidly expanding number of companies specializing in recreational vehicles. Some firms build standard product line models or special units on customer order.

This industry has learned a great deal from the auto industry, which accounts in part for its sudden success. The basic components are recognized brands of the major truck manufacturers and vehicle body builders.

Many in the industry also have background experience in the construction of mobile homes, which has enabled them to bring to the motor home such self-contained features as stove, refrigerator, heater, bathing and toilet facilities.

Interior combinations are many and varied, and only a period of time spent shopping will enable the potential purchaser to settle on a preferred unit.

A growing number of backpackers and wilderness hikers are using motor homes as base camp. Skiers and other enthusiasts of winter sports have found this to be a practical transportation unit that gets them to the snow areas and keeps them comfortable while there.

The industry's standards

The national trade association exclusively serving the recreational vehicle industry is the Recreational Vehicle Institute. The recreational vehicles pictured on these pages are made by RVI manufacturing members. Members include manufacturers of travel trailers, truck campers, camping trailers and motor homes as well as companies providing products and services to the industry. An "associates member division" welcomes firms and private groups who are "vitally interested in or associated with the industry: automotive and petroleum companies, park developers, campground owners, etc."

The RVI Standards Division has developed various recreational vehicle standards and code programs to meet consumer demands. A national code is expected to be adopted in 1970. The Standards Division also works with the U. S. Department of Transportation regarding regulations and legislation pertaining to recreational vehicles.

When you buy

Unless you have weighed all the factors and are prepared to buy a recreational vehicle, don't buy one the first time you go shopping. It is better to rent or borrow various types of units for two or three trips before purchasing one of your own. You may discover that towing a trailer makes you nervous, though that is not likely. Your wife may not wish to drive a motor home, though this, too, is doubtful. You may discover that you have no use for some of the luxury features; or you may find that more are necessary to your family's pleasure than you first thought.

Many dealers who sell recreational vehicles are also in the business of renting them. Rent one for a weekend. The dealer will usually mount a hitch on the family car for a trailer, wire up the lights, provide insurance protection and otherwise do what is necessary for you to drive away for a weekend or vacation. Rentals generally begin at $50 per week for camping trailers, more for other types of vehicles.

The Recreational Vehicle Institute makes the following recommendations for your consideration before buying a recreational vehicle:

1. Buy the one that fits your needs. Don't overbuy! How many people will be going along on your trips? Will you have room? Too much room?

2. Buy the one you can afford. Spend only what you can afford to spend. If the recreational vehicle you can afford is too small for your needs, consider renting instead.

3. Buy the one the family likes. Since this is a family venture in fun and recreation, let mom and the kids in on the selection.

4. Visit a local campground or state park. See recreational vehicles in actual use. Talk with the owners. Visit several families and evaluate this information in relation to your own needs.

In an information release to media, RVI succinctly sums up what makes the recreational vehicle so popular and useful:

"The family of recreational vehicle owners is constantly growing in America. Families have found that they can travel and go camping almost as cheaply as they can stay at home. Hunting, fishing and skiing enthusiasts can now pursue their hobbies without fear of bending the budget. People, who hertofore didn't enjoy traveling because of its accompanying discomforts, now feel free to sightsee the country because they carry their facilities with them.

"One of the greatest benefits of recreational vehicles is that, because this mode of travel is economical, many families who took few trips before, can now afford to go more often. Those who did take periodic vacations are utilizing their vehicle for weekends away from home.

"And, as the sun sinks silently in the West, silhouetted against the sky is no longer that old-time wagon train, but a new image—a train of recreational vehicles."

WINNEBAGO TRUCK CAMPER
Lightweight model designed for easy hauling, yet spacious enough inside for comfortable eating and sleeping.

RECREATIONAL VEHICLES POPULAR With CAMPERS

The recreational vehicles pictured on these pages have met the preference tests of many campers. A wide variety of styles, sizes and accommodations are available. For this reason, the wise shopper for a recreational vehicle will look over numerous makes and models before making his purchase.

A complete listing of leading recreational vehicle manufacturers follows this picture section. Descriptive folders and booklets are available from each manufacturer.

LEISURE TIME
Leisure Time Products, Inc., manufactures 16 models in three series.

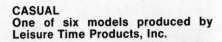

CASUAL
One of six models produced by Leisure Time Products, Inc.

THE FORESTER
Seven models are offered by Forest City Industries.

WINNEBAGO
Eight models by Winnebago Industries, Inc. 1970 Models include 15 and 17 foot travel trailers for young married people.

THE APACHE
Six new models have been introduced by Vesely Company. At left.

ASTRO-STAR
One of several models by the Starcraft Company. Below.

COACHMEN CITATION
Coachmen Industries, Inc., offers 14 models in sizes ranging from 13' to 26'. Bottom photo.

SERRO SCOTTY HI-LANDER
Economy is emphasized in several models by Serro Travel Trailer Company. Below

MONITOR MANOR
The Monitor Coach Company, Inc.,
line features models from 14′ to 26′.

HY-LANDER
The 24′ model of semi travel trailers
offered by Hyland Manufacturing,
Inc. Middle photo.

THE PHOENIX
A tandem model of
travel trailers manu-
factured by Cara-
vans International.

HI-LO BON VOYAGE
A deluxe 20' telescoping travel trailer by the Snyder Trailer Company. Unit height is reduced one-half with top lowered. Above.

MALLARD FLIGHT LEADER
Mallard Coach Corporation produces both luxury and economy models. Photo at left.

THE AVION
One of numerous models of riveted aluminum travel trailers produced by Avion Coach Corporation. Below.

SHASTA
One of several new designs by Shasta Trailer Company.

TROTWOOD
This is the 16′ Cub model by Trotwood Trailers, Inc.

WINNEBAGO
New 17′ 1970 economy priced unit is built ruggedly to give years of service over rough terrain. Left photo.

THE BLAZON
One of several models ranging up to 35′, manufactured by Blazon Mobile Homes Corporation. Below.

CORSAIR
This 23 footer sleeps five. Has range and oven, eight gallon hot water heater and shower. 12 volt lighting system.

BLAZON
This brand new 1970 Blazon is 21′6″ long and is thoroughly equipped for long cross country trips. Has refrigerator, range, oven, lavatory and shower in bath.

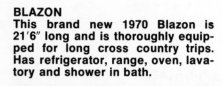

ARISTOCRAT
The low silhouette typifies this 20 ft. Landmark I trailer. It has a rear entrance and is offered in two floorplans—twin bed or side dinette.

The vast selection of interior layouts and furnishings available today assures satisfaction in finding the exact model to fit your needs and tastes. Some are fitted with materials designed to give excellent wear under hard use and are not easily stained or soiled by liquids or mud. Other interiors are outfitted in plush and expensive upholstery cloth and fine natural finish woods. You can have your choice of conveniences which include showers, wardrobes, air conditioning, television, inside toilets and bath tubs. All are of top quality and reasonably priced . . . will provide many years efficient on-the-spot living.

Interior of the Pan-O-Ramic Executive 28'.

Interior cutaway of the Hi-Lo Bon Voyage 20' telescoping travel trailer.

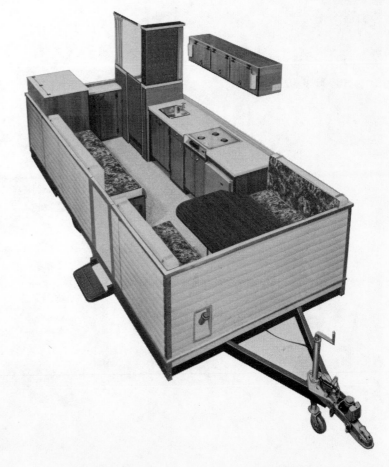

Kitchen in the Airstream.

The interior of this 31' Avion is a study in elegance.

A section of the Boles Aero 27' model 270-C.

Coachmen's 18' Carousel shows adaptability of modern travel trailer interiors.

Bedroom and bath section of the Airstream.

Kitchen and dining area of Starcraft's Trail Star.

TRUCK CAMPERS
gaining in popularity

Truck campers have advantages and disadvantages. The main reason they are chosen is because they are generally less expensive than a trailer. They are more in favor of farmers, hunters or fishermen who already have pick-up trucks. Another point in their favor is the fact that in some ways they handle better than a trailer-easier to drive over rough ground and through brushy woods. Backing up is no problem. The main drawback is lack of space in comparison to a trailer, though some now offered have as much space as a medium sized travel trailer.

WINNEBAGO
Winnebago manufactures four models of Camper Coaches.

LEISURE TIME
The Casual is one of four models in this series manufactured by Leisure Time Products, Inc.

YELLOWSTONE
Yellowstone, Inc., a pioneer in self-contained travel trailers, also produces this pickup camper.

THE AMERIGO
The Amerigo, made by Gardner, Inc., comes in three floor plans. Each plan is available with or without extension beds, as shown in the picture.

ECONO-CAMP
Shown here is the Econo-Camp, a pickup camper developed by Appleby Manufacturing Company. The camper may be easily removed from the truck as shown in the top picture.

FORESTER
This 11' Forester by Forest City Industries, Inc., offers two floor plans. Two other models are 8' and 8½'.

BLAZON
This Blazon 11' camper features a side door. It is one of three models manufactured by Blazon Mobile Homes Corporation. Photo at bottom.

COX CABANA

The recently introduced Cox Cabana series features the same interior and exterior, less tires and undercarriage, as the Cox camping trailer, Cadet series. This unit has quickly caught on with sportsmen and campers who like something handy for the pickup. This is actually the truck camper version of the tent trailer.

TROTWOOD TRUCK CAMPERS
Trotwood Trailers, Inc., makes two truck campers. This model is 10' 9" long. Has wide overcab window with big appeal for children.

CAVALIER COMPANION
Exterior view of Kamp-Craft's Cavalier Companion shows why it is attractive to sportsmen. Not too wide or heavy, it goes through rough, brushy areas without straining the truck frame or engine capacity.

STARCRAFT
The Starcraft Company has added this Starlighter camper to its line of recreational boats and vehicles. Roof design improves high speed travel performance by directing air flow. Bottom photo.

SNYDER HI-LO CUSTOM TELESCOPING CAMPER

The Hi-Lo custom camper, a telescoping unit, offered by the Snyder Trailer Company, fits ¾ ton pickups. Exterior and interior views are shown here. Sleeps four, has portable toilet, wardrobe, cooking facilities and extra storage space. Top raised with crank.

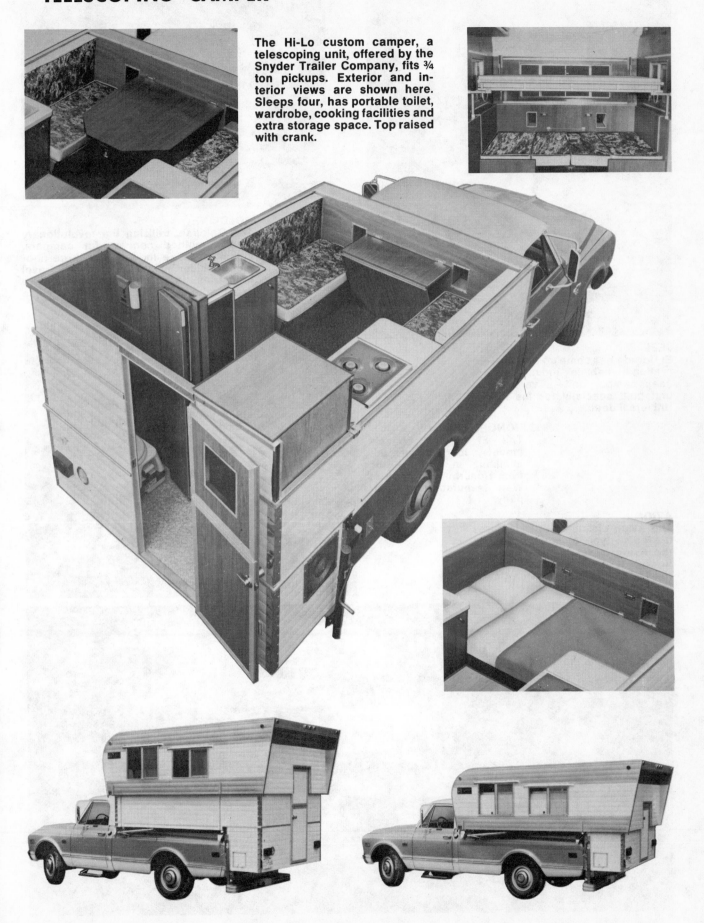

GOLDLINE
The Goldline, utilizing the revolutionary plastic molded concept for campers, comes in three models and three floor plan choices. Manufactured by Travel Industries, Inc., these pickup campers are marketed exclusively by franchise Ford dealers.

JEEP
El Dorado has come up with the recreational vehicle industry's first Jeep camper unit—a versatile 8' unit built specially for the Kaiser Universal Jeep.

HONORBUILT
The El Dorado chassis models, four in all, are available in two lengths from Honorbuilt Division of Ward Manufacturing Company.

AVION
The Avion pickup camper features the same type of construction as the Avion travel trailers. Rounded front cuts wind resistance on the road. Manufacturer is Avion Coach Corporation.

SURREY
A unique combination offered by Coachmen Industries, Inc., this 8½' Surrey truck camper and special deluxe Coachmen horse trailer is a convenience to campers who wish to do some trail riding.

CAMP KING LONGHORN
One of the largest slip-in campers in the industry, the new Camp King Longhorn, is manufactured by The John Plant Company of the Carolinas.

SKAMPER
Both the Skamper 10', shown here, and the 8' are popular with families and sportsmen. Manufacturer is Skamper Corporation. Roof unit can be raised for additional room . . . lowered for travel.

The Blazon 110 Side Dinette is built to last and give service over the roughest roads. Completely furnished with refrigerator, range and oven, shower, lavatory, stool, and pressure water system.

IMPERIAL SKYLOUNGE

The Del Rey Imperial Skylounge features a spacious overcab, by day a lounge area large enough for three adults, by night a roomy bed. This is one of several overcab units produced by Del Rey Industries, Inc., a division of Gladding Corporation. Photo below.

LEISURE TIME

Leisure Time Products, Inc., offers 10 models in the series bearing the company name.

MALLARD COACH
The Drift Wing series—three models—is a product of Mallard Coach Corporation.

THE SWISS CHALET
The Swiss Chalet sleeps six and is a product of Swiss Colony Travelers, Inc. Right photo.

TOWN CRIER
Six models, including this 11' Town Crier, are manufactured by Coachmen Industries, Inc.

Notice the placement of sleeping, cooking and lounging areas of this Avion camper.

TRUCK
CAMPER
INTERIORS

When truck camper bodies were first developed they didn't include much more than bunk space. Now they have been designed to provide just about every convenience of home. Some models for hunters and fishermen have just the facilities needed for eating and sleeping, others are outfitted for gracious comfort with upholstered seats and cushions, curtains, toilets, showers, the works.

Up-front eating-sleeping area marks the interior design of the Covered Wagon truck camper.

Interior view of the 11' Town Crier.

The dining area in the Del Rey Imperial Skylounge.

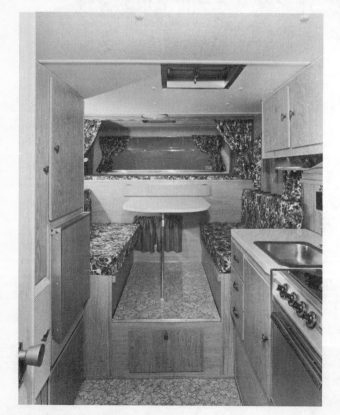

AQUA CAMP

Newest to hit the market is the Aqua/Camp, a very usable boat being the protective covering in transit. These units by Continental Products, Ltd., are made only for Chevrolet and Pontiac station wagons and are sold exclusively through Chevrolet dealers.

CAR-MOUNTED CAMPERS

Many campers have improvised shelters in connection with their automobiles, both station wagons and sedans. Several companies have gotten into the act and the commercial end products are both practical and economical. Some of the leaders are shown here.

CAMP'OTEL

The Camp'Otel Cartop Camper by Camp'Otel Corporation is an exciting camping concept. It includes everything needed for sleeping, cooking, eating and bathing.

JIFFY CAMP

The Jiffy-Camp Company has developed this automobile trunktop camper. Notice that on a station wagon it becomes in effect a two-story camper.

KAY-DEE KAMPER
This rooftop camper is a popular product of Kay-Dee Kampers, Inc. It can be adapted as a platform tent off the ground. An additional tent room may also be added. Top photo shows tent closed. Bottom photo shows tent erected.

SUNSET
The Sunset by Commodore Corporation.

CAMPING TRAILERS

A camping trailer provides an excellent way to take comfort and convenience into any type area from a private campground to a wilderness location beside a lake or river. Though smaller and lighter than a travel trailer they provide almost the same furnishings such as toilet, stove, running water, electric lights and refrigerator. Easier to pull on the road, and they also cost less.

JAYCO
Cranking the Jayco up and down is easy and simple with the company's new lifter system. Top and center photos.

WHEEL CAMPER
This is a ruggedly built model, almost all the work is done by hand and hand fitted. It is easy to erect and has a very efficient layout. The Packwagon shown here will sleep six comfortably. It is furnished with balloon tires and pulls smoothly. Bottom photo.

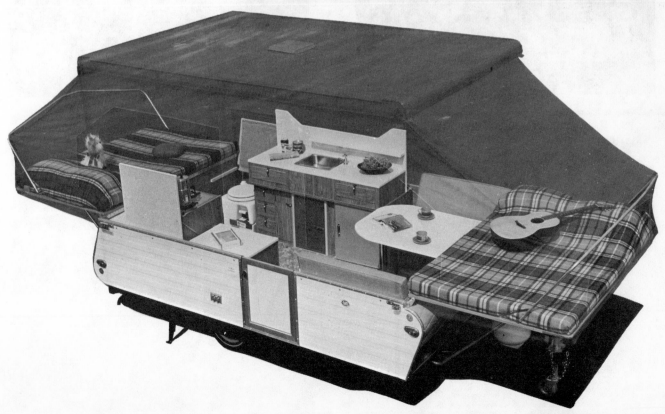

STARCRAFT
Starcraft's Stardust-8 is a favorite of hunters and the Galaxy-6 easily carries a boat.

APPLEBY
The Appleby Manufacturing Company's Econo Deluxe Camping Trailer.

COMMANDER
Unique tent trailer has canvas top. Bed extensions have windows. Features cloth awning. Made by Cox Trailers.

E-Z Kamper's Skylark-3.

PHOENIX
The Phoenix convertible by Caravans International. Has plastic top, aluminum covered body. Top photo.

TRADE WINDS
The Trade Winds Company manufacturers both campers and camper accessories. Center photo.

TRAVELMATE
Travelmate is manufactured by the Travel Equipment Corporation. They also market the Lark Mai-Kai Deluxe model. Bottom Photo.

WANDERER
The economy Wanderer produced by Pleasure Time Industry.

JAYCO
Canvas awning creates a ramada type area. Furnished with fixtures that make it easy to put up.

SKAMPER
Skamper Model CS-8 by Skamper Corporation. 8 foot model is easy to pull, simple to erect. Excellent for one day or weekend outings.

SCOUT
The 100 Scout by Leisure Time Products, Inc.

PLEASURE MATE
The Pleasure Mate Sunchaser produced by Pleasure Time Industry.

RAMADA
The Ramada, the Vesely Company's top-of-the-line. Photo below.

PALOMINO
All models in both the Mustang and Colt series have an inside height of 6' 4", but the closed height is only 48½" and doesn't obscure rear vision.

CAMEL
The Oasis III by Camel Manufacturing Company offers an extended canopy and three full size beds.

COLEMAN
Three models of the Coleman are shown here. Outer shells are made of durable plastic. Bottom photo.

CAMPING TRAILER INTERIORS

These interiors give examples of some of the many sleeping and working arrangements available in camping trailers. Sizes will range from eight to 16 feet and will accommodate four to eight sleepers. Sliding curtains, zippered windows provide privacy and air.

Coleman camping trailer

COMMANDER
Cox Trailers, Inc., produces six models in the Commander Series 500. This view shows comfortable interior. Above photo.

PUMA
The Puma Tent Trailer produced by The Ski-Tow Manufacturing Company. Left photo.

COLEMAN
Interior view of this Coleman model shows the modern sink and three burner stove with a fine window view. Right middle photo.

LARK
Interior of the Deluxe Model made by Travel Equipment Corporation. Left photo.

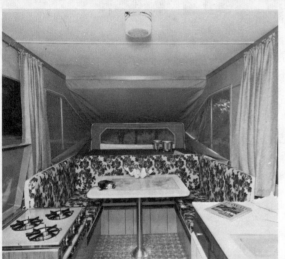

Interior view of the Steury, product of Steury Boat Company.

Motor homes are completely self-contained and self-propelled. Driving controls are part of the living room area at the front. They are the elite of the travel vehicles and this is reflected in the usually higher prices. Relatively easy to drive and furnished with all home comforts.

MOTOR HOMES

DODGE
Big and roomy is the Dodge Motor Home manufactured by Travco Corporation.

EL DORADO
Product of Honorbuilt Division of Ward Manufacturing Company.

KAMP KING
Two views of the Kamp King Ford Van-a-Home, a product of The John Plant Company of the Carolinas.

WINNEBAGO
The Winnebago by Winnebago Industries, Inc. Photos show both sides and interior from the front. Middle and bottom photos.

MINIHOME
The MiniHome is a conversion of Ford's Econoline van. It is sold through Ford dealers. Compact but has all the most wanted comforts. 1st and 2nd photos.

SHASTA
The Shasta Company has transferred many of its travel trailer features to the new Shasta Motorhome. Photo below.

TWIN COACH
The Twin Coach Cruiser by Highway Products, Inc.

GLASTRON
Featuring Fiberglas construction and a great deal of luxury is this Glastron by the Glastron Motor Home Company. Photo above.

FLXIBLE
The Flxible Cruiser, a motor home manufactured by the Flxible Company. Photo below.

WINNEBAGO
Upper left is the Winnebago 27 ft. Chieftain featuring both a back and front door. Above is the interior of the luxurious 24 ft. Chieftain.

WAYNE
Exterior and interior views of the Wayne Motor Home, made by Wayne Corporation. Interior is paneled in fine woods in more of classic design. Middle and bottom photos.

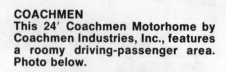

COACHMEN
This 24' Coachmen Motorhome by Coachmen Industries, Inc., features a roomy driving-passenger area. Photo below.

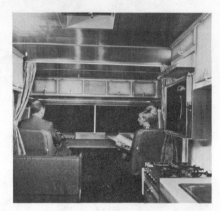

LIFETIME
There are four basic Lifetime models. The Imperial 25', the Continental 25', the Premier 23' and the Town & Country, 20'. Manufactured by Boise Cascade.

Model shown is the Imperial Model 22. Beechwood also makes an Imperial Model 24 and Vacationer Model 20. All have full comfort insulation, bonded construction and extra large glass area.

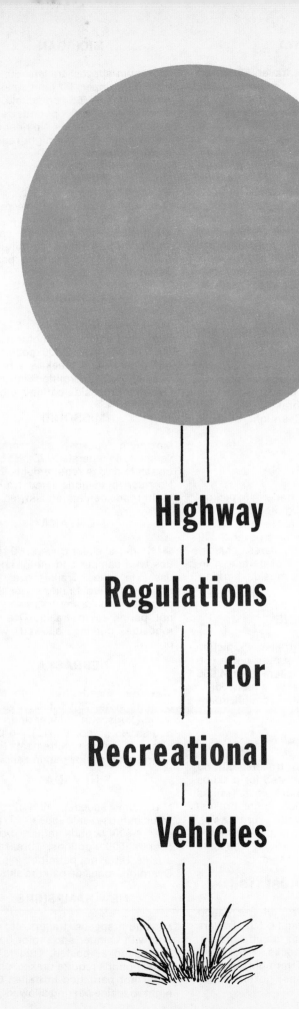

Highway Regulations for Recreational Vehicles

ALABAMA

Maximum speeds: trailer, 60; pickup with camper, 50; motor home, 50. Trailer brakes and flares required. Rider permitted in trailer. Overnight roadside parking permitted.

ALASKA

Maximum speeds: all recreation vehicles, 50. Trailers over 1,500 pounds require brakes; over 3,000 pounds, breakaway, flares, chains. Rider permitted in trailer. Overnight roadside parking allowed.

ARIZONA

Maximum speeds: as posted. Trailers over 1,500 pounds require brakes; over 3,000 pounds, breakaway, flares. Rider permitted in trailer. Overnight roadside parking allowed.

ARKANSAS

Maximum speeds: trailer 45; pickup with camper and motor home, 60. Trailers over 1,500 pounds require brakes; over 3,000 pounds, breakaway, flares, chains. Rider not permitted in trailer. Overnight roadside parking allowed where posted.

CALIFORNIA

Maximum speeds: trailer, 55; pickup with camper and motor home, 65. Trailers over 1,500 pounds require trailer and breakaway brakes, chains, mirrors, flares. Rider not permitted in trailer. Emergency overnight roadside parking only allowed.

COLORADO

Maximum speeds: trailer, 60; pickup with camper and motor home, 60 (interstate, 70). Trailers over 1,500 pounds require brakes; over 3,000 pounds, breakaway, chains. Rider permitted in trailer. No overnight roadside parking allowed.

CONNECTICUT

Maximum speeds: all recreation vehicles, 60 (interstate, 70). Trailers over 3,000 pounds, brakes on all wheels, mirrors. Rider permitted in trailer. Overnight roadside parking allowed where posted.

DELAWARE

Maximum speeds: trailer, 45; pickup with camper and motor home, 50 (interstate, 60). Trailers over 4,000 pounds require brakes, safety glass. Rider not permitted in trailer. Overnight roadside parking allowed.

DISTRICT OF COLUMBIA

Maximum speeds: as posted. Trailers over 1,500 pounds require brakes; over 3,000 pounds, breakaway, two chains. Rider permitted in trailer. No overnight roadside parking allowed.

FLORIDA

Maximum speeds: trailer, 50; pickup with camper and motor home, 65. Trailers over 3,000 pounds require trailer and breakaway brakes, mirrors, flares. Rider not permitted in trailer. No overnight roadside parking allowed.

GEORGIA

Maximum speeds: trailer, 60; pickup with camper, 55 (interstate, 60); no regulation listed for motor home speed. Trailers over 1,500 pounds require brakes; over 3,000 pounds, breakaway, chains, mirrors. Rider not permitted in trailer. No overnight roadside parking permitted.

IDAHO

Maximum speeds: all recreation vehicles, 60 (interstate, 70). Trailers over 1,500 pounds require brakes; over 3,000 pounds, breakaway, flares, chains, mirrors. Rider in trailer not recommended. Overnight roadside parking allowed.

ILLINOIS

Maximum speeds: trailer, 55; no regulations listed for pickup with camper and motor home speeds. Trailers over 1,500 pounds require brakes; over 3,000 pounds, breakaway, chains. Rider not permitted in trailer. Overnight roadside parking allowed.

INDIANA

Maximum speeds: all recreation vehicles, 65 (interstate, 70). Trailers over 1,500 pounds require brakes; over 3,000 pounds, breakaway, flares, chains, mirrors. Rider not permitted in trailer. Overnight roadside parking allowed with permit.

IOWA

Maximum speeds: trailer, 55 pickup with camper, 55 (interstate, 65); motor home, 70 (interstate 75). All trailers require trailer and breakaway brakes; trailers over 3,000 pounds, chains, flares. Rider permitted in trailer. Overnight roadside parking allowed.

KANSAS

Maximum speeds: trailer, 70; pickup with camper and motor home, 70 (interstate, 75). All trailers, brake type optional but must be safe; flares, chains required. Rider permitted in trailer. Overnight roadside parking allowed.

KENTUCKY

Maximum speeds: trailer 60; no speed regulations listed for pickups with camper and motor homes. All trailers require brakes. No rider regulation listed. Overnight roadside parking allowed.

LOUISIANA

Maximum speeds: trailer, 45; pickup with camper, 50; motor home, 60 (interstate, 70). Trailers over 1,500 pounds require brakes; over 3,000 pounds, breakaway, flares, chains, safety glass. Rider not permitted in trailer. Overnight roadside parking permitted.

MAINE

Maximum speeds: trailer, 45; pickup with camper and motor home, 60 (interstate, 70). Trailers over 4,000 pounds require brakes, chains. Rider permitted in trailer. Overnight roadside parking allowed.

MARYLAND

Maximum speeds: trailers, 50; no speed regulations listed for pickups with camper or motor homes. Trailers over 1,500 pounds require brakes; over 3,000 pounds, breakaway, flares, fire exiting. Rider permitted in trailer. No overnight roadside parking regulation listed.

MASSACHUSETTS

Maximum speeds: all recreation vehicles, 40 (interstate, 50). Trailers over 10,000 pounds require brakes, chains, wheel chocks. Rider permitted in trailer. Overnight roadside parking regulations governed locally.

MICHIGAN

Maximum speeds: trailers, 50; pickup with camper, 50 (interstate, 60); motor home, 65 (interstate, 70). Trailers over 1,500 pounds require brakes, flares, chains. No rider regulation listed. No overnight roadside parking allowed.

MINNESOTA

Maximum speeds: all recreation vehicles, 65. Trailers over 1,500 pounds require brakes, chains, safety glass. Rider permitted in trailer. Overnight roadside parking allowed.

MISSISSIPPI

Maximum speeds: trailers, 65; pickups with camper and motor homes, 50. Trailers over 2,000 pounds require trailer and breakaway brakes, chains. Rider permitted in trailer. Overnight roadside parking allowed.

MISSOURI

Maximum speeds: all recreation vehicles, 65 (interstate, 70). No brake or safety device requirements listed. No rider regulations listed. No overnight roadside parking allowed.

MONTANA

Maximum speeds: trailers, 50; pickups with camper and motor homes, use safe speed. Trailers over 1,500 pounds require brakes; over 3,000 pounds, breakaway, flares. Rider not permitted in trailer. Overnight roadside parking allowed where posted.

NEBRASKA

Maximum speeds: trailers under 23', 65 (interstate, 75); trailers over 23', 50; pickups with camper and motor homes, 65 (interstate, 75). No brake or safety device requirements listed. Overnight roadside parking allowed.

NEVADA

Maximum speeds: all recreation vehicles, use safe speed. Trailers over 1,500 pounds require brakes; over 3,000 pounds, breakaway, chains. Rider not permitted in trailer. Overnight roadside parking allowed.

NEW HAMPSHIRE

Maximum speeds: trailers, 45; pickups with camper and motor homes, use speed as posted. Trailers over 1,500 pounds require brakes, chains. Rider not permitted in trailer. Overnight roadside parking allowed.

NEW JERSEY

Maximum speeds: all recreation vehicles, 50. Trailers over 3,000 pounds require trailer and breakaway brakes, chains, safety glass. No rider regulations listed. Overnight roadside parking allowed.

NEW MEXICO

Maximum speeds: trailers, 60; pickups with camper and motor homes, 70. Trailers over 3,000 pounds require brakes, chains. Rider not permitted in trailer. Overnight roadside parking allowed.

NEW YORK

Maximum speeds: all recreation vehicles, 50 (interstate, 60). Trailers over 1,000 pounds require brakes. Rider permitted in trailer. Emergency overnight roadside parking allowed.

NORTH CAROLINA

Maximum speeds: trailers under 3,000 pounds, 55; trailers over 3,000 pounds, 45; pickups with camper under one ton, 55 (interstate, 65); pickups with camper one ton and over, 45; motor homes, 55 (interstate, 65). Trailers over 1,000 pounds require brakes, flares, safety glass. Rider permitted in trailer. Overnight roadside parking allowed.

NORTH DAKOTA

Maximum speeds: trailers, 50; pickups with camper and motor homes, 65 (interstate, 75). All trailers require trailer and breakaway brakes, chains, flares. Rider not permitted in trailer. Overnight roadside parking allowed.

OHIO

Maximum speeds: trailers, 60 (interstate, 70); pickups with camper, 50 (interstate, 55); motor homes, 60 (interstate, 70). Trailers over 2,000 pounds require trailer and breakaway brakes, chains, flares. Rider permitted in trailer. No overnight roadside parking allowed.

OKLAHOMA

Maximum speeds: trailers, 50; pickups with camper, 65 (interstate, 70); one-ton capacity pickups, 50 (interstate, 70); motor homes, 65 (interstate, 70). Trailers over 3,000 pounds require trailer and breakaway brakes, chains, flares. Rider permitted in trailer. Overnight roadside parking allowed where posted.

OREGON

Maximum speeds: all recreation vehicles, 55 (interstate, 70). All trailers require brakes when essential to safety, chains. Rider permitted in trailer. Overnight roadside parking allowed where posted.

PENNSYLVANIA

Maximum speeds: trailers, 45 (interstate, 55); pickups with camper and motor homes, 55 (interstate, 65). Trailers over 1,000 pounds require brakes; all trailers require breakaway, chains, safety glass, flares. Rider not permitted in trailer. Overnight roadside parking allowed.

RHODE ISLAND

Maximum speeds: trailers, 50; no speed regulations listed for pickups with camper and motor homes. Trailers over 4,000 pounds require trailer and breakaway brakes, chains, flares. No rider regulations listed. Overnight roadside parking allowed.

SOUTH CAROLINA

Maximum speeds: all recreation vehicles, 60 (interstate, 70). Trailers over 3,000 pounds require trailer and breakaway brakes, chains, mirrors, safety glass. Rider permitted in trailer. No overnight roadside parking allowed.

SOUTH DAKOTA

Maximum speeds: trailers, 70; pickups with camper and motor homes, 60 (interstate, 75). Trailer brakes required when essential to safety, chains, flares. Rider not permitted in trailer. Overnight roadside parking allowed.

TENNESSEE

Maximum speeds: trailers, 65; pickups with camper and motor homes, 50 (interstate, 65). Trailers over 1,500 pounds require brakes; over 3,000 pounds, breakaway. No rider regulations listed. Overnight roadside parking allowed.

TEXAS

Maximum speeds: trailers, 60; pickup with camper, 70; motor home, 60. Trailers over 3,000 pounds require trailer and breakaway brakes, flares. Rider permitted in trailer. Overnight roadside parking allowed.

UTAH

Maximum speeds: all recreation vehicles, use speed as posted. Trailers over 2,000 pounds require brakes; over 3,000 pounds, breakaway brakes, chains, flares, safety glass. Rider permitted in trailer. Overnight roadside parking allowed.

VERMONT

Maximum speeds: all recreation vehicles, use speeds as posted (interstate, 65). All trailers require brakes; over 3,000 pounds, breakaway brakes, chains, fire exiting. Rider permitted in trailer. Overnight roadside parking allowed.

VIRGINIA

Maximum speeds: trailers under 2,500 pounds, 55 (interstate, 65); trailers over 2,500 pounds, 45 (interstate, 55); pickups with camper and motor homes, 55 (interstate, 65). Trailer over 3,000 pounds require brakes, fire exiting, chains. Rider permitted in trailer. Overnight roadside parking allowed.

WASHINGTON

Maximum speeds: trailers, 60; pickups with camper and motor homes, use speed as posted. Trailers over 3,000 pounds require trailer and breakaway brakes, chains, flares. Rider not permitted in trailer. Overnight roadside parking allowed.

WEST VIRGINIA

Maximum speeds: trailers, 55 (interstate, 70); pickups with camper and motor homes, 50 (interstate, 70). Trailers over 3,000 pounds require trailer and breakaway brakes, chains, flares. Rider in trailer not recommended. No overnight roadside parking allowed.

WISCONSIN

Maximum speeds: all recreation vehicles, 65 (interstate, 70). All trailers require trailer and breakaway brakes, chains, safety glass. Rider not permitted in trailer. No overnight roadside parking allowed.

WYOMING

Maximum speeds: trailers, 65; pickups with camper and motor homes, 65 (interstate, 75). Trailers over 1,500 pounds require brakes; over 3,000 pounds, breakaway, flares. Rider not permitted in trailer. No overnight roadside parking allowed.

Recreational Vehicle Manufacturers

Members of the Recreational Vehicle Institute, Inc.

Note: These manufacturers subscribe to the standards and purposes of the Recreational Vehicle Institute, Inc., 2720 Des Plaines Avenue, Des Plaines, Illinois 60018.

Ace Traveler Corporation
Rt. 1, Box 43, Alfred, Maine 04002

Action Industries, Inc.
3300 W. Franklin St., Elkhart, Indiana 46514

Airstream, Inc.
North Dixie Highway, Sidney, Ohio 45365

American Duralite Corporation
P. O. Box B, Loudon, Tennessee 37774

American Sterling Enterprises, Inc.
Box 237, Blue Island, Illinois 60406

Appleby Manufacturing Company
Rt. 1, Lebanon, Missouri 65536

Aristocrat Travel Products
P. O. Box 817, Morgan Hill, California 95037

Avalon Mobile Homes, Inc.
P. O. Box 367, Bristol, Indiana 46507

Avco Corporation
10700 East Independence, Tulsa, Oklahoma 74115

Avion Coach Corporation
1300 East Empire Avenue, Benton Harbor, Michigan 49022

Barth, Inc.
Rt. 2, State Road 15, Milford, Indiana 46542

Beaver Enterprises, Inc.
P. O. Box 248, Fitzgerald, Georgia 31750

Beechwood Industries, Inc.
P. O. Box 1106, Elkhart, Indiana 46514

Bee Line Travel Trailers, Inc.
1322 North Nappanee Street, Elkhart, Indiana 46514

Bethany Fellowship, Inc.
6820 Auto Club Road, Minneapolis, Minnesota 55431

Blazon Mobile Homes Corporation
102 West Windsor Avenue, Elkhart, Indiana 46514

Boise Cascade Corporation
Recreational Products, 2746 Lamotte, Marlette, Michigan 48453

Boone Coach Manufacturing
3322 North Fifth Avenue, Laurel, Mississippi 39440

Boles-Aero, Inc.
8358 San Fernando Road, Sun Valley, California 91353

Bonanza Travelers, Inc.
Rt. 6, Box 168, Elkhart, Indiana 46514

Broken Arrow Mobile Home
Mfg., Inc.
P. O. Box 56, Broken Arrow, Oklahoma 74012

Camel Manufacturing Company
392 South Central, Knoxville, Tennessee 37902

Camper Corporation of America
Keenline Road, Jamestown, Indiana 46147

Camper Enterprises, Inc.
6501 Penn Avenue, South, Minneapolis, Minnesota 55423

Camp-Four Industries, Inc.
P. O. Box 849, Elkhart, Indiana 46514

Camp-Mor, Inc.
P. O. Box 147, Nappanee, Indiana 46550

Cannon Manufacturing Company
4916 Covington Highway, Decatur, Georgia 30032

Caravans International Mfg., Inc.
P. O. Box 32, Nappanee, Indiana 46550

Cascade Corporation
P. O. Box 636, Elkhart, Indiana 46514

Cavalier Industries, Inc.
P. O. Box 668, White Pigeon, Michigan 49099

Champion Home Builders Company
5573 E. North Street, Dryden, Michigan 48428

Char Mar Travel Trailers
P. O. Box 5080, Poland, Ohio 44514

Clay Camper Company
P. O. Box 65, Clay, West Virginia 25043

Coachmen Industries, Inc.
Box 379, Middlebury, Indiana 46540

Cobra Industries, Inc.
P. O. Box 1251, Elkhart, Indiana 46514

Coleman Camping Trailers, Inc.
250 North St. Francis Avenue, Wichita, Kansas 67202

Comanche Mobile Homes, Inc.
1200 Woodlawn Avenue, Elkhart, Indiana 46514

The Commodore Corporation
8712 West Dodge Road, Suite 4000, Omaha, Nebraska 68114

Concord Products, Inc.
3906 Main Avenue, Ashtabula, Ohio 44004

Condor Coach Corporation
11262 East Rush Street, S. El Monte, California 91733

Cox Trailers, Inc.
P. O. Box 338, Grifton, North Carolina

Cree Coaches, Inc.
M-119, Marcellus, Michigan 49067

Crossroad Travelers, Inc.
915 Country Club Drive, Elkhart, Indiana 46514

D & E Products, Inc.
Rt. 1, White Pigeon, Michigan 49099

Del Rey Industries, Inc.
3910 Cassopolis Street, Elkhart, Indiana 46514

Duke Travel Trailers
P. O. Box 397, Bristol, Indiana 46507

E-Z Kamper, Inc.
Loyal, Wisconsin 54446

Early Bird Industries, Inc.
P. O. Box 409, Three Rivers, Michigan 49093

Edgerton Enterprises
Edon, Ohio 43518

Elkhart Traveler Corporation
2211 West Wilden Avenue, Goshen, Indiana 46526

Explorer Motorhome Corporation
3021 Newport Blvd., Costa Mesa, California 97677

Fan Coach Company
Box 100, La Grange, Indiana 46761

Fleetwing Mobile Homes, Inc.
P. O. Box 83, Wakarusa, Indiana 46573

Fleetwood Enterprises, Inc.
3196 Meyers Street, P. O. Box 7638, Riverside, California 92503

The Flxible Company
326 N. Water Street, Loudonville, Ohio 44842

Forest City Industries
Highway 69 South, Forest City, Iowa 50436

Franklin Coach Company
Box 188, Nappanee, Indiana 46550

Gardner, Incorporated
Box 456, Bristol, Indiana 46507

Gem Industries, Inc.
7680 South Division, Grand Rapids, Michigan 49508

Giles Industries, Inc.
West Winchester Avenue, Middleboro, Kentucky 40965

Girard Metal Products, Inc.
P. O. Box 368, Newportville Road, Levittown, Pennsylvania 19058

Glastron Boat Company
Motor Home Division, P. O. Box 6249, Austin, Texas 78702

Globestar Industries, Inc.
P. O. Box 1248, Elkhart, Indiana 46514

Go-Tag-A-Long Manufacturing, Inc.
P. O. Box 55, Washingtonville, Ohio 44490

Golden Isles Travel Trailers, Inc.
P. O. Box 270, Douglas, Georgia 31533

Hawk Motor Homes, Inc.
142 Second St., Belleville, Michigan 48111

Highway Products, Inc.
789 Stow Street, Kent, Ohio 44240

Hillco, Incorporated
123 S. Shoop Avenue, Box 180 Wauseon, Ohio 43567

Holiday Rambler Corporation
400 Indiana Avenue, Wakarusa, Indiana 46573

The Huntsman, Incorporated
Highways 59 & 166, Chetopa, Kansas 67336

Hyland Manufacturing, Inc.
220 First Street, P. O. Box R, Carlisle, Iowa 50047

Islander Motorhome, Inc.
802 East Washington Street, Santa Ana, California 92701

Jayco, Incorporated
Rt. 1, Box 258, Goshen, Indiana 46526

Johnson Corporation
421 Monroe Street, Bellevue, Ohio 44811

The Johnson Corporation
111 Ohio Street, Monroeville, Indiana 46773

Juno Industries, Inc.
Rt. 3, Cassopolis, Michigan 49031

Kamp Craft Division
Fiber Tech, Inc., P. O. Box 475, Greensburg, Kansas 67054

Kamp King Division
The John D. Plant Company, Branford, Connecticut 06405

Kanzol Enterprises, Inc.
6345 Lumberjack Road, Riverdale, Michigan 48877

Kay-Dee Kampers, Inc.
P. O. Box 32, Rye, New York 10580

Krager Kustom Koach, Inc.
5676 Industrial Park Road, Winona, Minnesota 55987

Leisure Time Products, Inc.
Rt. 3, P. O. Box 232, Nappanee, Indiana 46550

Little Caboose Coach Company
Rt. 2, Maple Park, Illinois 60151

Lynn Manufacturing Corporation
Rt. 3, Industrial Park, Edwardsburg, Michigan 49112

Magnadyne Industries, Inc.
3580 Fisher Road, Columbus, Ohio 43204

Malcolm Industries
3 N. Hickory, Arlington Hts., Illinois 60004

Mallard Coach Corporation
P. O. Box 210, West Bend, Wisconsin 53095

McCain Industries Sales Corporation
3600 South Dixie Highway, Lima, Ohio 45804

McCoy Manufacturing & Sales Company
400 East Iowa, Indianola, Iowa 50125

Medford Industries, Inc.
P. O. Box 54, Elkhart, Indiana 46514

Midas-International Corporation
33 North Dearborn Street, Chicago, Illinois 60602

Mobile Scout Mfg. Corporation
2100 West Division, Arlington, Texas 76010

Mobile Tops, Incorporated
928 North Price, Junction City, Kansas 66441

Monitor Coach Company
P. O. Box 306, Wakarusa, Indiana 46573

Newmar Industries, Inc.
P. O. Box 42, Nappanee, Indiana 46550

National Merriway, Incorporated
1755 U. S. 90 West, Lake City, Florida 32055

Open Road Campers, Inc.
2601 Manhattan Beach Blvd., Redondo Beach, California 90278

Orbit Industries, Inc.
P. O. Box 98, Granger, Indiana 46530

Overland Manufacturing Company
855 East Lincoln Street, Nappanee, Indiana 46550

Pace Arrow Motor Homes
1126 North Fountain Way, Anaheim, California 92806

Park Hall, Inc.
1191 Dickman Road, P. O. Box 824, Battle Creek, Michigan 49016

Pathfinder Mobilehome, Inc.
400 Nason Street, Spencer, Wisconsin 54479

Plastimet Corporation
10801 North Lombard, Portland, Oregon 97203

Play-Mor Trailers, Incorporated
Highway 63, South, Westphalia, Missouri 65085

Pleasure Time Industries
P. O. Box 428, South Haven, Michigan 49090

Reco Division of Radio Equipment Co., Inc.
1202 S. Lafayette Boulevard, South Bend, Indiana 46618

Recreational Vehicles of America
Aalite Division, 1134 South Crystal Avenue, Benton Harbor, Michigan 49022

Ritz-Craft Travel Trailers
P. O. Box 107, Argos, Indiana 46501

Riviera Mfg. Company, Inc.
6899 East 49th Avenue, Commerce City, Colorado 80022

Rolite Trailer Division, Larson Industries, Inc.
P. O. Box 1370, Minneapolis, Minnesota 55440

Scully Industries, Incorporated
P. O. Box 1001, Elkhart, Indiana 46514

Serro Travel Trailer
Arona Road, Irwin, Pennsylvania 15642

Shasta Trailers, Incorporated
9401 Tampa Avenue, Northridge, California 91324

Sheergrain, Incorporated
Franklin and Loudon Streets, Chambersburg, Pennsylvania 17201

Siesta Travel Products, Inc.
926 East Lincoln Avenue, Goshen, Indiana 46526

Skamper Corporation
Box 338, Bristol, Indiana 46507

Ski Tow Mfg. Company, Inc.
3301 Phillips Street, Elkhart, Indiana 46514

Skyline Corporation
2520 By-Pass Road, Elkhart, Indiana 46514

The Snyder Trailer Company
Elm Street, Butler, Ohio 44822

Space Age Camper Company, Inc.
Rt. 1, Box 131B, Wakarusa, Indiana 46573

Starcraft Boat Division, Starcraft Corp.
P. O. Box 577, Goshen, Indiana 46526

Steury Boat Company, Inc.
924 East Lincoln Avenue, Goshen, Indiana 46526

Stutz Bearcat
P. O. Box 1184, Elkhart, Indiana 46514

Stutz Industries, Inc.
3199 West Mishawaka Road, P. O. Box 24, Elkhart, Indiana 46514

Swiss Colony Traveler, Inc.
P. O. Box 848, 1116 W. Mishawaka Road, Elkhart, Indiana 46514

Sycamore Mobile Homes, Inc.
P. O. Box 496, Goshen, Indiana 46526

Tennessee Travel Trailer Corporation
2714 N. Central Avenue, Knoxville, Tennessee 37917

Thunderbird Castles, Division of Alliance Machine Co.
P. O. Box 895, Alliance, Ohio 44601

TLR Corporation
630 Matteson, Bronson, Michigan 49028

Tour-A-Home, International
P. O. Box 467, Port Huron, Michigan 48060

Trade Winds Company, Inc.
1211 Depot Street, Manawa, Wisconsin 54949

Transit Industries
1044 North Nappanee, Elkhart, Indiana 46514

Travco Corporation
6894 Maple Valley Road, Brown City, Michigan 48416

Travel Equipment Corporation
Box 68, Elkhart, Indiana 46514

Travel Industries, Inc.
Box 108, Oswego, Kansas 67356

Travelier Industries, Inc.
P. O. Box 9036, Station A, Greenville, South Carolina 29604

Travel Queen Coaches, Inc.
7643 National Turnpike, Louisville, Kentucky 40214

Trotwood Trailers, Inc.
P. O. Box 3097, Trotwood, Ohio 45426

Utopia Coach Corporation
Box 456, Rt. 3, Elkhart, Indiana 46514

Vacation Homes, Incorporated
Silver Eagle Travel Trailer Division, P. O. Box 820, Elkhart, Indiana 46514

Vega Homes Corporation
P. O. Box 26, Syracuse, Indiana 46567

Vesely Company
2101 N. Lapeer Road, Lapeer, Michigan 48446

Wagnmaster Campers, Inc.
P. O. Box 309, Sturgis, Michigan 49091

Ward Manufacturing Company
500 Ford Boulevard, Hamilton, Ohio 45011

Wayne Division
Industries Road, Richmond, Indiana 47374

West Wind Trailer Company
Box 34, Long Point, Illinois 61333

Wheel Camper Corporation
580 W. Burr Oak, Centreville, Michigan 49032

Wick Building Systems
P. O. Box 378, Spencer, Wisconsin 54479

Williams Craft, Inc.
1701 West Division Street, Arlington, Texas 76010

Winnebago Industries, Inc.
Forest City, Iowa 50436

Winston Travelers, Inc.
P. O. Box 579, Haleyville, Alabama 35565

Wolverine Camper, Inc.
Rt. 1, Box 15, Lexington, North Carolina 27292

Wolverine Camper Company
East Cedar Street, Gladwin, Michigan 48624

Woods Motorhome, Inc.
10752 Gardena Avenue, Loma Linda, California 92354

Yellowstone, Inc.
2400 Mishawaka Road, Elkhart, Indiana 46514

Directory Section

- **National Parks**

- **National Forests**

- **Other Government Campsites**

- **State Parks**

- **Canadian Campsites**

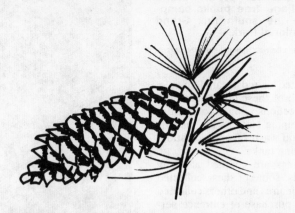

The spectacular beauty of America's national parks draws millions of visitors every year—including more campers in many places than the parks can adequately handle. Despite the fact that the government's Mission 66 program has enlarged and improved camping facilities, the problem of not enough room is greater today than ever.

The national parks were established primarily for preservation purposes. The more visitors the parks receive, the more problem there is in sticking to the purpose for their establishment. Too many facilities drawing too many visitors endanger preservation; on the other hand, it can be argued that the parks are of no real value unless they can be seen and enjoyed. This problem is one the Department of the Interior,

Without exception, the national parks are spectacular. Among those enjoying these outdoor attractions every year are millions of campers who seek and find peaceful solitude in the vast, healthful outdoors.

THE NATIONAL PARKS—
made for campers!

Congress and others in government are constantly wrestling with.

Be that as it may, millions of campers enjoy the scenic and recreational features of the National Park System. Each park is different and all of them offer a variety of recreational opportunities.

Limit stay

Because of the great influx of visitors, particularly in summer, it is usually necessary to limit the length of stay at the more popular campgrounds. Unfortunately, reservations are not accepted for campsites operated by the National Park Service. Assignments are made on a first-come, first-served basis.

Some sites are operated by concessionaires, and these may be reserved by direct contact with the concessionaire. Where special group camps exist, organizations may make advance reservations for camping in these areas. Each park issues detailed information on specific campgrounds,

which is made available to all camping residents.

Some of the national parks have wilderness areas. These afford opportunity for the self-sufficient camper, the backpacker, to hike into desert canyons or to tops of mountains where he will see few other humans. Improved facilities are not provided, and this type of camping should not be attempted by a novice. Because the dangers in such ventures are real and serious, it is required that the park superintendent or a park ranger be informed of plans for such trips and inspect the camper's gear.

Under extreme weather conditions or during a period of fire danger, a wilderness expedition may be ordered postponed until more favorable conditions prevail.

All of the national parks will supply information in advance, but you should write ahead of time. Allow at least one month for a reply. In connection with advance information the Park Service has made this announcement:

"No matter which type of camping you are contemplating, you may write to the superintendents of the areas you plan to visit, requesting full information on facilities available or possibilities of a wilderness trip, if that is your goal. When you arrive at the park, consult with the park ranger, who will answer your questions and attempt to make your stay enjoyable."

No fires

In many national park areas you will have to forego the joy of a campfire. Wood is short in many places. And because the campsites are often close together and grouped in large numbers, too many campfires may cause air pollution.

Most campgrounds encourage campers to use charcoal or campstoves that burn bottled fuel for campfire cooking. In some parks the gathering of deadwood from the ground is prohibited, and trees may not be cut in any.

Both tents and recreational vehicles are welcome in all parks and can be

Visitors make use of the Grand Canyon Village free public campground on the south rim, Grand Canyon National Park.

accommodated in most campgrounds. However, all of these do not have full utility connections. Some parks offer sanitary dumping stations for the disposal of liquid wastes from recreation-vehicle holding tanks.

Various fees are charged at many campgrounds, some of these collected by concessionaires and others collected through the purchase of entrance permits or user permits. The length of stay often is determined by the season, the facilities available and the demand for sites by newcomers.

Most parks offer interpretive programs such as nature walks, guided tours and campfire talks. These are conducted by park personnel.

Special regulations

Special regulations are few, but are strictly enforced. Here are the ones to pay special attention to:

1. Natural features. Every area of the National Park System is a museum of natural or human history; therefore, removal or destruction of any feature is not allowed. This also applies to manmade facilities.

2. Wildlife. Do not feed animals. Injuries to campers by bears or other animals are usually due to the campers' attempt to feed them. Observe them, but do not interfere with them. Food supplies should be locked up or hung out of reach.

3. Fire. Confine your fire to fireplaces in established campgrounds and picnic areas. Before you retire for the night or leave your campsite unattended for any reason, make certain that your campfire is entirely out. Wilderness campers usually are required to register for a fire permit.

4. Trash. Keep your camp clean by placing all garbage and trash in containers provided. All combustible material should be burned in the fireplaces. In wilderness camps, incombustible trash—including cans—should be carried out or disposed of as directed.

5. Pets. Pets are allowed in the parks if on leash or otherwise under physical restraint.

6. Noise. Common courtesy is the rule. Avoid noise, especially late at night and early in the morning.

Types of campgrounds

The National Park System offers three basic types of campground facilities. These are rated A, B and C.

Campground, Type A. This is the best campground and the Park Service's general descriptions of this type and the other two types are under-

stated descriptions. Often, you can expect more.

Type A is family camping area with roads, parking space and designated individual sites. Drinking water, toilets and refuse cans are provided on a community basis. Each campground has a designated capacity based upon the number of campsites therein.

Campsites in Type A campgrounds are designed to accommodate an individual, a family or a small party. Such sites include parking space, a fireplace

or grill, a table and bench combination and space for the campers' shelter. At walk-in campgrounds, or in the walk-in section, space for parking a vehicle is provided but not as an integral part of the campsite.

Camping area, Type B. An area (other than a campground) designated and used for camping by individuals, families or camping parties. Camping areas are accessible by either road or trail, and may be somewhat removed from the more developed areas of the

Campers in the national parks often get glimpses of wild animals, large and small, but seldom does one pose so willingly as this buffalo at Wind Cave National Park in South Dakota.

park. Facilities provided are minimum, generally limited to access roads, basic sanitary facilities, a limited number of fireplaces and tables.

Trail camps fall within this category, and shelters of the Adirondack or fully enclosed type may be divided. Each camping area has an "assigned," as differentiated from "designed," capacity based on the number of camping spaces therein. Superintendents assign to each camping area a capacity figure, in terms of camping spaces, based on a realistic evaluation of acreage involved, topography and facilities provided.

A camping space in a camping area is one which is normally occupied by an individual, family or party.

Group camp, Type C. A group camp is an area designated for use by organized groups, such as Boy Scouts, school groups or other large parties. It is composed of one or more group spaces, which is provided with a large fireplace, several tables and parking space for buses or a number of cars.

Capacity of group camps is rated on the basis of the number of group spaces within the camp.

On the following pages are photographs and abbreviated descriptions of America's national parks and other recreational lands administered by the Department of the Interior. Special attention is given to those features most applicable to camping and interesting to campers.

ACADIA NATIONAL PARK

Box 338
Bar Harbor, Maine 04609
Camping season — May 1-October 15

"Green waves and swirling kelp are Acadia's outer boundaries. Granite mountains and spruce-fringed lakes are its center. It is a place of many moods, sun-drenched islands in a sparkling sea . . . a fog-shrouded fiord . . . wind whispering in the trees.

"Teaming tide pools and a startled fawn hint of Acadia's animal life. Plants of the arctic mingle here with those of sunny clime. And the soaring bald eagle is lord of the sky—a friendly blue or forbidding gray realm that encompasses the Acadian archipelago.

"From the summit of Cadillac Mountain on a clear day, Mount Desert Rock can be seen 27 miles out to sea. This surf-lashed reef is losing its fight against the waves. Someday it will wear away and disappear beneath the water...."

This description is part of a booklet entitled "Acadia" which is published by the National Park Service and sold by the Superintendent of Documents for 20 cents. This is one

One of the most beautiful camping spots in all America is Paradise Campground, Mount Rainier National Park.

National Park Service Photo

publication that is a must for anyone contemplating a trip to Acadia National Park.

Acadia offers camping at two Type A campgrounds: Blackwoods, 355 sites; and Seawall, 218 sites. Both have water and flush toilets and Blackwoods provides a sanitary dumping station.

Recreational pursuits especially enjoyed are swimming, boating, fishing and horseback riding.

BIG BEND NATIONAL PARK

Big Bend National Park,
Texas 79834
Camping season—all year

This huge park of more than 700,000 acres is made up of spectacular mountain and desert scenery, enclosed in the great bend of the Rio Grande River. It is more suggestive of northern Mexico than the United States. Mountain ranges rise abruptly from arid flat lands and great expanses of desert sweep away to distant horizons.

Despite the fact that this national park is located on the southern border of the United States, it still has four seasons. Winter is described as being nippy in the mountains and comfortably warm during the day in the lowlands.

Once or twice a year snow falls in the mountains. Spring arrives early, and lingers. Some desert plants bloom all through the year, but a slow succession of blooms may be seen beginning in late February and continuing at higher elevations into May.

Temperatures

Summer temperatures in the desert and the river valley hover above 100° during the day. Obviously, this is the time of year to go to the mountains where the nights are cool and the daytime temperatures average about 85°.

Autumn is mostly sunshine and fresh air, not too hot and not too cold. This is a delightful time to visit Big Bend.

Big Bend offers two Type A campgrounds: Chisos Mountains Lower Basin, 59 sites; Rio Grande Village, 66 sites. The latter also offer facilities for trailers. This is operated by a concessionaire. Boating, fishing and horseback riding are the main recreational pursuits.

A modern camper travels the broad highways in scenic Glacier National Park.

Montana Highway Commission Photo

BRYCE CANYON NATIONAL PARK

Bryce Canyon, Utah 84717
Camping season—depends on weather

"Before you and below you, as you stand on the rim of Paunsaugunt Plateau, lies a city of stone: cathedrals, spires and windowed walls, structures of countless shapes and sizes delicately tinted in shades of pink and red and orange and softened by grays and whites and creams —all sculptured by the never-lagging forces of erosion. These are the Pink Cliffs of Bryce Canyon."

This is Bryce Canyon National Park, situated on a plateau ranging from 8,000 to 9,000 feet in elevation. The two Type A campgrounds are North, 111 sites, and Sunset, 114 sites. Sunset and Loops C and D of North are designed for use by tent, pickup camper units, motor homes

and tent-type trailers. House trailer-types, regardless of size, are allowed only in Loops A and B of North.

The chief recreational pursuits are trail hikes and horseback rides. Numerous scenic tours, audio-visual programs, exhibits and some wild scenery round out the other main attractions to campers.

CANYONLANDS NATIONAL PARK

Post Office Building
Moab, Utah 84532
Camping season—all year

This national park is a geological wonderland of rock, spires and mesas rising more than 7,800 feet. It is one of the newest national parks, established in 1964. It encompasses 257,640 acres.

The National Park Service describes this new national park as "indescribably diverse." This is apt, for the landscape is made up of arches, needles, spires and other amazing rock formations. Inside the park boundaries also are bold mesas, crenelated buttes, broad plains, rolling rapids, sandbars and intricately dissected tributary canyons.

The Colorado River slices through the center of the park and is joined within the park by the Green River. The park is bisected by the canyons of the rivers, dividing it into the Island in the Sky and the Needles districts.

Canyonlands encompasses 257,-640 acres and offers two small Type B campgrounds, one at "Island in the Sky" and the other at "Squaw Flat." No water is supplied at the campgrounds.

CRATER LAKE NATIONAL PARK

Box 7
Crater Lake, Oregon 97604
Camping season—varies from June to October

Crater Lake is Oregon's only national park. It is one of the nation's most beautiful, a paradise for hikers, campers and fishermen. Crater Lake itself is the result of Mt. Mazama "blowing its top." Those who have seen it say it is the world's most beautiful lake. More than 21 square miles, the lake is surrounded by towering walls 500 to 2,000 feet above the water and accented by rugged prominences, such as Cloud Cap and Llao Rock. Adding to the interest and beauty of the lake are the two islands, Phantom Ship and an inactive cone, Wizard Island.

Park campgrounds can accommodate trailers up to 18 feet, but there are no utility connections. The four Type A campgrounds are: Annie Springs, 26 sites; Lost Creek, 12 sites; Mazama, 198 sites; and Rim, 54 sites. All of these provide water and flush toilets, and Mazama provides a sanitary dumping station. Many species of wildlife, both flora and fauna, may be observed within the park's 160,290 acres.

EVERGLADES NATIONAL PARK

Box 279
Homestead, Florida 33030
Camping season—open all year

This is the largest remaining subtropical wilderness in continental United States. It embraces extensive fresh- and salt-water areas, open everglades prairies, mangrove forests and abundant wildlife. Contain-

A relatively new campground in Shenandoah National Park is this one at Loft Mountain, one mile from Skyline Drive. It accommodates 200 tents or recreational vehicles.

ing 1,400,533 acres, this national park was established in 1947, with subsequent boundary changes made as late as 1960.

Some of the habitats, such as the everglades themselves, and some of the animals--crocodiles, manatee, roseate spoonbill, reddish egret, wood ibis (really a stork) and bald eagles--are rare or unseen elsewhere in the United States. Among other inhabitants are the alligator, snook, tarpon, pink shrimp, royal palm, mahogany and mangroves.

Type A campsites are available at Long Pine Key, 108 sites, and Flamingo, 239 sites. Three Type B camping sites are available by boat only. Everglades back country is quite primitive and potentially dangerous. It's no place in which to be lost, and any comtemplated trips must be cleared with the proper authorities.

Fees

Camping fees at the two drive-in campgrounds are $2.25 (plus tax) per day per site. Flamingo offers some walk-in sites at $1.50 (plus tax) per day. Two sanitary dumping stations are located at Flamingo; there is none at Long Pine Key. Boating and fishing are enjoyed by most campers, and two trails have been marked for canoeists.

By all means, before traveling to this national park write the park headquarters for a packet of important information folders. The terrain

features, the wildlife and other factors make it mandatory that you be properly equipped and prepared for camping here. Type A campgrounds require no special preparation, but some of the activities do.

GLACIER NATIONAL PARK

West Glacier, Montana 59936
Camping season—open June-September

This park contains 1,013,129 acres of superb Rocky Mountain scenery, with numerous glaciers and lakes nestling among the highest peaks. It forms part of the Waterton-Glacier International Peace Park, established by the United States and Canada in 1932.

Glacier is one of the outstanding wilderness areas in the National Park System, an unspoiled primitive region. This is a place where a camper can enjoy almost unbelievable solitude, can find peace and quiet to sooth the jangled nerves and ease the tensions of a high-speed, mechanized civilization.

Many trails

This is one of the greatest trail parks, with more than 1,000 miles of trails inviting exploration. The trails are well marked, and there is no need to worry about venomous snakes or such unpleasant plants as poison oak or poison ivy. Trail trips vary from short, 15-minute walks along self-guided nature trails to hikes that may extend over several days. Some hikes are organized and led by ranger-naturalists. There are shelter cabins at numerous points.

Type A campgrounds include these: Apgar, 224 sites; Avalanche, 168 sites; Bowman Creek, 7 sites; Bowman Lake, 48 sites; Fish Creek, 180 sites; Logging Creek, 10 sites; Many Glacier, 132 sites; Mud Creek, 3 sites; Quartz Creek, 5 sites; Rising Sun, 82 sites; River, 7 sites; Sprague Creek, 42 sites; St. Mary Lake, 206 sites; and Two Medicine, 127 sites. There are three designated Type B campgrounds and 39 back-country camps, also rated Type B.

Study the maps and information brochures supplied by park headquarters before bringing large trailers into the park. Some campgrounds cannot accommodate these, although others have facilities for them. Six camps have sanitary dumping stations.

Hiking, horseback riding, fishing, boating and swimming are popular activities among campers. Camping limit in the park during July and August is 14 days.

This view of the east side of Lassen Peak is a favorite of visitors to Lassen Volcanic National Park.

National Park Service Photo

GRAND CANYON NATIONAL PARK

Box 129
Grand Canyon, Arizona 86023
Camping season—all year, except at 3 locations

The Grand Canyon of Arizona, which is inside the park boundaries, has also been called the greatest of the Seven Wonders of the World. The canyon walls are a mile deep, and at the bottom the Colorado River rushes toward the sea. The river's great canyon is 217 miles long and 4 to 18 miles wide. Rising from the depths of the canyon are whole mountain ranges, their tops only slightly below the rim of the gorge. The main canyon is fed by scores of side canyons and ravines that are almost as splendid as the famous canyon itself. By day the Grand Canyon is a picture of molten color; by moonlight it is a blue mystery.

A visit to the canyon affords opportunity for many kinds of recreation. One of the most famous is the pack trail which descends from the south rim to the very depths of the canyon. This is called Bright Angel Trail. Hikers may also follow this trail, and many do.

At the south rim, various facilities are offered such as barber shop and beauty shop, a camper's service building with shower facilities, a launderette, a snack bar and bags of ice.

The park operates three Type A campgrounds: Bright Angel Point, 78 sites; Desert View, 50 sites; and Mather (Grand Canyon Village), 331 sites. In addition are five Type B campgrounds. A sanitary dumping station is located at Mather.

Horseback riding, mule trains into the canyon and hiking are the main recreational pursuits by campers. Some 673,575 acres make up the Grand Canyon National Park, much of it perpendicular. In summer, early arrival is absolutely necessary. For those who plan to hike, it is important that they secure a copy of information for hikers issued at the park office.

GRAND TETON NATIONAL PARK

Box 67
Moose, Wyoming 83012
Camping season—May-October

Encompassed in Grand Teton National Park are 310,358 acres. These acres include the lofty peaks of the Grand Tetons, blue-gray pyramids of rock and glacier, their canyons and forested lower slopes and the basin called Jackson Hole. The mountains are exceptionally striking because they rise steeply 7,000 feet above the almost-level

basin of Sagebrush Flats and Morainal Lakes.

This is an unspoiled wilderness which offers limitless opportunities for recreation. You can camp by the lakes, swim, fish, watch and photograph birds, take float trips on the Snake River, horseback ride or hike the trails and climb a mountain, if you wish. Park facilities are crowded much of the time in summer, and many campers find these mountains more to their liking during the months of May, September and October.

In spring, willows, aspens and cottonwoods erupt from dormancy to add the soft glow of opening buds. Autumn is often the most colorful time of the year, with yellow, gold and red splashed about in generous fashion. The park may be visited in winter, of course, but camping is made by special arrangement. The campgrounds are closed.

Grand Teton National Park operates five Type A campgrounds and one excellent trailer village. The

A camping trip to Rocky Mountain National Park would not be complete without a hike to beautiful Bear Lake.

National Park Service Photo

trailer village is located at Colter Bay. The campgrounds are: Colter Bay, 520 sites; Gros Ventre, 207 sites; Jenny Lake, 85 sites; Lizard Point, 60 sites; and Signal Mountain, 80 sites. Sanitary dumping stations are located at Colter Bay and Gros Ventre. Activities include swimming, boating, fishing and horseback riding.

GREAT SMOKY MOUNTAINS NATIONAL PARK

Gatlinburg, Tennessee 37738
Camping season—all year, except at designated campgrounds

This is the most visited of all national parks. It forms the boundary between North Carolina and Tennessee and is a majestic climax of the Appalachian highlands. With outlines softened by a dense forest mantle, the mountains stretch in sweeping troughs and mighty billows to the horizon. The name, "Great Smokies," is derived from the smokelike haze that envelopes these mountains.

The forests of the park, composing most of it, are virtually unspoiled. They are very similar to those which the early settlers met. Some of the valleys of the Smokies held the settlers' isolated farms; many of the log cabins and barns stand today as

monuments to a pioneer way of life that is almost gone.

Some 1,400 kinds of flowering plants grow in the park. Broadleaf trees predominate in the forests, except along the crest of the mountains—which rise to more than 6,000 feet—where conifer forests like those of central Canada find suitable climate.

At the eastern entrance to the park lies the town of Cherokee, the home of the eastern tribe of the Cherokee Indians. Throughout the

park are some 600 miles of horse and foot trails, which wind along streams and through forests into the high country. Spectacular views and waterfalls along many of the trails are popular hiking objectives.

Eight campgrounds

There are eight developed campgrounds and four primitive camping areas in the park. There are no showers or hookups for trailers. From June 1 through Labor Day, the camping limit is 7 days. Disposal stations for trailer holding tanks are located at Smokemont, Cades Cove, Elkmont

the road from Sugarlands Visitor Center.

Primitive campgrounds have no developed water supply. All water in these areas must be boiled or chemically treated before it is safe to drink. Pit toilets are provided, and the camping limit is 14 days.

The Type A campgrounds include Balsam Mountain at Heintooga Overlook near the Blue Ridge Parkway, 47 sites; Cades Cove, 224 sites; Chimneys, 80 sites; Cosby, 230 sites; Deep Creek, 151 sites; Elkmont, 340

and Cosby campgrounds, and across sites; Look Rock, 92 sites; and Smokemont, 170 sites.

Along the Appalachian Trail, which traverses the park, are some 25 trail shelter sites. In addition to these and four Type B campgrounds, are some 56 miscellaneous camping sites, also rated Type B. Boating, fishing, horseback riding and hiking are enjoyed by many campers. Incidentally, some of the trout streams are reserved exclusively for children. The acreage of the Great Smoky Mountains National Park totals 515,225. The mountains constitute the loftiest range east of the Black Hills.

HALEAKALA NATIONAL PARK

Box 456
Kahului, Maui, Hawaii 96732
Camping season—open all year

This is a national park built around a volcano—the 10,023-foot Haleakala. Its crater is one of the largest and most colorful known. In it grows a species of the rare silver sword.

Only one campground is available within the park. This is Hosmer Grove, near the north entrance. It is a Type B facility with five campsites.

HAWAII VOLCANOES NATIONAL PARK

Hawaii Volcanoes National Park, Hawaii 96718
Camping season—all year

The celebrated author, James A. Michener, once described his introduction to Hawaii Volcanoes National Park in these words: "A smell of sulphur . . . a sound of crackling as if the surface of the earth were being torn apart . . . the sight of fire ebbing and exploding in the dark night . . . above me the snow-covered tip of the most massive single mountain in the world . . . around me the

tion of 13,250 feet. The trail is over lava rock and is marked with piles of rocks called *ahu's*. In places the trail may not be recognized. It is an extremely arduous climb, taking about three days for experienced climbers. No one is permitted to undertake the climb without proper equipment and a permit.

Camping and hiking regulations in this park are stringent, but by becoming properly oriented and equipped, a camper may enjoy both hiking and climbing.

Two Type A campgrounds are operated and one Type B. The Type A campgrounds are Kipuka Nene, 6 sites, and Namakani Paio, 6 sites.

Horseback riders survey Haleakala Crater in Haleakala National Park, Hawaii.

National Park Service Photo

The National Park Service maintains three cabins within the crater for visitor use. Each cabin has bunks, blankets, water, cookstove, firewood and kerosene lamps, and accommodates 12 persons. These cabins can be reached only by foot or horse. Travel is permitted within the crater only by hiking or horseback riding. Total acreage is 26,402.

density of the tropical jungle with exotic trees and lovely flowers. . . ."

The 220,344 acres that make up this park cover areas of impressive, active volcanism, luxuriant vegetation, rare plants and animals, and snow. You can enjoy all of these, one or two at a time, at elevations ranging from sea level to some 13,000 feet above sea level.

The most arduous trail is the trail to the top of Mauna Loa. This starts at an elevation of 6,662 feet and goes up the mountainside for 18 miles, ending near the summit at an eleva-

The Type B campground at Kamoamoa offers 10 campsites.

HOT SPRINGS NATIONAL PARK

Box 1219
Hot Springs National Park, Arkansas 71901
Camping season—open all year

As national parks go, this is a small one in terms of acreage. Within its boundaries are 3,535 acres, 47 mineral hot springs and one Type A

Canoe camping is preferred by many who visit Isle Royale National Park in Lake Superior.

National Park Service Photo

campground. This is at Gulpha Gorge, with 57 campsites. A sanitary dumping station is part of the modern facilities at Gulpha Gorge. Between May 1 and September 14, the time limit is 14 days, 30 days during the remainder of the year. Food, ice and other camping supplies may be obtained in the nearby city of Hot Springs. Walking trails lead from the campground up onto the mountainsides. Swimming is not available, but bathing in the hot springs at concessionaire-operated bathhouses is a major visitor activity.

ISLE ROYALE NATIONAL PARK

87 North Ripley Street
Houghton, Michigan 49931
Camping season—May-October

This park takes in a forested island of 539,341 acres. It is the largest island in Lake Superior and is distinguished for its wilderness character. It protects a great moose herd and such other animals as wolves. It is an excellent park for canoe and boat camping and for backpacking in the wilderness areas.

Numerous campsite locations are available to a limited number of persons. Three Type A campgrounds include: Daisy Farm (Rock Harbor), 18 sites; Tobin-Rock Harbor, 11 sites; and Washington Creek, 16 sites. The other 19 small campgrounds offer Type B facilities.

Several campgrounds charge a fee of $1 per night. Some are accessible only by boat, others only by trail and some by boat and trail. None is accessible by road. Swimming, boating and hiking are the main recreational features. A food store is operated at Rock Harbor.

KINGS CANYON NATIONAL PARK

Three Rivers, California 93271
Camping season—May-October

This park of 460,330 acres is a mountain wilderness dominated by two enormous canyons of the Kings River and by the summit peaks of the High Sierra. The former General Grant National Park, with its giant sequoias, is a detached section of Kings Canyon National Park.

All of the main campgrounds are Type A, and include Azalea, 114 sites; Cedar Grove I, 108 sites; Cedar Grove II, 81 sites; Cedar Grove III, 67 sites; Cedar Grove IV, 113 sites; Crystal Springs, 64 sites; Sunset, 225 sites; and Swale, 56 sites. A trailer camp with Type A facilities is also maintained at Cedar Grove.

Fishing, horseback riding and hiking are favored recreational activities. Wilderness areas attract many hikers and backpackers.

LASSEN VOLCANIC NATIONAL PARK

Mineral, California 96063
Camping season—varies, usually May to mid-October

Lassen Peak is the only recently active volcano in conterminous United States. It erupted between 1914 and 1917. It is an exhibit of impressive volcanic phenomena.

More than 100,000 acres of evergreen forest, a scattering of 50 wilderness lakes and almost as many mountains are dominated by the grandeur of Lassen Peak. This plug-dome of 10,457 feet is a sleeping volcano which lies at the southern tip of the Cascades. The Lassen Park

Many of the wonder spots in the national parks are reached only by the hiker.

National Park Service Photo

Road winds around three sides of the peak and affords many beautiful views of the volcano and views of woodlands and meadows, clear brooks and lakes. The park boasts of some 150 miles of foot trails, 50 kinds of mammals, 150 kinds of birds, stands of pines, firs, cedars and broadleaf trees, as well as aspens and cottonwoods and many wildflowers. Fishing, boating and hiking are favorite outdoor activities.

Of eight established campgrounds, four are Type A. These are Butte Lake, 98 sites; Manzanita Lake, 373 sites; Sulfur Works, 25 sites; and Summit Lake, 94 sites. There are no hookups for electricity, water or sewerage. Trailers are admitted, however.

MAMMOTH CAVE NATIONAL PARK

Mammoth Cave, Kentucky 45259
Camping season—April-October
(all year at one campground)

This is a national park whose main attraction is inside the earth. This is indeed a mammoth cave. It is a series of underground passages, 150 miles of which have been explored. The formations are of beautiful limestone, gypsum and cave onyx. It contains deep pits and high domes, and a river runs through its passages 360 feet below the land surface.

Numerous tours and programs are conducted the year around at the park, most of which require extra fees. Outside the cave are some 52,000 acres of woodlands, trails

and fields. A one-hour cruise is available on the Green River. Boating and fishing are popular pastimes.

Two of the campgrounds are Type A. These are Headquarters, New, 145 sites; and Headquarters, Old, 70 sites. A Type B campground offers 12 sites, and a Type C is available to groups. An extra charge of $2 per site per day is made at the Headquarters, New, campground. This campground also maintains a sanitary dumping station.

MESA VERDE NATIONAL PARK

Mesa Verde National Park, Colorado 81330
Camping season—April-October

Campfire sing at Crow Wing Wilderness Saddle Trail dedication at Huntersville, Minnesota. Ceremonies included a two day trail ride.

For many years, beginning about the time of the birth of Christ, Indians lived in this region. They farmed, fashioned tools and household utensils and traded with other Indian groups. For some reason, about 700 years ago, they abandoned their homes and moved to the south and east. Within the more-than-50,000-acre park today are preserved pit-nouses and masonry pueblos on mesa tops, and majestic cliff dwellings—the villages of the people who no longer live here.

The chief park ranger says that "Because of the need to protect the many archeological sites in the park, we restrict camping to only one area called Morfield campground."

This is a Type A facility and contains 475 sites. Facilities are available for 17 groups. A sanitary dumping station is maintained.

The chief recreational pursuit other than hiking is horseback riding.

MOUNT McKINLEY NATIONAL PARK

McKinley Park, Alaska 99755
Camping season—June 1-September 10

Mount McKinley National Park is a subarctic wilderness. It includes the highest mountain on the North American continent, 20,320-foot Mount McKinley. The park itself contains 300,030 square miles, embracing 1,939,493 acres—which constitutes only a small part of the vast wilderness area stretching out from the mountain.

Topographically, the park is varied. From its towering mountains to lowlands and stream valleys to the tundra, there is enough stark beauty to delight the photographer for a lifetime. The wild inhabitants are many, and some of them are huge, such as the grizzly bears. Caribou wander over the tundra as they have for centuries.

Since Alaska became a state more and more visitors from the other 49 states are visiting the national parklands in Alaska. Mount McKinley National Park boasts of four Type A campgrounds, Two Type B campgrounds and unlimited areas for back country camping. The Type A campgrounds are: Morino, 15 sites; Savage, 24 sites; Teklanika, 18 sites; and Wonder Lake, 28 sites. Other than hiking, fishing is the main outdoor sport here. The Morino campgrounds operates a camp food store, and at Savage and Wonder Lake trailers and motor homes may use sanitary dumping stations.

MOUNT RAINIER NATIONAL PARK

Longmire, Washington 98397
Camping season—varies all year

Mount Rainier is the greatest single-peak glacial system in the United States. On its lower elevations are dense forests and flowered meadows. The mountain is a towering, iceclad, dormant volcano. The national park is dominated by this peak. It rises 14,410 feet and is without doubt the most superb landmark of the Pacific Northwest. The park's 378 square miles extend from Mount Rainier eastward to the

Cascade range crest, embracing 241,992 acres.

Camping at established campgrounds is limited to 14 days from July 1 through Labor Day, 30 days after Labor Day. The campgrounds range from about 2,000 feet elevation to more than 6,000 feet elevation. You have several excellent ones to choose from.

Type A camping facilities offered are: Cougar Rock, 200 sites; Longmire, 110 sites; Ohanapecosh, 232 sites; Paradise, 65 sites; Sunrise, 63 sites; and White River, 125 sites. There are no sanitary dumping facilities at these campgrounds. Longmire is used for overflow campers only.

Other than hiking, the favorite outdoor sports are fishing and skiing.

OLYMPIC NATIONAL PARK

600 East Park Avenue
Port Angeles, Washington 98362
Camping season—varies all year

The 896,599 acres of this mountain wilderness contain the finest remnant of Pacific Northwest rain forest. Within the park are active glaciers and the rare Roosevelt elk. Wildflowers grow in profusion. The park is dotted with numerous lakes and gives off the many sounds of swift, mountain streams. Within the park is the wettest winter climate in the conterminous United States. On the west side of the Olympic Peninsula the yearly precipitation exceeds 140 inches in some sections. This park is a naturalist's delight.

Some of the campgrounds at lower elevations are open all year. In the height of the summer season, however, facilities are quite crowded and each site is limited to a maximum of 14 days use. The 16 Type A campgrounds are: Altaire, 29 sites; Deer Park, 10 sites; Dosewallips, 33 sites; Elwha, 23 sites; Fairholm, 90 sites; Graves Creek, 45 sites; Heart O'The Hills, 100 sites; Hoh, 95 sites; July Creek, 31 sites; Kalaloch, 180 sites; Mora, 91 sites; North Fork Quinault, 10 sites; Olympic Hot Springs, 50 sites; Queets, 12 sites; Soleduck, 84 sites; and Staircase, 50 sites. A trailer village is maintained at Lake Crescent and 100 sites are available. Extra fee is $2 per day. A primitive campsite is available at Ozette Lake for eight persons. Erickson's Bay campground offers 15 campsites, reachable only by boat. Camping is not allowed outside authorized campgrounds. A sanitary dumping

This campfire program at Acadia National Park is typical of nighttime scenes at campgrounds throughout the national park system.

National Park Service Photo

station is maintained at Kalaloch.

Fishing, boating, swimming and hiking are the chief pastime activities.

PLATT NATIONAL PARK

Box 201
Sulfur, Oklahoma 73086
Camping season—varies

Platt National Park is quite small in land area—911 acres—but it is popular because of the numerous cold mineral springs with distinctive properties in the water.

Actually, this national park is an oasis of woodlands in the prairie. It is a refreshing miniature of a broad sweep of nature: wooded valleys, rolling hills, mineral and fresh water springs and sparkling streams. Most of the springs can be classified as sulfur springs, three as bromide springs.

Camping is limited to 30 days except in summer when the limitation is 14 days. The two Type A campgrounds are at Cold Springs, 64 sites; and Rock Creek, 111 sites. Bicycling, fishing, horseback riding, swimming and hiking are popular pastimes.

ROCKY MOUNTAIN NATIONAL PARK

Estes Park, Colorado 80517
Camping season—varies

This park is one of the most diversified sections of the Rocky

Mountains, encompassing 262,324 acres and containing 107 named peaks in excess of 10,000 feet. High mountains, alpine lakes, glacier-sculptured valleys, rugged gorges and vast areas of alpine tundra are features of this park—one of the nost spectacular, yet most easily accessible high mountain areas in America.

Popular pastimes include fishing, skiing and ice skating. Horseback riding and hiking are favorite activities among campers. Back country camping is extremely popular in this park. A list of back country campsites is available from park rangers. A permit is required.

The six Type A campgrounds are: Aspenglen, 110 sites; Endovalley, 73 sites; Glacier Basin, 185 sites; Longs Peak, 35 sites; Moraine Park, 256 sites; Timber Creek, 97 sites. Several good Type B campgrounds are accessible by trail only. Sanitary dumping facilities are provided at Glacier Basin and Timber Creek.

SEQUOIA NATIONAL PARK

Three Rivers, California 93271
Camping season—varies

Sequoia's 386,862 acres include great groves of giant sequoias, world's largest and among the oldest living things. Within this park is some of the most magnificent High Sierra scenery, including Mount Whitney, highest peak in conterminous United States.

Self-guiding nature trails and the

more than 900 miles of high country trails attract thousands of hikers. Saddle horses are available for trails, and many of the trails are excellent saddle trails. Trout fishing is available in almost every lake and stream. The Type A campgrounds include: Buckeye Flat, 29 sites; Dorst One-Four, 257 sites; Lodgepole, 317 sites; Paradise, 62 sites; Potwisha, 44 sites; and Sunset Rock, 72 sites. A sanitary dumping station is maintained at Lodgepole.

SHENANDOAH NATIONAL PARK

Luray, Virginia 22835
Camping season—varies

The Shenandoah National Park represents an outstanding portion of the Blue Ridge Mountains. From north to south it is traversed by the Skyline Drive, a scenic road following the crest of the mountains. Overlooks and trails afford magnificent vistas of historic Shenandoah Valley. The park contains a wealth of wildflowers and is mostly covered in hardwood forests.

There are approximately 200 miles of foot trails in Shenandoah National Park. These include a 95-mile section of the famous Appalachian Trail, closely paralleling the Skyline Drive. This park is a favorite of Washingtonians and residents of Virginia and Maryland. Twenty-one open trailside shelters are located along the trail in the park. These have tables, spring water, garbage cans and toilets. There is no charge for their use. The open shelters are available for use throughout the

year. The park covers 193,538 acres.

Four Type A campgrounds are operated, the one at Big Meadows being open all year. It contains 251 campsites. The others are: Lewis Mountain, 32 sites; Loft Mountain, 240 sites; and Matthews Arm, 188 sites. Horseback riding and fishing are favorite pastimes. Dumping stations are available at all the Type A campgrounds.

VIRGIN ISLANDS NATIONAL PARK

Box 1707
Charlotte Amalie, St. Thomas, V.I. 00801
Camping season—all year

This park was established in 1956. Its 15,150 acres constitute and island of lush, green hills and white, sandy beaches. The park is rich in tropical plant and animal life. Favorite activities include swimming, snorkeling, fishing and hiking, One Type A campground at Cinnamon Bay has 47 sites. A Type B campground is operated at Lamsure.

WIND CAVE NATIONAL PARK

Hot Springs, South Dakota 57747
Camping season—May 19-September 20

The 28,059 acres of Wind Cave National Park are in the scenic Black Hills. The park is built around beautiful limestone caverns decorated by boxwork and calcite crystal formations. Within the park are elk, deer,

pronghorn, prairie dog towns and a bison herd.

The park preserves in relatively unspoiled condition part of the original prairie grassland. The strong currents of air that blow alternately in and out of the cave suggested the park's name. This strange phenomenon is believed to be caused by changes in atmospheric pressure. When outside pressure drops below that of the cave's interior, wind blows outward; when it rises, wind blows into the cave.

There is only one campground and this is at Elk Mountain. It is a Type A facility and has 100 sites. There are no utility connections for trailers.

YELLOWSTONE NATIONAL PARK

Yellowstone National Park, Wyoming 83020
Camping season—varies

This is the oldest of America's national parks, having been established in 1872. More than 2,000,000 acres of it lie in Wyoming, some 142,000 acres in Montana and more than 31,000 acres in Idaho. The gross acreage, including federal and non-federal lands, totals 2,221,772.

This is the world's greatest geyser area, with about 3,000 geysers and hot springs. Also in the park are spectacular falls and canyons of the Yellowstone River.

Yellowstone's main centers often are overrun with visitors in the summer months. But it is so large that the person who wishes to get away from people and crowds may find sanctuary off the beaten path. To most visitors, the four main subjects of interest at Yellowstone are thermal features, the Grand Canyon of the Yellowstone, Yellowstone Lake and the wildlife. The wildlife is extremely interesting in all seasons and includes pronghorn, elk, moose, bison, bighorn sheep and birds, as well as the famous park residents, the bears.

The eight Type A campgrounds are: Bridge Bay, 230 sites; Canyon, 240 sites; Fishing Bridge, 317 sites; Grant Village, 399 sites; Madison, 300 sites; Mammoth, 91 sites; Norris, 116 sites; Old Faithful, 323 sites. Within the park are five wilderness

A limited number of campsites have been developed thus far in Virgin Islands National Park, but many campers have already discovered this Caribbean beauty spot.

National Park Service Photo

camps rated Type B and nine other Type B facilities. The camping season for most campgrounds is from June 1 to mid-September; two or three stay open until October 15 and one, Mammoth, stays open all year. An extra fee is charged, a new regulation that went into effect in 1969. Facilities for 365 trailers are provided at Fishing Bridge. The charge is $2 per night. Boating, fishing, horseback riding and hiking are favorite pastimes.

YOSEMITE NATIONAL PARK

Box 577 (Yosemite Village)
Yosemite National Park,
California 95389
Camping season—varies

The official description of Yosemite National Park calls it "a 189 square-mile geological wonderland with sculptured peaks and domes, waterfalls tumbling from hanging valleys down the faces of shining granite cliffs; groves of giant sequoias and extensive forests of pine, fir and oak; wildflowers in alpine meadows; hundreds of species of birds and mammals; and scenic drives and trails to areas of high country grandeur with sparkling, glacial lakes." The total acreage is 761,320.

Within this beautiful park are more than 700 miles of trails. Opportunities are afforded for mountain climbing, horseback riding and pack trips. More than 200 miles of scenic roads traverse the park. Fishing, swimming and skiing are among miscellaneous other activities.

Ten campgrounds offer Type A facilities. These are: (in Yosemite Valley) Camp Seven, 152 sites; Camp Eleven, 300 sites; Camp Fifteen, 212 sites. Also Bridalveil Creek, 126 sites; Crane Flat, 164 sites; Hodgdon Meadow, 110 sites; Tenaya Lake, 50 sites; Tuolumne Meadows, 600 sites (some of these are Type B); Wawona, 187 sites; White Wolf, 86 sites. There are 12 Type B campgrounds. A sanitary dumping station is maintained at Camp Seven in Yosemite Valley. The only campground open all year is Camp Four in Yosemite Valley, a Type B facility.

Favorite pastime activities in the park are hiking, swimming, boating, fishing and horseback riding.

ZION NATIONAL PARK

Springdale, Utah 84767
Camping season—varies

Zion National Park is 147,034 acres of outstanding canyon and mesa scenery. To many of its visitors, it is the most beautiful place on the face of the earth. Clarence A. Dutton, a geologist, said about Zion in 1882: "Nothing can exceed the wonderful beauty of Zion. . . . In the nobility and beauty of the sculptures there is no comparison. . . . There is an eloquence to their forms which stirs the imagination with a singular power, and kindles in the mind a glowing response."

The park boasts of several spectacular scenic drives and several excellent trails. Persons who plan to make technical rock climbs must register at park headquarters. Climbing alone is not allowed. Horseback trips may be arranged for. Guides are necessary. Fishing is allowed all year in the Virgin River below Zion Narrows; a Utah fishing license is required. The park is a sanctuary for wildlife.

The campgrounds include three rated Type A. These are: Grotto, 55 sites; South, 150 sites; and Watchman, 280 sites. South is open all year. South and Watchman offer sanitary dumping station facilities. Interestingly, irrigation ditches run through the campgrounds to water the plants therein. Campers are asked to keep ditches clean and free from soapy water or other waste materials which may injure plants.

Horseback riding is the most popular pastime.

Youngsters love to fish in the streams and lakes of Yosemite National Park. They may not be "compleat anglers," but the trout don't mind if the bait is right.

National Park Service Photo

the beginning...

..days and months of a new tree are vitally important to its survival. Hundreds of thousands of tree seeds fall to the earth each year, but only a small percentage ever reach maturity. The tiny pine seedling in the photo above is one year old, small for its age, but it has survived in spite of a dry spell. This would indicate that it is well rooted in soil favorable to its growth. Someday it possibly will furnish shade and protection from wind for some camping family not even in existence now.

THE
a mecca
NATIONAL
for campers
FORESTS

154 national forests, 182 million acres, nearly 8,000 campgrounds, 88 wilderness areas — yours to enjoy, no matter where you live.

Seneca Creek in Spruce Knob-Seneca Rocks National Recreation Area of Monongahela National Forest, West Virginia.

U.S. Forest Service Photo

Of all the government agencies providing facilities for campers, the national forests have the most to offer. This is true in part because of their number and cumulative size: 154 national forests, spread over more than 182 million acres as diverse as the country's geography. But it is true in a larger measure because the management and personnel of the forest lands have performed so well in building and maintaining wonderful camping facilities.

And what makes all of this seem so ideal is the manner in which Forest Service workers deal with visitors. Their information efforts are well planned and well executed. Forest Service publications tell the story as it is, and in understandable language. Visiting a national forest is an education in itself, and any camper who stays more than a day or two should observe with appreciation the many other aspects of Forest Service programs.

A national forest camping vacation awaits you within a day's drive of anywhere, unless you live in Hawaii or certain parts of Alaska. You can take your choice of terrain and climate. In the south you'll find camping sites in cypress swamps, among sand pines, in river valleys and on high mountain peaks. In the Rocky Mountain region and among the Cascades, your national forest campsite may be in alpine meadows or great fir forests. In California, your tent may be in the midst of giant redwoods. In the Midwest, spreading hardwoods may be your canopy. Or you may prefer a desert site, a lakeshore, a snowfield or a meadow alongside a meandering brook.

Great variety

Whatever your preference, you'll find it in a national forest. Variety is the key. Recreation of all kinds goes with national forest camping. From swimming to skiing, hiking to canoeing, wild rivers to placid lakes, you'll be able to choose what you like best. Improved campgrounds with all the comforts of civilization are yours, if you choose; or primitive challenge deep in the wilderness may be your preference. It's all there, waiting for you!

Camping facilities

Within the national forests are nearly 8,000 developed campgrounds and picnic grounds, capable of accommodating some 500,000 people at one time. As many as 40 million visitor days are recorded at these sites in a year—double the number recorded per year a little more than a decade ago. The Forest Service continues to develop new campgrounds to meet the accelerated demand for this form of recreation.

Facilities vary, determined largely by the environment of the area. If the site is near a heavily populated area or is otherwise subject to a large influx of visitors, it is more highly developed. Paved roads, parking areas and modern sanitary facilities are provided. In remote areas, a primitive or rustic atmosphere is maintained.

Trailer locations

Trailers are permitted at many national forest campgrounds. In numerous locations, special areas have been designed for trailer camping (includes other types of recreational vehicles). Central sanitation stations are provided at some campgrounds for the disposal of sewage and waste water.

Overcrowding is not uncommon at more popular national forests, although not usually in the traffic-jam sense so often encountered at some national parks. At crowded sites, a notice may be posted that specifies a time limit on length of stay.

Forest Service personnel seem to have developed campgrounds in the most attractive surroundings available. They add to this attraction by providing some "breathing room" at each site. And usually the whole camping area is screened and otherwise protected

from highway traffic and other disconcerting noises of civilization. Many campgrounds are within easy access to main thoroughfares, but are not crowded close to them. Others may be reached only by quiet forest roads or by foot or horseback on wilderness trails.

The Forest Service admonishes campers to bring all their basics for outdoor living. Seldom are supplies and gear readily available at the site. Small towns and country stores are near many campgrounds. Other camping areas are many miles from a source of supplies.

Popular sports

The national forests boast of more than 70,000 miles of streams and rivers, plus thousands of lakes and ponds. Much of the nation's unpolluted water

resources are contained within the national forests. So are many of the water recreation resources.

Swimming, skindiving, sailing, boating, waterskiing, canoeing and fishing are some of the water sports enjoyed by campers and others in the national forests. The Boundary Waters Canoe Area in Minnesota offers one million acres of water and terrain for canoeing and portaging. In Arizona, national forest lakes have brought water sports to the desert. Throughout the nation, national forests offer campers the added attractions of water sports. In many places, from along a Florida

Purpose and Operation of The National Forest System

Following is the latest official information on the purposes and functions of the National Forest System, excerpted from "The National Parks, the National Forests: Their Purposes and Management":

"The National Forest System comprises 154 National Forests and 19 National Grasslands in 41 States and Puerto Rico. These public lands are administered by the Forest Service. U.S. Department of Agriculture.

"As directed by Congress, renewable forest resources—water, timber, forage, wildlife, recreation—are managed under the principles of Multiple Use and Sustained Yield. Multiple Use means that resource management is coordinated so that areas of land produce a combination of values that best serves the American people. Sustained Yield means that resources are managed so as to provide services and products at a level of supply as high as can be sustained without harming the land's ability to produce. Under such management, the National Forests represent the Nation's largest tangible accomplishment in forest resource conservation.

Water use

"Water from the forests irrigate millions of agricultural acres and is used for domestic and industrial purposes in hundreds of cities. Timber from the forests is manufactured into 5,000

products sold worldwide. National Forests and Grasslands provide habitat for millions of big and small game, game birds, and fish, and produce forage for 1,300,000 cattle and 2,600,000 sheep.

Forest recreation includes scenic drives, wilderness travel, picnicking, camping, hiking, skiing, swimming, boating and, subject to State conservation laws, some of the country's finest hunting and fishing. The National Forests are truly America's Playgrounds.

"The Forest Service pioneered in wilderness preservation in 1924 when it set aside the nation's first wilderness. The initial 9.1 million acres of the National Wilderness Preservation System created in 1964 are in 54 National Forest Wildernesses, previously classified as Wilderness, Wild, and Canoe Areas. Another 5½ million acres of the National Forests, set aside in 34 Primitive Areas, are being studied for possible inclusion in the wilderness system.

Experiment stations

"The Forest Service has two other equally important responsibilities. It maintains eight regional forest and range experiment stations, an Institute of Tropical Forestry, an Institute of Northern Forestry, and a Forest Products Laboratory. It also directs programs to encourage and support better management and protection of forest lands in State and private ownership."

Many backpackers head for Burden Falls, Shawnee National Forest, Illinois.

U.S. Forest Service Photo

shoreline to a snow-fed lake in the Rockies, completely equipped swimming facilities have been developed by the Forest Service.

OK to hunt and fish

Hunting and fishing are permitted in most national forests. A wide variety of mammals, birds and fishes inhabit forest lands and waters. National forests provide a home for more than half the big-game animals in the west, and also afford some of the best fishing in all areas of the country. State game laws apply to hunting and fishing, just as they do on private lands. Information on seasons, fees and the like may be obtained from the state game and fish department concerned.

Winter sports are big in the national forests. These include downhill skiing, ski touring, skating, tobogganing, snowshoeing, ice fishing and ski jumping. The most popular of these is downhill skiing. Deep mountain snows in many of the national forests provide

perfect settings for this popular pastime.

Most ski areas in the western states are in or partly in national forest land. The 1960 Winter Olympics were held on Tahoe National Forest land at Squaw Valley, California. In the Great Lakes states and in New England, national forests contain excellent slopes for skiing.

For full information on skiing in the national forests, send 30 cents to Superintendent of Documents, U. S. Government Printing Office, Washington, D. C. 20402, and ask for the booklet, "Skiing."

The wilderness

Nearly eight percent of national forest lands are managed as wilderness or primitive areas. This amounts to more than 14½ million acres, which is divided into 88 wilderness units. If you can ride a horse, hike or paddle a canoe, you may take advantage of

these roadless areas. The Boundary Waters Canoe Area already cited is part of the national forest wilderness domain. Other areas vary from Three Sisters in central Oregon to the Superstition Mountains in the Arizona desert, from remarkable Linville Gorge in North Carolina to the Wyoming and Montana lands pioneered by Jim Bridger.

In some areas, wilderness trips are sponsored by outdoor organizations. Only the most expert outdoorsmen should ever think to enter these remote places alone.

Forest trails

National forest trails may wind through magnificent forests, or follow the course of a river, or traverse some desolate looking desert country. Altogether, hiking and riding trails in the national forests add up to about 112,000 miles. Much of the Appalachian Trail passes through national forest lands, as does the Pacific Crest Trail in the West.

Thousands of miles are lesser known. Good trails are a part of all 154 national forests.

Rules to remember

Campfires may be built only in safe places. This means in desginated places when camping at improved areas, and not against logs, brush or trees when camping at primitive sites. Remember, wildfires destroy. Besides, they're illegal, no matter how they start.

Obey all posted rules and regulations.

Observe state and national game and fish laws.

Maintain high sanitary standards and avoid any action or procedure that could pollute streams and lakes.

Treat facilities such as tables, toilets and shelters as if they were your own— **which they are.**

Never discharge fireworks in national forests, nor firearms adjacent to or in recreation areas. Either act is a violation of law, in addition to being dangerous and inconsiderate.

Do not destroy the plant life. Protect trees, shrubs and flowers.

When camping in primitive areas, carry out all unburnables. And make certain that your fire is out—completely out—before leaving.

Finally, ask any questions of the ranger on duty and pay special attention to newly posted notices.

Now, scan the national forest descriptions (derived from official sources) which follow, and enjoy your national forest campout.

ALABAMA

WILLIAM B. BANKHEAD NATIONAL FOREST
(178,739 acres).

Office of Forest Supervisor: P. O. Box 40, Montgomery, Alabama 36101.
Camping facilities: 49 units at 21 locations.
Other facilities: Boating, picnicking, swimming, hunting and fishing.
Attractions: Limestone gorges, Lewis Smith Reservoir, two natural bridges, wildlife refuge and management area. Deer, turkey and squirrel hunting. Bass and bream fishing in Brushy Lake.
Nearby towns: Cullman, Decatur, Haleyville, Jasper and Russellville.

CONECUH NATIONAL FOREST
(83,900 acres).

Office of Forest Supervisor: P. O. Box 40, Montgomery, Alabama 36101.
Camping facilities: 11 units at 1 location.
Other facilities: Boating, picnicking and swimming.
Attractions: Large, clear ponds. Bass and bream fishing. Deer, turkey and small game hunting.
Nearby town: Andalusia.

TALLADEGA NATIONAL FOREST
(357,470 acres).

Office of Forest Supervisor: P. O. Box 40, Montgomery, Alabama 36101.
Camping facilities: 70 units at 4 locations.
Other facilities: Boating, picnicking and swimming sites. Resort, hotel and cabins at Cheaha State Park.
Attractions: South Sandy Wildlife Management Area; Skyway Motorway; Mount Cheaha, 2,407 feet, highest point in Alabama; Lake Cinnabee. Deer, turkey, duck and squirrel hunting. Bass, bream and perch fishing.
Nearby towns: Anniston, Centreville, Heflin, Marion, Selma, Sylacauga, Talladega and Tuscaloosa.

TUSKEGEE NATIONAL FOREST
(10,777 acres).

Office of Forest Supervisor: P. O. Box 40, Montgomery, Alabama 36101.
Camping facilities: 5 units at 1 location.
Other facilities: Picnicking.
Attractions: Pine plantation of advanced size. Bream fishing in streams.
Nearby towns: Auburn and Truskegee.

ALASKA

CHUGACH NATIONAL FOREST
(4,723,397 acres).

Office of Forest Supervisor: Anchorage, Alaska.
Camping facilities: 20 camp and picnic sites.
Other facilities: Fishing, hunting, picnicking, 1 swimming site. Two winter sports areas.
Attractions: Fiords and glaciers, lakes and rivers. Unexcelled scenery. Salmon spawning runs, salmon, crab and clam canneries. Kenai Mountains with access by road system throughout the Kenai Peninsula. Trout and saltwater fishing. Hunting for moose, sheep, mountain goats, Alaskan brown bear and elk; also for waterfowl and grouse.
Nearby towns: Anchorage, Cordova, Kodiak, Seward, Valdez and Whittier.

TONGASS NATIONAL FOREST—
North Division (16,011,643 acres).

Office of Forest Supervisor: Juneau, Alaska.
Camping facilities: None listed.
Other facilities: Boating, fishing, hunting, scenic wilderness trails, mountain climbing, picnicking, 1 swimming site, 2 winter sports areas. Hotel accommodations in all southeastern Alaska towns such as Juneau, Petersburg, Sitka and Skagway; all of these are served by plane.
Attractions: Rugged Alaska coast; hundreds of islands, fiords, snowcapped mountains above the sea; totems; territorial museum and Indian villages. Salmon canneries. Gateway to Canadian hinterland and Yukon, "Trail of '98'" gold mines. Glaciers; "Ice Cap" back of Juneau; fiords of Tracy Arm. Admiralty Island. Trout fishing, also salt water fishing for salmon and halibut. Hunting for Alaska brown and grizzly bear, mountain goat and deer. Boating on lakes and inland waterways.
Nearby towns: Juneau, Petersburg, Sitka and Skagway.

TONGASS NATIONAL FOREST—
South Division.

Office of Forest Supervisor: Ketchikan, Alaska.
Camping facilities: 2 camp facilities listed.
Other facilities: Picnicking, fishing, hunting, boating, 1 swimming site, 1 winter sports area. Hotel accommodations in all southeastern Alaska towns, such as Ketchikan and Wrangell; all these served by plane.
Attractions: Fiords of Walker Cove and Rudyerd Bay of the Behm Canal, and Portland Canal. Trout, salmon and halibut fishing. Hunting for Alaska brown, black and grizzly bear, boat and deer. Totems. Indian villages. Salmon canneries; pulpmill. Boating on inland waterways.
Nearby towns: Ketchikan and Wrangell.

ARIZONA

APACHE NATIONAL FOREST
(1,806,751 acres—partly in New Mexico).

Office of Forest Supervisor: Springerville, Arizona.
Camping facilities: 23 locations.
Other facilities: Boating, fishing, hunting, pack trips, scenic drives, picnicking, riding, hiking, historic points. Resorts and motels. Boats without motors for rent on Big and Luna Lakes.
Attractions: Scenic Coronado Trail and other drives through spruce and mountain-meadow country. Prehistoric Blue River cliff dwellings, Big Lake, Crescent Lake, Luna Lake. Blue Range and Mount Baldy Primitive Areas. Lake and stream trout fishing. Big game hunting for elk, deer, bear, antelope and wild turkey.
Nearby towns: Alpine, Greer, Springerville, Arizona. Luna and Reserve, New Mexico.

COCONINO NATIONAL FOREST
(1,800,738 acres).

Office of Forest Supervisor: Flagstaff, Arizona.
Camping facilities: 22 locations.
Other facilities: Boating, fishing, hunting, scenic drives, picnicking, riding. Arizona Snow Bowl Winter Sports Area. Resort hotels, dude ranches.
Attractions: Graceful San Francisco Peaks, 12,611 feet, highest in Arizona; Oak Creek Canyon and the Red Rock country near Sedona offer exceptional scenic and photographic opportunities; Sycamore Canyon Primitive Area and Mogollon Rim. Scenic drives: Lake Mary-Long Valley Road; Mogollon Rim Road; Baker Butte Fire Lookout offering vast view of Arizona timber. Numerous national monuments nearby, plus Lowell Astronomical Observatory, Museum of Northern Arizona, Flagstaff; Meteor Crater near Painted Desert. Hunting for deer, antelope, turkey, elk, mountain lion. Lake and stream fishing. Boating on Lake Mary.
Nearby towns: Camp Verde, Clarkdale, Cottonwood, Flagstaff, Sedona and Winslow.

CORONADO NATIONAL FOREST
(1,790,935 acres).

Office of Forest Supervisor: Tucson, Arizona.

Camping facilities: 616 units at 27 locations.
Other facilities: Boating, fishing, hunting, pack trips, scenic drives, hiking, skiing, swimming.
Attractions: Rugged mountains rising abruptly from surrounding deserts; cactus to fir trees, swimming to skiing in an hour's time—40 miles apart. Santa Catalina Mountains Recreation Area with Rose Canyon Lake, Sabino Canyon and Mount Lemmon Snow Bowl, southernmost winter sports area in the Continental U.S. Chiricahua Mountains with Chiricahua Wilderness and several small trout lakes. Pinaleno Mountains Recreation Area with Mount Graham, 10,713 feet, Riggs Flat Lake, Pena Blanca Lake, 52 acres of bass fishing 4 miles from the international boundary with Mexico. Galiuro Wilderness. Nearby are Arizona-Sonora Desert Museum, Colossal Cave State Park, Tucson Mountain Park. Hunting for deer, javelina, mountain lion, quail and dove. Pack trip and hiking trails in the rugged ranges of southern Arizona (caution: carry adequate water). Dude ranch and winter resort country.
Nearby towns: Benson, Bisbee, Mexican border towns of Douglas and Nogales, Fort Huachuca, Patagonia, Safford, San Simon, Tombstone, Tucson and Wilcox.

Office of Forest Supervisor: Williams, Arizona.
Camping facilities: 5 locations.
Other facilities: Fishing, hunting, scenic drives, riding, pack trips, picnicking. Motels, resorts, guest ranches. Hunting camps with groceries in season.
Attractions: Grand Canyon National Game Preserve with the famous North Kaibab deer heard, a wild buffalo herd and the only habitat of the Kaibab squirrel. Access to both north and south rims of the Grand Canyon and Supai Indian village in Havasu Canyon. Other points of interest are beautiful North Kaibab high country; pine, spruce and aspen forests with open meadows; East Rim, North Canyon, Bill Williams Mountain, Whitehorse Lake, Cataract Lake and Sycamore Canyon Primitive Area. Hunting of deer, elk, antelope, bear, mountain lion, turkey and limited buffalo. Photographic opportunities; wildlife and vivid geologic formations.
Nearby towns: Ashfork, Cottonwood, Flagstaff, Fredonia, Grand Canyon and Williams, Arizona. Kanab, Utah.

PRESCOTT NATIONAL FOREST
(1,247,834 acres).

Office of Forest Supervisor: Prescott, Arizona.

Camping facilities: 10 locations.
Other facilities: Fishing, hunting, scenic drives, horse trails, picnicking. Resorts, motels and dude ranches.
Attractions: Ideal year-round climate. Rugged back country, many roads primitive. Granite Basin Lake near Granite Mountain, Hassayampa Lake. Limited trout fishing. Sycamore Canyon and Pine Mountain Primitive Areas. Jerome, nation's largest ghost town. Deer, antelope, dove and quail hunting.
Nearby towns: Clarkdale, Cottonwood, Jerome, Mayer and Prescott.

SITGREAVES NATIONAL FOREST
(799,504 acres).

Office of Forest Supervisor: Holbrook, Arizona.
Camping facilities: 3 locations.
Other facilities: Fishing, hunting, rowboat rentals, saddle and pack trips, riding, hiking trails. Public golf and swimming at White Mountain Country Club. Numerous resorts, hotels, summer homes, guest ranches.
Attractions: Scenic Mogollon Rim Drive; pueblo ruins, Woods Canyon Lake. Hunting of deer, turkey, antelope and bear.
Nearby towns: Holbrook, Lakeside, Pinetop, Show Low, Snowflake and Winslow.

TONTO NATIONAL FOREST
(2,890,853 acres).

Office of Forest Supervisor: Phoenix, Arizona.
Camping facilities: 22 locations.
Other facilities: Boating, swimming, skindiving, water skiing, fishing, hunting, saddle and pack trips, scenic drives, picnicking. Swim with care, no lifeguards. Resorts, dude ranches.

Attractions: Semidesert to pine fir forests, elevations 1,500 to 7,300 feet. The lakes in the low country form an all-year haven in the desert; the cool pine forests along the Mogollon Rim are very popular in summer. Famous Mazatzal and Superstition Wildernesses, Pine Mountain Primitive Area; Sierra Ancha Wild Area. Thirty thousand acres of manmade lakes including Roosevelt, Apache, Canyon and Saguaro Lakes on the Salt River; Bartlett and Horshoe Lakes on the Verde River. Popular for boating, swimming, skindiving, water skiing, bass fishing. Public boat ramps at most lakes. Boats and tackle also for rent. Limited trout fishing in high country. Hunting for deer, elk, bear, javelina, turkey and moutain lion. Scenic

Even after a thousand looks, there still is good reason to pause and drink in the beauty of Hoodoo Basin in the North Absaroka Wilderness, Shoshone National Forest, Wyoming.

U.S. Forest Service Photo

drives: Apache Trail, Beeline Highway, Mogollon Rim drive.

Nearby towns: Globe, Mesa, Miami, Payson, Phoenix, Pine, Superior and Young.

ARKANSAS

OUACHITA NATIONAL FOREST
(1,563,383 acres—partly in Oklahoma).

Office of Forest Supervisor: Box 1270, Hot Springs, Arkansas 71902.

Camping facilities: 305 units at 18 locations.

Other facilities: Boating, hiking, picnicking and swimming sites. Hotels, resorts and cabin camps.

Attractions: Ouachita, Kiamichi and Winding Stair Mountains; 8 major and numerous smaller artificial lakes in or near the National Forest. Caddo Gap, where DeSoto fought Indians: lands explored by La Salle and De-Tonti, accounting for the many French names. Bass fishing. Deer, quail and squirrel hunting. Scenic drives.

Nearby towns: Booneville, Hot Springs and Mena, Ark. Heavener and Poteau, Okla.

OZARK NATIONAL FOREST
(1,088,164 acres).

Office of Forest Supervisor: Russellville, Arkansas 72801.

Camping facilities: 284 units at 17 locations.

Other facilities: Boating, picnicking and swimming sites. Mount Magazine Lodge and cabins. White Rock Mountain cabins, others nearby.

Attractions: Inviting summer climate, oak forest, rock cliffs and pools, scenic drives. Three recreational lakes; Mount Magazine. Stream and lake fishing. Deer and small game hunting. 2 large reservoirs near the National Forest.

Nearby towns: Clarksville, Fayetteville, Ft. Smith, Harrison, Ozark, Paris and Russellville.

ST. FRANCIS NATIONAL FOREST
(approx. 10,000 acres).

Office of Forest Supervisor: Russellville, Arkansas 72801.

Camping facilities: 34 units at 2 locations.

Other facilities: Boating, picnicking and swimming.

Attractions: Two recreational lakes. Fishing.

Nearby towns: Marianna and West Helena.

CALIFORNIA

ANGELES NATIONAL FOREST
(648,866 acres).

Office of Forest Supervisor: 1015 North Lake Ave., Pasadena, California 91104.

Camping facilities: 1,470 units at 94 locations.

Other facilities: Scenic drives, riding and hiking trails, skiing in season, fishing, hunting, some swimming, boating, picnicking. (Because of extreme fire danger in southern California, no open campfires are permitted in this forest.) Winter sports areas with ski lifts and other facilities. Resorts, cabins, pack and riding stables. Hotels and motels.

Attractions: Steep, rugged mountains adjoining Los Angeles metro-

The Eleven Point on the Mark Twain National Forest in Missouri is one of eight original Wild and Scenic Rivers created by act of Congress. This picture tells why.

U.S. Forest Service Photo

politan area; Old Baldy, 10,000 feet. Chiefly a chaparral forest that serves as a watershed for the Los Angeles area and as an easily reached mountain playground for the area's inhabitants. San Gabriel Wilderness. Scenic drives with wonderful views, especially of the city lights at night.
Nearby towns: Los Angeles and foothill towns.

CLEVELAND NATIONAL FOREST
(393,085 acres).

Office of Forest Supervisor: 1196 Broadway, San Diego, California 92101.
Camping facilities: 612 units at 20 locations. Plus 26 camps strictly for hunters.
Other facilities: Fishing, hunting, picnicking. (Because of extreme fire danger in southern California, no open campfires are permitted in this forest.) Dude ranches, resorts, motels.
Attractions: Primarily a watershed forest with an unusually mild climate, between the desert and the sea. Agua Tibia Primitive Area. The world's largest telescope at Palomar Observatory on Mount Palomar. Warm water fishing and duck hunting on the impounded lakes of the water systems. Hunting of deer is very popular with a necessarily short season; pigeon and quail hunting. The Mexico-to-Oregon Trail starts here.
Nearby towns: El Centro, Los Angeles, Oceanside and San Diego.

ELDORADO NATIONAL FOREST
(1,835,960 acres—partly in Nevada).

Office of Forest Supervisor: Placerville, California 95667.
Camping facilities: 1,205 units at 41 locations, plus group camps.
Other facilities: Fishing, hunting, geologic and nature walks, picnicking, hiking trails, water skiing, riding, boating, swimming, campfire circle, scenic drives, wilderness trips, winter sports. Resorts, motels and dude ranches.
Attractions: Rugged mountains in the Sierra Nevada. Hundreds of mountain lakes; including south shore of spectacular Lake Tahoe, 23 miles long, 13 miles wide, elevation 6,225 feet. California Gold Rush country, famous Mother Lode mining communities including site of Sutter's Mill. Mokelumne Wilderness and Desolation Valley Primitive Area. Lake and stream fishing. Deer and bear hunting. Scenic drives: Highway 50 to Lake Tahoe, Carson Pass Highway 88 (route of Fremont expe-

dition of 1844); Georgetown to Wentworth Springs.
Nearby towns: Placerville and Sacramento, California. Carson City and Reno, Nevada.

INYO NATIONAL FOREST
(1,835,960 acres—partly in Nevada).

Office of Forest Supervisor: Bishop, California 93514.

The White Mountains of Inyo National Forest boast this stand of bristlecone pines, the world's oldest living things (some 4,600 years old). Above.

U.S. Forest Service Photo

Camping facilities: 2,011 units at 66 locations.
Other facilities: Fishing, hunting, wilderness trips, winter sports, picnicking, self-guided nature trails, boating, swimming, geologic study, riding. Resorts, motels.
Attractions: John Muir Wilderness, Mt. Dana-Minarets Wilderness, Hoover Wilderness, Palisade Glacier, southernmost glacier in the United States. Ancient Bristlecone Pine

The Mt. Dana-Minarets Wilderness Area, Inyo National Forest, is kept in its natural state for wilderness-type recreation. The scenery rivals that of Yosemite National Park, which it adjoins. Below.

U.S. Forest Service Photo

Forest Botanical Area with many 4,000-year-old trees—the oldest living things on earth. Many wild granite peaks 12,000 to more than 14,000 feet in elevation. Mount Whitney, 14,495 feet, higest point in continental United States, and its closest approach road. Lake and stream fishing. Deer hunting. Dozens of natural lakes, some accessible by paved road up to 9,700 feet. Mammoth and Reversed Creek Recreation Areas.

Nearby towns: Bigpine, Bishop, Independence, Leevining and Lone Pine.

KLAMATH NATIONAL FOREST
(1,696,965 acres—partly in Oregon).

Office of Forest Supervisor: Yreka, California 96097.

Camping facilities: 359 units at 26 locations.

Other facilities: Boating, swimming, fishing, hunting, hiking, riding, pack trips, picnicking. Motels and resorts, dude ranches.

Attractions: Big timber forest. Klamath River and tributaries, famous for salmon and steelhead. Marble Mountain Wilderness and Salmon-Trinity Alps Primitive Areas. High mountain lakes and streams. Great scenic beauty in a wild setting. Deer hunting.

Nearby towns: Eureka, Mount Shasta, and Yreka, California. Medford, Oregon.

LASSEN NATIONAL FOREST
(1,045,624 acres).

Office of Forest Supervisor: Susanville, California 96130.

Camping facilities: 993 units at 54 locations.

Other facilities: Boating, fishing, hunting, swimming, riding, hiking trails, winter sports. Privately owned resorts, hotels, cabins.

Attractions: Caribou and Thousand Lakes Wildernesses. Many lakes; southern end of Cascade Wonderland; volcanic lava flow tubes, hot springs, mud pots. Indian pictographs and hieroglyphics, old emigrant trails. Lake and stream fishing for rainbow, Lochleven and steelhead trout. Deer and bear hunting.

Nearby towns: Chester, Chico, Mill Creek, Red Bluff and Redding.

LOS PADRES NATIONAL FOREST
(1,724,108 acres).

Office of Forest Supervisor: Federal Building, Santa Barbara, California 93101.

Camping facilities: 1,056 units at 114 locations.

Other facilities: Fishing, hunting, swimming, pack trips, scenic drives, wilderness trips, picnicking, riding, hiking trails, winter sports, hot baths, group and trail camps, rock collecting interests, sunbathing, barbecue pits, oceanside camping. (Because of extreme fire danger in Southern

A real beauty spot is Tumalo Falls, Deschutes National Forest, Oregon.

California, no open campfires are permitted in this National Forest.) Kern County Ski Lodge. Hotels, cabins and a few dude ranches.

Attractions: Undeveloped, rugged country, varying from lonely coast to semidesert, from brush to oak country to pine timber; elevations from near sea level to almost 9,000 feet; home of the rare California condor. Ventana Primitive Area and San Rafael Wilderness; snowcapped peaks in winter. Quail and pigeon hunting, some deer and wild boar hunting. Trout fishing.

Nearby towns: Atascadero, Carmel, King City, Monterey, Ojai, Paso Robles, Taft, San Luis Obispo, Santa Barbara, Santa Maria and Ventura.

MENDOCINO NATIONAL FOREST
(872,237 acres).

Office of Forest Supervisor: Willows, California 95988.

Camping facilities: 440 units at 51 locations.

Other facilities: Boating, fishing, hunting, swimming, saddle and pack trips, picnicking, air strip. Dude ranches, motels.

Attractions: Coast Range of California about 100 miles north of San Francisco. Peaks up to 8,600 feet. Beautiful lake country. Yolla-Bolly-Middle Eel Wilderness. Columbian black-tailed deer.

Nearby towns: Corning, Laytonville, Sacramento, Ukiah, Willits and Willow.

Thousands of acres of national forest grasslands, mostly in the West, are leased to sheep and cattle ranchers. This is one of a wide variety of programs conducted by the U. S. Forest Service.

MODOC NATIONAL FOREST
(1,689,508 acres).

Office of Forest Supervisor: Alturas, California 96101.
Camping facilities: 285 units at 23 locations.
Other facilities: Boating, fishing, hunting, swimming, scenic rides, wilderness trips, picnicking, riding, hiking, water sports, winter sports. Hotels, cabins; hunters' camps during deer season.
Attractions: Remote northeast corner of California. Scenic rides and wilderness trips on trails such as the summit trail through South Warner Wilderness, Glass Mountain lava flows, scene of Modoc Indian wars. Winter range of interstate deer herd, Clear Lake Reservoir migratory bird refuge. Stream and lake fishing. Mule deer and waterfowl hunting.
Nearby towns: Adin, Alturas, Canby, Cedarville and Tulelake.

PLUMAS NATIONAL FOREST
(1,146,732 acres).

Office of Forest Supervisor: Quincy, California 95971.
Camping facilities: 671 units at 32 locations.
Other facilities: Boating, fishing, hunting, scenic drives, picnicking, hiking, water skiing, winter sports. Resorts, hotels and cabins.
Attractions: Beautiful Feather River country; Feather Falls, one of the highest and most picturesque waterfalls in the United States. Historic gold mining areas of La Porte, Johnsville and Rich Bar; extensive hydroelectric developments. Limestone caves; large, beautiful, mountain valleys, such as Indian, American, Mohawk and Sierra Valleys. Lake and stream fishing. Hunting of mule and black-tailed deer, bear, duck, geese, quail and dove. Scenic drives include Feather River Canyon, Bucks Lake, Bald Rock Canyon, Quincy-La Porte and Lakes Basin Recreational Areas, and Little Last Chance Creek Pacific Crest Trail.
Nearby towns: Chico, Greenville, Marysville, Oroville, Quincy, Sacramento and Sierraville.

SAN BERNARDINO NATIONAL FOREST (616,315 acres).

Office of Forest Supervisor: Civic Center Bldg., 175 W. Fifth Street, San Bernardino, California 94201.
Camping facilities: 989 units at 42 locations.
Other facilities: Fishing, swimming, pack trips, picnicking, winter sports, ice skating, group camps by reservation, campfire circles. (Because of extreme fire danger in southern Cali-

These visitors to a California national forest learn "what to see and do" from a pretty, young Forest Service worker.

fornia, no open campfires are permitted in this National Forest.) Resorts, hotels, motels, cabins at Arrowhead, Big Bear Lakes, Idyllwild.
Attractions: Highest mountains in southern California: San Gorgonio, 11,485 feet; 6 others more than 10,000 feet. San Jacinto, San Gorgonio and Cucamonga Wilderness. Historic landmarks: Big Bear and Arrowhead Lakes; Mt. San Jacinto. Lake and stream fishing. Deer hunting. Life zones from desert to alpine within a few miles.
Nearby towns: Banning, Indio, Palm Springs, Riverside and San Bernardino.

SEQUOIA NATIONAL FOREST
(1,115,858 acres).

Office of Forest Supervisor: 900 W. Grand Avenue, Porterville, California 93258.
Camping facilities: 807 units at 53 locations.
Other facilities: Boating, fishing, hunting, swimming, scenic drives, picnicking, riding, hiking, skiing, winter sports, hot springs, group camps by reservation. Motels, resorts, lodges.
Attractions: Giant Sequoia trees, Hume Lake, Boydens Cave, Dome Land Wilderness, High Sierra Primi-

tive Area, Mineral King Game Refuge. High mountain lakes and stream fishing, home of the golden trout. Big game hunting, mule deer and bear. Scenic drives: Kern River Canyon, Kings River Canyon.
Nearby towns: Bakersfield, Fresno, Porterville and Visalia.

SHASTA-TRINITY NATIONAL FOREST (2,066,254 acres—two forests).

Office of Forest Supervisor: 1615 Continental St., Redding, California 96001.
Camping facilities: 1,426 units at 99 locations.
Other facilities: Boating, fishing, hunting, swimming, saddle and pack trips, picnicking, winter sports, group camps by reservation, skiing, scenic drives. Hotels, resorts, dude ranches.
Attractions: Beautiful Mount Shasta, 14,162 feet with eternal snow, 5 living glaciers. Whiskeytown-Shasta Trinity Recreation Area. Shasta and Trinity Lakes with outstanding boating. Lava beds, Glass Mountain and Castle Crags. Salmon-Trinity Alps Primitive Area and Yolla Bolly-Middle Eel Wilderness. Lake and stream fishing, home of Dolly Varden trout. Waterfowl, upland birds, deer, bear, small game hunting. Limestone

caves, lava caves and chimneys. Riding trails in the wilderness.

Nearby towns: Callahan, Dunsmur, McCloud, Mount Shasta, Redding, Weaverville and Weed.

SIERRA NATIONAL FOREST
(1,293,180 acres).

Office of Forest Supervisor: Federal Building, 1130 O Street, Fresno, California 93721.

Camping facilities: 1,326 units at 87 locations.

Other facilities: Boating, fishing, hunting, swimming, winter sports, mountain climbing, group campgrounds on reservation only. Many back country pack trips. Hotels, resorts and dude ranches.

Attractions: Huntington Lake, Florence Lake, Shaver Lake, Dinkey Creek and Bass Lake Recreation Areas. Nelder and McKinley Groves of Big Trees (giant sequoia), Central Sierra section of the John Muir Trail. John Muir and Minarets Wildernesses. Rainbow Falls in the Reds Meadow area. Lake and stream fishing. Deer, bear and quail hunting.

Nearby towns: Fresno and North Fork.

SIX RIVERS NATIONAL FOREST
(939, 399 acres).

Office of Forest Supervisor: 331 J St., Eureka, California 95501.

Camping facilities: 212 units at 14 locations.

Other facilities: Boating, fishing, hunting, swimming, scenic drives, picnicking, riding trails, winter sports. Resorts, hotels, cabins.

Attractions: Giant coast redwood and fir forests stretching 135 miles south from the Oregon line. Klamath, Smith, Eel and Mad Rivers. Mild, cool climate year-long in redwoods; rugged back country. Trout fishing, spring and summer; steelhead and salmon fishing, fall and winter in 6 rivers. Deer and bear hunting.

Nearby towns: Arcata, Crescent City, Eureka, Fortuna, Klamath, Orick and Orleans.

STANISLAUS NATIONAL FOREST
(896,312 acres).

Office of Forest Supervisor: 175 S. Fairview Lane, Sonora, California 95370.

Camping facilities: 978 units at 39 locations.

Other facilities: Boating, fishing, hunting, swimming, saddle and pack trips, scenic drives, picnicking, riding, winter sports, water skiing, historical points, pack station, group campgrounds by reservation, nature programs by forest naturalist. Resorts, cabins, stores.

Attractions: Nearest high mountain country to San Francisco Bay region and portion of San Joaquin Valley; elevations 1,100 to 11,575 feet. Deep canyons cut by Merced, Tuolumme, Stanislaus and Mokelumne Rivers; fine timber stands; Emigrant Basin Primitive Area. Gold Rush country with many a tall tale. Routes of pioneers, Sonora and Ebbets Passes, Calaveras Bigtree National Forest. Fishing in lakes and 715 miles of streams. Hunting for deer and bear.

Nearby towns: Angels Camp, Columbia, Groveland, Jamestown, San Andrews and Sonora.

TAHOE NATIONAL FOREST
(696,536 acres).

Office of Forest Supervisor: Nevada City, California 95939.

Camping facilities: 926 units at 58 locations.

Other facilities: Boating, fishing, hunting, swimming, scenic drives, picnicking, riding and hiking trails, winter sports, skiing, historic points, group campgrounds. Summer resorts, cabins, hotels.

Attractions: Squaw Valley, site of 1960 Winter Olympics. Outstanding conditions and facilities for winter sports; adjacent valleys being developed. Lakes and streams, including northwest shore of beautiful Lake Tahoe. Historic Donner Pass Emigrant Trail; Gold Rush country. Lake and stream fishing. Hunting for deer and bear. Scenic drives through historic gold mining towns.

Nearby towns: Downieville, Grass Valley, Nevada City, Sierra City, Sierraville and Truckee, California. Carson City, Reno, Nevada.

TOIYABE NATIONAL FOREST—
See Nevada listing.

Camping in the national forests is an education. A great deal can be learned about the multiple uses to which these lands are put by observing the work of Forest Service employees. Here a Forest Service worker is doing stream improvement work.

COLORADO

ARAPAHO NATIONAL FOREST (1,003,373 acres).

Office of Forest Supervisor: 1010 Tenth Street, Golden, Colorado 80401.
Camping facilities: 600 units at 26 locations.
Other facilities: Fishing, hunting, scenic drives, wilderness trips, picnicking, riding, winter sports. Seven winter sports areas. Resorts, hotels, cabin camps, dude ranches.

Attracions: Highest auto road in U. S. to the crest of Mount Evans, 14,-260 feet. Fold, silver mining; ghost towns. Gore Range-Eagle Nest Primitive Area. Moffat Tunnel, 6.2 miles long under Continental Divide. Lake and stream fishing. Big game hunting for elk, deer and bear. Small game hunting. Scenic high mountain routes; Loveland and Berthoud Passes, Peak to Peak Highway.
Nearby towns: Denver, Dillon, Golden, Granby, Grand Lake, Hot Sulphur Springs, Idaho Springs and Kremmling.

GRAND MESA—UNCOMPAGRE NATIONAL FORESTS (1,317,964 acres; two forests).

Office of Forest Supervisor: 11th and Main, Delta, Colorado 81416.
Camping facilities: 275 units at 15 locations.
Other facilities: Hunting, fishing, saddle trips, scenic drives, picnicking, winter sports. One winter sports area. Motels, resorts in and near the National Forest.
Attractions: Grand Mesa Plateau, 10,500 feet; 250 lakes and reservoirs; cliffs, canyons, waterfalls, wild flowers. Uncompahgre Plateau. Uncompahgre and Wilson Mountains Primitive Areas; Ouray and Telluride Scenic Areas. Lake and stream fishing. Deer, elk, bear, duck hunting.
Nearby towns: Delta, Grand Junction, Montrose, Norwood, Ouray and Telluride.

GUNNISON NATIONAL FOEST (1,662,860 acres).

Office of Forest Supervisor: 216 North Colorada, Gunnison, Colorado 81230.
Camping facilities: 481 units at 27 locations.
Other facilities: Fishing, hunting, saddle trips, wilderness trips, picnicking, winter sports. Seven winter sports areas. Commercial hotels, resorts, motels in and near the National Forest.
Attractions: Trout fishing streams, many high lakes. Twenty-seven mountain peaks more than 12,000 feet; Ruby Range. Taylor Park Reservoir and valley; ghost towns. West Elk Wilderness. Trout fishing. Hunting of elk, deer, mountain sheep and bear.
Nearby towns: Gunnison, Lake City, Montrose and Salida.

MANTI-LASAL NATIONAL FOREST —See Utah listing.

PIKE NATIONAL FOREST (1,106,101 acres).

This burned-over section of forest land was once lush and productive. What a lesson in forest fire prevention!

USDA Photo

Recreation of all kinds goes with national forest camping. Here Piedmont Trail Riders follow a forest road through Sumter National Forest in South Carolina.

Office of Forest Supervisor: 320 West Fillmore, Colorado Springs, Colorado 80907.

Camping facilities: 703 units at 46 locations.

Other facilities: Fishing, hunting, scenic drives, picnicking. Three winter sports areas. Commercial hotels, resorts, motels in and near the National Forest.

Attractions: Pikes Peak with highway to summit, historic Cripple Creek and Alma gold camps, scenic Rampart Range Road. Devil's Head Forest Fire Lookout, Monument Forest Nursery, Platte and Arkansas River watersheds. Abyss Lake and Lost Creek Scenic Area. Mountain

RIO GRANDE NATIONAL FOREST (1,799,389 acres).

Office of Forest Supervisor: Fassett Building, 914 First Avenue, Monte Vista, Colorado 81144.

Camping facilities: 621 units in 32 locations.

Other facilities: Fishing, hunting, saddle and pack trips, scenic drives, picnicking. One winter sports area. Motels in and near the National Forest.

Attractions: Mountain lakes and trout streams, Wolf Creek Pass, rugged high country. Upper Rio Grande Primitive Area and La Garita

Wilderness. Fishing. Deer, elk and duck hunting.

Nearby towns: Alamosa, Antonito, Creede, Monte Vista and Saguache.

ROOSEVELT NATIONAL FOREST (776,139 acres).

Office of Forest Supervisor: Rocky Mountain Bank & Trust Bldg., 211 Canyon, Fourth Floor, Fort Collins, Colorado 80521.

Camping facilities: 476 units in 16 locations.

Other facilities: Boating, fishing, hunting, saddle and pack trips, scenic drives, picnicking. One winter sports area. Motels and dude ranches in and near the National Forest.

Attractions: Arapaho, Isabelle and South St. Vrain Glaciers; rugged Continental Divide with many alpine lakes; Poudre, Big Tompson, St. Vrain and Boulder Canyons. Rawah Wilderness. Hunting for deer, elk, mountain sheep, bear, mountain lion, grouse and duck.

Nearby towns: Boulder, Denver, Estes Park, Fort Collins, Longmont and Loveland.

ROUTT NATIONAL FOREST (1,125,045 acres).

Office of Forest Supervisor: P. O. Box 1198, Steamboat Springs, Colorado 80477.

Camping facilities: 330 units at 20 locations.

Other facilities: Fishing, hunting, saddle and pack trips, scenic drives, picnicking. One winter sports area. Commercial cabins, motels in and near the National Forest.

Attractions: Continental Divide with perpetual ice and snow, trout streams and alpine lakes. Mount Zirkel Wilderness, Big Creek Lakes Recreation Area. Deer, elk, grouse and duck hunting.

Nearby towns: Craig, Kremmling, Steamboat Springs, Walden and Yampa.

SAN ISSABEL NATIONAL FOREST (1,106,510 acres).

Office of Forest Supervisor: Post Office Building, P. O. Box 753, Pueblo, Colorado 81002.

Camping facilities: 362 units at 20 locations.

Other facilities: Fishing, hunting, saddle and pack trips, scenic drives, picnicking. Two winter sports areas. Motels and dude ranches in and near the National Forest.

Attractions: Highest average elevation of any national forest; Sangre de Cristo Range; 12 peaks more than

14,000 feet; Mount Elbert, second highest in the United States. More than 40 timberline lakes. Snow Angel on Mount Shavano; molybdenum mines; Lake Isabel Recreation Area. Hunting for deer, elk, bear, mountain goat, grouse and duck.

Nearby towns: Canon City, Leadville, Pueblo, Salida and Walsenburg.

SAN JUAN NATIONAL FOREST
(1,850,405 acres).

Office of Forest Supervisor: Oliger Building, P. O. Box 341, Durango, Colorado 81301.
Camping facilities: 619 units at 31 locations.
Other facilities: Fishing, hunting, saddle and pack trips, scenic drives, picnicking, geological study, historical points. Two winter sports areas. Motels and dude ranches in and near the National Forest.
Attractions: Alpine lakes; Mount Wilson, 14,250 feet; canyons, waterfalls, cataracts, peculiar geological formations. Archeological ruins, historic mines. San Juan Primitive Area; Wilson Mountains Primitive Area. Hunting for deer, elk, bear, mountain lion, grouse and duck.
Nearby towns: Cortez, Durango, Pagosa Springs and Silverton Colorado. Farmington, New Mexico.

Some campers look for a unique way to relax. This relaxing scene depicts camping life at Stanley Lake, Challis National Forest, Idaho.

U.S. Forest Service Photo

WHITE RIVER NATIONAL FOREST
(1,960,183 acres).

Office of Forest Supervisor: Post Office Building, P.O. Box 948, Glenwood Springs, Colorado 81601.
Camping facilities: 640 units in 35 locations.
Other facilities: Fishing, hunting, saddle and pack trails, scenic drives, picnicking. Six winter sports areas. Motels and dude ranches in and near the National Forest.
Attractions: Spectacular Glenwood Canyon, Hanging Lake, Bridal Veil Falls, mineral hot springs, caves, alpine lakes. Source of marble for Lincoln Memorial and Tomb of the Unknown Solider. Flat Tops Primitive Area; Gore Range—Eagle Nest Primitive Area; Maroon Bells-Snowmass Wilderness. Elk, deer and bear hunting.
Nearby towns: Aspen, Craig, Eagle, Glenwood Springs, Gypsum, Leadville, Meeker and Rifle.

FLORIDA

APALACHICOLA NATIONAL
FOREST (556,972 acres).

Office of Forest Supervisor: Box 1050, Tallahassee, Florida 32302.
Camping facilities: 108 units at 9 locations.
Other facilities: Boating, picnicking and swimming.
Attractions: Pine hardwood forests, coastal Plain type. Natural sinks, bottom land hardwood swamps along large rivers with trees typically found far to the north. Old Fort Gadsen, old river landings. Three rivers and their tributaries with many miles of fishing waters—bass, bream, perch. Quail, deer and bear hunting. Numerous lakes, sinks and ponds provide water recreation.
Nearby towns: Apalachicola, Blountstown, Bristol and Tallahassee.

OCALA NATIONAL FOREST
(361,497 acres).

Office of Forest Supervisor: Box 1050, Tallahassee, Florida 32302.
Camping facilities: 333 units at 9 locations.
Other facilities: Boating, picnicking and swimming. Hunting camps; commercial accommodations near the forest.
Attractions: Juniper Springs and Alexander Springs, large clear, flowing streams through subtropical wilderness; botanical lore, palms,

hardwoods and pine. Hundreds of clear lakes. The Big Scrub, characterized by vast stands of sand pine, is unique. Wildlife management area, annual deer and bear hunts. Silver Springs is nearby. Numerous lakes, streams and ponds with fishing and camping sites.
Nearby towns: DeLand, Eustis, Leesburg, Mount Dora, Ocala and Palatka.

OSCEOLA NATIONAL FOREST
(680,618 acres).

Office of Forest Supervisor: Box 1050, Tallahassee, Florida 32302.
Camping facilities: 43 units at 1 location.
Other facilities: Boating, picnicking,

GEORGIA

CHATTAHOOCHEE NATIONAL
FOREST (680,618 acres).

swimming; opportunities for aquatic sports.
Attractions: Flat country, dotted with numerous ponds, sinks and cypress swamps. State game breeding ground. Bass, perch and bream fishing. Deer, turkey, quail and dove hunting.
Nearby towns: Jacksonville and Lake City.

Office of Forest Supervisor: Box 643, Gainesville, Georgia 30501.
Camping facilities: 534 units at 24 locations.
Other facilities: Boating, picnicking and swimming.
Attractions: Visitor Center at Brasstown Bald, 4,784 feet, highest point in Georgia; Blue Ridge Mountains;

lakes; Tallulah Gorge; waterfalls, southern end of Appalachian Trail. Deer and small game hunting, archery hunting for deer. Trout and bass fishing. Hiking.

Nearby towns: Clarksville, Clayton, Dahlonega, Dalton and Toccoa, Ga. Chattanooga, Tenn.

OCONEE NATIONAL FOREST
(102,911 acres).

Office of Forest Supervisor: Box 643, Gainesville, Georgia 30501.
Camping facilities: 42 units at 2 locations.
Other facilities: Boating, picnicking and swimming.
Attractions: Heavily forested Piedmont hills; archeological remains; Rock Eagle Lake; effigy of EAGLE; Mammoth 4-H Center; Piedmont Wildlife Refuge. Deer and small game hunting. Bass and bream fishing.
Nearby towns: Eatonton, Greensboro and Madison.

IDAHO

BITTERROOT NATIONAL FOREST
—See Montana listing.

BOISE NATIONAL FOREST
(2,632,321 acres).

Office of Forest Supervisor: 413 Idaho St., Boise, Idaho 83702.
Camping facilities: 826 units at 91 locations.
Other facilities: Boating, fishing, hunting, picnicking, scenic drives, swimming. Bogus Basin Winter Sports Area. Resorts, motels, dude ranches with horses, boats and other facilities.
Attractions: Rugged back country including portions of Sawtooth Primitive Area. Abandoned mines and ghost towns. Scenes of early Indian camps and massacres. Virgin stands of ponderosa pine. Arrowrock, Anderson Ranch, Cascade, Deadwood and Lucky Peak Reservoirs; other lakes. Includes headwaters of Boise, Payette and Salmon Rivers. Lake and stream fishing for trout and salmon. Hunting for bear, elk and deer. Spectacular scenic drives in Payette and Boise River Canyons, along Boise Ridge and edge of Sawtooth Primitive Area.
Nearby towns: Boise, Cascade, Emmett, Horseshoe Bend, Idaho City and Mountain Home.

CACHE NATIONAL FOREST—See Utah listing.

CARIBOU NATIONAL FOREST
(971,781 acres—partly in Utah and Wyoming).
Office of Forest Supervisor: 427 N. Sixth Ave., Pocatello, Idaho 83201.
Camping facilities: 302 units at 19 locations.
Other facilities: Boating, fishing,

National forest visitors swim in the Potomac River not far from where it begins.

hiking trails, hunting, picnicking, riding, scenic drives, swimming. Two winter sports areas. Resorts and motels.

Attractions: High country: towering mountain ranges divided by beautiful valleys. Historic markers and trails, natural soda springs, rushing streams and waterfalls. Stream fishing of cutthroat and rainbow trout. Game bird, deer, elk and bear hunting. Scenic drives: Mink Creek to Scout Mountain, Skyline Road, Snake River-McCoy Road along south bank of South Fork of Snake River, Georgetown Canyon—Diamond Creek and Snowslide-Crow Creek Roads. Numerous riding trails into wilderness country.

Nearby towns: Idaho Falls, Malad City, Montpelier, Pocatello, Soda Springs and Swan Valley, Idaho. Afton, Wyoming.

CHALLIS NATIONAL FOREST (2,447,243 acres).

Office of Forest Supervisor: Forest Service Bldg., Challis, Idaho 83226.

Camping facilities: 331 units at 24 locations.

Other facilities: Boating, fishing, hiking trails, hunting, picnicking, riding trails, scenic drives, wilderness trips. Resorts, hotels, cabins and dude ranches. Commercial packers and guides.

Attractions: Lost River Range with Mount Borah, 12,655 feet, highest peak in Idaho. Lemhi, Lost River and White Cloud Peaks; Salmon River and White Knob Mountain Ranges, headwaters of the Salmon River. Majestic Sawtooth Primitive Area and Stanley Basin; Middle Fork of the Salmon River in the Idaho Primitive Area. Stream and lake trout, salmon fishing. Hunting for deer, elk, mountain goat, mountain sheep, antelope and bear. Stanley Basin scenic drive.

Nearby towns: Challis, Mackay, Salmon and Stanley.

CLEARWATER NATIONAL FOREST (1,675,562 acres).

Office of Forest Supervisor: Federal Bldg., Orofino, Idaho.

Camping facilities: 204 units at 15 locations.

Other facilities: Fishing, hunting, picnicking, pack trip outfitters available, scenic drives. Motels, cabins.

Attractions: Famous Lolo Trail, Selway-Bitterroot Wilderness. Spring log drive on the Middle Fork and North Fork, Clearwater River; large stands of virgin white pine. Large timber operations. Trout and salmon fishing in back country. Hunting for elk, deer and bear. Lolo Pass Visitor Station. North Fork and Lewis & Clark Highway scenic drives.

Nearby towns: Kooskia, Lewiston, Orofino and Pierce, Idaho. Lolo, Hot Springs and Missoula, Montana.

COEUR D'ALENE NATIONAL FOREST (723,168 acres).

Office of Forest Supervisor: 218 N. 23rd, Coeur d'Alene, Idaho.

Camping facilities: 129 units at 12 locations.

Other facilities: Boating, fishing, hiking trails, hunting, picnicking. Lookout Pass Winter Sports Area. Resort hotels and cabins.

Attractions: Lovely Coeur d'Alene Lake, 30 miles long and with 104

A forest ranger talks to a group of young visitors at the annual Rhododendron Festival on Roan Mountain, Pisgah National Forest, North Carolina. This event draws up to 20,000 people from over the nation during two weekends.

U.S. Forest Service Photo

miles of shoreline. Cataldo Mission, built in 1846. Coeur d'Alene River; fishing. Hunting for elk, deer. Rich Coeur d'Alene mining district (zinc, lead, silver), several large sawmills.
Nearby towns: Coeur d'Alene, Kellogg, Spirit Lake and Wallace, Idaho. Spokane, Washington.

KANIKSU NATIONAL FOREST
(1,621,898 acres—partly in Montana and Washington).

Office of Forest Supervisor: Sandpoint, Idaho.
Camping facilities: 264 units at 18 locations.
Other facilities: Boating, fishing, hunting, nature trails, picnicking, scenic drives, swimming. Evening programs (movies, slides), forest "show-me" trips in summer. Schweitzer Basin Winter Ski Area. Resorts, hotels, lodges, cabins.
Attractions: Rugged back country, Selkirk Mountain Range. Massive Pend Oreille Lake (Loop Drive, 107 miles); Priest Lake. Kullyspell House, Clark Fork River; Roosevelt Ancient Grove of Cedars; Chimney Rock;

Among the many recreational opportunities offered by the national forests is skiing. The scene here is on Green Mountain National Forest in Vermont.

U.S. Forest Service Photo

Cabinet Mountains Wilderness. Lake and stream fishing. Big game hunting.
Nearby towns: Bonners Ferry, Clark Fork, Priest River and Sandpoint.

KOOTENAI NATIONAL FOREST—
See Montana listing.

LOLO NATIONAL FOREST—See
Montana listing.

NEZPERCE NATIONAL FOREST
(2,198,094 acres).

Office of Forest Supervisor: Grangeville, Idaho
Camping facilities: 84 units at 13 locations.
Other facilities: Boating, fishing, hiking trails, hunting, picnicking, pack trip outfitters, playground, scenic drives, wilderness pack trips. Resorts, hotels, cabins.
Attractions: Selway-Bitterroot Wilderness. Salmon River Breaks Primitive Area. Seven Devils Range between Salmon and Snake Rivers, Hells Canyon on the Snake River, Red River Hot Springs. Hells Canyon-Seven Devils Scenic Area. Historic Elk City. Wilderness big game hunting of elk, deer and bear. Lake and stream fishing. Scenic drives: Lochsa River, Salmon River, Selway River.

Nearby towns: Grangeville, Kamiah, Kooskia and Riggkins.

PAYETTE NATIONAL FOREST
(2,307,158 acres).

Office of Forest Supervisor: Forest Service Bldg., McCall, Idaho.
Camping facilities: 135 units at 30 locations.
Other facilities: Boating, fishing, hunting, picnicking, scenic drives, wilderness trips, ski tows, chair lift, warming hut. Payette Lake Winter Sports Area. Dude ranches.
Attractions: Idaho Primitive Area. Hells Canyon of Snake River, 5,500 to 7,900 feet deep, deepest gorge in the U. S., Payette Lakes Recreational Area, Seven Devils Mountains. Fishing for trout and salmon, 154 fishing lakes, 1,530 miles of fishing streams. Big game hunting for deer, elk, mountain goat, bighorn sheep and bear.
Nearby towns: Cascade, Council, McCall, New Meadows and Weiser.

SALMON NATIONAL FOREST
(1,767,585 acres).

Office of Forest Supervisor: Forest Service Bldg., Salmon, Idaho.
Camping facilities: 199 units at 17 locations.
Other facilities: Boating, boat trips, fishing, hunting, pack trips, swimming. Dude ranches.
Attractions: Idaho Primitive Area, Big Horn Crags, historic Lewis and Clark Trail, Salmon River Canyon. Fishing. Big game hunting including deer, elk, bighorn sheep, bear, mountain goat, cougar and antelope. Boat trips on "River of No Return" and Middlefork.
Nearby towns: Leadore and Salmon.

ST. JOE NATIONAL FOREST
(862,018 acres).

Office of Forest Supervisor: St. Maries, Idaho.
Camping facilities: 93 units at 10 locations.
Other facilities: Fishing, hunting, picnicking, scenic drives, swimming, hiking trails, "rockhounding" for garnets. North-South Winter Sports Area. Dude ranch nearby. Cabins on St. Joe River.
Attractions: Rugged Bitterroot

Range of Idaho-Montana divide; St. Joe River drainage; St. Maries River Valley; canyon areas of Little North Fork of Clearwater River, Clearwater-St. Joe divide, Palouse River area; virgin stands of white pine. Large timber operations. Big game hunting for elk, deer, bear and mountain goat. Lake and stream fishing. Scenic drives along St. Joe River from source to mouth in Coeur d'Alene Lake.
Nearby towns: Avery, Clarkia, Moscow, Potlatch and St. Maries.

SAWTOOTH NATIONAL FOREST (1,803,164 acres—partly in Utah).

Office of Forest Supervisor: 1525 Addison Avenue East, Twin Falls, Idaho 83301.
Camping facilities: 575 units at 43 locations.
Other facilities: Boating, fishing, golfing, hunting, ice skating, picnicking, riding, saddle and pack trips, scenic drives, swimming, skiing. Five winter sports areas including Magic Mountain, Mount Harrison, Soldier Creek and Sun Valley. Numerous dude ranches, camps and motels.
Attractions: Panoramic views of Snake River Valley, Sawtooth Primitive Area. Colorful mountains, lakes, developed hot springs. "Silent City of Rocks," fantastic formations worn by wind and water. Fishing. Big game and grouse hunting in season.
Nearby towns: Burley, Gooding, Sun Valley and Twin Falls.

TARGHEE NATIONAL FOREST (1,663,363 acres—partly in Wyoming).

Office of Forest Supervisor: 420 North Bridge Street, St. Anthony, Idaho 83445.
Camping facilities: 386 units at 25 locations.
Other facilities: Boating, fishing, hiking trails, hunting, picnicking, riding trails, scenic drives, swimming. Bear Gulch, Moose Creek and Pine Basin Winter Sports Areas. Resorts, motels, dude ranches, pack outfits for hunting parties, fishing camps.

Attractions: Island Park Reservoir; Grand Canyon of the Snake River; Teton and Snake Ranges, Big Falls; North Fork of Snake River; Cave Falls; Falls River; Palisades Dam. Lake and stream fishing. Hunting for bear, deer, elk and moose. Many riding and hiking trails into remote mountain country.
Nearby towns: Ashton, Driggs, Dubois, Idaho Falls, Rexburg Rigby, St. Anthony and Victor, Idaho. Afton and Jackson, Wyoming.

ILLINOIS

SHAWNEE NATIONAL FOREST (217,982 acres).

Office of Forest Supervisor: Harrisburg, Illinois 62946.
Camping facilities: 303 units at 13 locations.
Other facilities: Boating, fishing, hunting, swimming, riding trails, nature trails, geological study. Hotels and cabins.
Attractions: Prehistoric stone forts and Indian mounds; interesting rock formations. Much of the Illinois shore of the Ohio River and some of the Mississippi; their confluence nearby at Cairo, Ill. Stream and river fishing. Hunting for quail, migratory waterfowl,, squirrel, rabbit, fox and raccoon. Artificial lakes in and adjacent to the National Forest provide fishing, boating and swimming.
Nearby towns: Anna, Cairo, Carbondale, Harrisburg, Marion, Metropolis and Murphysboro, Illinois. Paducah, Kentucky. St. Louis, Missouri.

INDIANA
HOOSIER NATIONAL FOREST (134,779 acres).
Office of Forest Supervisor: Bedford, Indiana 47421.

Midwestern campground with trailer and tent sites spaced for plenty of elbow room.

Not all fires are destructive. This is a controlled burn by the Forest Service on the Chequamegon National Forest. The purpose of the burn: to create better sharptail grouse habitat.

Camping facilities: 215 units at 4 locations.
Other facilities: Boating, fishing, swimming, scenic drives, picnicking, forest trails. Hotels and motels.
Attractions: Pioneer Mothers Memorial Forest containing the nation's outstanding specimen of black walnut. Final outlet of Lost River; Ten O'-Clock Indian Boundary Line crosses the forest. Old trail of migrating buffalo between Western Plains and French Lick. Squirrel, fox and quail hunting. Fishing in the East Fork of the White River, Salt Creek and the Ohio. Lost and Patoka Rivers for catfish, bass and bluegill. Scenic drives among spring flowers (dogwood and redbud) and fall coloring.
Nearby towns: Bedford, Bloomington, Evansville, Jasper, Paoli and Tell City.

KENTUCKY
DANIEL BOONE NATIONAL FOREST
(464,683 acres).
Office of Forest Supervisor: P. O. Building, Winchester, Kentucky 40391.
Camping facilities: 169 units at 12 locations.
Other facilities: Boating, picnicking and swimming. Hotels and cabins at Cumberland Falls and Natural Bridge State Parks. Motels and cottages at the boat docks on Lake Cumberland at confluence of Laurel and Rockcastle Rivers.
Attractions: Western rim of Cumber-

land Plateau, sandstone cliffs 100 feet high, Red River Gorge, natural rock arches, numerous limestone caves and mineral springs. Cumberland Falls and Natural Bridge State Parks within the National Forest shoreline. About 500 miles of fishing streams. Hunting for squirrel, deer, cottontails and upland game birds.
Nearby towns: Boonesboro, Corbin and Lexington.

LOUISIANA

KISATCHIE NATIONAL FOREST
(593,064 acres).

Office of Forest Supervisor: 2500 Shreveport Highway, Pineville, Louisiana 71360.
Camping facilities: 174 units at 11 locations.
Other facilities: Boating, picnicking and swimming. Hotels.

Attractions: Colonial homes; Natchitoches, oldest town in Louisiana on Old San Antonio Trail; Stuart Forest Service Nursery, one of the largest pine nurseries in the world. Extensive plantations of longleaf, loblolly and slash pine. Many bayous and lakes screened with Spanish moss. Fishing in lakes and bayous. Hunting

for deer, quail and migratory birds. Scenic drives.
Nearby towns: Alexandria, Leesville, Minden and Winnfield.

MICHIGAN

HIAWATHA NATIONAL FOREST
(839,960 acres—
two separate sections).

Office of Forest Supervisor: Escanaba, Michigan 49829.
Camping facilities: 688 units at 23 locations.

Other facilities: Boating, fishing, swimming, scenic drives, picnicking, winter sports, forest trails, group campgrounds, canoeing. Resorts, hotels, many cabins. Gladstone Winter Sports Area.
Attractions: Lakes Huron, Michigan and Superior; some shoreline in the national forest. Many small lakes among mixed evergreen and hardwood forests. Pictured Rocks on Lake Superior; Mackinac Island country; waterfalls. Lake and stream fishing for trout, bass, northern and walleyed pike, perch; smelt dipping. Deer, black bear, ruffed and sharptailed grouse hunting.
Nearby towns: Escanaba, Gladstone, Manistique, Munising, Rapid River, Saint Ignace, Sault Sainte Marie and Trout Lake.

HURON NATIONAL FOREST
(415,493 acres).

Office of Forest Supervisor: Cadillac, Michigan 49601.
Camping facilities: 203 units at 13 locations.
Other facilities: Boating, fishing, hunting, swimming, picnicking, winter sports, forest trails. Au Sable and Silver Valley Winter Sports Areas. Many resorts, hotels and cabins.
Attractions: Lumberman's Monument. A national forest easily reached from heavily populated southern Michigan, northern Ohio, Indiana and Illinois. Trout fishing in the Au Sable River and smaller streams. Deer, small game and bird hunting. At eastern edge, Lake Huron with excellent beaches.
Nearby towns: Grayling, Harrisville, Mio, Oscoda and Tawas City.

MANISTEE NATIONAL FOREST
(465,140 acres).

Office of Forest Supervisor: Cadillac, Michigan 49601.
Camping facilities: 395 units at 17 locations.
Other facilities: Boating, fishing, swimming, hunting, scenic drives, picnicking, winter sports, skiing, forest trails, canoeing, snowmobile

trail. Caberfae and Manistee Winter Sports Areas. Many resorts, hotels and cabins.

Attractions: Another national forest less than a day's drive from Chicago, South Bend, Detroit, Toledo and Cleveland. Lake and stream fishing for trout, bass, northern and walleyed pike, perch. Deer and small game hunting. Good skiing on northern part of the national forest. Many of the lakes, including Lake Michigan, have fine beaches for swimming. Chittenden Forest Service Nursery at Wellston.

Nearby towns: Big Rapids, Cadillac, Ludington, Manistee, Muskegon and Reed City.

OTTAWA NATIONAL FOREST
(886,484 acres).

Office of Forest Supervisor: Ironwood, Michigan 49938.
Camping facilities: 368 units at 23 locations.
Other facilities: Boating, fishing, hunting, swimming, scenic drives, picnicking, winter sports, forest trails. Numerous hotels and cabins.
Attractions: Sylvania Recreation

Travel trailers are ideal for long stays in more remote areas of national forests. Photo courtesy of Airstream.

Area. Numerous accessible lakes and streams; Bond, Agate, Sturgeon, Conglomerate, Gorge, Sandstone and Rainbow Falls. Victoria Dam, James Toumey Forest Service Nursery, State Fish Hatchery, forest plantations, Porcupine Mt. State Park. Lake and stream fishing, deep water trolling in Lake Superior. Deer and bear hunting. Several winter sports areas nearby.
Nearby towns: Bessemer, Iron River, Ironwood, Ontonagon, Trout Creek, Wakefield and Watersmeet, Michigan. Duluth, Minnesota.

MINNESOTA

CHIPPEWA NATIONAL FOREST
(644,602 acres).

Office of Forest Supervisor: Cass Lake, Minnesota 56633.
Camping facilities: 513 units at 25 locations.
Other facilities: Boating, fishing, hunting, swimming, scenic drives, hiking and forest trails, winter and water sports. Shingobee Winter Sports Area. 300 resorts in and adjacent to the national forest. Hotels, cabins.
Attractions: Headwaters of the Mississippi River; Leech Lake, Lake

Winnibigoshish, Cass Lake and hundreds of smaller lakes; stands of virgin red pine. Home and present headquarters of the Chippewa Indians. Lake fishing for walleyes, northern pike and pan fish. Waterfowl and upland game bird hunting; big game hunting for deer and black bear. Hundreds of miles of good roads and scenic drives; Winter sports include skiing, tobogganing, snowshoeing and ice fishing.
Nearby towns: Bemidji, Blackduck, Cass Lake, Deer River, Grand Rapids, Remer and Walker.

SUPERIOR NATIONAL FOREST
(2,040,569 acres).

Office of Forest Supervisor: Duluth, Minnesota 55801.
Camping facilities: 714 units at 35 locations. 1600 wilderness campsites available in Boundary Waters Canoe Area.
Other facilities: Boating, fishing, hunting, swimming, scenic drives, picnicking, winter sports, forest trails, canoe routes. Resorts, hotels, cabins outside the wilderness area.
Attractions: 5,000 lakes, rugged shorelines, picturesque islands, sand beaches, more than a million acres of virgin forest. Boundary Waters Canoe Area, part of the National

Forest Wilderness System. Finest canoe country in the United States here in the land of the French *voyageurs,* along their historic water route to the Northwest. Unusual canoe routes in wilderness country. Adjacent Quetico Provincial Park in Canada also maintains a canoe-wilderness character over a large area. Lake and stream fishing. Deer hunting. Two ski areas nearby. Scenic drives: Honeymoon and Ely Buyck Roads, Gunflint and Sawbill Trails.
Nearby towns: Duluth, Ely, Grand Marais, International Falls, Two Harbors and Virginia, Minnesota. Port Arthur and Winnipeg, Canada.

MISSISSIPPI

BIENVILLE NATIONAL FOREST
(175,697 acres).

Office of Forest Supervisor: Box 1291, Jackson, Mississippi 39205.
Camping facilities: 70 units at 4 locations.
Other facilities: Boating, picnicking and swimming.
Attractions: Coastal Plain second growth pine and hardwood forest; numerous forest management demonstration areas. Eighty acres of virgin loblolly pine surrounding

Bienville Ranger Station. Quail hunting. Fishing.
Nearby towns: Jackson and Meridian.

DELTA NATIONAL FOREST
(58,923 acres).

Office of Forest Supervisor: Box 1291, Jackson, Mississippi 39205.
Camping facilities: 4 units at 1 location.
Other facilities: Boating and picnicking.
Attractions: Greentree Reservoir (2,000 acres) popular for waterfowl hunting in the fall. Red Gum Natural Area is an example of a natural bottom land hardwood stand. Hunting and fishing.
Nearby towns: Rolling Fork and Vicksburg.

DESOTO NATIONAL FOREST
(501,548 acres).

Office of Forest Supervisor: Box 1291, Jackson, Mississippi 39205.

Camping facilities: 25 units at 4 locations; camping permitted at five of the picnic areas.
Other facilities: Boating, picnicking and swimming.
Attractions: Site of South Mississippi Gun and Dog Club field trials. Quail hunting. Fishing. Ashe Forest Service Nursery.
Nearby towns: Biloxi, Gulfport, Hattiesburg, Laurel and Wiggins.

HOLLY SPRINGS NATIONAL FOREST (143,729 acres).

Office of Forest Supervisor: Box 1291, Jackson, Mississippi 39205.
Camping facilities: 9 units at 2 loca-

tions; camping permitted at 1 other picnic site.
Other facilities: Boating, picnicking and swimming.
Attractions: Intensive erosion control projects. Annual bird dog field trials at Holly Springs. Quail and small game hunting.
Nearby towns: Holly Springs, New Albany and Oxford.

HOMOCHITTO NATIONAL FOREST
(189,053 acres).

Office of Forest Supervisor: Box 1291, Jackson, Mississippi 39205.
Camping facilities: 23 units at 1 location; camping permitted at 3 other picnic sites.
Other facilities: Boating, picnicking and swimming.
Attractions: One of the finest natural timber growing sites in the United States; numerous forest management demonstration areas. Picturesque eroded loess country near Natchez. Fishing.

Tent campers relax on a peaceful afternoon in the Homochitto National Forest Mississippi. USDA Photo.

TOMBIGBEE NATIONAL FOREST
(65,254 acres).

Office of Forest Supervisor: Box 1291, Jackson, Mississippi 39205.

Camping facilities: 37 units at 2 locations.
Other facilities: Boating, fishing, picnicking and swimming.
Attractions: Upper Coastal Plain pine and hardwood forests. Indian mounds; Davis and Choctaw Lakes; Natchez Trace Parkway. Deer and quail hunting.
Nearby towns: Ackerman, Houston, Kosciusko and Tupelo.

MISSOURI

CLARK NATIONAL FOREST
(768,254 acres).

Office of Forest Supervisor: Rolla, Missouri 65401.
Camping facilities: 262 units at 16 locations.
Other facilities: Boating, fishing, hunting, swimming, picnicking, riding and hiking trails.
Attractions: Clear, fast-flowing streams, Ozark Mountains covered with oak and pine forests, spring bloom of redbud and dogwood and brilliant fall coloring. Smallmouth bass and other fishing. Squirrel, coon and fox hunting. Black and St. Francis Rivers and others provide hundreds of miles of streams for float trips. Riverbank campsites in places. Several lakes.
Nearby towns: Fredericktown, Ironton, Piedmont, Poplar Bluff, Potosi, St. Louis and Salem.

MARK TWAIN NATIONAL FOREST
(608,719 acres).

Office of Forest Supervisor: Springfield, Missouri 65806.
Camping facilities: 151 units at 11 locations.
Other facilities: Boating, fishing, hunting, swimming, horse trails, forest trails, forest tours. Resorts and hotels.
Attractions: Ozark Mountains, numerous caves, rock cairns and Big Springs. Current and Eleven Point Rivers; hundreds of miles of streams for "John-boat" float trips. Fishing for pan fish, bass and walleye. Deer, quail and small game hunting. Fall color tours. Several state parks.
Nearby towns: Branson, Doniphan, Springfield, Van Buren, West Plains and Willow Springs.

MONTANA

BEAVERHEAD NATIONAL FOREST
(2,111,070 acres).

Office of Forest Supervisor: Federal Bldg., Dillon, Montana.
Camping facilities: 194 units at 19 locations.
Other facilities: Boating, fishing, horseback riding, picnicking, wilderness trips. Dude ranches and resorts in and near the National Forest.
Attractions: Anaconda-Pintlar Wilderness Area; Big Hole Battlefield Monument; Sacajawea Memorial Area; Bannack, the first capital of Montana. Gravelly Range self-guided auto tours. Tobacco Root, Madison, Gravelly, Snowcrest, and Continental Divide Ranges; Madison, Ruby, Beaverhead and Big Hole Rivers; alpine

lakes. Fishing. Hunting for deer, elk, moose, antelope and bear. Hot springs, scenic drives. Rainy Mountain Winter Sports Area.
Nearby towns: Dillon, Ennis, Jackson, Lima, Sheridan, Virginia City and Wisdom.

BITTERROOT NATIONAL FOREST
(1,575,919 acres).

Office of Forest Supervisor: 316 North 3rd St., Hamilton, Montana.
Camping facilities: 95 units at 15 locations.
Other facilities: Boating, fishing, hunting, nature trails, picnicking, riding, wilderness trips. Resorts, hotels, cabins and dude ranches.
Attractions: Bitterroot Valley and spectacular Bitterroot Mountains, scores of mountain lakes and hot springs. Ancient Indian hieroglyphics, Saint Mary's Mission and Fort Owen. Selway-Bitterroot Wilderness; Anaconda-Pintlar Wilderness. Lewis and Clark Trail. Lake and stream fishing. Hunting for elk, deer and mountain goat. Lost Trail Pass Visitor Station. Bitterroot Valley scenic drives.
Nearby towns: Corvallis, Hamilton, Missoula and Stevensville.

CUSTER NATIONAL FOREST
(1,185,663 acres).

Office of Forest Supervisor: 1015 Broadwater, Billings, Montana.
Camping facilities: 219 units at 15 locations. There are three Custer Forests. One in South Central Montana, another in the southeastern area east of Ashland and a third on the North and South Dakota border in East Central Montana.
Other facilities: Fishing, hunting, picnicking, saddle and pack trips, wilderness trails. Red Lodge and Grizzly Peak Winter Sports Areas. Resorts, hotels, cabins and dude ranches.
Attractions: Spectacular Beartooth Highway; snowclad peaks and alpine plateaus; Granite Peak, 12,799 feet, highest point in Montana; hundreds of lakes; Woodbine Falls, 900 feet high; glaciers and ice caverns. Rich fossil beds, Indian hieroglyphics and burial grounds. Beartooth Primitive Area. Trout fishing. Big game hunting.
Nearby towns: Absarokee, Ashland, Billings, Columbus, Hardin, Laurel and Red Lodge.

DEERLODGE NATIONAL FOREST
(1,181,276 acres).

Office of Forest Supervisor: 107 E. Granite St., Butte, Montana.
Camping facilities: 201 units at 19 locations.

Other facilities: Boating, fishing, hunting, picnicking, riding, wilderness trails and trips. Wraith Hill Winter Sports Area. Resorts, hotels, cabins and dude ranches.
Attractions: Anaconda-Pintlar Wilderness, Tobacco Root Mountains, Mount Powell and Flint Creek Range, numerous alpine lakes. Lake and spring fishing. Big game hunting of bear, deer, elk, and special moose seasons.
Nearby towns: Anaconda, Boulder, Butte, Deer Lodge, Phillipsburg and Whitehall.

FLATHEAD NATIONAL FOREST
(2,341,664 acres).

Office of Forest Supervisor: North Main at Washington, Kalispell, Montana.
Camping facilities: 171 units at 8 locations.
Other facilities: Boating, canoeing, fishing, hunting, nature trails, picnicking, riding, scenic drives, swimming, wilderness trips. Big Mountain Winter Sports Area. Resorts, hotels, cabins and dude ranches.
Attractions: Spectacular geological formations, including massive Chinese Wall and jagged Mission Mountains; hanging valleys; glaciers and scores of glacial lakes. Hungry Horse Dam Visitor Center and lake. Mission Mountains Primitive Area; Bob Marshall Wilderness. Big game hunting of elk, deer, moose, bear, mountain sheep and goats.
Nearby towns: Belton, Bigfork, Columbia Falls, Coram, Kalispell and Whitefish.

GALLATIN NATIONAL FOREST
(1,701,338 acres).

Office of Forest Supervisor: Post Office Bldg., Bozeman, Montana.
Camping facilities: 323 units at 20 locations.
Other facilities: Climbing, fishing, hiking trails, hunting, picnicking, riding, scenic drives, wilderness trips, Bridger Bowl and Lionhead Winter Sports Areas. Resorts, hotels, cabins and dude ranches.
Attractions: Fertile Gallatin Valley; Crazy Mountains; snowclad peaks; 11 outstanding waterfalls; more than 200 lakes and thousands of miles of trout streams. Madison River Canyon earthquake area and Visitor Center. Spanish Peaks, Beartooth, and Absaroka Primitive Areas. Lake and stream fishing. Hunting for bear, moose, elk and deer. Gallatin Canyon, Boulder Canyon, and Yankee Jim Canyon.
Nearby towns: Big Timber, Bozeman, Gardiner, Livingston and West Yellowstone.

HELENA NATIONAL FOREST
(969,000 acres).

Office of Forest Supervisor: Steamboat Block, Helena, Montana.
Camping facilities: 134 units at 10 locations.
Other facilities: Boating, summer excursion boat, fishing, hiking trails, hunting, picnicking, riding, scenic

Jewel lake in the beautiful rolling hill country of Virginia.

drives, wilderness trips. Grass Mountain Winter Sports Area. Resorts, hotels, cabins and dude ranches.
Attractions: Continental Divide; Big Belt and Elkhorn Mountain Ranges. Boat trip up through Gates of the Mountain Wilderness on Missouri River; old Fort Logan original blockhouse; ghost towns: Diamond City, Marysville, Crow Creek Falls. Lake and stream fishing. Hunting for deer and elk. Trout and Beaver Creek Canyons.
Nearby towns: Helena, Lincoln, Townsend, Boulder and White Sulphur Springs.

KANIKSU NATIONAL FOREST—
See Idaho listing.

KOOTENAI NATIONAL FOREST
(1,819,545 acres—partly in Idaho).

Office of Forest Supervisor: 418 Mineral Ave., Libby, Montana.
Camping facilities: 164 units at 14 locations.
Other facilities: Boating, fishing, hunting, picnicking, riding, scenic drives. Turner Mountain Winter Sports Area. Hotels, cabins and dude ranches.
Attractions: Cabinet Mountains Wilderness; Yaak River, Kootenai Canyon and Fisher River. Libby Dam and lake. Lake and stream fishing. Hunting for black bear and deer. Ten Lakes and Northwest Peaks Scenic Area.
Nearby towns: Eureka, Libby and Troy.

LEWIS AND CLARK NATIONAL
FOREST (1,834,612 acres).

Office of Forest Supervisor: Federal Building, Great Falls, Montana.
Camping facilities: 145 units at 13 locations.
Other facilities: Fishing, hunting, riding, scenic drives, wilderness trips. Kings Hill Winter Sports Area. Many resorts, cabins and dude ranches.
Attractions: Bob Marshall Wilderness. Chinese Wall and Continental Divide, scenic limestone cayons and rolling mountains with many open parks. Stream and lake fishing. Hunting for deer, elk, antelope, grizzly and black bear. Kings Hill, Judith River, Crystal Lake, Sun River and Teton River.
Nearby towns: Augusta, Choteau, Great Falls, Larlowton, Lewistown and White Sulphur Springs.

LOLO NATIONAL FOREST
(2,086,234 acres—partly in Idaho).

Office of Forest Supervisor: Post

Tent set up on prepared sight in the new Oconee National Forest in the Piedmont section of Georgia.

office Building, Missoula, Montana.
Camping facilities: 151 units at 14 locations.
Other facilities: Boating, fishing, hiking trails, hunting, picnicking, riding, saddle and pack trips, scenic drives, swimming, wilderness trips. Snow Bowl Winter Sports Area. Resorts, dude ranches.
Attractions: Selway-Bitterroot Wilderness; Rattlesnake, Bitterroot and Swan Ranges. Clark Fork and Blackfoot Rivers. Stream and lake fishing. Hunting for native grouse, elk, deer and bear. Lochsa River, Seeley Lake, Buffalo Park, Rock Creek.
Nearby towns: Alberton, Drummond, Ovando, Plains, St. Regis, Superior, Thompson Falls and Missoula.

NEBRASKA

NEBRASKA NATIONAL FOREST &
OGLALA NATIONAL GRASSLAND
(339,716 acres).

Office of Forest Supervisor: Post Office Building, Lincoln Nebraska 68508.
Camping facilities: 44 units at 3 locations.
Other facilities: Fishing, swimming. Nearby hotels.
Attractions: Bessey Nursery; extensive forest plantations on sand hills; entire forest in game refuge; mule deer, antelope; nesting ground of great blue heron, grouse and prairie chicken, pheasant and wild turkeys.
Nearby towns: Broken Bow, Valentine, Halsey and Chadron.

NEVADA

HUMBOLDT NATIONAL FOREST
(2,512,258 acres).

Office of Forest Supervisor: 976 Mountain City Highway, Elko, Nevada 89801.
Camping facilities: 274 camping units, 213 trailer spaces at 23 locations.
Other facilities: Boating, fishing, hunting, swimming, saddle and pack trips, scenic drives, wilderness trips. Ward Mountain Winter Sports Area. Resort and dude ranch at Wildhorse Reservoir. Hotels.
Attractions: Jarbridge Wilderness; Wildhorse Reservoir; Owyhee River Canyon: Humboldt, Independence, Ruby and Santa Rosa Mountains. Spectacular canyons, colorful cliffs, old historic mining camps. Fishing in streams and Wildhorse Reservoir. Deer hunting.
Nearby towns: Ely, Elko, Mountain City, Wells and Winnemucca.

TOIYABE NATIONAL FOREST
(3,119,593 acres—partly in
California).

Office of Forest Supervisor: P. O. Box 1331, Reno, Nevada 89504.
Camping facilities: 704 camping units, 512 trailer spaces in 29 locations.
Other facilities: Boating, fishing, hunting, swimming, saddle and pack trips, scenic drives, wilderness trips, picnicking, horse rentals, ski rentals and lifts. Lee Canyon and Reno Ski Bowl winter Sports Areas. Motels, resorts, dude ranches.
Attractions: Lake Tahoe; Nevada

Beach Forest Camp; historic ghost towns; rugged High Sierra country. Many beautiful lakes and streams. Notable trout fishing. Hoover Wilderness. Big game hunting. Scenic drives: Mt. Rose, Lake Tahoe, Ebbetts and Sonora Passes.

Nearby towns: Austin, Carson City, Minden, Reno and Tonopah.

NEW HAMPSHIRE

WHITE MOUNTAIN NATIONAL FOREST (716,157 acres—partly in Maine).

Office of Forest Supervisor: Laconia, New Hampshire 03246.

Camping facilities: 741 units at 18 locations.

Other facilities: Boating, fishing, hunting, swimming, scenic drives, picnicking, hiking, winter sports, forest trails, rock climbing, skiing, group campgrounds, high-country cabins for hikers. Wildcat, Tuckermans Ravine, Waterville Valley Winter Sports Areas. Cabins, motels, hotels.

Attractions: Very popular mountains and forest including a major part of the White Mountains. Mount Washington, 6,288 feet, highest point in New England; Presidential Range; Great Gulf Wilderness; Glen Ellis Falls; Tuckerman Ravine; the Dolly Copp Recreation Area. Some 650 miles of streams, 39 lakes and ponds, provide brook trout fishing. Deer, bear and small game hunting. Scenic drives through famous notches and over mountain highways. Outstanding skiing with spring skiing often lasting into June. 1,000 miles of foot trails.

Nearby towns: Berlin, Conway, Gorham, Lancaster, Littleton, Pinkham Notch.

NEW MEXICO

CARSON NATIONAL FOREST (1,419,732 acres).

Office of Forest Supervisor: Taos, New Mexico

Camping facilities: 19 locations.

Other facilities: Fishing, scenic drives, historic points, picnicking, skiing, hunting, riding, pack trips, hiking trails. Three winter sports areas. Resorts, motels, dude ranches on nearby private land.

Attractions: Massive timbered Sangre de Cristo Mountains and other ranges flanking the upper Rio Grande Valley. Wheeler Peak, 13,151 feet, highest in New Mexico. Pecos Wilderness; Wheeler Peak Wilderness; alpine lakes and timberline country. Trout streams, 12,000-13,000-foot peaks. High green valleys

with Spanish-speaking villages. Scenic drives: Taos-Questa-Red River-Eagle Nest Loop. Tres Piedras-Lagunitas lake country. Santa Barbara Canyon near Penasco. Taos: Indian Pueblo. Near Abiquiu, Ghost ranch Museum.

Nearby towns: Chama, Cimmaron, Espanola, Farmington, Taos and Tierra Amarilla, New Mexico. Alamosa and Pagosa Springs, Colorado.

CIBOLA NATIONAL FOREST (1,599,337 acres).

Office of Forest Supervisor: Albuquerque, New Mexico.

Camping facilities: 11 locations.

Hillman Ferry campground

Other facilities: Fishing, hunting, scenic drives, picnicking. Sandia Peak Ski Area in Sandia Mountains. Motels, hotels, dude ranches.

Attractions: Magdalena, Manzano, Sandia, San Mateo and Zuni Mountain Ranges. Mount Taylor, 11,389 feet. Sandia Crest, 10,700 feet, accessible by car and aerial tramway. Deer and antelope hunting. Bighorn sheep often visible at Sandia Crest in summer. Nearby are Pueblo Indian villages, prehistoric ruins, ancient "sky city" of Acoma. Fishing at Bluewater and McGaffey Lakes.

Nearby towns: Albuquerque, Belen, Bernalillo, Gallup, Grants, Magdalena, Mountainair, Scorro.

GILA NATIONAL FOREST (2,694,447 acres).

Office of Forest Supervisor: Silver City, New Mexico.

Camping facilities: 15 locations.

Other facilities: Fishing, hunting, riding, pack trips, picnicking, scenic drives, hiking trails. Some motels, resorts, dude ranches.

Attractions: Semidesert to alpine country, most of it very remote and undeveloped. Elevation 4,500 to 10,700 feet. Pack trips into the Gila Wilderness and Black Range Primitive Area. Magollon Rim; many prehistoric ruins. Lake fishing in Wall Lake, Lake Roberts and Bear Canyon Reservoir. Stream fishing in the three forks of the Gila, other streams; most of it "packing in" to little used streams. Abundant game; uncrowded big game hunting; black bear, mule deer, white tailed deer, antelope, elk, mountain lion, turkey. Scenic drives: Outer Loop, Inner Loop; ghost town of Mogollon.

Nearby towns: Deming, Las Cruces, Lordsburg, Reserve, Silver City and Truth or Consequences, New Mexico. Clifton and Springerville, Arizona.

LINCOLN NATIONAL FOREST (1,085,302 acres).

Office of Forest Supervisor: Alamogordo, New Mexico.

Camping facilities: 11 locations.

Other facilities: Fishing, big game and turkey hunting, horseback riding, saddle and pack trips, scenic drives, picnicking, hiking trails. Golfing at Ruidoso (7,000 feet) and at Cloudcroft (9,000 feet). One winter sports area. Resorts, hotels, dude ranches, organization camps.

Attractions: Sierra Blanca, 12,000 feet (summit is in Mescalero Apache

Indian Reservation) with beautiful scenery. White Mountain Wilderness. Sacramento, Capitan and Guadalupe Mountain Ranges with extensive ponderosa pine and fir stands. Resort cities of Cloudcroft, Ruidoso.
Nearby towns: Alamogordo, Artesia, Capitan (birthplace of Smokey the Bear), Carlsbad and Roswell, New Mexico. El Paso, Texas.

SANTA FE NATIONAL FOREST (1,440,511 acres).

Office of Forest Supervisor: Santa Fe, New Mexico.
Camping facilities: 27 locations.
Other facilities: Fishing, hunting, hiking trails, skiing, wilderness pack trips, saddle trails, picnicking. Winter sports at Santa Fe Basin; scenic double chair lift to 11,600 feet, operates summer by appointment. Resorts, hotels, guest ranches on Pecos River up as far as Cowles and Jemez River near Jemez Springs.
Attractions: Southern Sangre de Cristo Range including 13,000-foot Truchas Peaks; across Rio Grande to the west, Jemez and San Pedro Ranges, 10,000-12,000 feet. Headwaters Pecos, Jemez and Gallinas Rivers; mountain streams and lakes; Pecos Wilderness; San Pedro Parks Wilderness. A dozen living Indian Pueblos nearby, great vistas, ancient ruins, Spanish missions, cliff dwellings. Turkey, elk, deer and bear hunting.
Nearby towns: Albuquerque, Bernalillo, Cuba, Espanola, Las Vegas, Pecos and Santa Fe.

NORTH CAROLINA

CROATAN NATIONAL FOREST (152,373 acres).

Office of Forest Supervisor: Box 731, Asheville, North Carolina 28802.
Camping facilities: 13 units at 1 location.
Other facilities: Boating, fishing, picnicking and swimming.

Attractions: Historic New Bern, founded in 1710; Civil War breastworks. Five large lakes; pine and swamp hardwoods, 3 miles from Atlantic Ocean. Neuse River Estuary. Deer, bear, turkey, quail and migratory bird hunting.
Nearby towns: Goldsboro, Morehead City, New Bern and Wilmington.

NANTAHALA NATIONAL FOREST (449,281 acres).

Office of Forest Supervisor: Box 731, Asheville, North Carolina 28802.
Camping facilities: 311 units at 8

locations; camping permitted at 1 picnic area; 6 group campsites.
Other facilities: Boating, hiking, picnicking and swimming.
Attractions: Fontana, Hiwassee, Santeetlah, Nantahala, Cheoha, Glenville and Apalachia Lakes; Fontana Dam, 8 resorts, Cullasaja, White Water River, Bridal Voll, Toxaway and Dry Falls. Joyce Kilmer Memorial Forest; 60 miles of Appalachian Trail. Annual big game hunts: European wild boar, deer; also turkey and bird hunting. Southern Appalachian Mountains, famous for azaleas and rhododendrons. Lake and stream fishing for bass and trout. Scenic drives.
Nearby towns: Bryson City, Franklin, Hayesville, Highlands, Murphy and Robbinsville.

PISGAH NATIONAL FOREST (478,297 acres).

Office of Forest Supervisor: Box 731, Asheville, North Carolina 28802.
Camping facilities: 288 units at 9 locations; two picnicking sites permit camping.
Other facilities: Hiking, horseback riding, picnicking and swimming. Resorts and cabins available nearby.
Attractions: Mount Mitchell, 6,684 feet, highest point east of the Mississippi; Shining Rock Wilderness; Linville Falls and Gorge. Annual hunts for deer, bear; also small game hunting. Craggy Gardens and Roan Mountain, famous for purple rhododendron; Cradle of American Forestry Visitor Center; Appalachian Trail. Trout, bass, and perch fishing. Scenic roads and trails.
Nearby towns: Brevard, Burnsville, Canton, Hot Springs, Lenoir, Marion and Waynesville.

UWHARRIE NATIONAL FOREST (43,571 acres).

Office of Forest Supervisor: Box 731, Asheville, North Carolina 28802.
Attractions: Regulated hunting on the Uwharrie wildlife management area. Fishing in the Uwharrie River and Badin Lake.
Nearby towns: Asheboro, Troy and Albemarle.

OHIO

WAYNE NATIONAL FOREST (118,944 acres).

Office of Forest Supervisor: Bedford, Indiana 47421.
Camping facilities: 106 units at 2 locations.
Other facilities: Boating, fishing, hunting, swimming, picnicking,

horseback riding, forest trails, auto tours. Overnight accommodations at numerous motels, tourist homes and hotels along the main highways and at the larger towns.
Attractions: Particularly beautiful fall coloring of hardwoods. Nearby are historic Marietta, Gallipolis, Blennerhasset's Island and Amesville "Coonskin Library." Old charcoal furnaces. Small game hunting. Fishing on numerous streams and lakes. Scenic lookout points.
Nearby towns: Athens, Ironton, Jackson, Marietta.

OREGON

DESCHUTES NATIONAL FOREST (1,587,690 acres).

Office of Forest Supervisor: P. O. Box 751, Bend, Oregon 97701.
Camping facilities: 1,756 units in 88 locations.
Other facilities: Berry picking, boating, fishing, hunting, swimming, saddle and pack trips, scenic drives, picnicking, riding, nature trails, hiking trails; skiing, water sports, geological study, playground. Dude ranches, motels and resorts.

Attractions: Beautiful southern Cascade Range. Snow-clad peaks, ice caves, waterfalls and over 300 lakes; lava caves; Deschutes River; Newberry Crater; scenic Cascades Lake Highway; Bend Forest Service Nursery; historic Willamette Military Road; Mount Jefferson Primitive Area and Three Sisters, Mount Washington and Diamond Peak Wildernesses. Sections of Oregon Skyline Trail from Mount Jefferson to Mount Thielsen. Cast Forest and Lava Butte. Geological areas in a ponderosa pine setting. Rainbow trout fishing. Deer hunting.
Nearby towns: Bend, Crescent, Redmond and Sisters.

FREMONT NATIONAL FOREST (1,208,302 acres).

Office of Forest Supervisor: P. O. Box 551, Lakeview, Oregon 97630.
Camping facilities: 166 units at 22 locations.
Other facilities: Boating, fishing, hunting, winter sports, picnicking, geological study. Motels.
Attractions: Indian paintings and writings. Protected herds of antelope; Oregon Desert; Gearhart Mountain Wilderness. Drier inland forests. Deer and bird hunting. Abert geologic fault east of Lake Abert, second largest vertical fault in the world.
Nearby towns: Bly, Chemult, Kla-

math Falls, Lakeview, Paisley and Silver Lake.

MALHEUR NATIONAL FOREST
(1,204,974 acres).

Office of Forest Supervisor: 139 N. E. Dayton Street, John Day, Oregon 97845.
Camping facilities: 205 units at 18 locations.
Other facilities: Berry picking, boating, fishing, hunting, saddle and pack trips, scenic drives, picnicking, hiking trails, geological study. One winter sports area. Motels and cabins in and near the National Forest.
Attractions: Mountains, fishing streams, archers' hunting reserve, fossil beds of prehistoric plants and animals, extensive stands of ponderosa pine. Strawberry Mountain Wilderness. Steelhead and rainbow trout fishing. Elk and deer hunting. Cabin of Joaquin Miller.
Nearby towns: Burns, Dayville, John Day and Prairie City.

MOUNT HOOD NATIONAL FOREST
(1,115,746 acres).

Office of Forest Supervisor: P. O. Box 16040, Portland, Oregon 97216.
Office of Forest Supervisor: P. O. Box 16040, Portland, Oregon 97216.
Camping facilities: 1,181 units in 104 locations.
Other facilities: Winter sports, huckleberry picking, boating, fishing, hunting, swimming, saddle and pack trips, scenic drives, picnicking, riding, mountain climbing, hiking trails, geological study. Six winter sports areas. Timberline Lodge, Multomah Falls Lodge and other resorts in and near the National Forest.
Attractions: Beautiful Mount Hood with Timberline Lodge; Multomah Falls; glaciers, lakes, hot springs and flower filled alpine meadows. Mount Hood Wilderness and Mount Jefferson Primitive Area. Mount Hood Loop and Columbia Gorge scenic drives; Oregon Trail route. North end of Oregon Skyline Trail, a segment of the Pacific Crest Trail system. Stream and lake fishing.
Nearby towns: Gresham, Hood River, Maupin, Oregon City and Portland.

OCHOCO NATIONAL FOREST
(845,855 acres).

Office of Forest Supervisor: P. O. Box 490, Prineville, Oregon 97754.
Camping facilities: 144 units at 11 locations.
Other facilities: Boating, fishing, hunting, swimming, scenic drives, picnicking, hiking trails, water sports, geological study, playground. Motels, cabins.

Attractions: Park-like ponderosa pine forest, many beaver colonies. Fort Watson and Camp Maury, frontier day army posts; scenes of early day range wars. Steins Pillar, geological landmark. Trout fishing. Elk and deer hunting.
Nearby towns: Bend, Burns and Prineville.

ROGUE RIVER NATIONAL FOREST
(621,473 acres—partly in California).

Office of Forest Supervisor: P. O. Box 520, Medford, Oregon 97501.
Camping facilities: 285 units at 27 locations.
Other facilities: Community kitchens, historical points, berry picking, fishing, boat launch, hunting, swimming, saddle and pack trips, scenic drives, riding, hiking trails, skiing. Union Creek and Mt. Ashland Sports Areas. Resorts, motels, cabins.
Attractions: Beautiful Rogue River, lakes, trout streams and waterfalls; extensive sugar pine and Douglas fir forests; mammoth sugar pine roadside specimen. Table Rock, site of bloody war with Rogue River Indians. Rainbow and steelhead trout fishing. Deer hunting. Oregon Skyline trail extends through National Forest from Crater Lake almost to California line.
Nearby towns: Ashland, Grants Pass, Klamath Falls and Medford.

SISKIYOU NATIONAL FOREST
(1,081,006 acres—partly in California).

Office of Forest Supervisor: P. O. Box 440, Grants Pass, Oregon 97526.
Camping facilities: 190 units at 21 locations.
Other facilities: Boat trips, boating, fishing, hunting, saddle and pack trips, scenic drives, picnicking, hiking trails. Resorts, outfitters and cabins in and near the National Forest.
Attractions: Beautiful Oregon coast, famous salmon fishing in lower Rogue River Gorge; early day gold camps. Home of rare species, including Port Oxford cedar, Oregon myrtle, rock rhododendron, Brewer weeping spruce and Saddler oak. Profuse growth of wild lilac, rhododendron, azaleas and pitcher plants. Kalmiopsis Wilderness. Cutthroat and steelhead trout and salmon fishing. Deer, bear and cougar hunting. Boat trips up the pristine Rogue.
Nearby towns: Brookings, Gold Beach, Grants Pass, Port Orford and Powers.

SIUSLAW NATIONAL FOREST
(618,685 acres).

Office of Forest Supervisor: P. O. Box 1148, Corvallis, Oregon 97330.

Snowmobiling, skiing are attracting more outdoor enthusiasts every year. Photo courtesy Banner Motor Homes.

Camping facilities: 570 units at 30 locations.

Other facilities: Boating, fishing, hunting, swimming, clam digging, sand dunes, ocean beaches, amphitheaters, berry picking, scenic drives, picnicking, nature trails, hiking trails, water sports, geological study. Resorts, motels.

Attractions: Heavy stands of Sitka spruce, western hemlock, cedar and Douglas fir; pitcher plants, rhododendron, azaleas. Bordered by Pacific Ocean; 34 miles of public beach, shoreline and sand dunes. Cape Perpetua Recreation Area and Visitor Center. Marys Peak, highest in the Coast Range, with road to campsites near summit. Ocean, lake and stream fishing. Deer, bear, cougar and migratory bird hunting.

Nearby towns: Corvallis, Eugene, Florence, Mapleton, Reedsport, Tillamook and Waldport.

UMATILLA NATIONAL FOREST
(1,389,709 acres—partly in Washington).

Office of Forest Supervisor: 2517 SW Hailey Ave., Pendleton, Oregon 97801.

Camping facilities: 326 units at 39 locations.

Other facilities: Boating, fishing, hunting, swimming, berry picking, community kitchens, historical points, saddle and pack trips, scenic drives, picnicking, riding, hiking trails, skiing. Resorts, motels.

Attractions: Skyline trip along summit of Blue Mountains on the Kendall-Skyline Forest Road. Spectacular views of Touchet and Wenaha River Canyons. Wenaha Backcountry Area. Extensive stands of ponderosa pine. Oregon Trail route; hot sulfur springs. Stream fishing for steelhead and rainbow trout. Elk, deer, pheasant and other bird hunting.

Nearby towns: La Grande and Pendleton, Oregon. Clarkston, Pomeroy, Waitsburg and Walla Walla, Washington.

UMPQUA NATIONAL FOREST
(984,497 acres).

Office of Forest Supervisor: P. O. Box 1008, Roseburg, Oregon 97470.

Camping facilities: 661 units at 35 locations.

Other facilities: Boating, fishing, hunting, swimming, berry picking, saddle and pack trips, scenic drives, picnicking, riding, hiking trails, skiing, water sports, playground. Taft Mountain Winter Sports Area. Resorts, dude ranches, motels.

Attractions: Spectacular North Umpqua Cateracts, Steamboat and Watson Falls, Umpqua River; a little

Matterhorn, Mount Thielsen, rising above beautiful Diamond Lake. Unique stands of incense cedar. Steelhead and rainbow trout fishing. Deer, bear, cougar hunting. Oregon Skyline Trail from Windigo Pass to Crater Lake.

Nearby towns: Canyonville, Cottage Grove and Roseburg.

WALLOWA-WHITMAN NATIONAL FORESTS (2,497,094 acres—two national forests).

Office of Forest Supervisor: P. O. Box 471, Baker, Oregon 97814.

Camping facilities: 510 units at 46 locations.

Other facilities: Boating, fishing,

hunting, swimming, saddle and pack trips, scenic drives, picnicking, riding, hiking trails, water sports, geological study, berry picking, historical points, community kitchens. Anthony Lake Winter Sports Area. Resorts, dude ranches, motels.

Attractions: Snowcapped peaks; Wallowa and many other lakes; glaciers; alpine meadows and rare wild flowers; Minam River, famous fishing stream. Grand spectacle of Snake River and Imnaha Canyons from Grizzly Ridge Road and Hat Point. Blue and Wallowa Mountains, Anthony Lakes, Eagle Cap Wilderness. Stream and lake trout fishing. Elk, deer and bear hunting.

Nearby towns: Baker, Enterprise, Halfway, La Grande and Union,

WILLAMETTE NATIONAL FOREST
(1,665,979 acres).

Office of Forest Supervisor: P. O. Box 1272, Eugene, Oregon 97401.

Camping facilities: 949 units at 68 locations.

Other facilities: Boating, fishing, hunting, swimming, saddle and pack trips, scenic drives, picnicking, riding, mountain climbing, hiking trails,

water sports, geological study, berry picking, winter sports, hot springs. Two winter sports areas. Motels, cabins, pack trip outfitters.

Attractions: Most heavily timbered national forest in the United States. Snowcapped peaks, lakes, waterfalls and hot springs; McKenzie Pass Highway and lava beds. Historic Willamette Military Road. Three Sisters Wilderness Area including extensive volcanic formations; Mount Jefferson Primitive Area and the Mount Washington and Diamond Peak Wildernesses. Sections of Oregon Skyline Trail from Mount Jefferson south to Maiden Peak. Stream and lake fishing. Deer and bear hunting.

Nearby towns: Albany, Eugene, Lebanon and Salem.

WINEMA NATIONAL FOREST
(908,984 acres).

Office of Forest Supervisor: P. O. Box 1390, Klamath Falls, Oregon 97601.

Camping facilities: 221 units in 9 locations.

Other facilities: Boating, fishing, hunting, swimming, picnicking, rid-

ing, hiking trails, skiing, water sports, geological study. Tomahawk Ski Bowl. Resorts, cabins, motels, pack trip outfitters.

Attractions: Peaks and mountain lakes of southern Oregon Cascades, including Mt. McLoughlin, 9,495 feet, and Lake of the Woods and Fourmile Lake. Half the forest consists of former tribal lands of Klamath Indians; has great historical interest. Mountain Lakes Wilderness; teeming waterfowl areas in adjacent Upper Klamath Lake, Oregon's largest lake. Oregon Skyline Trail meanders along crest of the Cascades through the forest from Crater Lake to the forest boundry and on to the California line. Trout fishing. Deer, both black tailed and mule, and migratory bird hunting.

Nearby towns: Chemult, Chiloquin and Klamath Falls.

PENNSYLVANIA

ALLEGHENY NATIONAL FOREST
(475,749 acres).

Office of Forest Supervisor: Warren, Pennsylvania 16365.

Camping facilities: 442 units at 16 locations.

Other facilities: Boating, fishing, hunting, swimming, scenic drives, picnicking, interpretive forest trails. Hotels nearby; cabins in Cook Forest and Allegheny State Parks.

Attractions: Hearts Content and Tionesta virgin timber stands; Allegheny Reservoir; 260 miles of trout streams, 85 miles of bass fishing in Allegheny and Clarion Rivers, 32 acres of lake fishing in Twin Lakes and Beaver Meadows Pond. Hunting for deer, turkey and bear.

Nearby towns: Bradford, Kane, Ridgway, Sheffield, Tionesta and Warren.

SOUTH CAROLINA

FRANCIS MARION NATIONAL FOREST (245,657 acres).

Office of Forest Supervisor: 1813 Main Street, Columbia, South Carolina 29201.

Camping facilities: 31 units at 4 locations.

Other facilities: Boating and picnicking. Hotels and motels nearby.

Attractions: Ruins and remnants of early colonial settlements and plantations. Many "Carolina bays," small lakes, believed to be caused by meteors; picturesque moss-hung oaks, flowering yucca, dogwood, redbud and holly. Bass and other fishing. Alligator, deer, turkey and quail hunting.

Nearby towns: Charleston, Georgetown, McClellanville and Moncks Corner.

SUMTER NATIONAL FOREST .
(342,082 acres).

Office of Forest Supervisor: 1813 Main Street, Columbia, South Carolina 29201.

Camping facilities: 112 units at 5 locations.

Other facilities: Boating, picnicking and swimming. Hotels and motels near the National Forest.

Attractions: Piedmont and Blue Ridge Mountains, rank growth of rhododendron and other flowering shrubs; Walhalla Trout Hatchery. Trout and some bass fishing. Quail hunting. Scenic drives.

Nearby towns: Abbeville, Clinton, Edgefield, Greenwood, Newberry, Union and Walhalla.

SOUTH DAKOTA

BLACK HILLS NATIONAL FOREST (1,221,411 acres—partly in Wyoming).

Office of Forest Supervisor: Forest

Boaters on Lakes Mead and Mohave in the Lake Mead National Recreation Area will find many coves and sandy beaches where they may set up camp for overnight or an extended period.

Service Office Building, P. O. Box 792, Custer, South Dakota 57730.

Camping facilities: 629 units at 23 locations.

Other facilities: Boating, fishing, hunting, swimming, saddle trips, scenic drives, picnicking, historic points. One winter sports area. Motels and dude ranches in and near the National Forest.

Attractions: Spectacular canyons and waterfalls, crystal caves. Historic gold rush area where famous early day characters lived and were buried, including Calamity Jane, Wild Bill Hickok, Deadwood Dick and Preacher Smith; famous Homestake Mine. Harney Peak, highest east of Rocky Mountains. Mount Rushmore National Memorial. Lake and stream fishing. Deer and elk hunting.

Nearby towns: Belle Fourche, Custer, Deadwood, Edgemont, Hot Springs and Rapid City, South Dakota. Newcastle and Sundance, Wyoming.

CUSTER NATIONAL FOREST—See Montana listing.

TENNESSEE

CHEROKEE NATIONAL FOREST (600,437 acres).

Office of Forest Supervisor: Box 400, Cleveland, Tennessee 37312.

Camping facilities: 435 units at 24 locations.

Other facilities: Boating, hiking, picnicking and swimming.

Attractions: Rugged mountain country, rhododendron and laurel blooming in season. Lake and stream fishing, rainbow and brook trout. Hunting for small and big game, including wild boar. Ducktown Copper Basin, one of the nation's worst examples of deforestation through air pollution, with consequent erosion.

Nearby towns: Cleveland, Erwin, Etowah, Greeneville, Johnson City, Madisonville, Mountain City, Newport, Parksville and Tellico Plains.

TEXAS

ANGELINA NATIONAL FOREST (154,389 acres).

Office of Forest Supervisor: Box 969, Lufkin, Texas 75902.

Camping facilities: 167 units at 6 locations.

Other facilities: Boating, picnicking and swimming.

Attractions: Flat to rolling sandy hills with longleaf pine hardwood forest. Sam Rayburn Reservoir. Bass and catfish fishing in rivers and lakes. Quail and dove hunting.

Nearby towns: Jasper, Lufkin and San Augustine.

DAVY CROCKETT NATIONAL FOREST (161,556 acres).

Office of Forest Supervisor: Box 969, Lufkin, Texas 75902.
Camping facilities: 59 units at 3 locations.
Other facilities: Boating picnicking and swimming.
Attractions: Flat, shortleaf loblolly pine woods; hardwoods in bottoms; timber management demonstration area at Ratcliff Lake. Bass and catfish fishing in rivers and lakes. Some deer hunting.
Nearby towns: Alto, Crockett, Groveton, Lufkin.

SABINE NATIONAL FOREST (183,842 acres).

Office of Forest Supervisor: Box 969, Lufkin, Texas 75902.
Camping facilities: 43 units at 3 locations.
Other facilities: Boating, picnicking and swimming.
Attractions: Southern pine and hardwood forest; Toledo Bend Reservoir; Boles Field Fox Hunt Area. Bass and catfish fishing in river and lakes. Fox hunting.
Nearby towns: Center, Hemphill, Jasper and San Augustine.

SAM HOUSTON NATIONAL FOREST (158,235 acres).

Office of Forest Supervisor: Box 969, Lufkin, Texas 75902.
Camping facilities: 73 units at 2 locations.
Other facilities: Boating, picnicking and swimming.
Attractions: Flat, shortleaf loblolly pine woods, hardwoods in bottoms; numerous lakes and small streams; part of "Big Thicket" area. Bass and catfish fishing in rivers and lakes.
Nearby towns: Cleveland, Conroe and Huntsville.

UTAH

ASHLEY NATIONAL FOREST (1,271,146 acres).

Office of Forest Supervisor: 437 East Main Street, Vernal, Utah 84078.
Camping facilities: 612 units at 37 locations.
Other facilities: Boating, fishing, hunting, pack trips, wilderness pack trips, wilderness trails, riding trails.

One winter sports site. Resorts, motels, dude ranches.
Attractions: East half of Uinta Range; Kings Peak, 13,498 feet, highest point in Utah; Red Gorge of the Green River, 1,500 feet deep; exposed ancient geological formations; site of new Flaming Gorge dam; new High Uintas Primitive Area, mostly above 10,000 feet; numerous scenic gorges, natural erosion formations. Lake and stream fishing. Big game hunting of deer, elk and antelope.
Nearby towns: Duchesne, Manila, Roosevelt and Vernal, Utah. Green River and Rock Springs, Wyoming.

CACHE NATIONAL FOREST (673,035 acres — partly in Idaho).

Office of Forest Supervisor: 429 South Main Street, P. O. Box 448, Logan, Utah 84321.
Camping facilities: 370 units at 24 locations.
Other facilities: Boating, fishing, hunting, swimming, scenic drives,

Hematite Lake nature trail.

picnicking, riding trails, nature trails, mountain climbing, hiking trails. Beaver Mountain and Snow Basin Winter Sports Areas.

Attractions: Rugged mountains, Bear River and Wasatch Ranges, Minnetonka Cave, Logan and Ogden Canyons, Monte Cristo Mountain. Bear Lake nearby. Fishing. Deer and elk hunting.

Nearby towns: Brigham, Logan and Ogden, Utah. Montpelier, Preston and Soda Springs, Idaho.

CARIBOU NATIONAL FOREST— See Idaho listing.

DIXIE NATIONAL FOREST
(1,883,688 acres).

Office of Forest Supervisor: 500 South Main Street, Cedar City, Utah 84720.
Camping facilities: 508 units in 19 locations.
Other facilities: Boating, fishing, hunting, swimming, scenic drives, picnicking. Cedar Canyon Winter Sports Area. Resorts, motels, dude ranches.
Attractions: Red Canyon, Panguitch and Navajo Lakes; Pine Valley Mountains; Boulder Top Plateau and its many lakes not accessible by road. Table Cliff Point with vista into 4 states (Colorado, Arizona, Nevada and Utah). Spectacularly colored cliffs. Deer, elk and cougar hunting Lake and stream fishing.
Nearby towns: Cedar City, Enterprise, Escalante, Panguitch, Parowan and St. George, Utah. Las Vegas, Nevada.

FISHLAKE NATIONAL FOREST
(1,424,538 acres).

Office of Forest Supervisor: 170 North Main, Richfield, Utah 84701.
Camping facilities: 166 units at 16 locations.
Other facilities: Boating, fishing, hunting, scenic drives, picnicking. Resorts, hotels and motels.
Attractions: Beaver Mountains, Thousand Lake Mountain Scenic Area. Fish Lake, Petrified Wood Scenic Area. Lake and stream fishing. Big game hunting of deer and elk. Beaver Canyon, Wayne Wonderland, Fish Lake-Salina, Marysvale-Belknap, and other scenic drives.
Nearby towns: Beaver, Delta, Fillmore, Kanosh, Loa, Monroe, Richfield and Salina.

MANTI-LASAL NATIONAL FOREST
(1,263,473 acres—partly in Colorado).

Office of Forest Supervisor: 350 East Main Street, Price, Utah 84501.

Hiker on trail leading through DeSoto Falls Scenic Area in Georgia. This trail leads to several sets of waterfalls. Much of the way the trail follows Frogtown Creek.

Camping facilities: 231 units at 14 locations,
Other facilities: Boating, fishing, hunting, scenic drives, picnicking, riding and hiking trails, limited skiing. Bluebell Flat Winter Sports Area.
Attractions: Wasatch Plateau; Skyline Road penetrates high alpine meadows and sylvan glades; unique geology, Indian hieroglyphics and cliff dwellings. World's largest aspen trees. La Sal and Abajo Mountains. Fishing. Deer and elk hunting.
Nearby towns: Blanding, Ferron, Huntington, Manti, Moab, Monticello, Mount Pleasant and Price.

SAWTOOTH NATIONAL FOREST— See Idaho listing.

UINTA NATIONAL FOREST
(794,686 acres).

Office of Forest Supervisor: 290 North University Avenue, P. O. Box 1428, Provo, Utah 84601.
Camping facilities: 706 units at 32 locations,

Other facilities: Fishing, hunting, scenic drives, picnicking, hiking trails. 2 winter sports areas; 4 valley view overlook points. Hotels, motels.

Attractions: Cool, high mountains rising out of desert. Near Provo, deep canyons with spectacular waterfalls cutting through upthrust Wasatch limestone. Timpanogos Cave; Alpine Scenic Highway around Mount Timpanogos; Nebo Scenic Loop Road; maple, aspen and oak make brilliant colored landscapes in fall. Fishing in mountain streams. Deer and elk hunting. Six-mile hiking trail to top of 12,000-foot Mount Timpanogos.

Nearby towns: American Fork, Heber, Nephi, Provo and Spanish Fork.

WASATCH NATIONAL FOREST
(876,820 acres—partly in Wyoming).

Office of Forest Supervisor: 4438 Federal Bldg., 125 South State, Salt Lake City, Utah 84111.
Camping facilities: 1,220 units at 42 locations.
Other facilities: Boating, fishing, hunting, pack trips, scenic drives, wilderness trips, picnicking, riding and hiking trails, mountain climbing, skiing and ski lift, skating. 4 winter sports areas including the famous developments at Alta and Brighton. Numerous resorts, motels and dude ranches.
Attractions: Big, cool mountains on the city's doorstep; rugged back country: Wasatch, Uinta, Stansbury, Onaqui Mountain Ranges; High Uintas Primitive Area, with 12-13,000-foot peaks. Mirror Lake; Granddady Lakes; Bridger Lake; many others; picnic sites in Mill Creek and Big Cottonwood Canyons Lake and stream fishing Deer and elk hunting.
Nearby towns: Heber, Kamas, Murray, Ogden, Provo and Salt Lake City, Utah. Evanston, Wyoming.

VERMONT

GREEN MOUNTAIN NATIONAL FOREST (233,463 acres).

Office of Forest Supervisor: Rutland, Vermont 05702.
Camping facilities: 78 units at 5 locations.
Other facilities: Boating, fishing, hunting, swimming, scenic drives, picnicking, riding and hiking trails, winter sports, skiing, forest trails, historic points. Five Adirondack shelters on Long Trail. Mount Snow and Sugarbush Winter Sports Areas. Summer resorts and famous New England inns, hotels and cabins.
Attractions: Rugged mountains, scenery, picturesque valleys, quaint New England villages. Green Mountain Range traversed by the Long Trail. Champlain Valley and points of historic interest such as famous battlegrounds of Revolutionary and French and Indian Wars. Hunting for big and small game: deer, ruffed grouse, rabbit and black bear. Fishing in some 400 miles of streams and 30 lakes and ponds.
Nearby towns: Brandon, Burlington, Manchester, Middlebury, Rochester and Rutland.

VIRGINIA

GEORGE WASHINGTON NATIONAL FOREST (1,018,221 acres).

Office of Forest Supervisor: Federal Building, Harrisonburg, Virginia 22801.
Camping facilities: 233 units at 10 locations.
Other facilities: Boating, hiking, picnicking and swimming.
Attractions: Rugged mountainous terrain with elevations up to 4,500 feet; Blue Ridge, Shenandoah, Allegheny and Massanutten Ranges. Outstanding scenery: Crabtree Falls, limestone caverns, Lost River sinks, Devils Garden, Trout Run sinks, and other unusual geological sites. Duncan, Bald, High, Reddish and Elliott Knobs. Shenandoah and Warm Springs Valleys. Civil War iron furnaces. Sherando Lake Recreation Area, with 20-acre swimming and fishing lake. Trout and bass fishing, 208 miles of cold water fishing streams. Hunting, including black bear, deer, turkey, grouse and squirrel. Panoramic views, scenic drives, Blue Ridge Parkway and 391 miles of foot trails.
Nearby towns: Front Royal, Luray,

A favorite of campers in Colorado and surrounding states is the Curecanti Recreation Area, with facilities built around three huge reservoirs.

Photo Courtesy Bureau of Reclamation

Harrisonburg, Staunton, Lesington, Lynchburg, Waynesboro, Charlottesville and Winchester, Va.; Franklin and Moorefield, W. Va.; Washington, D. C.

JEFFERSON NATIONAL FOREST (565,712 acres).

Office of Forest Supervisor: Carlton Terrace Building, 920 Jefferson St., S. W., Roanoke, Virginia 24001.
Camping facilities: 142 units at 7 locations.
Other facilities: Boating, picnicking and swimming.
Attractions: Blue Ridge Mountains; Mount Rogers, 5,719 feet, highest in Virginia. Mt. Rogers National Recreation Area. Transitional zone between northern and southern flora; rhododendron. Glenwood and Roaring Run Civil War iron furnaces; Appalachian Trail; Blue Ridge Parkway. More than 200 miles of fishing streams, 3 fishing lakes. Principal game species: white-tailed deer, grouse, squirrel, bear, raccoon and elk.
Nearby towns: Bristol, Bluefield, Lexington, Lynchburg, Marion, Radford, Roanoke and Wytheville.

WASHINGTON

COLVILLE NATIONAL FOREST (939,919 acres).

Office of Forest Supervisor: Colville, Washington.
Camping facilities: 126 units at 13 locations.
Other facilities: Boating, fishing, hunting, swimming, scenic drives, picnicking, berry picking, winter sports, community kitchen. Chewelah Peak Winter Sports Area. Resorts and cabins.
Attractions: Roosevelt Lake, 151 miles long, 82,000 acres. Old mission near Kettle Falls. Hunting in area noted for large mule deer, record weight of 440 pounds. Water transportation from Roosevelt Lake to Arrow Lakes in Canada. Huckleberries and mushrooms. Lake and stream fishing: Thomas, Swan, Sullivan Lakes and others.
Nearby towns: Chewelah, Colville and Republic, Washington. Grand Forks, British Columbia, Canada.

GIFFORD PINCHOT NATIONAL FOREST (1,259,910 acres).

Office of Forest Supervisor: P. O. Box 449, Vancouver, Washington 98660.
Camping facilities: 1,186 units at 63 locations.
Other facilities: Boating, fishing, hunting, swimming, saddle and pack

trips, scenic drives, picnicking, riding, nature trails, mountain climbing, hiking trails, water sports, geological study, berry picking, winter sports, community kitchens. Resorts, motels, cabins.
Attractions: Mount Adams, 12,300 feet, reached by scenic Evergreen Highway; Spirit Lake, many other lakes; snow-capped peaks; Mineral Springs. Wind River Forest Nursery. Goat Rocks and Mount Adams Wilderness. Lake and stream trout fishing. Deer and bear hunting. Historic Indian huckleberry fields. Cascade Crest Trail extends through the National Forest. Spectacular auto tours.
Nearby towns: Castle Rock, Morton, Stevenson, Vancouver and White Salmon.

KANIKSU NATIONAL FOREST — See Idaho listing.

MOUNT BAKER NATIONAL FOREST (1,818,182 acres).

Office of Forest Supervisor: P. O. Box 845, Bellingham, Washington 98225.
Camping facilities: 649 units at 50 locations.
Other facilities: Boating, fishing, hunting, swimming, saddle and pack trips, picnicking, riding, nature trails, mountain climbing, hiking trails, skiing, water sports, winter sports, historical points. Mount Baker and Mount Pilchuch Winter Sports Areas. Hotels, resorts; experienced guides.
Attractions: Superb mountain scenery; snowcapped peaks, including Glacier Peak; numerous glaciers; alpine lakes; heavy stands of Douglas fir up to 200 feet in height. Glacier Peak Wilderness and North Cascade Primitive Area. Mount Bker Recreation Area featuring both summer and winter sports and recreation. Segments of Cascade Crest Trail from Harts Pass to Glacier Peak. Steelhead and rainbow trout fishing. Deer and bear hunting.
Nearby towns: Bellingham, Darrington, Everett and Granite Falls.

OKANOGAN NATIONAL FOREST (1,520,448 acres).

Office of Forest Supervisor: P. O. Box 950, Okanogan, Washington 98840.
Camping facilities: 325 units at 53 locations.
Other facilities: Boating, fishing, hunting, saddle and pack trips, picnicking, riding, mountain climbing, hiking trails, water sports, playground, winter sports, community kitchens. Loup Loup Winter Sports Area. Dude ranches, motels.
Attractions: Alpine meadows, snow

peaks and glaciers. Cascade Crest Trail, a segment of the Pacific Crest Trail system, originates at Canadian boundary and extends southward to Harts Pass. North Cascade Primitive Area. Lake and stream fishing.
Nearby towns: Brewster, Okanogan, Tonasket and Twisp.

OLYMPIC NATIONAL FOREST (621,756 acres.).

Office of Forest Supervisor: Federal Building, Olympia, Washington 98501.
Camping facilities: 309 units in 20 locations.
Other facilities: Boating, fishing, hunting, swimming, saddle and pack trips, scenic drivers, picnicking, nature trails, geological study, berry picking. Resorts, motels, dude ranches.
Attractions: Dense rain forests, big trees, spectacular snow peaks, scores of lakes and streams. Fishing includes salmon and steelhead trout. Hunting for deer, bear, cougar and elk.
Nearby towns: Aberdeen, Olympia, Port Angeles, Quilcene and Shelton.

SNOQUALMIE NATIONAL FOREST (1,211,901 acres).

Office of Forest Supervisor: 905 Second Avenue Building, Room 208, Seattle, Washington 98104.
Camping facilities: 832 units at 57 locations.
Other facilities: Boating, fishing, hunting, saddle and pack trips, scenic drives, picnicking, riding, nature trails, mountain climbing, hiking trails, skiing, water sports, berry picking, historical points, community kitchens. Five winter sports areas. Motels and outfitters locally available.
Attractions: Snoqualmie Falls, 250 feet high; scenic Chinook and White Pass Highways; giant Douglas firs; snow peaks, lakes, fishing streams. Sections of Cascade Crest Trail from Cady Pass to Goat Rocks. Mather Memorial Parkway, Goat Rocks Wilderness. Stream and lake fishing, including salmon and steelhead trout. Hunting black tailed and mule deer, bear and elk.
Nearby towns: Cle Elum, Everett, Seattle, Tacoma and Yakima.

UMATILLA NATIONAL FOREST — See Oregon listing.

WENATCHEE NATIONAL FOREST (1,731,076 acres).

Office of Forest Supervisor: P. O.

Box 811, Wenatchee, Washington 98801.
Camping facilities: 782 units at 88 locations.
Other facilities: Boating, fishing, hunting, swimming, saddle and pack trips, scenic drives, picnicking, riding, nature trails, mountain climbing, hiking trails, water sports, geological study, playgrounds, berry picking, winter sports, historical points, community kitchens, boat trips. Four winter sports areas. Motels and dude ranches.
Attractions: Lake Chelan, 55 miles long, between precipitous mountain ranges; lake bottom 389 feet below sea level. Glacier Peak Wilderness. Snowcapped peaks, lakes, alpine meadows, rare wild flowers in Tumwater Botanical Area. Fishing streams; Lake Wenatchee. Stream and trout fishing. Deer and bear hunting. Cascade Crest Trail between Rainy Pass and Blowout Mountain. Lake Chelan boat trip.
Nearby towns: Cashmere, Chelan, Cle Elum, Ellensburg, Leavenworth and Wenatchee,

WEST VIRGINIA

MONONGAHELA NATIONAL
FOREST (808,898 acres).

Office of Forest Supervisor: Elkins, West Virginia 26241.
Camping facilities: 326 units at 15 locations.
Other facilities: Boating, fishing, hunting, swimming, scenic drives, picnicking, horseback riding, forest trails, group campground. Tourist homes and motels.
Attractions: Appalachian and Allegheny Mountains; Spruce Knob, 4,860 feet, highest in West Virginia; Blackwater Canyon and 60-foot falls; spectacular Seneca Rocks on historic Seneca Indian Trail. Botanically curious Cranberry Glades; rhododendrons in early July; unexplored limestone caves; bear colonies. Parsons Forest Nursery, Smoke Hole, rugged mountain scenery. Some 1,900 miles of trout and bass fishing streams. Hunting for deer, turkey, squirrel, bear, grouse and other game. Manmade lakes at Spruce Knob, Summit and Sherwood offer trout and bass fishing with good campsites nearby.
Nearby towns: Charleston, Elkins, Lewisburg and Petersburg.

WISCONSIN

CHEQUAMEGON NATIONAL
FOREST (831,327 acres).

Office of Forest Supervisor: Park Falls, Wisconsin 54552.

Fisherman working an Oregon river. Family enjoys fine campsite across river.

Camping facilities: 351 units at 20 locations.
Other facilities: Boating, fishing, hunting, swimming, picnicking, winter sports, forest trails, skiing, group campgrounds by reservation, canoeing, forest tours. Resorts and cabins.
Attractions: Hundreds of large and small lakes. Pine, spruce and balsam forests; extensive jack pine plantations. Lake and stream fishing, particularly for muskellunge. Hunting for deer and small game. Canoe travel on Flambeau and Chippewa Rivers.
Nearby towns: Ashland, Eau Claire, Hayward, Medford, Park Falls, Superior and Washburn.

NICOLET NATIONAL FOREST
(643,875 acres).

Office of Forest Supervisor: Rhinelander, Wisconsin 54501.
Camping facilities: 539 units at 24 locations.
Other facilities: Boating, fishing, hunting, swimming, picnicking, winter sports, forest trails, skiing, canoeing, snowmobile trail, forest tours. Sheltered Valley Ski Area. Numerous resorts and private cabins on private lands within and near the national forest.
Attractions: Northern Wisconsin lake region, trout streams and scenic rivers. Pine, spruce-balsam, hardwood and cedar-spruce swamp forests. Lake and stream fishing for muskellunge, pike, bass and trout. Deer, bear, grouse and duck hunting.
Nearby towns: Eagle River, Green Bay, Marinette and Rhinelander.

WYOMING

BIGHORN NATIONAL FOREST
(1,113,769 acres).

Office of Forest Supervisor: P. O. Box 914, Sheridan, Wyoming 82801.
Camping facilities: 335 units at 39 locations.
Other facilities: Fishing, hunting, saddle and pack trips, scenic drives, picnicking. Motels, resorts and dude ranches in and near the National Forest.
Attractions: Big Horn Mountains, snowcapped peaks; glaciers; scenic canyons; more than 300 lakes and reservoirs with 2,350 acres of water; 850 miles fishing streams. Curious prehistoric Indian Medicine Wheel near Medicine Mountain. 137,000-acre Cloud Peak Primitive Area. Elk, deer, moose and bear hunting.
Nearby towns: Buffalo, Dayton, Greybull, Lovell, Ranchester, Sheridan, Story, Ten Sleep and Worland.

BRIDGER NATIONAL FOREST
(1,700,029 acres).

Office of Forest Supervisor: Forest Service Building, Kemmerer, Wyoming 83101.
Camping facilities: 314 units at 22 locations.
Other facilities: Boating, fishing, hunting, swimming, scenic drives, wilderness trips, picnicking, horses. Divide and Surveyor Park Winter Sports Areas. Resorts, hotels, cabins and dude ranches.
Attractions: Salt River, Wyoming and Wind River Mountain Ranges, live glaciers, Bridger Wilderness; Gannett Peak, highest in Wyoming at 13,785 feet. Lots of remote country. Lake and stream fishing. Hunting for bear, moose, elk, mountain sheep and deer. Scenic drives: Pinedale Skyline Drive, Greys River Road.
Nearby towns: Afton and Pinedale.

CARIBOU NATIONAL FOREST—
See Idaho listing.

MEDICINE BOW NATIONAL FOREST (1,094,824 acres).

Office of Forest Supervisor: Box 3355, University Station, Laramie, Wyoming 82070.
Camping facilities: 329 units at 16 locations.
Other facilities: Fishing, hunting, saddle and pack trips, scenic drives, picnicking. Three winter sports areas, motels and dude ranches in and near the National Forest.
Attractions: Medicine Bow, Sierra Madre, Laramie and Pole Mountains. Many lakes and fishing streams; numerous beaver colonies. Fishing and deer hunting.
Nearby towns: Centennial, Cheyenne, Douglas, Encampment, Laramie and Saratoga.

SHOSHONE NATIONAL FOREST
(2,424,937 acres).

Office of Forest Supervisor: Blair Building No. 1, 1731 Sheridan Avenue, Cody, Wyoming 82414.
Camping facilities: Boating, fishing, hunting, saddle and pack trips, scenic drives. Two winter sports areas. Motels and dude ranches in and near the National Forest.
Attractions: Rugged Absaroka Mountains and Beartooth Plateau, Wind River Range with perpetual snow; Gannett Peak, 13,785 feet, highest in Wyoming; largest glaciers in Rocky Mountains; hundreds of lakes. North and South Absaroka Wildernesses. Glacier, Stratified and Popo Agie Primitive Areas. Hunting for mountain sheep, elk, moose, deer, antelope, black and grizzly bear and game birds. Scenic drives: Red Lodge-Cooke City Highway, Sunlight Basin Road, Cody-Yellowstone Road, Togwotee Pass Road.
Nearby towns: Cody, Dubois and Lander, Wyoming. Cooke City and Red Lodge, Montana.

TARGHEE NATIONAL FOREST—
See Idaho listing.

TETON NATIONAL FOREST
(1,700,820 acres).

Office of Forest Supervisor: Forest Service Building, Jackson, Wyoming 83001.
Camping facilities: 143 units at 10 locations.
Other facilities: Boating, fishing, hunting, swimming, scenic drives, picnicking, skiing. Three winter sports areas including Jackson and Teton Pass Ski Runs. Resorts, dude ranches, cabins.
Attractions: Unspoiled scenic back country famous for big game herds. Gros Ventre Slide; Gros Ventre, Teton and Wind River Ranges; Continental Divide. Teton Wilderness; famous Jackson Hole country. Outstanding skiing. Stream and lake fishing. Big game hunting: moose, elk, deer, mountain sheep, grizzly bear. Scenic drives: Hoback Canyon, Snake River Canyon, Wind River Highway.

Check These

Camping Areas -

A popular campground in Badlands National Monument, South Dakota.

National Park Service Photo

Many Almost Unknown,

Scarcely Used

Motion pictures and slide programs are frequently featured at the campgrounds of national monuments. This one is taking place at Craters of the Moon National Monument, Idaho.

The U. S. Government is BIG in the outdoor recreation field. Here are some federal land areas for camping that may be new to you.

IN addition to national parks and national forests, the United States Government owns hundreds of millions of acres—managed by various agencies—on which have been built numerous recreational facilities. Many camping facilities improved and primitive, are provided. And in most instances, backpacking and all kinds of wilderness-type adventure beckon.

Agencies providing camping opportunities on the lands they manage include the National Park Service, Bureau of Land Management, Bureau of Reclamation, Corps of Engineers, Tennessee Valley Authority, Bureau of Sport Fisheries and Wildlife (limited facilities) and others.

Included in the National Park System are recreation areas, national monuments, national seashores, parkways, national historical parks, national battlefields, a memorial park and special parks.

National Recreation Areas

Recreation areas catering to campers include these:

Arbuckle, 8,851 acres in Oklahoma; Bighorn Canyon, 63,000 acres in Wyoming and Montana; Coulee Dam, 98,500 acres in Washington; Curecanti, 41,103 acres in Colorado; Delaware Gap, 68,826 acres along the Delaware River; Flaming Gorge, 108,400 acres in Utah and Wyoming.

Glen Canyon, 1,196,545 acres surrounding one of the highest dams in the world, in Arizona and Utah; Lake Mead, 1,936,978 acres in Arizona and Nevada; Sanford, 41,097 acres in Texas; Shadow Mountain, 18,240 acres in Colorado; and Whiskeytown-Shasta-Trinity, 41,987 acres in California.

National Monuments

The national monuments offering camping facilities are: Arches, 34,009 acres in Utah; Badlands, 111,529 acres in South Dakota; Bandelier, 29,661 acres in New Mexico; Black Canyon of the Gunnison, 13,689 acres in Colorado; Canyon de Chelly, 83,840 acres in Arizona; Capital Reef, 39,185 acres in Utah.

Capulin, 775 acres in New Mexico; Cedar Breaks, 6,154 acres in Utah; Chaco Canyon, 21,509 acres in New Mexico; Channel Islands, 18,166 acres in California; Chesapeake and Ohio Canal, 4,477 acres in Maryland and West Virginia; Chiricahua, 10,645 acres in Arizona; Colorado, 17,362 acres in Colorado; Craters of the Moon, 53,545 acres in Idaho; Death Valley, 1,907,760 acres in California and Nevada.

Devils Postpile, 798 acres in California; Devils Tower, 1,346 acres in Wyoming; Dinosaur, 206,233 acres in Utah and Colorado; El Morro, 1278 acres in New Mexico; Glacier Bay, 2,803,840 acres in Alaska; Grand Canyon (not to be confused with Grand Canyon National Park), 198,-280 acres in Arizona; Great Sand Dunes, 36,740 acres in Colorado.

Hovenweep, 505 acres in Utah and Colorado; Joshua Tree, 557,992 acres in California; Lava Beds, 46,238 acres in California; Natural Bridges, 7,600 acres in Utah; Navajo, 360 acres in Arizona; Organ Pipe Cactus, 330,874 acres in Arizona; Pinnacles, 14,497 acres in California; and Tipanogos Cave, 250 acres in Utah.

National Seashores

National seashores in which the National Park Service provides camping facilities are these:

Assateague Island, 39,630-acre barrier island in Maryland and Virginia; Cape Cod, 44,600 acres along the coast of Massachusetts; Cape Hatteras, 28,500 acres along the coast of North Carolina.

Fire Island, 19,311-acre barrier island off the south shore of Long Island; Padre Island, 133,918 acres comprising an 80-mile stretch of barrier island along the gulf coast of Texas; and Point Reyes, 64,546-acre peninsula north of San Francisco, California.

National Parkways

The two national parkways providing camping facilities are purely scenic roads, perhaps the most beautiful routes on the continent totally unhampered by commercialism. These are the Blue Ridge Parkway, 469 miles and 72,773 acres along the crest of the Blue Ridge Mountains from Roanoke, Virginia, to the Great Smoky Mountains National Park (eventually to a point near Atlanta, Georgia); and Natchez Trace Parkway, 450 miles (more than 300 completed) and 45,297

Thus far, campers have created no space problems in Glacier Bay National Monument. The reason: it is a vast area at the northwest end of the Alexander Archipellago in southeastern Alaska. It is reached only by boats and aircraft. Those who do camp there see both unique ice designs and unique forest floors.

National Park Service Photos

acres along the Old Indian Trail between Nashville, Tennessee, and Natchez, Mississippi.

Detailed information on the national recreation areas, the national monuments, the national seashores, the national parkways and other outdoor areas administered by the National Park Service is included in two valuable publications available from the Superintendent of Documents, Government Printing Office, Washington, D. C. These are *Camping in the National Park System,* 25 cents; and *National Parks and Landmarks,* 55 cents.

TVA Camping

The Tennessee Valley Authority was established to supply electricity to parts of seven states comprising the Tennessee River Valley and the river's tributaries. It has done that, and more. TVA's 36 reservoirs provide more than 600,000 acres of water surface and 11,000 miles of shoreline. All types of water craft are seen on the lakes and rivers comprising the TVA system. These waterways and hundreds of roads lead to all types of recreational areas. Camping is a popular activity all the way from Fontana Dam high in the Smokies to Kentucky Lake strad-

dling the Kentucky-Tennessee border several hundred miles to the west.

Some facilities are private, others are public. A total of 14 state parks, in addition to many federal facilities, have been established on TVA shores by Alabama, Kentucky, Mississippi and Tennessee. Nine of these are in Tennessee.

Nearly 100 improved camping sites are maintained on the shores of TVA lakes and almost 150 primitive-type areas have been designated as unimproved other than available sanitary facilities. Many thousands of campers can be provided for each day. Some improved areas are for tents only, others are for recreational vehicles only and many are for both. Water, sanitary facilities, fireplace, picnic table and electricity are standard for most "improved" campgrounds.

For a copy of *Recreation on TVA Lakes* and other colorful reading matter, write Information Office, Tennessee Valley Authority, Knoxville, Tennessee 37902.

Corps of Engineers

If you think of Army engineers as rugged soldiers building bridges and unrolling barbed wire in a combat zone, if you see them as builders of great

dams and waterways and levees, you are right on both counts. But they also are concerned with your recreation—including camping. You may be surprised to know that Corps of Engineer projects receive almost 200 million visits each year. Not a few of these are for recreational purposes.

Corps of Engineers recreation areas, offering a great variety of outdoor fun in conjunction with reservoirs and waterways, are strategically located in some 40 states. Millions of acres of water surface and land areas are involved, incorporating thousands of miles of shoreline. General facilities usually include public boat launching lanes, picnic areas, swimming beaches, rental boats, fishing aids, scenic trails and roads and tent and trailer spaces.

Any Corps of Engineers office or facility will gladly provide you with a copy of *Recreation,* a very colorful booklet describing in detail the recreational opportunities available at all facilities maintained by this army unit. Camping statistics and directions are included.

Bureau of Reclamation

The National Reclamation Act was passed in 1902, opening the way for the Bureau of Reclamation to construct

The Tennessee Valley Authority has established an amazing network of recreational facilities along lakes and rivers of seven states. Camping is a popular activity all the way from Fontana Dam, high in the Smokies, to Kentucky Lake, a vast body of water straddling the Kentucky-Tennessee border and backing up the Tennessee River for many miles. These photos show some of the activities in this vast recreation area.

dams, reservoirs and canal systems that now bring irrigation to more than 8 million acres in the 17 western states. If you live in these areas or plan to vacation in the west, don't overlook the recreational opportunities these reclamation facilities afford. Some of the national recreation areas, already cited, are built in conjunction with reclamation projects.

Hundreds of lesser known areas have been developed to offer many types of outdoor recreation. Most of these welcome campers. In recent years, the Bureau of Reclamation has intensified its efforts to develop outdoor playgrounds at its projects. The bureau explains its efforts this way:

"Recreation has always been an important byproduct of the projects, but today this function is being accelerated to provide millions of hours of exciting and satisfying experiences in the woods, along the streams, on the mountainsides and, especially, on beautiful, man-made lakes behind reclamation dams often set in surroundings of incomparable grandeur."

These efforts are popular, this tact borne out by some statistics: 44.9 million annual visitor days at 219 public recreation areas on 3.7 million acres of land, 11,000 miles of shoreline and 1.6 million acres of water surface.

About 450 campgrounds are maintained, with 18,500 tent and trailer spaces. Sanitary facilities, swimming beaches, bathhouses, boat moorings, launching ramps, fireplaces and plenty of room are usually provided.

Reclamation's Recreation Opportunities is a "must" publication if you plan to visit one of the many projects maintained by this federal agency. Send 20 cents to Superintendent of Documents, Government Printing Office, Washington, D. C. 20402, or ask for a copy at any Reclamation project.

Bureau of Land Management

This agency recently published a runaway bestseller, *Room to Roam.* It is a beautiful publication and is available for 75 cents per copy from the Superintendent of Documents.

Room to Roam is a recreation guide to the public lands. It opens with this significant paragraph:

"From the arid deserts to Arctic tundra, through all imaginable types of climate and terrain, stretch some 450 million acres of public domain land. The citizens of the United States own this land, which lies mostly in the western states and Alaska. Its resources are hardly tapped, its beauty is relatively unknown and its potential for recreation and wildlife is virtually unlimited. This wide-open space offers an invigorating change from the hurry and press of urban life; it offers re-

Hiking and backpack trips are part of the program at Point Reyes National Seashore, California.

National Park Service Photo

Rangers of the Glen Canyon National Recreation Area headquarter in this floating unit as they keep a lookout on the activities of both boaters and campers.

Photo Courtesy Bureau of Reclamation

freshment for the spirit in its multitude of scenes."

Room to Roam offers exciting descriptions and maps of these areas. The Bureau of Land Management has outstanding maps and brochures covering all major areas under its jurisdiction. Camping information is presented in detail.

In addition to the headquarters office in the U. S. Department of the Interior, the Bureau of Land Management maintains these regional offices:

ALASKA—555 Cordova Street, Anchorage 99501

ARIZONA—Federal Building, Room 3022, Phoenix 85025

CALIFORNIA—Federal Building, Room E 2820, 2800 Cottage Way, Sacramento 95825

COLORADO—Federal Building, Room 14023, 1961 Stout Street, Denver 80202

IDAHO—Federal Building, Room 334 (P. O. Box 2237), Boise 83702

MONTANA, NORTH AND SOUTH DAKOTA—Federal Building and U. S. Courthouse, 316 N. 26th Street, Billings, Montana 59101

NEVADA—Federal Building, Room 3008, 300 Booth Street, Reno 89502

NEW MEXICO—Federal Building, South Federal Place (P. O. Box 1449), Santa Fe 87501

OREGON AND WASHINGTON—729 N. E. Oregon Street (P. O. Box 2965), Portland, Oregon 97208

UTAH—125 South State (P. O. Box 11505), Salt Lake City 84111

WYOMING—Courthouse Building, 2120 Capitol Avenue, (P. O. Box 1828), Cheyenne 82001

On the public domain lands are more than 100 developed campgrounds. In these you will find variety, from deserts to forests, sagebrush canyons to snow-capped mountains. If you prefer, you may make camp away from developed facilities. This you are privileged to do, if you observe a few rules for off-the-road travel:

■ Keep your vehicle on the road unless the ground is firm enough to allow off-road travel without leaving ruts; careless driving can cause soil erosion.

■ Leave fences and gates as you find them.

■ In range country, camp at least one quarter of a mile from watering places; don't frighten livestock.

■ Be careful with fire. Build campfires only in safe places where flames can't spread. Make sure your fire is completely dead when you leave.

■ Keep a clean camp, leave a clean camp.

■ Be careful with firearms. Don't shoot near cattle. .

■ Be a courteous driver. Give logging trucks plenty of room; watch out for people and wildlife on the road. Walk on left, facing traffic.

■ Respect public and private property. Treat the land as you would your own.

■ Be prepared. When you head into back country, leave word where you're going. Take plenty of water, a good map, compass, first aid kit, spare rations, extra clothing.

Some areas charge fees. Game and fish regulations of the respective states are enforced, and you may be required to purchase licenses.

Within these states are Bureau of Land Management improved camping sites that may be made to order for you: Alaska, Arizona, California, Colorado, Idaho, Montana, Nevada, New Mexico, Oregon, South Dakota, Utah and Wyoming. For more information, send five cents to the Superintendent of Documents and ask for *Camping on the Public Lands,* Information Bulletin No. 3. All the improved camping facilities are described.

State Parks Ideal

for Weekend or

Weeklong Camping

What the States Offer Campers

Wherever you are, at home or on the road, you are not far from a state park. It may be the ideal site for your overnight stop, that outdoor weekend you promised the family or for your full-length vacation.

Practically every state operates a good state park system, and in recent years millions of dollars have been spent in upgrading existing facilities and adding new ones. A few states where federal lands predominate have not felt the need to develop much in the way of state parks, but even these are taking a new look at the possibilities.

The main reason for much state park enjoyment is proximity. Many state parks are outdoor meccas to millions of city residents because they are located reasonably close to urban populations. Some are not so close, to be sure, and these attract vacationers and others—including many campers—who spend more than a day or two there.

Recreation variety

Many parks offer all kinds of fun and recreation. Some are quite large, totaling thousands of acres. Some are laid out like a resort. Games and sports, swimming and boating, food services, safe play areas for the youngsters—are a few of the attractions of state parks. Possibly it is the way the camping areas are laid out that makes them seem less crowded than, say, the roadside campgrounds in the Smokies or Yellowstone. Not a few campers choose state parks over other areas.

In well developed state parks you often will find paved roads, flush toilets, hot showers (sometimes), a supervised swimming pool or beach,

One of Wyoming's favorite devices for luring the traveler to her spots of beauty and wilderness is the pack trip.

Wyoming Travel Commission

Colorado camping, either rugged or refined, is a vacation experience the entire family will long remember. The state boasts more than 210 free campgrounds.

ample campsite space and firewood. Electrical hookups are becoming more common. In some states you can make reservations, a good idea in the summer months.

For all of this there usually is a fee. Two dollars per night per family seems to be about the norm. That isn't much —if you find a state park that your whole family can enjoy.

You'll have no difficulty in discovering the charms of one not far from where you live. The following descriptions may suggest to you that you should not overlook your state's parks when planning that camping trip. Unfortunately, a very few states do not readily honor out-of-state requests for camping information. These won't be named here, lest you be prejudiced unnecessarily. But be forewarned.

ALABAMA

"Alabama's . . . variety of landscapes is preserved in nine major state parks, plus minor parks and recreational areas. Camping is permitted in all state parks, national forests and in numerous private campgrounds through the state. Spring comes early and fall lingers, and Alabama's gentle climate . . . makes life in the outdoors a favorite family sport nine months of the year."

Of the dozen state parks operating campgrounds, only two or three with

special attractions charge for camping. Fees are $2 per day per family.

Alabama, Guide to Family Funland and an official state map are available on request from Bureau of Publicity, State of Alabama, Montgomery 36104. For specific information on state parks, write Department of Conservation, State Capitol, Montgomery 36104.

ALASKA

By 1980, Alaska expects to host 325,000 tourists a year. New accommodations and transportation facilities are making Alaska one of America's most attractive travel destinations. Scores of campgrounds, from the most primitive to the most modern, dot the state.

No state parks, as such, are operated, as most recreational areas are on federal lands. McKinley National Park in interior Alaska offers 106 camping units at 7 locations. Some 1,640 other camping units can be found throughout the state in areas maintained by the Bureau of Land Management, Alaska Division of Lands, U. S. Fish & Wildlife Service and the U. S. Forest Service. Boat launching, canoeing, fishing, sanitary facilities and drinking water and shelters are provided.

In addition to the campgrounds, there are literally thousands of places to camp, depending upon the degree to which you may want to rough it. There are many others accessible only by horseback, airplane or on foot and are pretty much as nature has provided. There are many places where you could be the first ever to set foot.

A color-keyed sectional map containing much helpful information will be sent on request from Alaska Travel Division, Pouch E, Juneau 99801. For information on state campgrounds and camping, write Alaska Division of Lands, 344 Sixth Avenue, Anchorage 99501.

ARIZONA

Arizona's park program is relatively new on the state level and is being developed at this writing. See sections on national forests and national parks for camping information in Arizona.

For a listing of campgrounds in national parks, national forests and Indian reservations, write to Travel Promotion Dept., Arizona Development Board, 3443 North Central Avenue, Phoenix 85012.

For information on state parks, write to Arizona State Parks Department, 1611 West Adams, Phoenix 85007.

ARKANSAS

Seventeen Arkansas state parks provide developed camping areas and offer a wide variety of activities. The parks are located throughout the state and feature the diverse geography of Arkansas. Campsites (979 of them) within the state park system are offered on a first-come, first-served basis with a charge of $1.50 per night per family camping unit, $1.75 with electric hookup.

For a copy of **Arkansas Camper's Guide** and a state parks folder, write Arkansas Publicity and Parks Commission, Room 149, Capitol Building, Little Rock 72201.

CALIFORNIA

About 7,000 campsites are available in the California State Park System at 79 state parks. Of this number, 48 are Type A campgrounds which ordinarily include flush toilets, piped drinking water, hot showers, laundries, campsites with a table, stove and cupboard, and surfaced roads. Type B and Type C campgrounds have adequate but fewer facilities.

Rates per night for Types A, B and C sites without hookup are $3, $2 and $1 respectively from May 1 through September 30. From October 1 through April 30 the rates are $1.50, $1 and $1 respectively. Hookup rates for trailers, campers and motor homes, at six parks only, are $3.50 per night May 1 through September 30, $2 per night October 1 through

North Dakota campers have a choice of 123 camping areas in the state.
North Dakota Travel Division

April 30. The required advance reservation fee is $1.

For a copy of **"California State Park System,"** write Department of Parks and Recreation, P. O. Box 2390, Sacramento 95811.

COLORADO

"Camping in Colorado is the real thing," says the promotion folder, and this is no exaggeration. "All outdoors, wrapped in the silence of primeval forest. Big mountains, big white stars. Indian country that gets you back to nature. Many of the highways to the campgrounds follow moccasin trails, some lead to historic ghost towns."

Overnight camping is permitted at most of the 53 Colorado state parks. Most campsites have fire grates, garbage containers, picnic

tables, sanitation facilities and adequate room for tents. Camp trailers may not exceed 22 feet in length and are limited to length of stay in many areas.

A state use fee permit is required to enter state campgrounds. The calendar year cost of the permit is $5; one-day permits may be purchased for $1. This use fee sticker should not be confused with the federal Golden Eagle Passport.

All campgrounds are available on a first-come, first-served basis. Reservations are not accepted.

For a copy of **Colorful Colorado Invites You,** maps, brochures and specific camping information, write Travel Development, State Capitol, Denver 80203.

CONNECTICUT

Connecticut provides for year-round use and enjoyment 82 state parks totaling 23,981 acres. Annual attendance has reached nearly 7,000,000 visitors of which approximately three quarters of a million

are campers. Campsites numbering 1,523 are located throughout the state in 10 state parks. The ranger in charge must be contacted. The camping fee is $2 per campsite per day.

Long-term camping is for Connecticut residents only. No reservations are necessary for camping up to 14 days. Services provided by the Connecticut Park Commission on the larger campgrounds are drinking water, sanitary facilities and safety lighting. Not provided are individual connections for electricity, water or sanitary facilities, nor are there laundry units or tubs. Vendors deliver milk, baked goods, vegetables and ice to organized camp areas.

For additional information, write Connecticut State Park and Forest Commission, Hartford 06115.

DELAWARE

Camping sites are available at Trap Pond, Cape Henlopen and Delaware Seashore State Parks. The fee is $2 per night or $12 per

week with a limit of 2 weeks in any 30-day period. The length of any trailer plus towing vehicle must not exceed 40 feet.

Facilities and recreation provided in most of these areas are picnicking, pavilions, toilets, drinking water, swimming, fishing, boating, boat rental, refreshments, historic interests and unusual flora.

The rustic beauty of Delaware's state forests awaits the outdoorsman. Redden, Ellendale, Appenzellar and Owens forest areas are favorite sites for tenters (no trailers.)

Direct further questions to State Park Commission, 3300 Faulkland Road, Wilmington.

FLORIDA

Of the 65 Florida state parks, 29 provide tent and trailer campsites (more than 2,500). Other facilities include picnicking, swimming, fishing, boating, skin and scuba diving, museum exhibits, historic structures, nature trails, youth tent areas, guided tours and concessions. Each campsite includes picnic tables, grills and safe water. Complete bathhouse facilities are the rule. Standard fee per night per campsite. Extra fee for electricity. Stays limited to two weeks.

A map featuring state parks only and a copy of a state parks folder are available upon request from Florida Board of Parks, 101 W. Gaines Street, Tallahassee 32304.

GEORGIA

The 44 parks in Georgia's state park system encompass approximately 40,000 acres. These are well distributed throughout the state and are conveniently located near principal highways. Some 1,800 campsites are provided in 32 catering to campers. No advance reservations are accepted.

The fee is $2 per site per night for each family in tent-trailer areas. Facilities include comfort station with flush toilets and hot showers, picnic tables, grills, water and electricity.

In the truck and travel trailer areas the rate is $2.50 per site per night for each family. Facilities are dump station, water, electricity. Comfort station in this area not yet available in all parks.

Added facilities in many state parks are concessions, swimming, fishing, water skiing, launching ramps, fishing boat rentals, reserved shelters, nature and hiking trails, museum exhibits, group camps and pioneer campgrounds.

For further information, write to Georgia State Parks, 7 Hunter Street, S. W., Atlanta 30334.

HAWAII

Camping in Hawaii is not well developed. Campers from the mainland have joined with local groups to urge expansion of facilities and camping opportunities. Five state parks permit some camping on request. The picture is sure to improve soon.

For general information and listing of camping facilities, write Hawaii Visitors Bureau, 2051 Kalakaua Avenue, Honolulu.

IDAHO

This state maintains 26 state parks, 14 permitting tent camping and six admitting trailers. Most offer boating, fishing, historical sites, picnicking and swimming. Stoves, tables, safe drinking water and toilets are standard. Six parks charge fees of $1 per vehicle per night, $1.50 per unit for water and electricity, $2 for water, sewer and electricity hookups; the remainder of the parks have no fees.

A copy of **Idaho Is What the Rest of the World Would Like to Be** and a campgrounds folder are available from the Idaho Parks Department, Boise 83707.

ILLINOIS

This is a good camping state and almost any state park is a sure bet for camping satisfaction. Modern facilities are offered in 48 parks. Advance reservations are not accepted. Fees are charged, usually $1.50 per site per day. For maps, brochures and general information, write Illinois Information Service, 406 Capitol Building, Springfield.

INDIANA

This state offers more than 40 excellent camping areas, and residents of the Hoosier State make good use of them. Entrance and camping fees are charged, the entrance fee varying with the group and the camping fee $1 per family per day. Campgrounds feature playgrounds, full bath facilities, good-size sites and hookups.

Brochures and maps are available from Indiana Department of Natural Resources, 612 State Office Building, Indianapolis.

IOWA

Iowa lists its parks as State Owned Recreation Areas, which includes park preserve areas, multiple use areas, state forests and state areas under management of local government agencies. There are 81 such areas throughout the state, 66 of which permit camping.

All camping permits are issued by the park officer. The State Conservation Commission has fixed the fees for tent and trailer camping as follows:

$1 per night per camping unit.
$1.50 per night per camping unit in

areas where modern restroom and shower facilities are available. Camping fees do not include use of boat and beach facilities.

Most camping areas include electrical outlets, sewage dumps, shower and are a short walk to swimming.

Additional information is available from the State Conservation Commission, State Office Building, 400 Fourth Street, Des Moines 50319.

KANSAS

Since its creation in 1955, the Kansas Park and Resources Authority has made tremendous strides toward developing an outstanding park system. Along with state lakes and game refuges and well preserved historical sites, Kansas State Parks beckon the vacationer to exciting and hospitable country.

Camping is restricted to areas specified. All campers must register and are limited to a length of stay of two weeks in any one park per season. A camping charge in the developed campgrounds of $1.50 is assessed on a per-night basis for utility hookups—electricity, water and sewer for trailers.

Kansas has 17 state parks; only one does not have camping facilities. Most areas feature boat launching, marinas and picnic areas.

For more details, write to State Park and Resources Authority, 801 Harrison, Topeka 66612.

KENTUCKY

More than $20 million, a lot of know-how and some natural beauty have combined during the 1960s to make the state parks of Kentucky a camper's paradise. Some 28 state parks offer nearly 2,000 campsites for tents and trailers. Four permit camping at primitive sites.

Most of the campgrounds are built around excellent central service buildings that provide plenty of hot water, modern toilet facilities, showers, telephone. The charge is $3 per day for up to six people, 25 cents additional for each extra person. Most areas have free electrical hookups. There is a $1 per day charge for the primitive camping sites at Buckhorn, Falmouth, Jenny Wiley and Rough River Dam State Parks.

A folder, "**Kentucky Tent and Trailer Camping**," a directory of Kentucky campgrounds and a highway map may be obtained free by writing to Travel Division, Department of Public Information, Frankfort 40601.

LOUISIANA

The eight state parks of Louisiana all provide camping facilities for families and larger groups. Refreshment stands, shelters, pits and tables, bathhouses and comfort stations are standard. Recreation includes boating, fishing and swim-

ming. Two parks provide pools, pavilions, museums and nature trails. A fee of $1 per campsite per night is charged, plus 25 cents for electricity, plus $1 for trailers with air conditioners.

For more state park information, write State Parks and Recreation Commission, P. O. Drawer 1111, Baton Rouge 70821.

MAINE

Maine has stressed relaxing camping vacations in the campgrounds of the state parks. The parks are strategically placed, on the sea coast, others on lake shores and many others in the wilderness areas. One can pull into any one of these parks and set up a tent or unhook his travel trailer and spend his vacation in beautiful surroundings. He may fish, swim, go boating, hiking, mountain climbing—and enjoy these at their best.

Of Maine's 19 state parks, 11 permit camping and two provide trailer sites. Fees are $2 to $2.50 per night, depending on the services offered, plus 25 cents for wood. No electricity for trailers is provided. No reservations can be accepted for camping except at Baxter State Park. Children under 12 are admitted free in all areas when part of a family group.

A leaflet, "**State Parks and Historic Sites in Maine**," and a sheet showing facilities may be obtained by writing to the Department of Economic Development, State House, Augusta 04330.

The Maine Forest Service, whose authorized campsite program is administered in cooperation with private landowners, is designed to provide safe, sanitary camping and picnicking areas for the general public. Site development is kept to a minimum, and every effort is made to maintain a natural environment. Many sites are accessible only by water and provide the ultimate in solitude and privacy. Campsites are usually equipped with a minimum of one safe fireplace, one picnic table and one pit toilet.

Other facilities commonly found at the more heavily used sites include trash barrels, a registration board and drinking water. No charge is made for the use of Maine Forest Service campsites. Some 205 areas permit camping; 82 provide trailer space. More details may be received by writing to Campsite Coordinator, Maine Forest Service, Augusta 04330.

MARYLAND

State parks and other state recreation areas offer camping variety

Many state and federal recreation areas include museums depicting the heritage of America. This museum in Nebraska commemorates the Homestead Act, which gave 160 acres of land to anyone willing to settle on it.

Nebraska Game Commission Photo

in more than a dozen locations—from mountain vistas in the west to the Atlantic shore in the east. Hiking, boating, museums, nature trails and heavily forested areas are some of the attractions. Fees range from $1.25 to $2 per day, depending on the quality of facilities. For further information, write Maryland Department of Forests and Parks, State Office Building, Annapolis.

MASSACHUSETTS

Massachusetts state parks, forests, beaches and other outdoor areas have been equipped to accommodate the growing numbers of families and others who like to camp and otherwise enjoy the outdoors. Fun activities include swimming, hiking, fishing and hunting.

Twenty-two of the 58 state parks and forests offer about 1,900 campsites. Campsites are available on a first-come, first-served basis, and between the last Saturday in June and Labor Day, the occupancy of a campsite is limited to two weeks. Camping trailers which can fit into a standard tentsite will be accepted. There are no available trailer services—gas, electricity and water connections—in any state park or forest.

Fees: campsite—$2 per day; tent platform—$2.50 per day; fireplace wood—50 cents per bushel.

A camping regulations folder and other information may be obtained from Division of Forests and Parks, Dept. of Natural Resources, State Office Building, 100 Cambridge St., Boston 02202.

Nebraska's Lake Maloney near North Platte lures campers to its playground shores.

Nebraska Game Commission Photo

MICHIGAN

Tourists from throughout the country visit Michigan each year, enjoying the long stretches of beautiful open country, interspersed with forests, rivers and lakes. The 67 state parks with campgrounds boast 13,394 campsites, 10,985 of these sites with electricity.

Motor vehicle permits are required on all vehicles entering state parks and recreation areas. An annual permit costs $3 for Michigan residents and $5 for non-resident visitors. Daily permits cost $1 and $2 respectively.

Campsite rental in state parks varies from $1.50 to $2 per night depending on what facilities are available. Permits for camping are issued by each park, reservations are not accepted and all facilities are on a first-come, first-served basis.

A Michigan campground directory is available from the Michigan Department of Conservation, Lansing 48926.

MINNESOTA

More than 70 state parks and forests offer the camper a wide variety of sites. Many boast both lake and forest features. The thousands of streams and lakes make canoe camping popular. Annual entry permits are available, admitting the holder to all state parks. A two-day permit costs 50 cents. Campsites are $1.50 per day; in some primitive areas, 50 cents.

Detailed information and maps may be obtained from Minnesota Division of State Parks, State Office Building, St. Paul.

MISSISSIPPI

Mississippi offers outstanding recreation and relaxation through its 19 state parks, which are open throughout the year. Camping reservations may be made in advance through park rangers. Visitors admitted free to parks but must pay $1

camping fee, plus 50 cents for electricity where available.

The various recreational outlets offered in the state parks include swimming, boating, fishing, surf riding, softball, hiking and a good Southern pastime, relaxing. Piers, diving boards and protection by lifeguards make swimming one of the most popular fun activities. At some of the parks, lights are installed on the piers, making night swimming possible.

A copy of **Mississippi, the Hospitality State** and further camping details are available from Mississippi Park System, 1102 Woolfolk State Office Building, Jackson.

MISSOURI

This is a state with forests and streams and offers pleasant campground facilities. Part of the Ozark range lies in the southern part of the state, affording mountain pleasures to the campers.

More than 30 state parks contain excellent camping facilities. The campgrounds are open all year, but some facilities are not available in winter. Campsite fees range from 75 cents to $1.50 per day. Time limit is 15 days.

Information will be sent on re-

Rugged, picturesque wilderness and a large game refuge attract backpackers and other wilderness campers to Nebraska's Wildcat Hills.

Nebraska Game Commission Photo

quest by State Park Board, Jefferson Building, Jefferson City.

MONTANA

Montana maintains camping facilities in most of its 40 state parks and forests.

Whether you plan overnight campouts just off interstate highways, or a more adventurous stay in out-of-the-way state parks or recreational areas, Montana has a lot to offer. For those who take camping seriously, there is primitive country where travel is limited to horses or foot trails. Here you'll have miles of green-timbered forests and cool streams all to yourself.

For a list of camping areas and a copy of **Your Vacation in Montana, the BIG SKY Country,** write Advertising Department, Montana Highway Commission, Helena 59601.

NEBRASKA

Sprinkled across Nebraska's expansive and diverse landscape are hundreds of campgrounds to accommodate the ever-increasing number of Americans who want to get away from the humdrum of life for awhile and move in with Mother Nature.

There are rustic, primitive areas, but there are also some modern, fully-equipped, convenient sites. These feature such luxuries as playgrounds for the kids, laundries and showers and game rooms. Virtually all camps provide crystal-clear drinking water, picnic tables, grills and sanitary facilities. Most all sites have a lake or stream to provide the visiting camper with fishing, swimming and boating. Some have swimming pools, rental horses, concessions and shelter houses.

Of the 49 state parks and recreation areas, four provide special trailer parking. Fees are 50 cents to $1 per night, depending on facilities.

For a copy of **Discover NEBRAS-KAland** and camping specifics, write Information and Tourism Division, Nebraska Game and Parks Commission, State Capitol, Lincoln 68509.

NEVADA

Nevada is sometimes referred to as "one of the last frontiers of the United States." Its state park system is still young; consequently some of the park areas are not yet entirely improved. To date, nine state parks ranging in size from a few acres to several thousand acres have been established and the Nevada State Park System is conducting an active program to acquire, improve and maintain additional state park areas.

There are no charges for camping or picnicking in the state park areas. It is always a good idea to make local inquiry of road conditions when visiting state park areas situated at some distance from paved highways, and to carry some water.

Eight state parks provide 103 camping units. For copies of **"Your Guide to Camping in Nevada"** and "Guide to Nevada State Parks," write Nevada State Park System, Room 221, Nye Building, Carson City 89701.

NEW HAMPSHIRE

Far from the beaten path but close to many famous tourist attractions, most New Hampshire state parks are in wooded settings. Several are nestled in the White Mountains, famous for their scenic, rugged grandeur.

Ten parks have public campgrounds with many conveniences; several have well-maintained hiking trails; some are close to trails of the Appalachian system. The mountaintop parks offer magnificent views.

Some may be reached by road. Two have aerial rides—a tramway and gondola.

Fourteen lakeside parks with sandy beaches appeal to family groups for swimming and picnicking; two offer bathing in the Atlantic Ocean. Many have boats for rent to fishermen and pleasure boaters.

Most state parks are open through the fall foliage season. During winter, the New Hampshire Division of Parks operates two major ski areas at Cannon Mountain in Franconia and Mt. Sunapee in Newbury.

Each campsite has an open, outdoor fireplace, picnic table and car parking space. Running water and toilets are nearby. Wood and charcoal are available at all campgrounds.

Tentsites cannot be reserved. Two weeks is the camping period, unless attendance is low. Trailers will be admitted only if they fit conveniently into available tentsites. There are no special facilities for them. Fees range from $1 to $3, depending on facilities furnished.

Request camping and state park folders from State Division of Economic Development, P. O. Box 856, Concord 03301.

NEW JERSEY

The state parks in New Jersey have been established to provide facilities for healthful outdoor recreation, to preserve the native flora and fauna in their natural conditions and to preserve areas of outstanding historic significance. Most of the parks have been set aside as wildlife sanctuaries and hunting is not permitted.

Many state parks in lake and river country attract thousands of canoe campers.

Michigan Department of Conservation

Kentucky state parks, strategically located in all parts of the state, offer a variety of camping pleasures.

Kentucky Department of Public Information

Travel trailers and camp trailers can be accommodated at all parks and forests except High Point State Park. Electric, water and sewage connections are not provided. Water and toilet facilities are located nearby. Flush toilets, hot showers and laundry facilities are available only at Bass River and Belleplain.

Wilderness sites are accessible by road, canoe and backpack. No facilities of any kind are provided. Open and closed, equipped lean-tos are provided in some areas. Water and toilet facilities are located nearby.

Family campsites are on a first-come, first served basis. From May 25 to September 7 one-third of the family campsites and all lean-tos may be reserved for exactly a 7- or 14-day period. Payment in full

must accompany the application for reservation. If facility is not available, the remittance will be returned promptly.

Fees: family campsite, $1.50 per night without reservation, $2 with reservation; open lean-to, $2.50 per night without reservation, $3 with reservation; closed lean-to, $3 per night without reservation, $3.50 with reservation.

For folders and further information, write Bureau of Parks, P. O. Box 1889, Trenton 08625.

NEW MEXICO

The 22 parks now in New Mexico's State Park System are scattered about the Land of Enchantment as jewels in a fabulous setting. Park facilities are constantly being expanded and improved with the most modern equipment.

Most parks contain picnic areas with sheltered and unsheltered tables, grills or fireplaces for cooking, sanitary facilities (some with hot and cold showers), domestic water, playgrounds, overnight camping sites— many with electrical outlets—trash receptacles and, above all, courteous park attendants to maintain the park and assist the visitor in every way possible.

Service fees: annual camping permit (electricity, 50 cents extra per day)—$15; overnight camping, electricity available—$1.50 per day, $7.50 per week; overnight camping, no electricity—$1 per day, $5 per week.

For a copy of **"New Mexico's State Parks and How to Get to Them"** and further details, write New Mexico State Park and Recreation Commission, P. O. Box 1147, Santa Fe 87501.

NEW YORK

New York was among the first to anticipate the camping boom, and both the number of public campgrounds and the number of tentsites in state parks have steadily increased.

There are over 120 state parks and camping areas in the New York State Park System. Each of these has a large number of tent and trailer campsites, with a charge of $1.50 per day, and campsites with electricity at $1.75 per day.

For copies of **"New York State Parks"** and **"Camping in New York State,"** write to Division of State Parks, 1220 Washington Ave., Albany 12226.

NORTH CAROLINA

North Carolina's state parks are located from the top of Mount Mitchell, highest peak in Eastern America, to the Atlantic Coast near Morehead City and Beaufort. All parks are free to visitors and are open all year (except for Mount Mitchell State Park, which is closed during winter). Refreshment stands and swimming areas are open from early June through Labor Day. Camping is available at developed campgrounds in eight of the parks.

Each campsite has parking space, a table, outdoor fireplace, tentsite and parking space for a car or trailer, except for Mount Mitchell, which has a central parking area and tent camping only. Each campground has a central washhouse with lavatories, flush toilets and showers, approved drinking water and sewage disposal. There are no electrical, sewage or water connections for trailers.

The fee is $1.50 per day per campsite for four persons or less, plus 25 cents per day for each person in excess of four. Reservations for periods of seven days or more may be made and are payable in advance. Maximum stay is 14 days. Campers for shorter periods of time are assigned sites and pay on arrival.

For full description of all parks and copies of "North Carolina State Parks" and "Outdoors in North Carolina," write Division of State Parks, Dept. of Conservation & Development, Raleigh 27602.

Only the Indians ever had it so good. This is typical of many ideal campsites in Utah parks.

Utah Tourist and Publicity Council.

NORTH DAKOTA

North Dakota—roughrider country —has 10 state parks and areas, all with camping facilities. Three provide campsite electricity, and most of the others feature fireplaces, drinking water, picnic tables, swimming, fishing, boating, toilets and playgrounds.

Entry fees are required at state parks as follows: 50 cents per vehicle for a one-day permit; $2 per vehicle for an annual permit; in addition, a $1 per night or $3.50 per week camping fee.

For official highway map and a copy of "Camping in North Dakota" leaflet and state park information, write to Travel Division, North Dakota Highway Department, Bismarck 58501.

OHIO

All Ohio state park campgrounds are open year-round. Thirty nine parks maintain camping facilities. Class A sites generally have approved water under pressure, drinking fountains, waste water drains, flush toilets, laundry and shower facilities, numbered lots, picnic tables and fire rings or outdoor grill. Sites where electricity is available, $2 per night during season; $1.25 off season.

Class B sites generally have approved well or hydrant water, pit-type latrines, waste water drains, either marked or unmarked lots, picnic tables and fire ring or outdoor grill. Sites where electricity is available, $1.50 per night; where no electricity is available, $1.25 per night.

Primitive sites have only pit-type latrines and waste containers and there is no charge at any time. Reservations are not accepted for family campsites.

Camping information folder may be secured on request from Division of Parks and Recreation, Room 913, Ohio Departments Bldg., Columbus 43215.

OKLAHOMA

The "Oklahoma State Parks Have Everything" folder says: "Oklahoma hasn't yet found a vacation pocketbook it can't fit. . . . For campers, Oklahoma is one of the few states which does not levy a user charge for use of campsites, and as a result, millions of enthusiastic campers annually enjoy the great Oklahoma out-of-doors."

Oklahoma maintains 21 state parks, 14 special recreational areas and 11 monuments, shrines and memorials. Most have electric-sewer-water hookups, charcoal grills, picnic shelters, shower/latrines, plus many recreational facilities. There is a small charge for electricity.

For a copy of "Oklahoma State Parks Have Everything" and "Oklahoma Camper's Directory," write Oklahoma Park Department, 500 Will Rogers Memorial Building, Oklahoma City 73105.

OREGON

"One of Oregon's most popular vacation attractions is its extensive system of state parks, offering hundreds of overnight camping and trailer sites and a variety of recreation accommodations for people seeking fun and relaxation in the outdoors." This is not just a promotion blurb. Oregon maintains more than 200 state parks, some 60 of them located along the scenic Oregon coast. Many others are situated on the banks of sparkling rivers and streams, in fertile valleys and woodlands and among juniper trees.

Oregon parks, for the most part, offer electric stoves or fireplaces, water supply, picnic tables, special recreation and play areas, comfort stations and a free supply of firewood. Travel trailer sites have hookups for electricity, water and waste disposal.

Length of stay at any one park is limited to 7 days in any 10-day period. At parks with camper registration booths, campsites are assigned by the attendant. Camping fees are based on the type of campsite occupied: Trailer campsite—$2 per night; facilities include hookups for water, electricity and sewage disposal at each site, with a table, stove and access to a modern utility building with toilets, showers and laundry facilities. Improved campsite—$1.50 per night; facilities include a table, stove and water nearby, with access to a utility building or rest station

Camping is one of Oregon's most popular pastimes. Many campers prefer Tumalo State Park, seen here with the snow-clad Three Sisters towering in the distance.

Oregon State Highway Department Photo

with flush toilets. Unimproved campsite—$1 per night; facilities include a table and stove, but water and sanitary facilities may be some distance from the site.

The Highway Department has a brochure, "Oregon Parks," with a map and detailed information on local, state and federal recreation areas popular with travelers vacationing in Oregon. Write Travel Information, 102 State Highway Bldg., Salem 97310.

PENNSYLVANIA

Forty-one Pennsylvania state parks welcome campers to 4,004 campsites. Many Pennsylvania campgrounds have modern sanitary facilities. The charge is $1.75 per site per night. Sites without these facilities cost $1.25. Advance reservations are not accepted. The camping period is limited to 14 consecutive nights.

Brochures on "Family Camping Pennsylvania State Parks" and "Pennsylvania State Parks" are available from the Department of Forests and Waters, Harrisburg 17120.

RHODE ISLAND

More than 700 campsites—improved and primitive—are maintained in five state parks and recreation areas, plus several good sites reached only by canoe. The largest campground is at Burlingame State Park, where more than 650 tent and trailer sites are available.

The rate for most sites is $2 per night. Many privately owned camping areas are operated near the state sites. For maps and information on both public and private campgrounds, write Rhode Island Development Council, Publicity and Recreation Division, Hayes Street, Providence 02908.

SOUTH CAROLINA

Climate, variety of scenery, forests, mountains, beaches, lakes and a vast embroidery of streams make South Carolina ideal for family camping. Some campsites are as modern as tomorrow, with a full range of facilities. Others are more rustic so you can get closer to nature. The Palmetto State's even climate makes camping attractive year-round.

South Carolina's state parks encompass quiet seaside beaches, the crisp air of the Blue Ridge Mountains and beautiful lakes. Twenty-eight state parks enhance the state with well stocked lakes, nature trails, picnic tables, fishing facilities and campgrounds.

Fees at all parks are $1.75-$3.75 a day per family for each site. No advance reservations. One week maximum stay.

Greenleaf Lake State Park draws many Oklahoma camping fishermen.

Oklahoma Industrial Development and Park Department

Nearly all parks have the following facilities: flush toilets, hot showers, electrical and water connections, tables and grills, nature trails, boating, fishing and swimming.

For copies of "South Carolina State Parks & Campgrounds" and "South Carolina Vacationland," write Department of Parks, Recreation & Tourism, Box 1358, Columbia 29202.

SOUTH DAKOTA

South Dakota, "a big, broad-shouldered land of infinite pleasure matched only in dimension by its western hospitality," offers several state parks and recreational areas in which to camp. Drinking water, toilets, picnic tables and fireplaces are provided. There is a 14-day camping limit in all areas.

Charges vary. An average charge is $1 per unit per night or $5 per unit per week.

"South Dakota Visitor's Directory" may be obtained upon request from Department of Highways, Publicity Division, Pierre 57501.

TENNESSEE

Tennessee has 21 state parks. Activities are many and varied: camping, swimming, boating, fishing, hiking, archery, tennis and golf, to name a few. Most parks offer equipped playgrounds, nature trails, beautiful scenery and more. There are tent and trailer camping facilities and more are being developed each year to meet the growing demands. Most have central restrooms with hot and cold running water, showers and laundry tubs. Many have electric, water and sewerage hookups.

Rates for camping in state parks are $2 a day for four persons or less; 25 cents for each additional person. No person under six years of age will be charged. An electrical hookup is 25 cents a day or 75 cents a day for electric, water and sewerage (where available) hookup.

Camping and water recreation go together in Wisconsin. Fishing and canoeing seem to be in the plans for this camping couple.

Wisconsin Natural Resources Department

For copies of **"Camping Tennessee"** and **Three 'States' of Tennessee,** write Tennessee Dept. of Conservation, 2611 West End Avenue, Nashville 37203.

TEXAS

Texas' 59 state parks offer a variety of outdoor recreational activities in interesting and attractive settings. The 59 parks encompass 61,000 acres. Most operate year-round.

Overnight camping is a part of almost all state parks. Camping permits are required, and fees are as follows:

Camping (tent or trailer) $1 per car per night without electricity; $1.50 per car per night with electricity. Screened shelters, $2.50 per night, plus $1 per car.

For copies of **"Texas State Parks,"** **"99 Tips on Camping in Texas State Parks,"** and **"Parks Information — Rules and Regulations,"** write Texas Parks & Wildlife Dept., John H. Reagan Bldg., Austin 78701.

UTAH

Most of Utah's state-operated recreation areas are located in cool aspen or evergreen forests, in canyons and mountains that are only a few miles from main highways. Many are established in stream or lake country, affording the opportunity to fish and boat. Hiking, sightseeing, nature study and hunting are also pursued avidly by campers.

Camping is provided for in 21 of 35 state parks. The usual facilities are provided, with a few offering electricity and showers. Fees are charged, commensurate with other states.

"A Guide to Utah's Camp and Picnic Areas," "A Guide to Utah's State Parks," and **Utah!,** state publications, may be secured from Utah Travel Council, Council Hall, State Capitol, Salt Lake City 84114.

VERMONT

Vermont has 32 state forests totaling 87,343 acres, and 34 state parks totaling 12,087 acres. Recreational facilities in these forests and parks are administered by the Vermont Division of Parks. Some of the largest and most frequently used recreation areas are in the state forests in contrast to other states where the majority of the outdoor recreation areas are in state parks. Altogether Vermont has 36 state-owned campgrounds with approximately 1,900 individual sites.

Fees for camping: Tentsite (with or without platform)—$3 per night minimum; $1.50 per night per adult. Lean-to, $4 per night minimum; $2 per night per adult. Small camping trailers and small house trailers or pickup campers can be parked on most tentsites. Special trailer hookups for utilities are not available.

All campgrounds operate on a first-come, first-served basis, but reservations are available for a minimum period of six nights up to three weeks.

For copies of a very helpful Vermont official map and a state parks and forests camping sites leaflet, write to Department of Forests and Parks, Montpelier 05602.

VIRGINIA

Virginia maintains ten state parks, all with good camping facilities. Rates at state parks are $2 per campsite per night. Sites can accommodate tents and trailers alike. A few have electrical and water hookups.

Many have washrooms with hot showers, restrooms, flush toilets, washtub, outdoor cooking facilities, tables, garbage disposal, drinking water, ice and supply stores. Fishing, nature study, horseback riding and hiking are pleasant pastimes.

On request, Virginia State Travel Service, 911 East Broad Street, Richmond 23219, will gladly send a copy of "**Camping in Virginia.**"

WASHINGTON

The Evergreen State has nearly 200 state parks ranging from ocean beaches to high mountain peaks and subterranean caverns. Some park sites have been intentionally left in a primitive state, while others are highly developed. One maintains a gold course. Another is set aside for the exclusive use of horseback riders. Four have ski slopes and snow play areas, and three have areas reserved for snowmobiling. Altogether, there are 4,000 campsites, and hookups for 700 trailers.

Some 50 marine parks are accessible only by boat. Twenty-five others have either ocean beaches or frontage on the salt water of Puget Sound or the Hood Canal.

Camping fees: $1.50 per night per car; $2 per night where special hookups for water, electricity and waste disposal are provided; a state sales tax is added to all charges. Only one vehicle per campsite is permitted. No reservations are taken for overnight camping. A seven-day camping limit is enforced. Vacation trailers up to 20 feet long normally can be accommodated.

A great variety of trails abound for beginning and experienced hikers, as well as self-guiding nature trails. A number of trails have been designated primarily for travel on horseback. Horses are available for hire at selected parks throughout the state.

"**Washington Outdoor Recreation Guide**" is available from State Parks and Recreation Commission, Box 1128, Olympia 98501.

WEST VIRGINIA

Standard campgrounds in West Virginia state parks and state forests are designed to cater to more demanding tastes. Many have modern central sanitary facilities with hot

Camping out is a memorable experience in Montana, the "Big Sky Country." This family chose Lake Como for its camping vacation.

Montana Highway Commission Photo

Checking facts with one who knows, a visitor gets guidance from a park ranger at Anastasia State Park, near St. Augustine, Florida.

showers, coin-operated laundry equipment, trailer dumping stations and a few will have electricity and water connections at selected sites.

Other sites are more rustic, with drilled wells, hand pumps and pit toilets. Both standard and rustic sites have picnic tables, fireplace grills and refuse containers at each pad. Advance reservations are not accepted.

Camping fees in state parks and forests are $2 per night in standard areas, and $1.50 per night in rustic areas, both for a party of six or less, plus 25 cents per night for each additional camper.

"West Virginia has pioneered an 'honor system' for the payment of camper fees on an experimental basis at a number of its areas," the Department of Natural Resources reports. "A master board has slots for each available campsite. Each morning envelopes are placed in all slots, and campers merely take the envelope for their numbered site,

drop in the required fee and deposit the envelope in a box for that purpose. Campers may thus keep the same site up to the two-week maximum. Added advantage is that newcomers can see at a glance which sites are available."

For copies of "**West Virginia State Parks and Forests**" and "**Tent and Trailer Camping in West Virginia State Parks & Forests,**" write West Virginia Dept. of Natural Resources, State Capitol, Charleston 25305.

WISCONSIN

The nine state forests, comprising more than 200,000 acres of scenic lakes, pine-wooded retreats, glacial terrains and wildlife preserves, offer the camper all that he could wish for. Camping, boating and fishing facilities will be found in most areas.

There are family campgrounds, canoe campsites and primitive campsites. A few family campgrounds offer flush toilets, showers, concessions and electrical outlets. Rates are $2.50 per unit per day for modern campgrounds and $2 for rustic campgrounds; firewood, 25 cents;

electricity, 25 cents per day. Admission sticker, $1 daily or $3 per season.

From Vacation and Travel Service, Wisconsin Department of Natural Resources, Box 450, Madison 53701, you may obtain copies of "**Wisconsin Campground Directory**" and "**Guide to Scenic Parks, State Forests and Recreational Areas.**"

WYOMING

State parks are splashed across the map of Wyoming. "Camp next to nature," the ads say, and they paint a true picture. Fishing, boating, exploring wilderness areas—these are some of the exciting by-products of camping in Wyoming. Of course, considerable western history was made here, and many state parks are in location with history.

Camping in Wyoming state parks is free. Facilities run the gamut from primitive to ultra-modern.

For further information on Wyoming state parks, write Wyoming Recreation Commission, Box 309, Cheyenne 82001. For a copy of **This is BIG Wyoming,** write Wyoming Travel Commission, 2320 Capitol Ave., Cheyenne 82001.

Tunnel Mountain soars high above the campground that bears its name near the town of
Banff in Banff National Park.

Camping in Canada

You can't begin to total the good camping sites in Canada, for Canada is 90 percent outdoorsman's country.

No country in the world is more aware of its outdoor heritage than is Canada. Canada holds all the lure of a new frontier. Canadians themselves have long since understood this and benefited from it. Others, too, first by the thousands and now by the millions, have journeyed to this second-biggest country in the world for vacation purposes. Many of these are campers.

Canada is overwhelming in every respect. Take a look at a map of Canada. If you travel from St. John's, Newfoundland, to Victoria, British Columbia, you will traverse more than one-fifth of the earth's circum-ference. A modern highway, the Trans-Canada, links these two port cities, following some 5,000 miles along a scenic route that mere words cannot describe.

Canada is not only wide from east to west, but also from north to south. If a citizen of Detroit, Michigan, started traveling south and a resident of Windsor, across the border, started going north, both traveling at the same rate of speed, the person from Detroit would be sightseeing along the head-waters of the Amazon River before the Windsorite stepped off the Cana-dian soil onto the icecap covering the Arctic Ocean.

Most of Canada's 20 million citizens live within a narrow ribbon 200 miles or so wide along the border just north of the United States. Most of the rest of Canada is almost uninhabited, having a population of about one person per square mile. There are 3 million square miles of this, and any camper will know that that's a lot of outdoors.

Ten provinces

Canada is composed of ten prov-inces and two territories. The prov-inces are Newfoundland (includes Labrador), Prince Edward Island, Nova Scotia, New Brunswick, Quebec, Ontario, Manitoba, Sas-katchewan, Alberta and British Colum-bia. The territories are the Yukon and the Northwest Territories. In all of the provinces except Quebec there is at least one national park. The provinces themselves, as well as the territories, maintain many parks and recreational areas.

An American citizen is welcome to Canada with practically no red tape at any one of many border points, but he should have adequate identification

Mount Assiniboine, 11,870 feet, is the reward for these ri-ders as they ride through the Cana-dian Rockies. Riding the trails and passes of the Rockies offers an incomparable va-cation experience.

–driver's license, usually – for re-admission to the United States. It is important that the visitor to Canada avail himself of highway regulations and other laws with which he may not be familiar. This kind of information can be supplied by the courteous customs people at the border crossings.

Before being admitted to the Alaska Highway, a traveler may be asked to show that he is financially supplied for the trip.

By all means, ask your automobile insurance agent to supply you with a special Canadian rider on your insurance policy. Many an American has discovered to his dismay that his insurance policy without such a guarantee held no weight with authorities

In the parks of Newfoundland, individual campsites are spaced to provide uncrowded privacy.

Newfoundland Tourist Development Office

when he had an accident north of the border.

Canada's national parks

Canada boasts of 19 national parks, and they are all different. Ranging from the immense forests and mountains of the west to the steep cliffs and sun-tanned beaches of the Atlantic, they bear such romantic names as Yoho (Indian for "How Wonderful!"), Kootenay, Wood Buffalo and Terra Nova.

The Canadian Government Travel Bureau, Ottawa, Ontario, has published two excellent descriptive booklets of Canada's national parks, which are free upon request. If you are interested in information on national parks from Manitoba west, ask for **Canada National Parks West;** if you desire information on eastern Canada's national parks, ask for **Canada National**

Parks East. Both booklets are profusely illustrated in beautiful color.

The Canadian Government Travel Bureau also maintains offices in Boston, Chicago, Cincinnati, Cleveland, Detroit, Hartford, Indianapolis, Los Angeles, Minneapolis, New York, Philadelphia, Pittsburgh, Rochester, San Francisco, Seattle and Washington, D. C. Full information is available at any of these.

Admission to Canada's national parks is free, but motorists must register and buy a license in some of the parks. The license generally is 25 cents per car per visit; 50 cents if you are pulling a trailer. For in-and-out privileges, a special license good during the year ending March 31 is available for $1 per car, $2 for car and trailer.

To avoid all license problems, a visitor may purchase one license good for the entire season in all national parks in Canada. This license costs $2 for cars and $3 for cars and trailers.

No hunting

No hunting is permitted in Canada's national parks. They are game sanctuaries. Unsealed firearms are prohibited. You can't even pick flowers: plants and trees are as rigidly protected as are the animals.

A $2 fishing license is required in all national parks except in Ontario. In these areas, nonresidents of Ontario must purchase a provincial fishing license. It costs $3.25 for three consecutive days, $6.50 for the entire season.

TERRA NOVA NATIONAL PARK

Glovertown, Newfoundland
Area, 153 square miles

This national park, located in Newfoundland, is Canada's newest in full operation. The park is marked by a rugged coastline, with fiord-like sounds cleaving into bold headlands. The cold Labrador current bathes these shores, and the unusual sight of an iceberg, dazzling and shimmering in the blue water, is common. The Trans-Canada Highway crosses Terra Nova for a distance of about 25 miles. Park headquarters, with such services as public wharf and an information bureau, is situated about midway between the park's northern and southern boundaries. Visitors to Terra Nova often arrive by sea. Excellent docking facilities are in the headquarters area.

There is a campground in idyllic surroundings near the park's headquarters on the shore of Newman Sound. It boasts such services as kitchen shelters, showers and laundry facilities and a children's playground. There is room for 200 tents. Other campgrounds are being developed.

Nature trails are popular, and it is the rule rather than the exception that hikers, motorists and those traveling by watercraft frequently see animals such as bear lynx and moose.

PRINCE EDWARD ISLAND NATIONAL PARK

Stanhope, Prince Edward Island
Area, 7 square miles

This is a unique park, consisting of 25 miles of glimmering, sandy beaches, backed by sandstone cliffs, and caressed by the warmth of the Gulf Stream. Three areas have been developed for recreational purposes, with cabins, serviced trailer parks and campsites, supervised swimming, golf, nature trails and recreation halls available to the visitor.

Campgrounds include Stanhope (serviced), 157 tents and 14 trailers; Stanhope (primitive), 12 tents: Rustico Island, 148 tents; and Cavendish, 226 tents and 78 trailers.

The miles and miles of beaches are lapped by the warmest ocean water north of Florida. Horseback riding along the vast stretches of open beach is one of the most popular pastimes.

KEJINKUJIK NATIONAL PARK

Maitland Bridge, Nova Scotia
Area, 150 square miles

This is a new national park located west of Maitland Bridge on Highway 8. A forested area with many lakes, it has no visitor facilities, except for one campground at Jeremy which accommondates 88 tents. The park is made—to—order for canoeing.

CAPE BRETON HIGHLANDS NATIONAL PARK

Ingonish Beach, Nova Scotia
Area, 367 square miles

This park in Nova Scotia is encircled by the Cabot Trail, a 184-mile, all-weather paved highway that climbs four mountains to provide breath-taking panoramas of rock and sea and valley. This area was settled by Scots, many of whom still speak Gaelic, and the park's 367 square miles remind visitors of the highlands of Scotland.

Campgrounds within the park are Ingoish Beach, 108 tents; Broad Cove, 186 tents and 83 trailers; Black Brook, 86 tents or trailers; Big Intervale, 5 tents and 5 trailers; MacIntosh Brook, 15 tents and 15 trailers; Corney Brook, 10 tents and 10 trailers; and Cheticamp, 150 tents and 24 trailers (additional space may be provided for 38 tents or trailers).

There is a campground right on the Gulf of St. Lawrence where the Cabot Trail nears the town of Cheticamp. At the eastern entrance is a safe, quiet beach which is attractive to many families. Other beaches and numerous lakes and fresh-water streams within the park provide all kinds of water recreation opportunities.

FUNDY NATIONAL PARK

Alma, New Brunswick
Area, 97.5 square miles

This park in the province of New Brunswick skirts the Bay of Fundy for eight miles and extends inland for more than nine miles. The park is beautiful and boasts of excellent beaches, a golf course, a large, saltwater swimming pool overlooking the bay, tennis courts, playgrounds, nature trails and many special art and crafts features during the summer months.

Campgrounds are Park Headquarters, 125 tents and 29 trailers; Pointe Wolfe, 250 tents; Chignecto, 620 tents; Bennett Lake, 35 tents; Wolfe Lake, 60 tents; and Pointe Wolfe, 200 persons.

This campground along the Trans-Canada Highway is one of many strategically placed in the province of Nova Scotia.

Nova Scotia Information Service

A noticeable feature of campgrounds in Nova Scotia is the attractive way they are laid out. Bottom photo.

Nova Scotia Information Service

ST. LAWRENCE ISLANDS NATIONAL PARK

Mallorytown, Ontario
Area, 260 acres

Thirteen small islands in the Thousand Island area of the St. Lawrence River between Kingston and Brockville, and Mallorytown Landing on the mainland, comprise this scenic recreation park. The islands can be reached by boat or by comercial water-taxi. All have docks, campsites and wells; on the mainland there is a campground with a nearby bathing beach. Fishing, swimming and boating are popular pastimes.

Camping is permitted on all of the islands. Developed campgrounds are located at Mallorytown Landing,

75 tents; and Grenadier Island, 20 tents.

GEORGIAN BAY ISLANDS NATIONAL PARK

Honey Harbour, Ontario
Area, 5.40 square miles

This park consists of 30 islands or parts of islands in Georgian Bay, Ontario. The largest is Beausoleil Island—five square miles. This island was once the home of the Chippewa Indians and is reached only by boat. There are excellent bathing beaches, docks and well-equipped campsites.

Campgrounds include Cedar Spring, 150 tents; Thumb Point, 10 tents; Tonch Point, 25 tents; Sandpiper Bay, 6 tents, McCabe Rock, 5 tents; The Oaks, 15 tents;

Chimney Bay, 10 tents; Little Dog, 2 tents; Minnehaha, 10 tents; Codettes Grove, 6 tents; Cherry Pointe, 3 tents; Panhawke, 3 tents; Frying Pan Bay, 8 tents; Sunset, 6 tents; Beausoleil Pointe, 10 tents; Island No. 92, 6 tents; and Island No. 95B, 5 tents.

POINTE PELEE NATIONAL PARK

Leamington, Ontario
Area, 6 square miles

This park is small but unique. Pointe Pelee is a V-shaped sandspit jutting into Lake Erie. It is the southernmost area of Canada's mainland and is on the same latitude as California. It boasts of sand beaches and a unique 2,000-acre freshwater swamp. It is also on the spring and fall bird migration routes.

Within this park will be found plants and wildlife unique in Canada. Such trees as cottonwood, sycamore, white sassafras and shagbark hickory are found here. Even prickly pear cactus and wild potato vine grow in this park. Animal life includes such unusual characters as the mole, the katydid and many varieties of turtles. Unusual birds include the scarlet ebis, orchard oriole, blue-gray gnatcatcher and yellow-breasted chat.

Swimming, boating and canoeing—on the four large ponds within the park—are enjoyed by visitors. The park provides an unusually large number of facilities for picnickers; it can accommodate 7,600 people at picnic tables at any one time.

Campgrounds include Pointe Pelee, 132 tents; Little Racoon, 20 tents; and Marsh Hawk, 20 tents. In

Quiet beaches that echo over the noise of pounding surf, like this one near Cheticamp, Nova Scotia, are found almost everywhere along the province's 4,625 miles of coastline, as well as along the coastlines of other eastern provinces.

The Trans-Canada Camp and Picnic Ground at McLean, Saskatchewan, 30 miles east of Regina, is a completely modern, 40-acre tourist stop with facilities for picnicking and camping.

addition, there is a large, serviced campground for groups.

RIDING MOUNTAIN NATIONAL PARK

Wasagaming, Manitoba
Area, 1,148 square miles

A four-lane highway leads into this park, a vast area dotted with fish-filled lakes and streams. It offers a unique mixture of untamed wilderness and modern resort convenience. It boasts of an 18-hole golf course, tennis, lawn bowling, sailing, swimming, riding and other popular pastime opportunities.

The park is situated on the vast plateau of Riding Mountain, which rises to 2,200 feet above the sprawling prairie. Clear Lake, the largest body of water in the park, is nine miles long and two miles across at the widest point. Free swimming classes are offered for children. Boating and sight-seeing launches are popular lake pleasures. Trail riding and a closeup look at a buffalo herd are among the interesting variety of pastime pleasures.

A museum building, constructed of natural logs and stone, contains exhibits of mounted wildlife and Indian, geological and other displays relating to the area.

Camping accommodations are located at these campgrounds: Clear Lake, 665 tents and trailers; Wasagaming, 437 tents and 95 trailers; Loon Lake, 25 tents; Lake Audy, 50 tents; Lake Catherine, 100 tents; and Whirlpool Lake, 15 tents.

You bring the tent and the government will provide the rest—plenty of space, cooking facilities, picnic tables, and recreation. This is Norquay Beach, near Portage la Prairie, Manitoba.

PRINCE ALBERT NATIONAL PARK

Prince Albert, Saskatchewan
Area, 1,496 square miles

Located in central Saskatchewan, this park is a fascinating example of lake and woodland country lying north of the prairies. It has many lakes, rimmed with sandy beaches, and many connecting rivers which form exciting waterways for canoe safaris. Within the park are tennis courts, a golf course, a bowling green, children's playgrounds and boat launching and docking facilities. Leafy forest trails are excellent for hiking and riding, and there are saddle horses for hire.

Campgrounds include: Waskesiu, 200 tents and 120 trailers; Beaver Glen, 214 tents; The Narrows, 60 tents; Halkett (Sandy) Lake, 25 tents; Namekus Lake, 30 tents; Kingsmere Kitchen, 20 tents; Bagwa Lake, 10 tents; Crean Lake, 10 tents; Trappers Lake, 5 tents. Also in the Kingsmere Lake area are these camping sites: Bladebone Bay, 10 tents; Ajawaan Portage, 10 tents; Sandy Beach, 10 tents; and Peare Pointe, 10 tents. In the Crean Lake area are camping sites at Moose Bay, 5 tents, and Big Island, 10 tents. Many camping sites are accessible by boat only.

WATERTON LAKES NATIONAL PARK

Waterton Park, Alberta
Area, 203 square miles

This is the Canadian part of the Waterton-Glacier International Peace Park, the first of its kind in the world, which was inspired by Rotary Clubs of Alberta and Montana. It is located where the mountains arise abruptly from the prairie in southwest Alberta. The park boasts spectacular mountain scenery. Nature trails to high emerald lakes and alpine meadows are ample rewards for riders or hikers who climb to these spots of unforgettable beauty and grandeur. A chain of lakes forms the main valley, providing boating, fishing and excellent sight-seeing, whether by foot or boat.

More than 100 miles of wide trails crisscross the park, often leading to the more remote beauty spots. Saddle horses and ponies are for hire at several locations, and guides are also available.

Campground accommodations include Townsite, 200 tents; Campgrounds, 95 trailers; Cameron Lake, 25 units; Crandell Mountain, 132 units; Belly River, 24 units; Alderson Lake (primitive), 12 persons; Bertha Lake No. 1 (primitive), 12 persons; Bertha Lake No. 2 (primitive), 10 persons; Crandell Lake (primitive), 20 persons; Crypt Lake, 10 persons; Twin Lakes (primitive), 10 persons; Wishbone, 20 persons; Bertha Bay (primitive), 10 persons; and Snowshoe (primitive), 10 persons.

ELK ISLAND NATIONAL PARK

Lamont, Alberta
Area, 75 square miles

This park is located some 30 miles east of Edmonton, Alberta. It is the

largest fenced wild animal preserve in Canada. Apart from elk, moose, mule deer and numerous smaller animals, it contains a herd of some 600 buffalo. North America's largest herd, some 12,000 buffalo, is in Wood Buffalo National Park, a huge undeveloped area on the Alberta-Northwest Territories boundary.

One campground is available at Elk Island. This is Sandy Beach with a capacity for 50 tents and 8 trailers.

JASPER NATIONAL PARK
Jasper, Alberta
Area, 4,200 square miles

Lying along the eastern slopes of the Canadian Rockies, this vast park was named after Jasper Hawes, clerk in the first trading post at Brulé Lake about 1813. Within Jasper National Park are Whistlers Mountain, the 7,350-foot summit reached by a 35-passenger cable car; Maligne Lake, a real beauty spot; part of the Columbia Icefield; and the Miette Hot Springs, one of which gushes forth at a temperature of 129 degrees. Much of the park's most impressive scenery is accessible by road and improved trail. The whole area is a photographer's dream.

All kinds of camping opportunities are afforded. Campgrounds include Cottonwood Creek, 225 tents and 53 trailers; Whistlers, 510 tents and 241 trailers; Snaring River, 50 tents or trailers; Rocky River, 40 tents or trailers; Fiddle River, 30 tents or trailers; Miette Hot Springs, 100 tents; Wapiti, 182 tents or trailers; Wabasso, 44 tents; Mount Kerkeslin, 18 tents; Honeymoon Lake, 20 tents and 10 trailers; Jonas Creek, 16 tents; Columbia Icefield, 12 tents; Wilcox Creek, 46 tents or trailers; and Celestine Lake, 18 tents.

BANFF NATIONAL PARK
Banff, Alberta
Area, 2,564 square miles

This park is a magnificent scenic playground in the central Rockies.

Many of Canada's national and provincial parks provide cooking shelters for campers. This one is located in Waterton Lakes National Park on the eastern slopes of the Rockies.

It contains two noted resorts, Banff and Lake Louise. Here, too, is the Columbia Icefield, from which flows impressive glaciers, some as much as 1,000 feet deep. The Trans-Canada Highway bisects Banff and touches on some of the park's finest camping areas. Big horned sheep, Rocky Mountain goats, elk and deer as well as bear can often be glimpsed on the forest-clad slopes of the lower elevations. Some of the best fishing anywhere is found in the crystal clear lakes and rushing mountain streams.

Campgrounds in the park offer these accommodations: Tunnel Mountain, 310 tents or trailers in one area, 700 tents or tent-trailers in another, and 322 trailers in a third area; Two Jack Lake, 408 units; Johnston Canyon, 148 units; Mount Eisenhour, 44 units; Protection Mountain, 72 units plus facilities for 14 trailers; Lake Louise, 219 units, including accommodations

Saskatchewan is great for wilderness campers who travel the canoe route.

for 157 trailers; Moraine Lake, 24 tents; Mosquito Creek, 25 units; Bow Lake, 10 tents; Waterfowl Lake, 50 units; Rampart Creek, 50 units; and Cirrus Mountain, 16 units.

KOOTENAY NATIONAL PARK

Radium Hot Springs, British
Columbia
Area, 543 square miles

The hot springs at Radium were a favorite meeting place for generations of Indians from the area. Today a modern bathing center is fed by a daily flow of 475,000 gallons from the odorless mineralized springs.

Kootenay is a "valley" park which extends five miles on each side of the Banff-Windermere Highway for 65 scene-filled miles. It follows a natural course formed by the Vermilion and Kootenay Rivers. Both the highway and many self-guiding nature trails lead the visitor to such beauty spots as Marble Canyon, erroded out of gray-white marble limestone.

Campground facilities include Red

Streak, 153 tents and 88 trailers; Olive Lake, 16 units; McLeod Meadows, 100 units; Dolly Varden, 10 units; Vermilion Crossing, 15 units; and Marble Canyon, 56 units.

YOHO NATIONAL PARK

Field, British Columbia
Area, 507 square miles

Yoho means "How wonderful!" This is the name the Indians gave it. It is part of the roof of the Rockies and is perfect for the mountaineer. It has 250 miles of improved trails which lead riders and hikers to unforgettable natural wonders: the Curtain of Mist at Laughing Falls, the exciting Twin Falls, Yoho Glacier, the Ice River Valley and the strangely-shaped pillars in Hoodo Valley. The park is well known for its sparking, alpine lakes.

Campgrounds in Yoho include Kicking Horse, 160 tents and 35 trailers; Hoodo Creek, 106 tents; Chancellor Peak, 50 tents; and Takakkaw Falls, 50 tents.

GLACIER NATIONAL PARK

Revelstoke, British Columbia
Area, 521 square miles

This park is located 29 miles east of Revelstoke and is reached by the Trans-Canada Highway. Snow-capped peaks, flanked by immense icefields and sparkling glaciers, look down forest-clad slopes to canyons and caverns, turbulent rivers and waterfalls, alpine meadows and silent woods. A network of trails provides hikers with a choice of scenery. Autumn fishing is extremely popular here.

Modern campgrounds include Illecillewaet, 60 units; Loop Creek, 20 units; and Mountain Creek, 200 units.

MOUNT REVELSTOKE NATIONAL PARK

Revelstoke, British Columbia
Area, 100 square miles

Climb any mountain in this national park and you will see another that seems higher. An extraordinary experience for good mountain walkers is provided by the nine-mile trail on the summit of Mount Revelstoke. It winds through flower-strewn meadows and forested slopes to climax in unsurpassed vistas of sharp peaks, ridges clad in snow, glaciers and mountain lakes. The park is situated in the Selkirk Range, mountains more jagged and spiky than those in the Rockies. There are no accommodations in this park, but excellent campground facilities are operated in the vicinity.

Camping Regulations

Campsites in Canada's national parks are allocated on a first-come, first-served basis, and no reservation can be made. There is a limit on occupying a campsite, usually two weeks.

Camping is allowed only at designated campgrounds, unless permission and the necessary camping and fire permits are obtained from a park warden. The normal camping season is from late May to October, but the season may be shorter in campgrounds located in the mountains.

Daily fees at all campgrounds are $1 for an unserviced site; $1.50 for a site with electricity; and $2 for a site with water, electricity and sewer connections. Electrical services in campgrounds are 60 cycle.

Nearly all campgrounds offer free firewood. Trailer areas are designed for trailers and camping vehicles equipped to use the services provided. Tenters and other campers who do not need these services are requested to use the other campsites, which are equipped with picnic tables and barbeque grills for cooking over a wood fire. Wood fires are permitted only in stoves,

A covered bridge, a rushing stream and a clearing at the foot of wooded slopes combine to make this New Brunswick campground ideal for the summer vacationer.

New Brunswick Travel Bureau

grills and fireplaces especially constructed for this purpose.

Information on camping techniques in Canada is provided in the book, **Family Camping,** available at 75 cents per copy at all national park information offices or by mail from Queen's Printer, Ottawa, Ontario.

The Trans-Canada Highway

Almost 5,000 miles in length, the Trans-Canada Highway stretches from Victoria, in British Columbia, to historic St. John's, capital of Newfoundland.

In designing the highway and its facilities, those in charge gave much thought to the vacationer and

The 5,000-mile Trans-Canada Highway, longest in the world, offers the traveler many recreational opportunities in addition to camping.

traveler who likes to camp. All along this mighty artery federal and provincial authorities have carefully selected campgrounds and picnic grounds that are never far from a center of interest.

Beginning in British Columbia, on Vancouver Island, and continuing uninterrupted except for ferry steamer to the mainland and ferry steamer in the east between the mainland and Newfoundland, the highway runs close to more than 220 national and provincial camping and picnicking areas. In addition, near its route are many privately operated campgrounds. Fees are nominal, capacity often is enormous and facilities in most instances are good to excellent.

Any camper who plans to travel along the Trans-Canada Highway should carry a copy of **Campgrounds Along the Trans-Canada Highway.** For a copy. of this excellent guide and a map, write Canadian Govern-

Typical of Canada's many ideal campsites is this one in Quebec, north Montreal.

ment Travel Bureau, Ottawa, Canada.

The Provinces

In addition to the national parks, each provincial parks and other areas that welcome campers. In most locations, one or more park officers will be found on duty at all times.

Any province will gladly send maps and detailed information on camping opportunities within its boundaries. Publications promoting outdoor activities in Canada are colorful, interesting and packed with useful information.

NEWFOUNDLAND

Since the Trans-Canada Highway was completed across Newfoundland a few years ago, the province has made progress by leaps and bounds. Travelers from the United States and elsewhere in Canada have come to this province by the thousands—many in automobiles towing trailers or packing tents in the trunk. Newfoundland has met the demand

by accelerating its construction of campgrounds. Presently, there are about a dozen provincial parks catering to campers and some 34 parks open to picnickers. Interestingly, a bona fide traveler caught on the road after 6 p.m. may be permitted to camp in an area generally reserved for picnickers. A campsite permit must be obtained from the park officer, and this costs $1.

On visiting the first park in Newfoundland the camper will be required to purchase a $1 seasonal sticker for his vehicle. This entitles him to enter any and all provincial parks during the current season. In addition, a camping permit is necessary. This may be purchased from the officer on duty, and the charge is $1 per day.

All provincial parks are situated near either fresh or saltwater. Most have suitable areas for swimming. All swimming spots are equipped with basic lifesaving equipment. Each family has an individual site of approximately 40 feet in diameter. These are seeded in wild, white clover. Wherever possible, camp-

sites are 100 feet apart and are surrounded by a screen of trees.

There are no electrical or water hookups for recreational vehicles. Sanitary facilities are carefully maintained and each site is provided with a garbage can. It is recommended that campers bring gas cooking stoves as there are days when wood fires are banned due to high fire hazard. However, when outdoor fires are permissible, plenty of firewood is available on a do-it-yourself basis.

For a copy of **Camp in the 10th Province, Newfoundland** and color-ful brochures and maps, write Resources Branch, Department of Mines, Agriculture and Resources, St. John's, Newfoundland.

NOVA SCOTIA

Nova Scotia offers, largely through its provincial parks, 12 camping areas. The outstanding camping sites are in or near Cape Breton Highlands National Park. (See "Cape Breton Highlands National Park" for more details.) Other good facilities are at designated areas along the Trans-Canada Highway.

Various privately owned camp-grounds are open in the summer, and these are well used.

Fees in the provincial parks are $1.50 per day per campsite. Complete information is available from Nova Scotia Travel Bureau, Department of Trade and Industry, Halifax, Nova Scotia.

NEW BRUNSWICK

Some 30 provincial parks offer camping facilities, many of these providing electrical hookups. Numerous municipalities and private citizens also operate campgrounds with facilities comparable to those under provincial direction.

A camp area permit covers one motor vehicle and one tent or trailer, and the maximum length of stay where permits are required is 14 days. Some campsites, where the more elaborate services are missing, are free. Close to 200,000 campers utilize New Brunswick's provincial parks each year, and approximately 25 percent of these are from the United States.

Canoe camping is extremely popular in New Brunswick, and one of Canada's largest canoe and boat building factories is located in Fredericton. Six of the main rivers and their tributaries offer more than 817 miles suitable for canoe travel.

Some of the most interesting activities for campers are in and around the Bay of Fundy parks.

On request to Department of Lands and Mines, Fredericton, New Brunswick, you may receive a copy of **New Brunswick Parks, Campgrounds and Picnic Sites.**

Campers traveling through Yukon Territory on the Alaska Highway, an all-weather, gravel-surfaced road, view many vistas of forests and mountains and clouds.

A popular pastime in most Canadian national parks is trail hiking. This trail is part of the vast trail system in Banff National Park, Alberta.

PRINCE EDWARD ISLAND

In addition to its four national park campgrounds, Prince Edward Island boasts 24 provincial park campgrounds and more than 30 privately operated camping sites. More than 160,000 tenters and trailerites, one and a half times the normal population of the province, stay at island campsites each year.

Provincial park fees are as follows: tents and trailer sites, unserviced, $1.50 per day; tent and trailer sites, serviced, $2 per day. Privately operated campground and trailer fees range from a nightly charge of 75 cents to $1.75, and by the week from $8 to $10.50. Trailer fees are from $2 to $2.50 per night, and from $10.50 to $15 per week.

Running water, picnic tables, electricity, toilets, fireplaces and kitchen shelters are standard facilities at most island campgrounds. Trailer hookups are also available at many. All campgrounds are supervised, and most are close to towns and villages where the visitor has access to stores, restaurants, theatres, churches and medical help if needed. Some are adjacent to golf and fishing, and all provide some form of entertainment such as pony rides, playgrounds and games.

For a copy of **Campsites, Trailer Parks, Picnic Grounds in Prince Edward Island,** write Prince Edward Island Travel Bureau, Charlottetown, P. E. I.

QUEBEC

A wide variety of attractions and services awaits the camper in Quebec. The campgrounds are under the jurisdiction of the parks division of the Department of Tourism, Fish and Game. Several are in huge, wooded parks. Many excellent camping facilities are also operated by private citizens.

Quebec operates six types of parks: parks for short-stay camping, parks with special attractions, parks and reserves with virgin forest, re-

The lake-dotted Prince Albert National Park sprawls over 1,496 square miles of Saskatchewan.

gional parks with full recreational facilities, salmon-fishing parks and hunting and fishing parks.

These range in size from a few acres along a main highway to many thousands of acres remote from human activity. Campgrounds range from those with all essential services to primitive sites. Some are relatively close to metropolitan areas such as Montreal and Quebec City; others are in some of the most remote wilderness areas on the North American Continent. Fees in the serviced campgrounds range from $1 to $2 daily.

For a copy of **Quebec,** address a request to Quebec Provincial Park Service, Parliament Buildings, Quebec City, Quebec.

ONTARIO

The province of Ontario operates some 97 parks, the oldest and best known being Algonquin Park with an area of 2,910 square miles.

Some campsites in Ontario are conveniently placed along highways —particularly along the remote sec-

tions of the Trans-Canada route. Others are located at or near beach and lakeland resort areas. In southern Ontario, mainly, campsites are conveniently located near major historic sites and urban centers. All have some form of supervised sanitary arrangements, some have flush toilets. Many provide covered cooking and dining pavilions. All drinking water sources are tested regularly to conform to requirements of the public health authorities.

Some camping parks accommodate recreational vehicles of all kinds; many offer electric hookups and sewage service.

All commercial camping establishments in Ontario are licensed and are inspected periodically by the officers of two or three provincial government departments or by municipal authorities.

Permits needed

Forest travel permits are required for bush and lake travel. Campsite permits (including vehicle entry fee) at all parks cost $2.50 daily. A fee of $1 per day is charged for ve-

hicle entry. An annual vehicle entry permit may be purchased for $10, which lowers the daily rates to campers. Electricity, where available, is charged for at the rate of 50 cents per day.

Old-time prospectors, like "Yukon Bud" Fisher, take the time to show visitors how to pan for gold in the Yukon's famous Klondike Valley.

Yukon Department of Travel and Publicity

A permit is also necessary for camping in the interior of a provincial park, away from organized campsites. These interior areas are reached by boat, and the permit is $5 per boat.

The Department of Tourism and Information, Toronto, Ontario, issues an excellent guidebook, **Ontario Campsites.** A map and information folder on Algonquin Provincial Park is available from Ontario Department of Lands and Forests, Toronto.

MANITOBA

This province in central Canada has six established provincial parks, and three more are in the process of being developed. The parks are located in all parts of the province, including the northern area. In addition to these parks, there are more than 150 picnic, camping and trailer grounds maintained by the government, plus 110 similar sites operated privately. Nine provincial forests in Manitoba contain a total of approximately 5,500 square miles. Some of the provincial parks are contained within these areas.

Camping is a popular pastime for many Manitobans, and each year thousands of campers come to Manitoba from all over Canada and many parts of the United States. Some 5,000 public campsites are maintained and another 5,000 sites are operated by various groups and individuals. Facilities range from simple, in wilderness sites for those who desire complete solitude, to fully serviced campgrounds for the camper who likes to rough it in style.

Tables and benches and firewood are supplied at all government-operated campgrounds and picnic sites where cooking facilities are indicated.

Open in May

All government campgrounds are open by the third weekend in May and generally close the last weekend in September. Most park areas charge a daily entrance fee of 50 cents. Seasonal permits are available for $3 and those are honored at all provincial parks and recreational areas. Camping permits also are required in provincial campgrounds.

Camping fees are as follows: Day, $1, $1.50 with electricity, $2 with water, sewer and electricity; by the week, $6, $9 with electricity, $12 with added services. Some areas limit camping to from seven days to three weeks. All campsites are offered on a first-come, first-served basis.

For a copy of **Manitoba Vacation Handbook,** which lists and describes all the main camping areas within the province, address a request to Tourist Branch, Department of Tourism and Recreation, Legislative Building, Winnipeg, Manitoba.

Some outdoor lovers might pay more attention to the falls, but these Canadian youngsters are oblivious to the beauties surrounding them.

Algonquin Provincial Park's 2,910 miles of virgin forest land and lakes in Ontario is a natural habitat for wildlife. It offers just about every variety of camping, too.

SASKATCHEWAN

A network of provincial parks throughout Saskatchewan has been established and these are located in scenic areas. They provide such outdoor activities as fishing, swimming and boating. Many additional attractions enhance these parks, such as playground equipment, camp and picnic sites and golf courses. Altogether, more than 100 provincial facilities offer camping opportunities.

Saskatchewan, the "land of Swift Running Water," tempts the camper to spend weeks—even months—exploring through forests, up and down rivers, over glistening lakes and through vast areas practically untouched by the hand. The provincial parks provide the best base of operations for such adventuring.

For a current copy of **Saskatchewan Travel Guide,** write to Tourist

Campers come to Bon-Ami Park on one of the extreme eastern points of the famous Gaspe Peninsula, Quebec, to see the great forillon, or rock, which juts 900 feet out of the sea opposite the Gaspe coast.

Development Branch, Department of Industry and Commerce, Power Building, Regina, Saskatchewan. Also request a copy of **Saskatchewan, Land of Outdoor Fun.**

ALBERTA

This has been aptly labeled "Princess Province," not entirely after Princess Louise Caroline Alberta, fourth daughter of Queen Victoria. The fertile prairies, rolling parklands, evergreen-clad foothills to towering glacial-crowned mountains offer enough variety to designate a "royalty" name for this area.

In addition to its outstanding national parks, provincial facilities for camping total some 97 locations. A

unique service offered by the Forestry Trunk Road System, built originally as access roads in case of forest fires, has become a popular attraction to those seeking to "rough it" just a few miles from a paved highway. Campgrounds are frequent and well maintained. Modern facilities, of course, are limited, but for the back country camper it is near ideal. At least 100 locations are open to primitive camping.

Literally hundreds of campsites have been constructed and are maintained by the Department of Highways, and wherever you travel on Alberta's highways you will be within easy access to an improved camp-

A truck and trailer pull into the camping area at Jan Lake, northern Saskatchewan.

ground. All of these offer picnic tables and practically all are supplied with approved drinking water, fireplaces, firewood, sanitary facilities (sometimes primitive but clean) and various types of recreation. Ice is available at some, and so are boat rentals and camping supplies.

Among the publications available to campers in Alberta are two very helpful ones: **Alberta, Canada's Princess Province** and **Alberta Tourist Guide.** Both are available from Alberta Government Travel Bureau, Edmonton, Alberta.

BRITISH COLUMBIA

This is the most westerly and third largest of Canadian provinces. To

the camper, it offers a wide variety of outdoor fun: sunny beach resorts, salt and freshwater fishing, mountains, lakes and rivers and beautiful campgrounds.

Campgrounds total almost 100, and nearly every one offers outstanding scenery, ample space, clean facilities and many recreational opportunities.

Camping is permitted only in designated campsites, but these are plentiful. No trailer hookups are provided, but basic facilities are maintained.

A camper may take his choice to camp near populated centers or in unbelievably beautiful shangri-las along the coast or high in the mountains.

For copies of **British Columbia Tourist Directory** (includes details on campgrounds) and **Beautiful British Columbia,** write Department of Travel and Industry, Government of British Columbia, Victoria, British Columbia.

THE TERRITORIES

For the experienced camper who wants to be individualistic and really get away from it all, the Yukon and the Northwest Territories in Canada offer as much opportunity as will be found anywhere.

The Yukon is a virtual paradise for outdoor enthusiasts and nature lovers. This country of mountains, lakes and rivers, with its everchanging moods of a northern summer's long daylight hours and the great variations of the seasons, offers a complete range of outdoor enjoyment.

When you use a camper, tent or trailer, you will find over 30 government campgrounds ready for you at regular intervals along the network of excellent gravel roads throughout the territory. A number of privately owned campgrounds offer added luxuries such as electricity, water hookups, showers and laundry rooms.

Lakes and rivers offer thousands of miles of undisturbed wilderness travel on unpolluted waters, which can be navigated with all manner of small craft. The same waters are teeming with many species of fish.

YUKON

The network of campgrounds in the Yukon is under the supervision and maintenance of the Yukon Forest Service. Their use is provided free of charge and all are situated amidst natural scenic beauty, usually at a lake, river or stream. Firewood, outdoor cookstoves, tables, benches, garbage cans and outdoor privies are provided at each site. Most campgrounds also have an enclosed kitchen shelter, containing table and benches plus a large wood range where several families can be accommodated at one time.

The campgrounds are open from May to October. Many are located along the Alaska Highway. For those wishing to have adventure in the deep wilderness areas, special guides and outfitters are available at Whitehorse, Yukon.

A copy of **Your Yukon Guide to Outdoor Recreation** is available from Travel and Publicity Branch, Yukon Branch Territorial Government, Whitehorse, Yukon Territory, Canada.

The Northwest Territories, which lie to the east of Yukon, constitute a territory of 1,300,000 square miles with a population of about 35,000. This is Canada's arctic. It is larger than half the continental United States. It's a land that has known fantastic adventures and heroic journeys. It is a land on the verge of emerging.

Now it can be reached by car, and many campers are "discovering" the Northwest Territories each year.

Yellowknife

Yellowknife is the seat of the territories. Located almost directly north of Edmonton, Alberta, and only some 300 miles from the Arctic Circle, Yellowknife is a modern little city which is a center for outfitting and for pushing off to the vast wilderness to the north. Much of the surrounding territory is virtually unexplored.

For a safe and successful venture into the untamed McKinsey Mountains and many other areas, you need good guides, equipment and all that is necessary for rough living in the bush. This is no place for the inexperienced.

Along the highway from Alberta to Yellowknife are several well-planned campgrounds and picnic places. Placed at beauty spots along the way, they include areas for tenting or trailer parking, sanitary facilities, picnic tables, fireplaces and covered camp kitchens. There are no fees. Just be sure you have adequate food and gasoline supplies. Your next source may be 100 miles down the highway.

If you wish to spend the night at an arctic outpost camp or in an igloo, this can be arranged in the Northwest Territories.

For full information on all types of outdoor adventure, write to Travel Arctic, Yellowknife, Northwest Territories, Canada. Ask for copies of **Accommodation in Canada's Arctic Northwest Territories** and **Explore Canada's Arctic.**

Canadian, Minnesota

Boundary Waters

Canoe Area

On the eastern Minnesota - Canadian border are about 1,000,000 acres of streams, lakes, forests and rocky crags of amazing beauty. Much of the beauty comes from the deep solitude, a feeling that one is traveling and living in the tradition of the early fur traders who were the first white men to venture into this area.

This, a paradise for canoe campers, is the American half of the famed Quetico-Superior canoe area straddling the border between Canada and Minnesota. It is a unique wilderness land. Within the area — covering both sides of the border — are more than two million acres. On the Canadian side, the canoe area lies within Ontario's Quetico Provincial Park. On the American side, the area is called Boundary Waters Canoe Area.

The land is covered mostly in jack pine, balsam, spruce, hemlock, birch and poplar. These vast forests are interlaced with an unbelievable variety of lakes and streams. The fringe areas are places of easy access, from which you can start a journey beyond civilization.

Nature sounds

The sounds of nature are varied, too. Solitude broken by the spine tingling call of a loon may be shattered in a few hours by thunderstorms and rain squalls. The nights are cool, even in summer. If you like islands and peninsulas offering ideal camping sites and if you enjoy the exercise that comes from canoeing and portaging — and if you are a camper — sometime you must journey into the Boundary Waters Canoe Area.

A party of four campers in a canoe pauses at the base of a cliff in the Boundary Waters Canoe Area of Superior National Forest. They are at a point on the international boundary between the United States and Canada. USDA Photo

If you are also a fisherman you'll want to take advantage of the fine walleye, northern and smallmouth bass angling in this area. These will not only provide excellent sport, but will supplement your camp fare. Northerns run five to 15 lbs., walleyes average up to five lbs. with catches up to 10 lbs. not being unusual.

Smallmouth bass run 1½ to an occassional 5 pounder. All coming from these cool clear waters have excellent meat, flaky, mild and sweet in taste.

In planning a trip to the BWCA, write first for information. The best source probably is the Forest Supervisor, U. S. Forest Service, Federal Building, Duluth, Minnesota 55802. Maps and other information will be supplied gladly.

Also write to the Chamber of Commerce at Ely or Grand Marais, Minnesota. The Minnesota Arrowhead Association in Duluth will send folders and a list of outfitters.

Plan early

Write early for your information, contact one or more outfitters for prices and reservations, and when you have settled on an outfitter, let him know when you will arrive, how long you will be there and about how many are in your party.

Many canoe campers in this area arrive a little early and stop by the Forest Service Voyageur Visitor Center, one mile east of Ely on Highway 169. Many of your questions can be answered there, and you can pick up the latest folders and announcements.

Study the literature and listen to the advice of the outfitters. You may need special clothing and you will need a detailed briefing on routes, safety precautions and such.

Expect pleasure

A summation of what you can expect from canoe camping in the Boundary Waters Canoe Area has been well phrased by Arthur W. Greeley and Clifford D. Owsley in **Outdoors U. S. A.**

"When you have paddled these calm waters for a week, when you've been lulled into another world by the panorama of woods, sky and water, when you've snagged a lake trout and cooked it over a campfire, when you have toted packs and a canoe overland and rested while feasting your eyes on nature's wonderland, when you've slept in a tent with the song of the rain outside — when you've done these things all on your own, you just won't be quite the same person that entered this truly unique area. You'll feel different somehow — and the workaday world won't seem quite so formidable." You will agree that a million dollars would hardly buy such an enjoyable vacation.

A NEVER TO BE FORGOTTEN EXPERIENCE FOR BEGINNERS OR VETERAN CAMPERS

This is typical scene of the wilderness of Boundary Waters Canoe Area. U. S. Forest Service Photo

This is an excellent example of a privately owned camping facility. Called Whippoorwill, it is located in an isolated valley surrounded by deep green forests and streams that wind their way down to the Mississippi River about 20 miles away. Open the year around, it offers sites for trailers, tent campers or tents. Has modern shower and toilet accommodations and a communal barbecue center. A one-acre spring fed pool with sand beach and sand bottom offers swimming for both children and adults. It provides electricity, picnic tables and safety lighting. Winter time activities center on snomobiling and skating. Six spring fed ponds are filled with beautiful hybrid rainbow-cutthroat trout-the most delicious eating fish- in the midwest. Excellent fighters, they are sold by the pound or by the inch. Owned and operated by Emil and Myra Funke, Whippoorwill is located at the intersection of County Roads # 4 and 86, 2 miles south of Theilman, Minnesota.

The Attractions

and Advantages of

Private Campgrounds

Some 60 percent of all campsites open to the public are on private campgrounds. These run from wilderness-type sites to posh facilities offering the extras you would expect at a sleek AAA motel. Many are used by travelers as overnight stops. Most offer a real camping flavor and are situated in scenic or otherwise attractive areas.

As these words are being printed, one of the most ambitious recreation-oriented, private camping developments to date will be opening for business.

Pineola Land Harbor, a 900-acre, stream-and-lake-studded tract just off the Blue Ridge Parkway near Linville, North Carolina, is the first in a series of "resorts for campers" to be developed by Land Harbors of America, a new division of Carolina Carribbean Corporation.

According to executive vice president Harry C. Robbins, Land Harbors will be "the Waldorf" of camping.

The new Land Harbor camper resorts, he said, "are being designed to offer seclusion in the most beautiful of mountain settings. One may say that we will provide the finest of complete resort hotels except that one brings his own room."

Featured at the Pineola Land Harbor is a 70-acre lake with a three-mile shoreline. Recreational offerings include canoeing and sailboating, swimming pools, tennis courts, playgrounds, club and an open pavilion for rainy day activities. In addition there will be a nursery for small children, camp counselors for teenage programs and an area embracing convenient shops and first aid facilities.

Tram trips

Rubber-tired trams will make regularly scheduled trips through the campsite areas for the purpose of transporting campers to the various activity areas.

The new company plans to sell some campsites, rent others and devote more than half the land to recreational purposes, wilderness trails, bridal paths and gardens.

The story of this new super resort for campers is cited here to illustrate

Commercial campgrounds advertise their attractions and facilities.

the "bigness" of private campground operations. This is by no means the first camping resort of its kind, though it possibly will be the largest to date.

The president of the National Campground Owners Association—U.S.A., Harry J. Jensen, is owner of the Lazy J Trailer Park and Kampground at Rapid City, South Dakota. Harry and his wife, Ellen, came out of retirement to get into the campground business. They formerly were in the manufacturing business in southeastern South Dakota. In 1962 they decided to retire and bought themselves a 23-foot Holiday Rambler. They traveled to many points of the United States, Canada and Mexico—for almost two years.

Harry became bored with retirement and decided that he would build an overnight trailer park. The Lazy J wouldn't be just another trailer park. Harry called in service engineers to design drive-through parking and terracing. He decided that every space should have complete hookup with water, sewer and electricity. Here is what the Lazy J now offers campers:

- Grocery story
- Hiking trails
- Children's playground

- Adult-only patios
- A reserved drive-through space
- Complete hookups
- Free showers
- Recreation room
- Laundry facilities, ironing facilities, ladies hair dryers, etc.

Promote scenery

Harry and Helen didn't stop there. Situated in South Dakota's tourist country, they set out to promote the Black Hills, Mount Rushmore, Wind Cave National Park and other natural attractions. Teaming up with many businesses, the Jensens issue a "Free Courtesy Coupon Book" which offers everything from free meals and free entertainment tickets to discounts on haircuts and auto services.

All privately operated campgrounds don't offer this variety of enticements, of course. But thousands do offer special advantages to campers, particularly the traveling variety.

The biggest success story in commercial campground operations is the KOA story. Kampgrounds of America is a franchised chain of modern campgrounds aimed at accommodating the whole spectrum of campers—from tenters to traveling residents of motor homes.

Began in Billings

The idea began in 1960 in the mind of Dave Drum of Billings, Montana. In 1961 Mr. Drum and a few associ-ates built a trial campground at Billings.

Today more than 200 KOA's are in operation coast to coast and another 200 are in the planning stages. Observers have likened this to the success of the Holiday Inns. And there is some similarity in the two operations.

A camper knows what to expect in the way of standard facilities at any KOA stop. He knows that the Kampgrounds are easy to reach from the main highways, and he can secure confirmed reservations at any KOA, free of cost.

The home office in Billings issues a seasonal directory of all Kampgrounds which lists charges, standard and "extra" facilities, proximity to recreational and entertainment attractions and a map showing how to get there.

Each KOA Kampground offers an attractive location, adequate spacing, showers, restrooms, laundry facilities, staple groceries, sundries, adequate lighting, recreation areas, level parking, clean grounds, camp supervision, insect and weed control, ice, firewood, briquettes, propane, white gas, utilities,

Top-rated, commercial campgrounds always offer clean and well-maintained bathroom facilities. Photo Courtesy CamParks of America, Inc.

Automatic laundries have become standard at the better commercial campgrounds. Photo Courtesy KOA

telephone, bulletin board, fireplaces, picnic tables, area activities and tourist information, and mail and messenger service. In addition, the organization sponsors a camping club and recently began Ranch Kamps of America, a chain of dude ranches.

New franchise

Some of the more elaborate campgrounds are moving nearer to the cities. A new franchise chain, based in Mobile, Alabama, CamParks of America, Inc., is establishing its facilities close to cities as well as at locations near main highways.

Sidney J. Gerhardt, vice president, says CamParks will "have the appearance and the environment of a park rather than a parking lot. . . . We believe in landscaping, trees, shrubbery and flowers to provide a natural camping environment. Because we are convinced that travel trailers will become more luxurious in time, and more of them will be equipped with air conditioning and stereo, we provide heavier electrical wiring to accommodate this load."

In an expression of personal views relative to commercial campground operation, Mr. Gerhardt said this:

"I have tried to get away from using the word, campground, too frequently as I believe its connotation conveys a more primitive type of camping facility. Since in recent years camping equipment has come a long way in design and luxury, so have camping facilities.

Our own concept embodies a park rather than a campground, incorporating the more desirable features of campground and travel trailer park as well as the more desirable features of overnight park and destination or vacation park."

The standard CamPark includes these basic features:
- Swimming pool or swimming beach
- Children's playground
- Various types of recreation for all ages
- Pavilion or area for groups and meetings
- Modern sanitary comfort stations containing private flush toilets and showers
- Launderettes
- Store featuring camping equipment and supplies

Top. The biggest success story in commercial campground operation is the KOA story.

Middle. Camp stores are operated at the better equipped private campgrounds. Photo Courtesy KOA

Bottom. Swimming pools and the like are becoming quite common at modern commerical campgrounds catering to the traveling public. Photo Courtesy KOA

Kampgrounds of America now operate more than 200 complete facilities, with another 200 in the planning stages.

What This Means To You, the Camper

What has brought on this sudden boom in privately operated campgrounds? What does it mean to you, the camper? How will it affect the camping offerings of our national parks, national forests and other public lands?

Several factors have influenced the growth of this phase of the camping industry. Not the least of these is the ingenuity of American businessmen who also have an affinity for good living out-of-doors. The population explosion and the migration to urban areas have contributed to the added interest in camping, and of course to the necessities involved in traveling.

A great many people like to save money when traveling, and they have discovered that camping is a comfortable way to do so. Still others have become attracted to the amazingly efficient recreational vehicles and other modern camping gear to the point that millions are spending a great deal of money to outfit themselves for recreational travel.

Why stop?

But why can't you take your recreational vehicle straight to a national forest or national park without ever stopping at a private campground? You can, and many do. But more and more, as the trips become longer, families find it quite convenient to stop overnight at a good campground near the interstate. Once they've stopped, chances are they will enjoy the experience so much that they'll do it again.

Another reason for utilizing private campgrounds is the fact that public facilities at certain times of the year are often overcrowded and inadequate. And there are some campers who wish to have a good time out-of-doors, on the trail or on the lake during the day, but prefer the relative security and privacy at night that commercial campgrounds often provide.

These are not the only reasons for using privately owned campgrounds. Many excellent facilities do not cater to the highway traveler. Some are as secluded as a remote canyon in a national forest. In the state of Maine, for example, it is estimated that more campers use remote, privately owned facilities than public facilities. Sometimes this is by choice, sometimes by necessity, due to overcrowded public facilities.

Destroy beauty

In some circles, particularly among conservationists, there is a growing concern over "proliferation" of public lands. It is claimed by some that more campgrounds and overcrowded campgrounds, with the numerous associated people-activities, will endanger and possibly destroy the beauty of many natural landmarks.

Considering the millions of visitors to national parks and other public outdoor attractions, this constitutes a problem. The great influx of motor vehicles creates traffic jams, parking problems and even air pollution problems.

It has been suggested that future development of recreational facilities, including camping, be severely curtailed in the national parks and in certain other "endangered" areas. It is argued that private enterprise can offer shelter and other accommodations near enough to natural attractions that heavy traffic and heavy use might be avoided.

Should restrictive use of government lands for camping become more pronounced, this could mean severe limitations to recreational vehicles' admittance to certain areas. Also, it could have a similar effect on tent campers, except for backpackers.

What the conclusions and whatever the solutions, it is certain that private campground operation is here to stay. It is growing by leaps and bounds, and as more urban-confined Americans rediscover the outdoor heritage of the nation, the more demands will be made on camping facilities of all kinds. Private enterprise will play an important role in meeting that demand. A survey taken early in 1970 has shown that 38% of the campers prefer private grounds.

Owning Your Own Private Campsite

Private campgrounds in the context of this discussion are not private in the full sense of the word. They are privately owned, but cater to the general public.

It is possible, however, to have a completely private campground, and some individuals buy or rent ground for this purpose. Many groups, of course, own and operate for their own members private campgrounds, from small family layouts to facilities accommodating hundreds.

If your interests turn in this direction, whether toward a private campground for personal use or for public use, there are several publications which will be helpful. **Profitable Private Campground Construction and Operation,** by Rea Agnew, sells for $2 from Rajo Publications, Inc., P. O. Box 2576, Palos Verdes Peninsula, California 90274. For 50 cents the American Camping Association, Bradford Woods, Martinsville, Indiana, will send you a copy of **Guidelines for the Development and Operation of Family Campgrounds and Sites.** From the Superintendent of Docu-ments, Government Printing Office, Washington, D. C., you may secure Agriculture Information Bulletin #264, **Working Drawings of Basic Facilities for Campground Development.** The cost is 20 cents.

Private Campgrounds Are "Rated"

Among the organizations serving campers and campground owners is the Family Camping Federation, a division of American Camping Association, Bradford Woods, Martinsville, Indiana. This is a nationwide nonprofit organization representing national, regional and state organizations as well as family campground owners, operators and developers. The FCF subscribes to the principle that "all campers be provided with adequate campground facilities, and considers it desirable for the camping leadership to establish its own standards and to regulate itself, rather than to have regulatory legislation imposed upon it."

Accordingly, the federation has set up an accrediting list of mandatory standards and a list of desirable standards. These and similar efforts by state and local groups have done a great deal to improve standards in private campgrounds. For a copy of the FCF standards, address a request to the Indiana headquarters office.

Numerous organizations and publications rate privately operated campgrounds. See the bibliography for these.

Many commercial campgrounds guarantee reservations. Photo Courtesy KOA

MAPS

Showing the locations of
National Parks in the
Continental United States
and Alaska

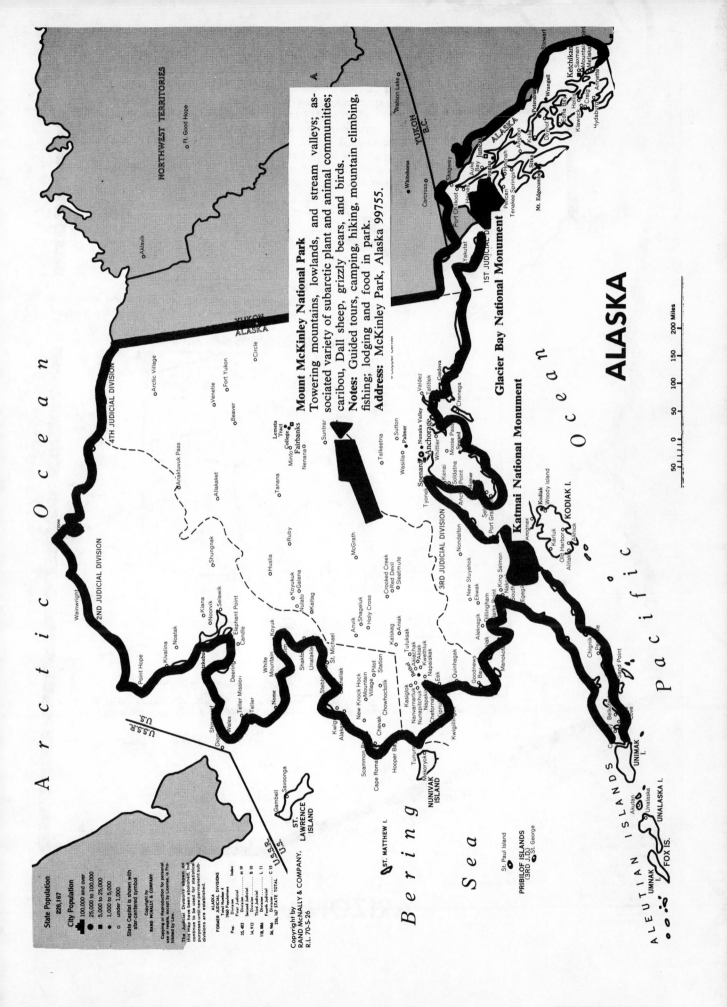

ALASKA

Mount McKinley National Park

Towering mountains, lowlands, and stream valleys; associated variety of subarctic plant and animal communities; caribou, Dall sheep, grizzly bears, and birds. **Notes:** Guided tours, camping, hiking, mountain climbing, fishing; lodging and food in park. **Address:** McKinley Park, Alaska 99755.

Glacier Bay National Monument

Katmai National Monument

NORTHWEST TERRITORIES

YUKON
B.C.

Arctic Ocean

Pacific Ocean

Bering Sea

U.S.S.R.

U.S.

State Population
226,167

City Population
■ 100,000 and over
■ 25,000 to 100,000
■ 5,000 to 25,000
• 1,000 to 5,000
○ under 1,000

State Capital is shown with star-centered symbol

Copyright by
RAND McNALLY & COMPANY

The Judicial Division shown on this map have been abolished, but continue to be used for statistical purposes until new permanent subdivisions are established.

ALASKA
FORMER JUDICIAL DIVISIONS
Total Population
1960 Populations   Index
Pop.
First Judicial
Division .... N 19
35,403
Second Judicial
Division .... B 10
14,912
Third Judicial
Division .... L 11
118,886
Fourth Judicial
Division .... C 15
56,966
226,167 STATE TOTAL

Copyright by
RAND McNALLY & COMPANY.
R.L. 70-S-26

1ST JUDICIAL D.

2ND JUDICIAL DIVISION

3RD JUDICIAL DIVISION

4TH JUDICIAL DIVISION

ALEUTIAN ISLANDS

FOX IS.
UNMAK I.
UNALASKA I.
UNIMAK I.

PRIBILOF ISLANDS
(3RD J.D.)
St. Paul Island
St. George

ST. MATTHEW I.

ST. LAWRENCE ISLAND

NUNIVAK ISLAND

KODIAK I.

0 50 100 150 200 Miles

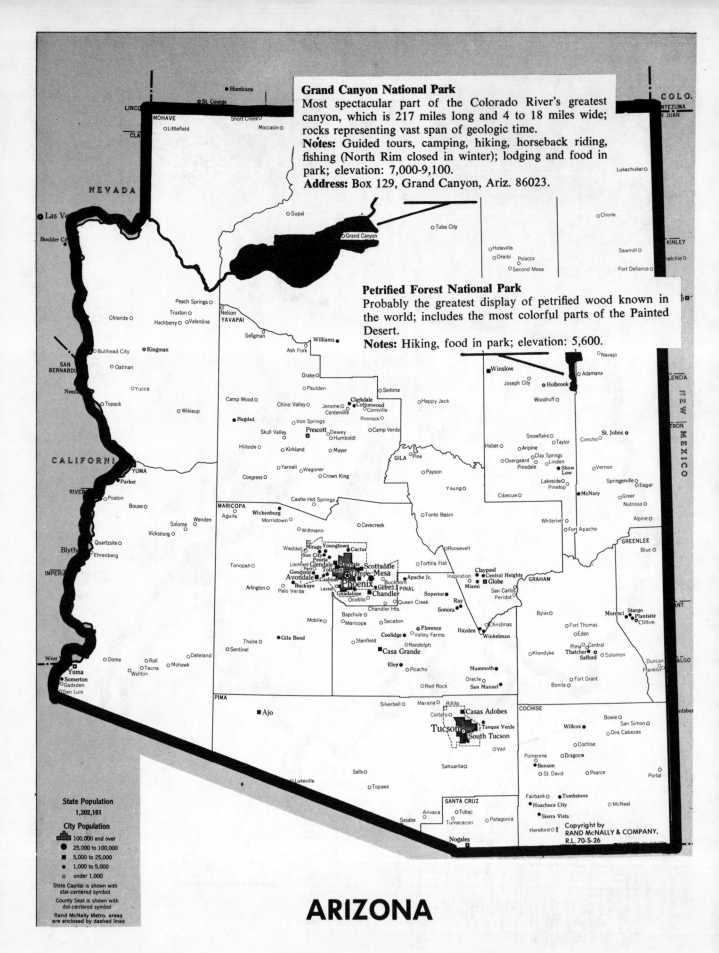

Grand Canyon National Park

Most spectacular part of the Colorado River's greatest canyon, which is 217 miles long and 4 to 18 miles wide; rocks representing vast span of geologic time.

Notes: Guided tours, camping, hiking, horseback riding, fishing (North Rim closed in winter); lodging and food in park; elevation: 7,000-9,100.

Address: Box 129, Grand Canyon, Ariz. 86023.

Petrified Forest National Park

Probably the greatest display of petrified wood known in the world; includes the most colorful parts of the Painted Desert.

Notes: Hiking, food in park; elevation: 5,600.

State Population
1,302,161

City Population

- 100,000 and over
- 25,000 to 100,000
- 5,000 to 25,000
- 1,000 to 5,000
- under 1,000

State Capital is shown with star-centered symbol

County Seat is shown with dot-centered symbol

Rand McNally Metro. areas are enclosed by dashed lines

Copyright by
RAND McNALLY & COMPANY,
R.L. 70-S-26

ARIZONA

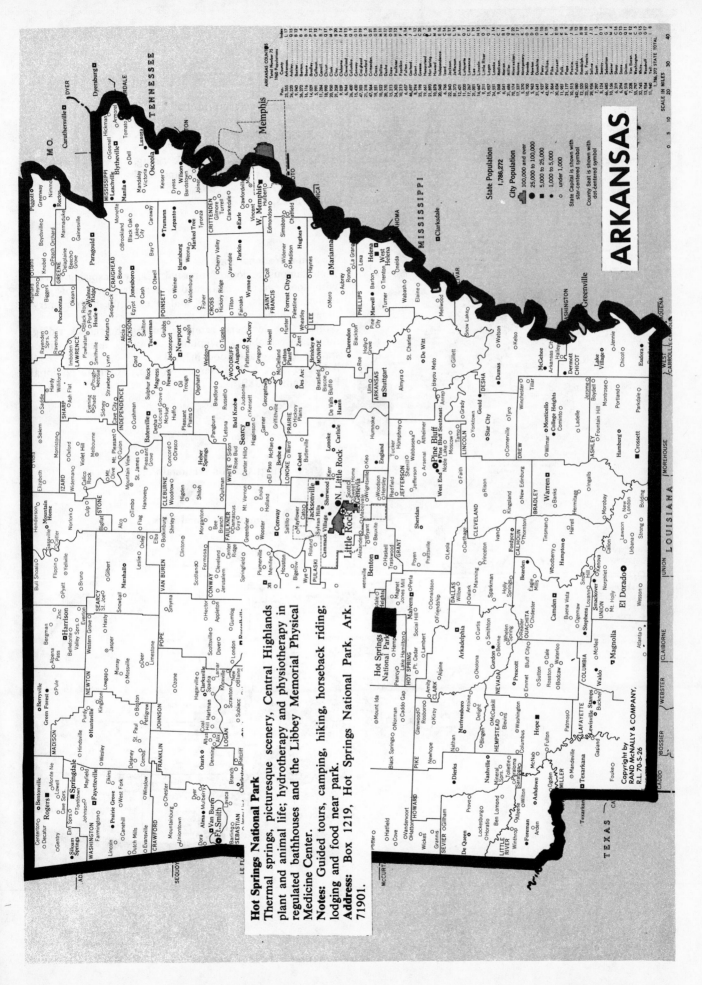

ARKANSAS

Hot Springs National Park

Thermal springs, picturesque scenery, Central Highlands plant and animal life; hydrotherapy and physiotherapy in regulated bathhouses and the Libbey Memorial Physical Medicine Center.

Notes: Guided tours, camping, hiking, horseback riding; lodging and food near park.

Address: Box 1219, Hot Springs National Park, Ark. 71901.

State Population 1,786,272

City Population
● 100,000 and over
● 25,000 to 100,000
● 5,000 to 25,000
• 1,000 to 5,000
○ under 1,000

☆ State Capital is shown with star-centered symbol

County Seat is shown with dot-centered symbol

SCALE IN MILES
0 5 10   20   30   40

Copyright by
RAND McNALLY & COMPANY,
R.L. 70-S-26

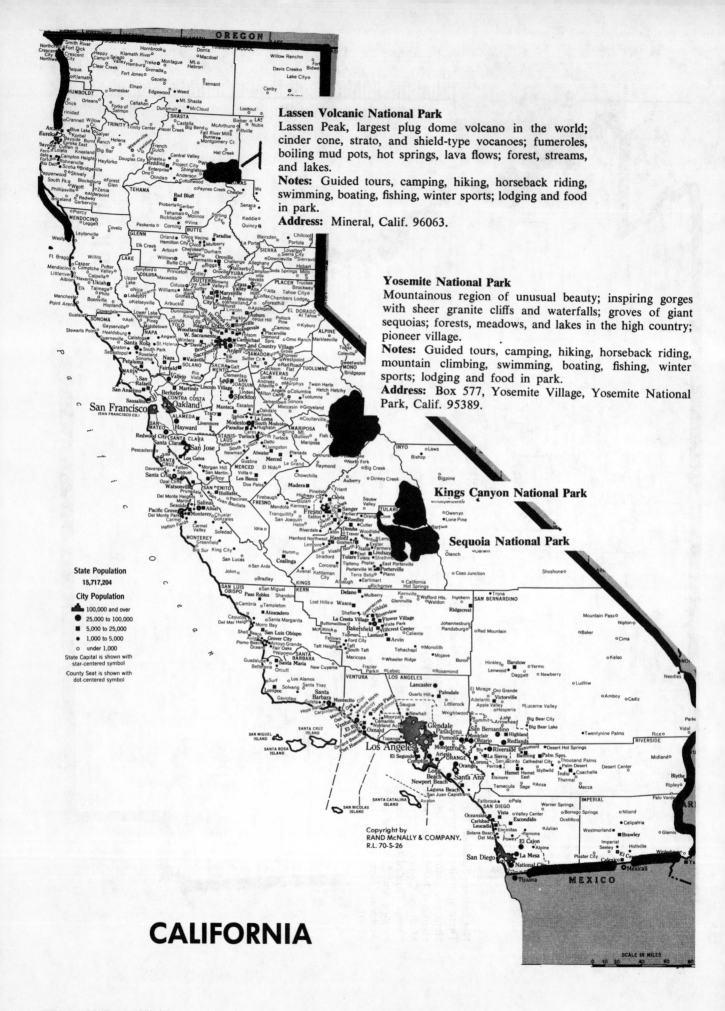

Lassen Volcanic National Park

Lassen Peak, largest plug dome volcano in the world; cinder cone, strato, and shield-type vocanoes; fumeroles, boiling mud pots, hot springs, lava flows; forest, streams, and lakes.

Notes: Guided tours, camping, hiking, horseback riding, swimming, boating, fishing, winter sports; lodging and food in park.

Address: Mineral, Calif. 96063.

Yosemite National Park

Mountainous region of unusual beauty; inspiring gorges with sheer granite cliffs and waterfalls; groves of giant sequoias; forests, meadows, and lakes in the high country; pioneer village.

Notes: Guided tours, camping, hiking, horseback riding, mountain climbing, swimming, boating, fishing, winter sports; lodging and food in park.

Address: Box 577, Yosemite Village, Yosemite National Park, Calif. 95389.

Kings Canyon National Park

Sequoia National Park

State Population
15,717,204

City Population

- 100,000 and over
- 25,000 to 100,000
- 5,000 to 25,000
- 1,000 to 5,000
- under 1,000

State Capital is shown with star-centered symbol

County Seat is shown with dot-centered symbol

Copyright by
RAND McNALLY & COMPANY,
R.L. 70-S-26

MEXICO

SCALE IN MILES
0 10 20   40   60   80

CALIFORNIA

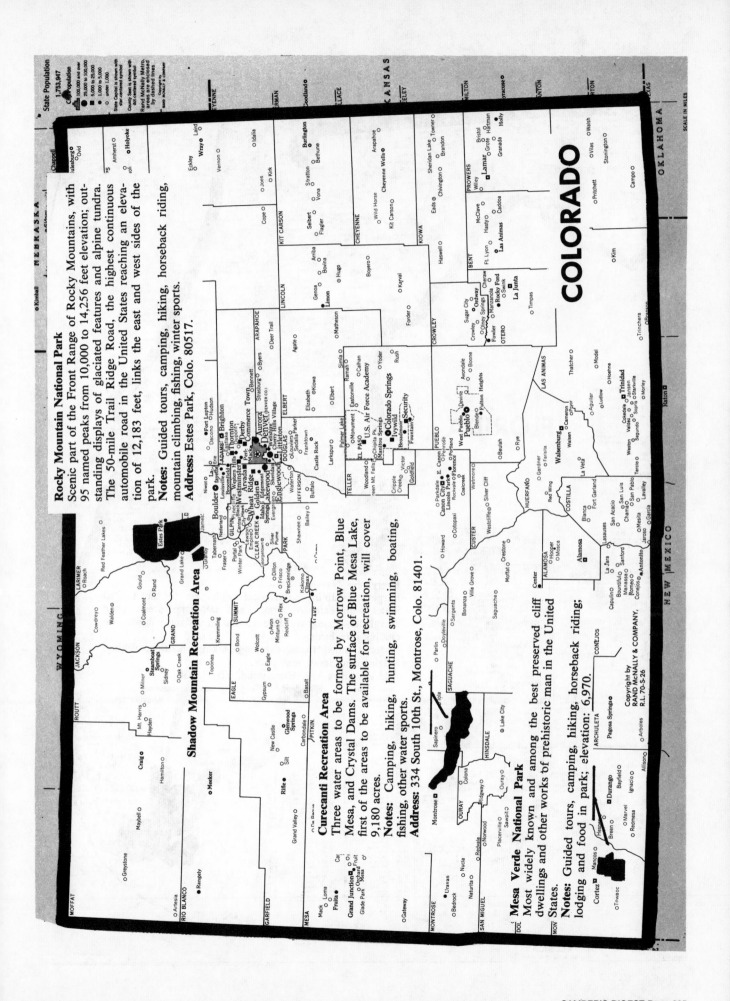

Rocky Mountain National Park

Scenic part of the Front Range of Rocky Mountains, with 95 named peaks from 10,000 to 14,256 feet elevation; outstanding displays of glaciated features and alpine tundra. The 50-mile Trail Ridge Road, the highest continuous automobile road in the United States reaching an elevation of 12,183 feet, links the east and west sides of the park.

Notes: Guided tours, camping, hiking, horseback riding, mountain climbing, fishing, winter sports.

Address: Estes Park, Colo. 80517.

Shadow Mountain Recreation Area

Curecanti Recreation Area

Three water areas to be formed by Morrow Point, Blue Mesa, and Crystal Dams. The surface of Blue Mesa Lake, first of the areas to be available for recreation, will cover 9,180 acres.

Notes: Camping, hiking, hunting, swimming, boating, fishing, other water sports.

Address: 334 South 10th St., Montrose, Colo. 81401.

Mesa Verde National Park

Most widely known and among the best preserved cliff dwellings and other works of prehistoric man in the United States.

Notes: Guided tours, camping, hiking, horseback riding; lodging and food in park; elevation: 6,970.

COLORADO

State Population 1,753,947

Copyright by
RAND McNALLY & COMPANY,
R.L. 70-S-26

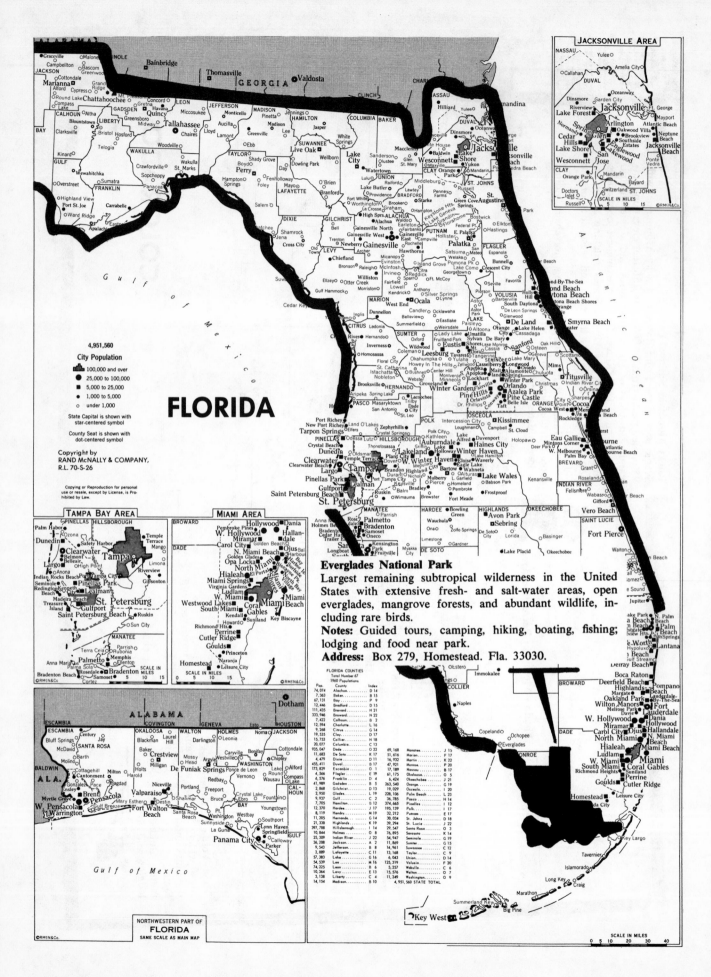

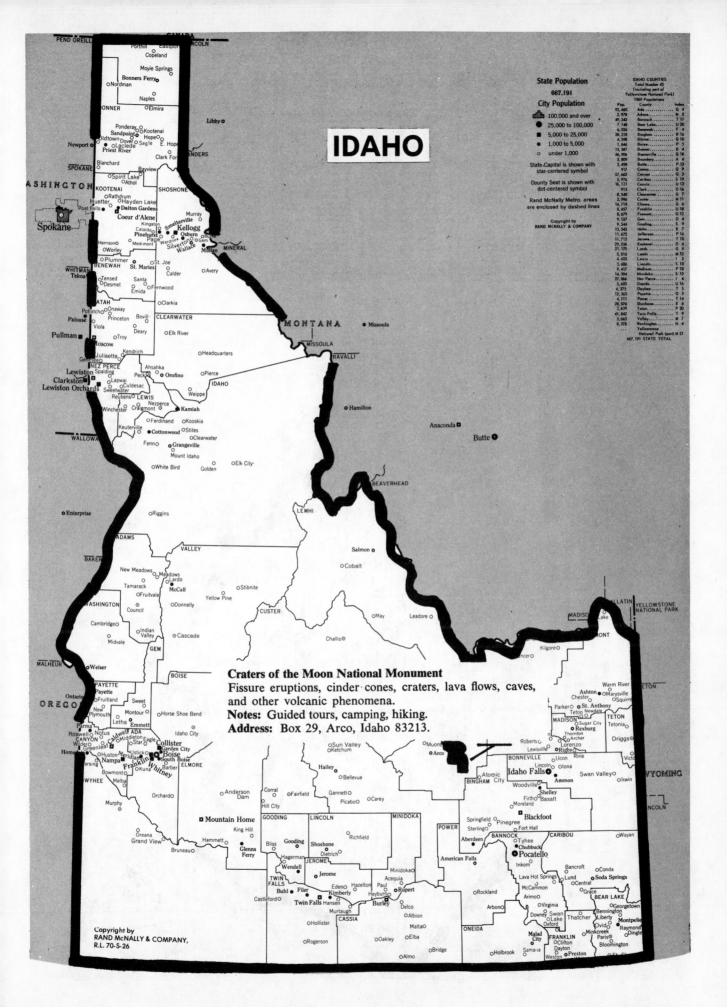

IDAHO

Craters of the Moon National Monument
Fissure eruptions, cinder cones, craters, lava flows, caves, and other volcanic phenomena.
Notes: Guided tours, camping, hiking.
Address: Box 29, Arco, Idaho 83213.

State Population
667,191
City Population

⬛ 100,000 and over
⬤ 25,000 to 100,000
■ 5,000 to 25,000
• 1,000 to 5,000
○ under 1,000

State Capital is shown with
star-centered symbol

County Seat is shown with
dot-centered symbol

Rand McNally Metro. areas
are enclosed by dashed lines

Copyright by
RAND McNALLY & COMPANY

IDAHO COUNTIES Total Number 45 (including part of Yellowstone National Park) 1960 Populations		
	Pop.	County	Index
Ada	93,460	Q 4
Adams	2,978	M 5
Bannock	49,342	T 17
Bear Lake	7,148	U 20
Benewah	6,036	F 4
Bingham	28,218	R 16
Blaine	4,598	Q 10
Boise	1,646	P 5
Bonner	15,587	B 4
Bonneville	46,906	Q 18
Boundary	5,809	A 4
Butte	3,498	P 13
Camas	917	Q 9
Canyon	57,662	S 19
Caribou	5,976	S 19
Cassia	16,121	U 12
Clark	915	O 16
Clearwater	8,548	G 7
Custer	2,996	N 11
Elmore	16,719	R 8
Franklin	5,457	U 18
Fremont	8,679	O 12
Gem	9,127	O 4
Gooding	9,544	S 9
Idaho	13,542	K 7
Jefferson	11,672	P 16
Jerome	11,712	T 10
Kootenai	29,556	D 4
Latah	21,170	G 4
Lemhi	5,816	M 12
Lewis	4,423	I 5
Lincoln	3,686	S 10
Madison	9,417	P 18
Minidoka	14,394	S 12
Nez Perce	27,066	H 4
Oneida	3,603	U 16
Owyhee	6,375	T 3
Payette	12,363	Q 3
Power	4,111	T 14
Shoshone	20,876	E 6
Teton	2,639	P 20
Twin Falls	41,842	T 9
Valley	3,663	M 7
Washington	8,378	N 4
Yellowstone National Park (part)		M 21
667,191 STATE TOTAL		

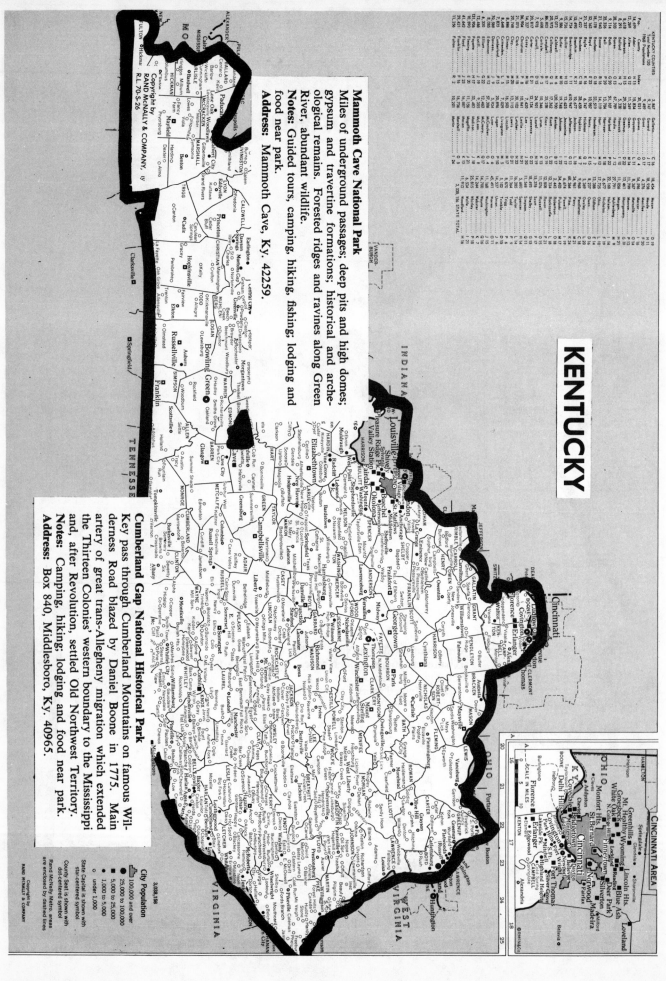

KENTUCKY

Mammoth Cave National Park

Miles of underground passages; deep pits and high domes; gypsum and travertine formations; historical and archeological remains. Forested ridges and ravines along Green River; abundant wildlife.

Notes: Guided tours, camping, hiking, fishing; lodging and food near park.

Address: Mammoth Cave, Ky. 42259.

Cumberland Gap National Historical Park

Key pass through Cumberland Mountains on famous Wilderness Road blazed by Daniel Boone in 1775. Main artery of great trans-Allegheny migration which extended the Thirteen Colonies' western boundary to the Mississippi and, after Revolution, settled Old Northwest Territory.

Notes: Camping, hiking; lodging and food near park.

Address: Box 840, Middlesboro, Ky. 40965.

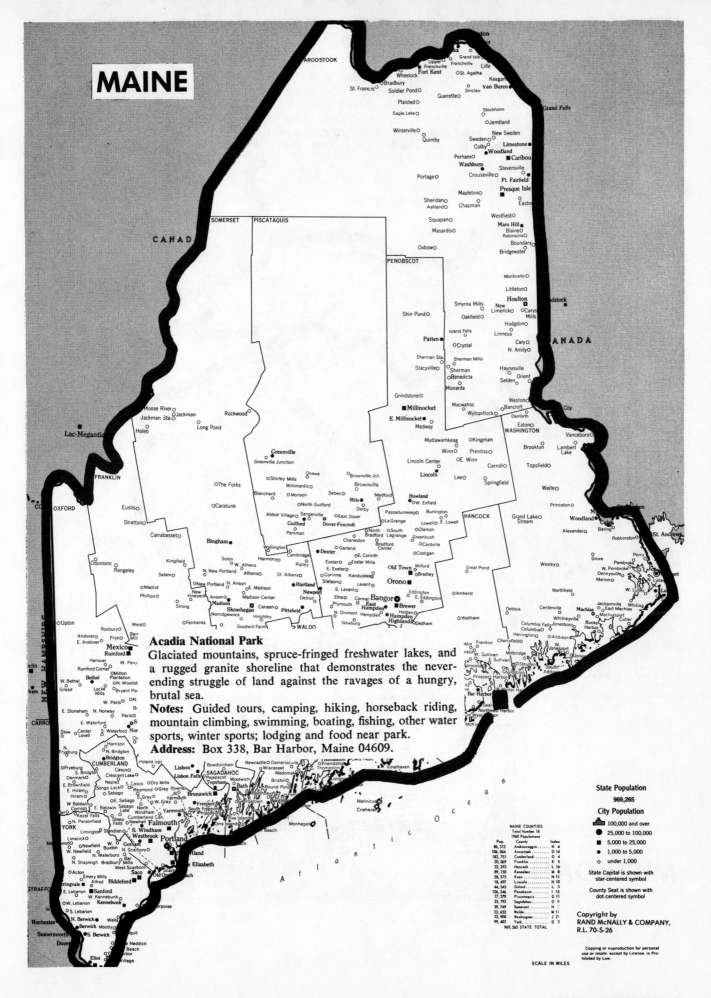

MAINE

Acadia National Park

Glaciated mountains, spruce-fringed freshwater lakes, and a rugged granite shoreline that demonstrates the never-ending struggle of land against the ravages of a hungry, brutal sea.

Notes: Guided tours, camping, hiking, horseback riding, mountain climbing, swimming, boating, fishing, other water sports, winter sports; lodging and food near park.

Address: Box 338, Bar Harbor, Maine 04609.

State Population
969,265

City Population

- 100,000 and over
- ● 25,000 to 100,000
- ■ 5,000 to 25,000
- ● 1,000 to 5,000
- ○ under 1,000

State Capital is shown with
star-centered symbol

County Seat is shown with
dot-centered symbol

MAINE COUNTIES
Total Number 16
1960 Populations

Pop.	County	Index
86,312	Androscoggin	N 6
106,064	Aroostook	D 14
182,751	Cumberland	O 4
20,069	Franklin	K 5
32,293	Hancock	L 16
89,150	Kennebec	M 8
28,575	Knox	N 11
18,497	Lincoln	L 3
44,345	Oxford	L 3
126,346	Penobscot	I 15
17,379	Piscataquis	G 11
22,793	Sagadahoc	O 8
39,749	Somerset	H 7
22,632	Waldo	M 11
32,908	Washington	J 21
99,402	York	Q 3
969,265	STATE TOTAL	

SCALE IN MILES

Isle Royale National Park

An island archipelago in western Lake Superior noted for its moose herd, magnificent shorelines and seascapes, and 210 square miles of unspoiled forests.

Notes: Guided tours, camping, hiking, swimming, boating, fishing, other water sports; lodging and food near park.

Address: Box 27, Ripley St., Houghton, Mich. 49931.

MICHIGAN

State Population
7,823,194

City Population

100,000 and over
25,000 to 100,000
5,000 to 25,000
1,000 to 5,000
under 1,000

State Capital is shown with star-centered symbol

County Seat is shown with dot-centered symbol

Rand McNally Metro. areas are enclosed by dashed lines

Copyright by
RAND McNALLY & COMPANY

Copying or Reproduction for personal use or resale, except by License, is Prohibited by Law.

Copyright by
RAND McNALLY & COMPANY,
R.L. 70-S-26

SCALE IN MILES
0 5 10   20   30   40   50   60

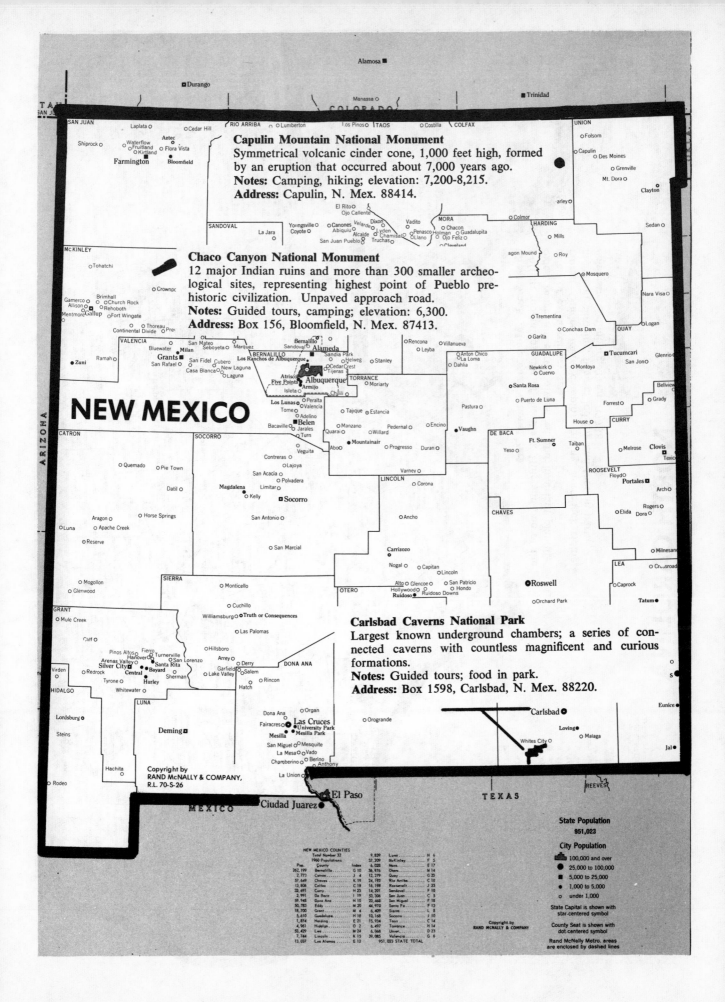

NEW MEXICO

Capulin Mountain National Monument

Symmetrical volcanic cinder cone, 1,000 feet high, formed by an eruption that occurred about 7,000 years ago.
Notes: Camping, hiking; elevation: 7,200-8,215.
Address: Capulin, N. Mex. 88414.

Chaco Canyon National Monument

12 major Indian ruins and more than 300 smaller archeological sites, representing highest point of Pueblo prehistoric civilization. Unpaved approach road.
Notes: Guided tours, camping; elevation: 6,300.
Address: Box 156, Bloomfield, N. Mex. 87413.

Carlsbad Caverns National Park

Largest known underground chambers; a series of connected caverns with countless magnificent and curious formations.
Notes: Guided tours; food in park.
Address: Box 1598, Carlsbad, N. Mex. 88220.

Copyright by
RAND McNALLY & COMPANY,
R.L. 70-S-26

Copyright by
RAND McNALLY & COMPANY

State Population
951,023

City Population

- 100,000 and over
- 25,000 to 100,000
- 5,000 to 25,000
- 1,000 to 5,000
- under 1,000

State Capital is shown with star-centered symbol

County Seat is shown with dot-centered symbol

Rand McNally Metro. areas are enclosed by dashed lines

NEW MEXICO COUNTIES		
Total Number 32		
1960 Populations		
Pop.	County	Index
262,199	Bernalillo	G 10
2,773	Catron	J 4
57,649	Chaves	K 19
13,806	Colfax	C 18
32,691	Curry	H 23
2,991	De Baca	J 19
59,948	Dona Ana	N 10
50,783	Eddy	M 20
18,700	Grant	M 4
5,610	Guadalupe	H 18
1,874	Harding	E 21
4,961	Hidalgo	O 2
35,429	Lea	M 24
7,744	Lincoln	K 15
13,037	Los Alamos	E 12
9,839	Luna	N 6
37,209	McKinley	F 5
6,028	Mora	E 17
36,976	Otero	M 14
12,279	Quay	G 23
24,193	Rio Arriba	C 10
16,198	Roosevelt	J 23
14,201	Sandoval	F 10
53,306	San Juan	C 3
23,468	San Miguel	F 16
44,970	Santa Fe	F 13
6,409	Sierra	L 8
10,168	Socorro	H 9
15,934	Taos	C 14
6,497	Torrance	H 14
6,068	Union	D 23
39,085	Valencia	G 6
	951,023 STATE TOTAL	

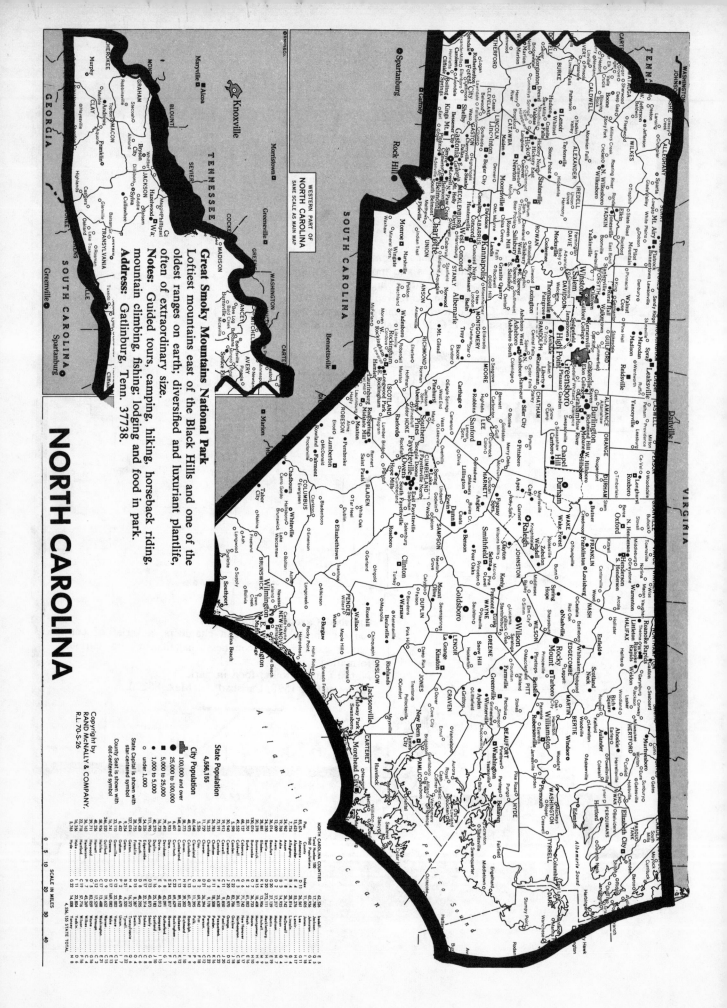

NORTH CAROLINA

Great Smoky Mountains National Park

Loftiest mountains east of the Black Hills and one of the oldest ranges on earth; diversified and luxuriant plantlife, often of extraordinary size.

Notes: Guided tours, camping, hiking, horseback riding, mountain climbing, fishing; lodging and food in park.

Address: Gatlinburg, Tenn. 37738.

WESTERN PART OF
NORTH CAROLINA
SAME SCALE AS MAIN MAP

Copyright by
RAND McNALLY & COMPANY,
R.L. 70-S-26

State Population
4,556,155

■	100,000 and over
■	25,000 to 100,000
●	5,000 to 25,000
●	1,000 to 5,000
○	under 1,000

City Population

State Capital is shown with star-centered symbol

County Seat is shown with dot-centered symbol

SCALE IN MILES
0   5   10   20   30   40

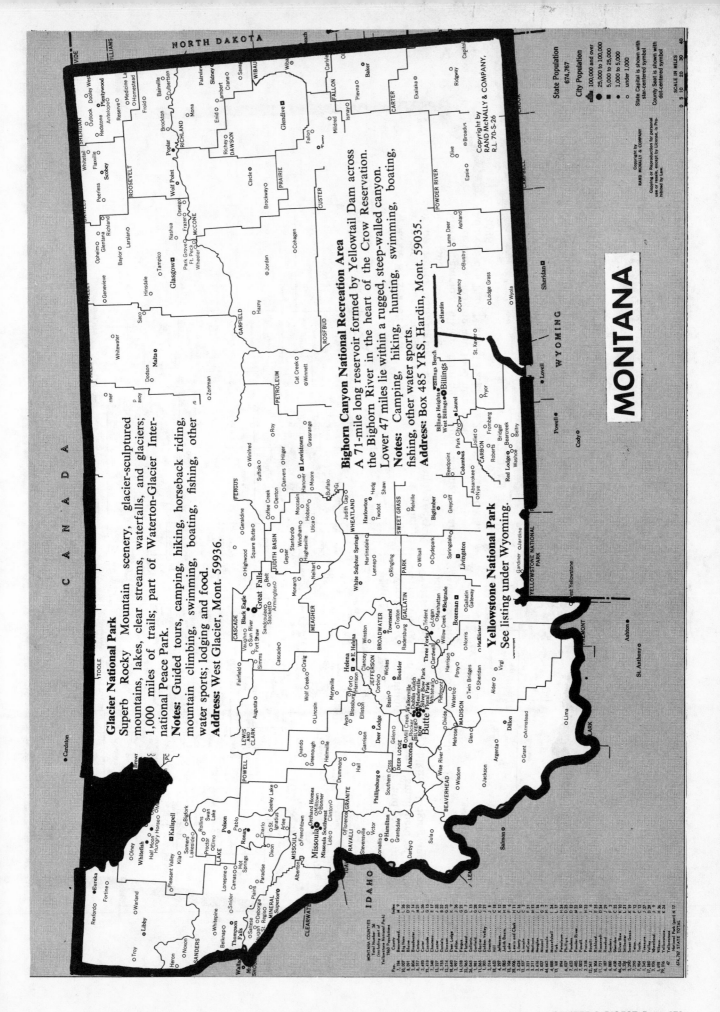

MONTANA

Glacier National Park
Superb Rocky Mountain scenery, glacier-sculptured mountains, lakes, clear streams, waterfalls, and glaciers; 1,000 miles of trails; part of Waterton-Glacier International Peace Park.
Notes: Guided tours, camping, hiking, horseback riding, mountain climbing, swimming, boating, fishing, other water sports; lodging and food.
Address: West Glacier, Mont. 59936.

Bighorn Canyon National Recreation Area
A 71-mile long reservoir formed by Yellowtail Dam across the Bighorn River in the heart of the Crow Reservation. Lower 47 miles lie within a rugged, steep-walled canyon.
Notes: Camping, hiking, hunting, swimming, boating, fishing, other water sports.
Address: Box 485 YRS, Hardin, Mont. 59035.

Yellowstone National Park
See listing under Wyoming.

State Population
674,767

City Population
▲ 100,000 and over
● 25,000 to 100,000
● 5,000 to 25,000
○ 1,000 to 5,000
○ under 1,000

State Capital is shown with star-centered symbol
County Seat is shown with dot-centered symbol

SCALE IN MILES
0 5 10 20 30 40

Copyright by
RAND McNALLY & COMPANY,
R.L. 70-S-26

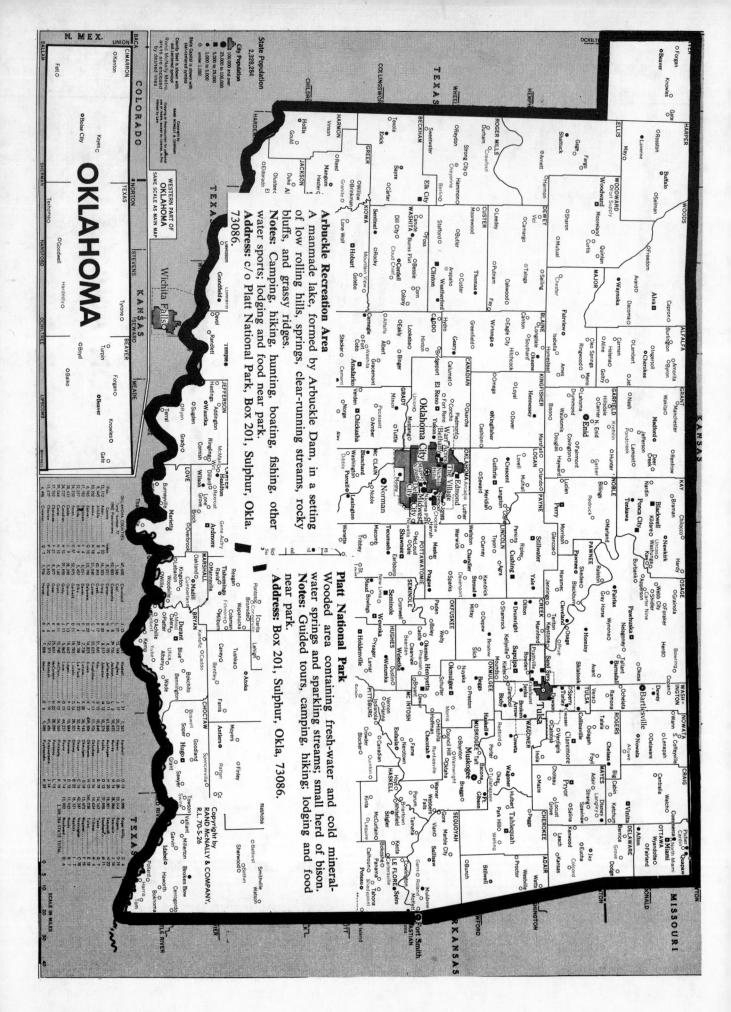

Arbuckle Recreation Area

A manmade lake, formed by Arbuckle Dam, in a setting of low rolling hills, springs, clear-running streams, rocky bluffs, and grassy ridges.

Notes: Camping, hiking, hunting, boating, fishing, other water sports; lodging and food near park.

Address: c/o Platt National Park, Box 201, Sulphur, Okla. 73086.

Platt National Park

Wooded area containing fresh-water and cold mineral-water springs and sparkling streams; small herd of bison.

Notes: Guided tours, camping, hiking; lodging and food near park.

Address: Box 201, Sulphur, Okla., 73086.

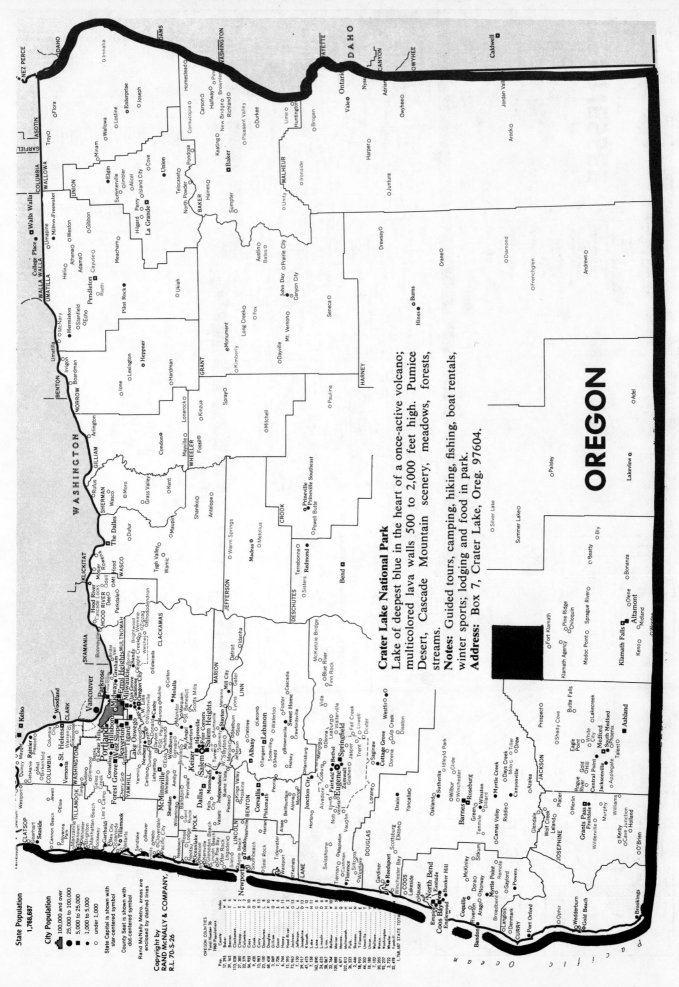

Crater Lake National Park

Lake of deepest blue in the heart of a once-active volcano; multicolored lava walls 500 to 2,000 feet high. Pumice Desert, Cascade Mountain scenery, meadows, forests, streams.

Notes: Guided tours, camping, hiking, fishing, boat rentals, winter sports; lodging and food in park.

Address: Box 7, Crater Lake, Oreg. 97604.

OREGON

State Population
1,768,687

City Population
● 100,000 and over
■ 25,000 to 100,000
■ 5,000 to 25,000
● 1,000 to 5,000
○ under 1,000

State Capital is shown with star-centered symbol
County Seat is shown with dot-centered symbol
Rand McNally Metro. areas are enclosed by dashed lines

Copyright by
RAND McNALLY & COMPANY.
R.L. 70-S-26

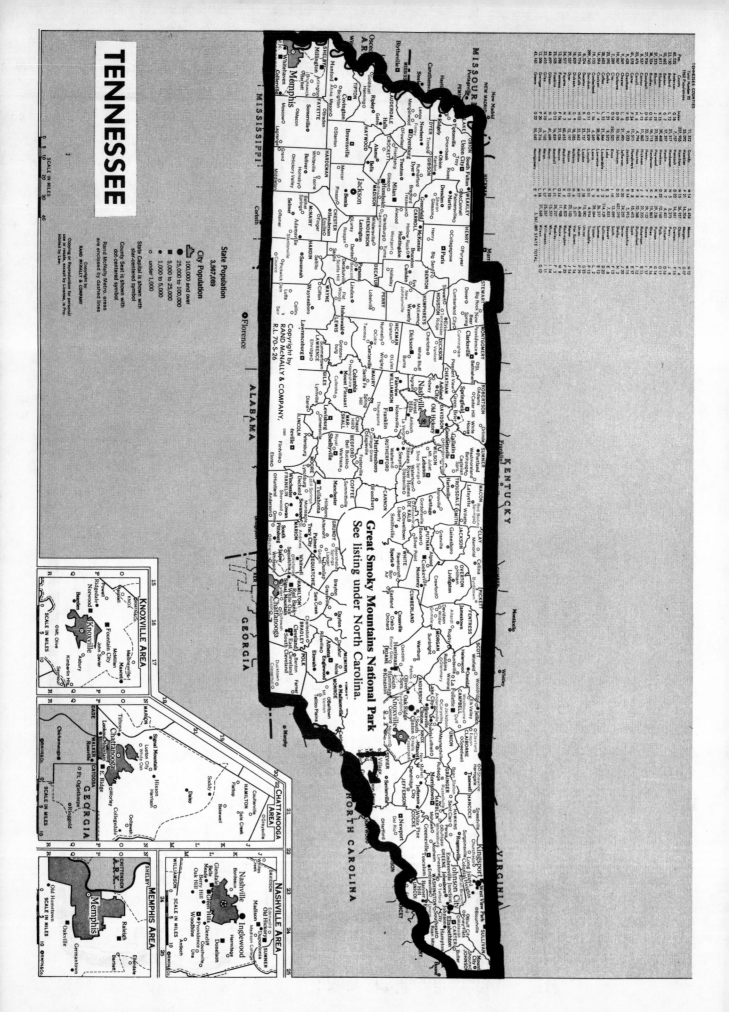

TENNESSEE

State Capital is shown with star-centered symbol

County Seat is shown with dot-centered symbol

Rand McNally Metro. areas are enclosed by dashed lines

Copyright by RAND McNALLY & COMPANY

Copying or Reproduction for personal use or resale, except by License, is Prohibited by Law.

State Population
3,567,089

City Population

■ 100,000 and over
■ 25,000 to 100,000
■ 5,000 to 25,000
● 1,000 to 5,000
○ under 1,000

SCALE IN MILES
0 5 10 20 30 40

Copyright by RAND McNALLY & COMPANY, R.L. 70-S-26

Great Smoky Mountains National Park
See listing under North Carolina.

KNOXVILLE AREA
SCALE IN MILES

CHATTANOOGA AREA
SCALE IN MILES

MEMPHIS AREA
SCALE IN MILES

NASHVILLE AREA
SCALE IN MILES

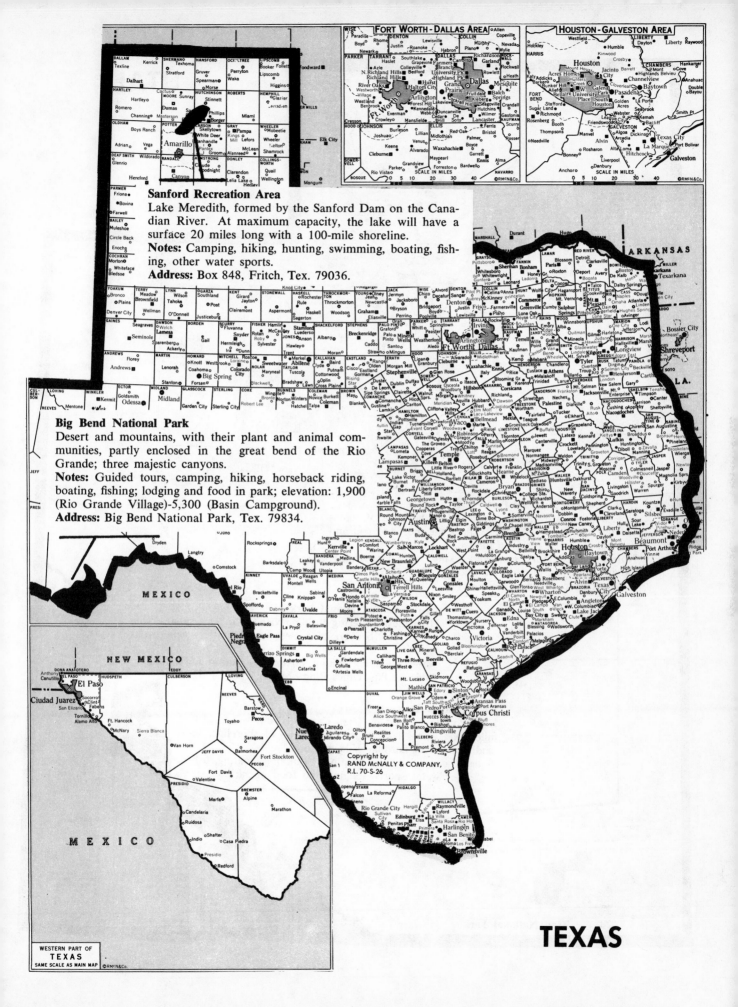

Sanford Recreation Area

Lake Meredith, formed by the Sanford Dam on the Canadian River. At maximum capacity, the lake will have a surface 20 miles long with a 100-mile shoreline.

Notes: Camping, hiking, hunting, swimming, boating, fishing, other water sports.

Address: Box 848, Fritch, Tex. 79036.

Big Bend National Park

Desert and mountains, with their plant and animal communities, partly enclosed in the great bend of the Rio Grande; three majestic canyons.

Notes: Guided tours, camping, hiking, horseback riding, boating, fishing; lodging and food in park; elevation: 1,900 (Rio Grande Village)-5,300 (Basin Campground).

Address: Big Bend National Park, Tex. 79834.

Copyright by
RAND McNALLY & COMPANY,
R.L. 70-S-26

TEXAS

WESTERN PART OF
TEXAS
SAME SCALE AS MAIN MAP

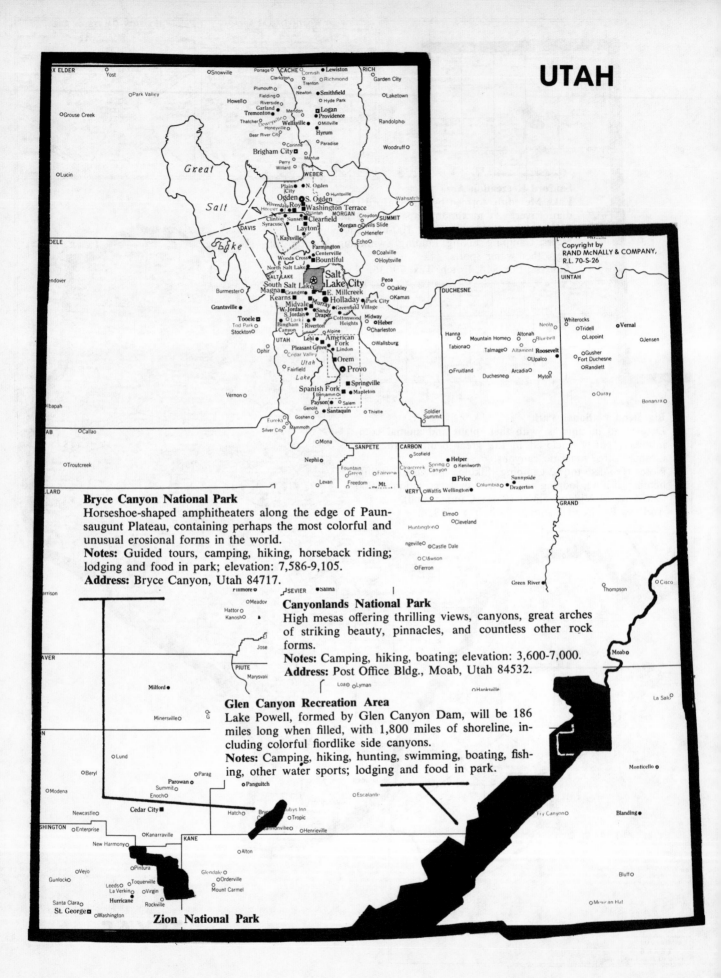

UTAH

Bryce Canyon National Park

Horseshoe-shaped amphitheaters along the edge of Paunsaugunt Plateau, containing perhaps the most colorful and unusual erosional forms in the world.

Notes: Guided tours, camping, hiking, horseback riding; lodging and food in park; elevation: 7,586-9,105.

Address: Bryce Canyon, Utah 84717.

Canyonlands National Park

High mesas offering thrilling views, canyons, great arches of striking beauty, pinnacles, and countless other rock forms.

Notes: Camping, hiking, boating; elevation: 3,600-7,000.

Address: Post Office Bldg., Moab, Utah 84532.

Glen Canyon Recreation Area

Lake Powell, formed by Glen Canyon Dam, will be 186 miles long when filled, with 1,800 miles of shoreline, including colorful fiordlike side canyons.

Notes: Camping, hiking, hunting, swimming, boating, fishing, other water sports; lodging and food in park.

Zion National Park

VIRGINIA

WESTERN PART OF
VIRGINIA
SAME SCALE AS MAIN MAP
KENTUCKY
TENNESSEE
NORTH CAROLINA
WEST VIRGINIA
Atlantic Ocean
State Population
3,966,949
City Population
100,000 and over
25,000 to 100,000
5,000 to 25,000
1,000 to 5,000
under 1,000
State Capital is shown with star-centered symbol
County Seat is shown with dot-centered symbol
Rand McNally Metro. areas are enclosed by dashed lines
Copyright by RAND McNALLY & COMPANY
Copying or Reproduction for personal use or resale, except by License, is Prohibited by Law.
Copyright by
RAND McNALLY & COMPANY,
R.L. 70-S-26

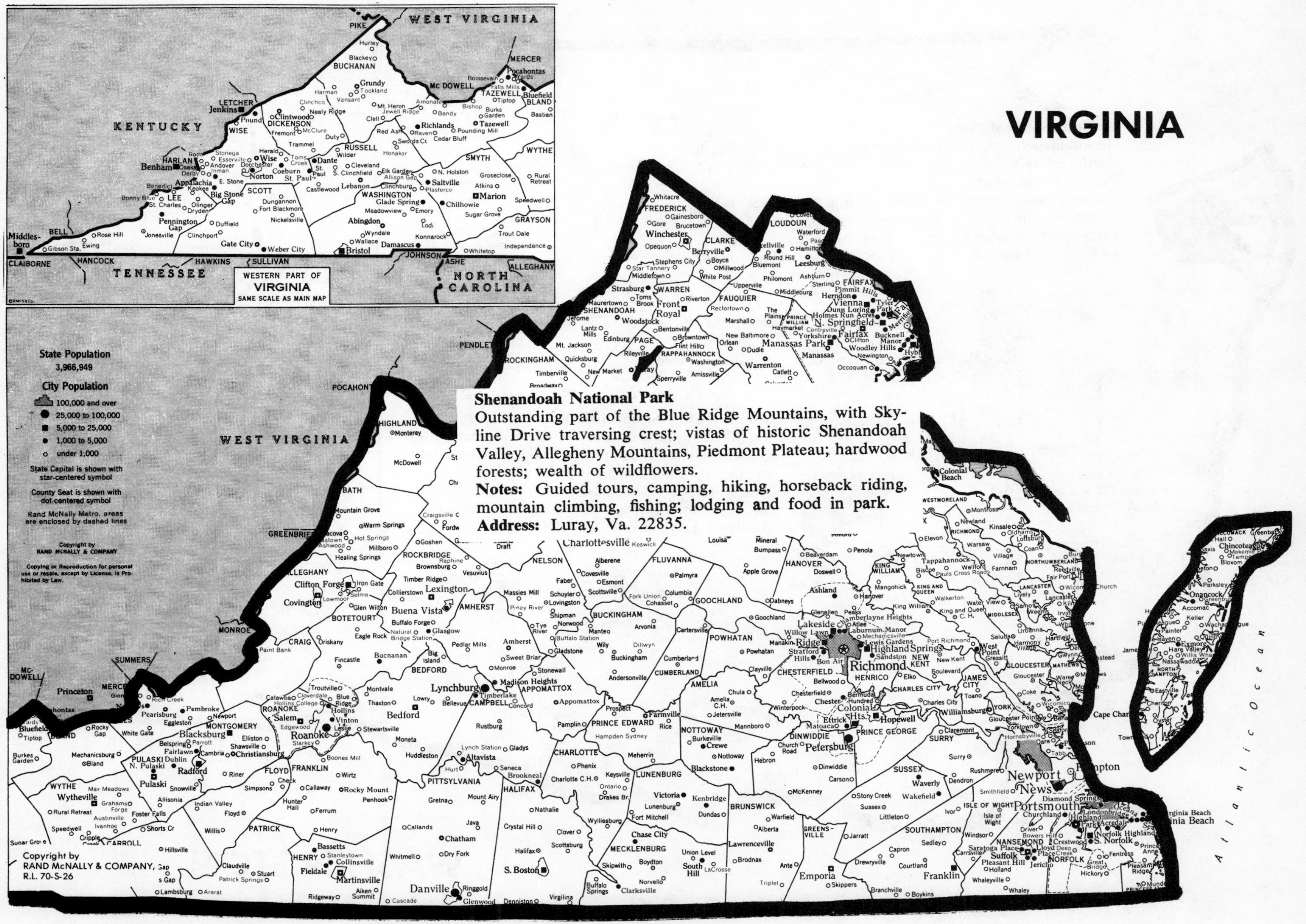

Shenandoah National Park
Outstanding part of the Blue Ridge Mountains, with Skyline Drive traversing crest; vistas of historic Shenandoah Valley, Allegheny Mountains, Piedmont Plateau; hardwood forests; wealth of wildflowers.
Notes: Guided tours, camping, hiking, horseback riding, mountain climbing, fishing; lodging and food in park.
Address: Luray, Va. 22835.

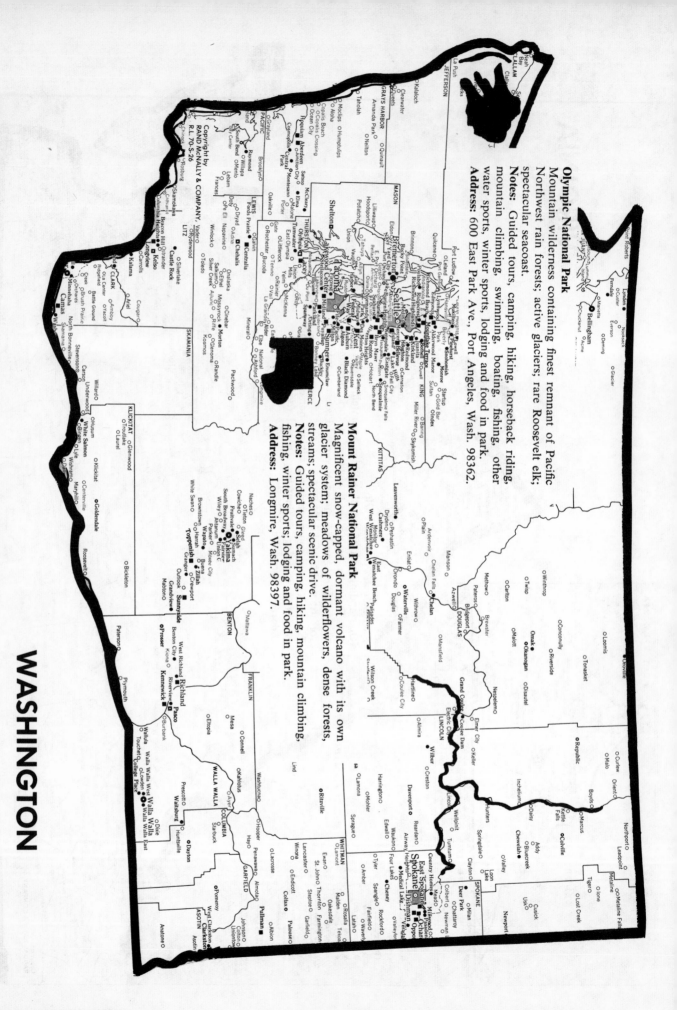

Olympic National Park

Mountain wilderness containing finest remnant of Pacific Northwest rain forests; active glaciers; rare Roosevelt elk; spectacular seacoast.

Notes: Guided tours, camping, hiking, horseback riding, mountain climbing, swimming, boating, fishing, other water sports, winter sports, lodging and food in park.

Address: 600 East Park Ave., Port Angeles, Wash. 98362.

Mount Rainer National Park

Magnificent snow-capped, dormant volcano with its own glacier system; meadows of wilderflowers, dense forests; spectacular scenic drive.

Notes: Guided tours, camping, hiking, mountain climbing, fishing, winter sports; lodging and food in park.

Address: Longmire, Wash. 98397.

WASHINGTON

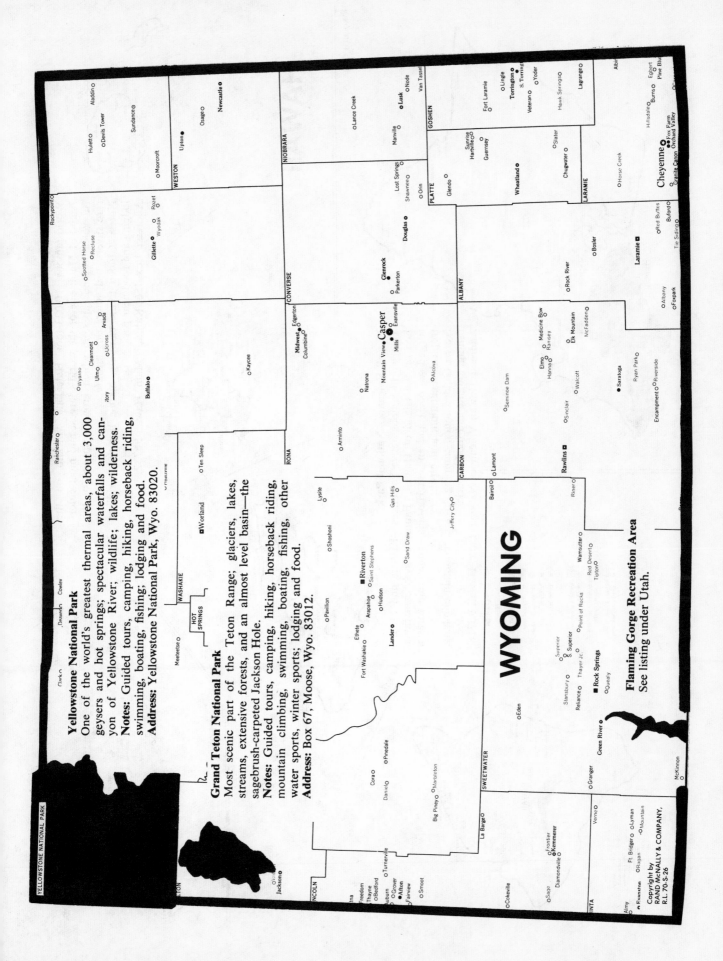

WYOMING

Yellowstone National Park

One of the world's greatest thermal areas, about 3,000 geysers and hot springs; spectacular waterfalls and canyon of Yellowstone River; wildlife; lakes; wilderness.
Notes: Guided tours, camping, hiking, horseback riding, swimming, boating, fishing; lodging and food.
Address: Yellowstone National Park, Wyo. 83020.

Grand Teton National Park

Most scenic part of the Teton Range; glaciers, lakes, streams, extensive forests, and an almost level basin—the sagebrush-carpeted Jackson Hole.
Notes: Guided tours, camping, hiking, horseback riding, mountain climbing, swimming, boating, fishing, other water sports, winter sports; lodging and food.
Address: Box 67, Moose, Wyo. 83012.

Flaming Gorge Recreation Area
See listing under Utah.

Copyright by
RAND McNALLY & COMPANY,
R.L. 70-S-26

HAWAII

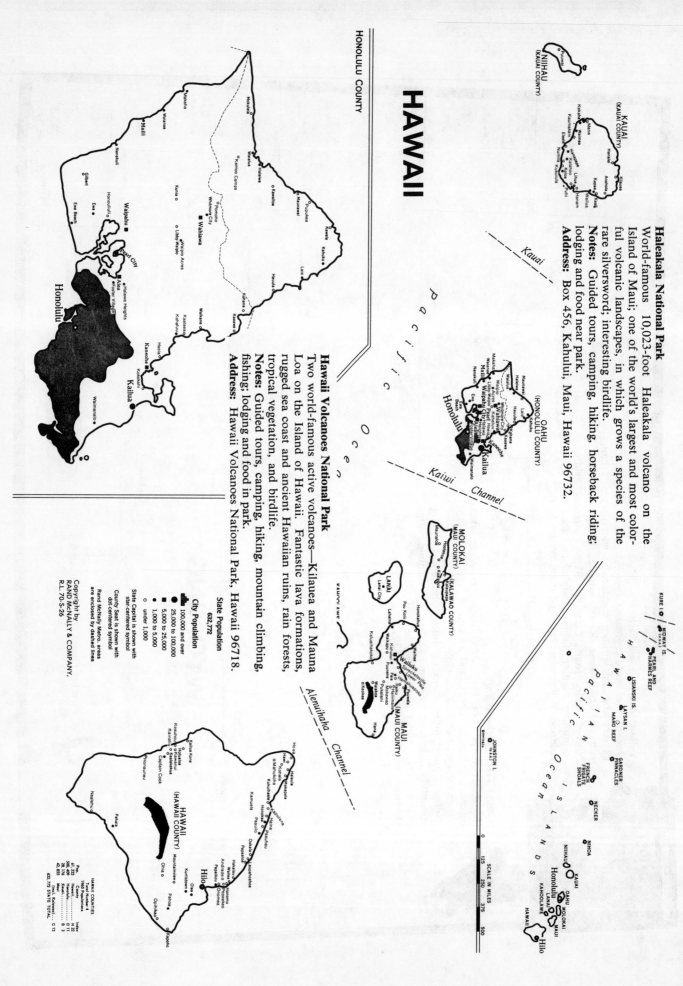

Haleakala National Park
World-famous 10,023-foot Haleakala volcano on the Island of Maui; one of the world's largest and most colorful volcanic landscapes, in which grows a species of the rare silversword; interesting birdlife.
Notes: Guided tours, camping, hiking, horseback riding; lodging and food near park.
Address: Box 456, Kahului, Maui, Hawaii 96732.

Hawaii Volcanoes National Park
Two world-famous active volcanoes—Kilauea and Mauna Loa on the Island of Hawaii. Fantastic lava formations, rugged sea coast and ancient Hawaiian ruins, rain forests, tropical vegetation, and birdlife.
Notes: Guided tours, camping, hiking, mountain climbing, fishing; lodging and food in park.
Address: Hawaii Volcanoes National Park, Hawaii 96718.

State Population
632,772

City Population

■ 100,000 and over
■ 25,000 to 100,000
■ 5,000 to 25,000
● 1,000 to 5,000
○ under 1,000

State Capital is shown with star-centered symbol

County Seat is shown with dot-centered symbol

Rand McNally Metro. areas are enclosed by dashed lines

Copyright by
RAND McNALLY & COMPANY.
R.L. 70-S-26

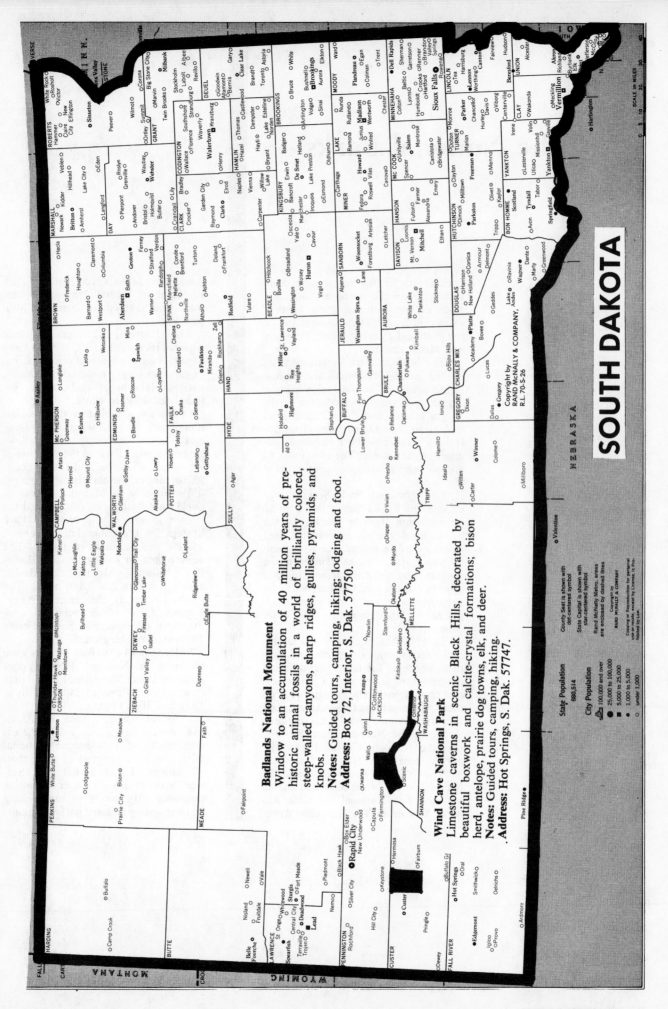

SOUTH DAKOTA

Badlands National Monument

Window to an accumulation of 40 million years of prehistoric animal fossils in a world of brilliantly colored, steep-walled canyons, sharp ridges, gullies, pyramids, and knobs.

Notes: Guided tours, camping, hiking, lodging and food.
Address: Box 72, Interior, S. Dak. 57750.

Wind Cave National Park

Limestone caverns in scenic Black Hills, decorated by beautiful boxwork and calcite-crystal formations; bison herd, antelope, prairie dog towns, elk, and deer.

Notes: Guided tours, camping, hiking.
Address: Hot Springs, S. Dak. 57747.

State Population
680,514

City Population
- 100,000 and over
- 25,000 to 100,000
- 5,000 to 25,000
- 1,000 to 5,000
- under 1,000

County Seat is shown with dot-centered symbol
State Capital is shown with star-centered symbol

Copyright by
RAND McNALLY & COMPANY

Rand McNally Metro. areas are enclosed by dashed lines

Copying or Reproduction for personal use or resale, except by License, is Prohibited by Law.

Copyright by
RAND McNALLY & COMPANY,
R.L. 70-S-26

SCALE IN MILES

The National Parks—

Following is the latest official information on the purposes and functions of the National Park System, excerpted from "The National Parks, the National Forests: Their Purposes and Management":

"The National Park System consists of 263 natural, historical and recreational areas of national significance. These areas range from Alaska to the Virgin Islands and from Puerto Rico to Hawaii. The Department of the Interior's National Park Service administers 251 areas. The remaining 12 are managed under agreement with the Service.

"The National Park Service was established by Congress in 1916 'to promote and regulate the use of the . . . national parks, monuments and reservations' in accordance with their purpose which 'is to conserve the scenery and the natural and historic objects and the wild life therein . . . by such means as will leave them unimpaired for the enjoyment of future generations.'

"In 1964 the Secretary of the Interior recommended separate management concepts for the 'three different categories of areas, natural, historical and recreational.' On January 1, 1968 there were 67 Natural Areas, 165 Historical Areas, and 30 Recreational Areas in the National Park System, plus the National Capital Parks, the park system of the Nation's Capital.

"The Natural Areas comprise 32 national parks, 34 national monuments and Ice Age National Scientific Reserve, Wisconsin. The Historical Areas range from Mesa Verde National Park to Statue of Liberty National Monument and Gettysburg National Military Park.

The Recreational Areas include national recreation areas, such as Lake Mead National Recreation Area, national parkways, national seashores, national lakeshores and Ozark National Scenic Riverways.

"Congress established the first national park in 1872 when it set aside more than two million acres as Yellowstone National Park at the junction of Wyoming, Montana, and Idaho; about 95 percent of the park is in Wyoming.

Yellowstone is still the largest of our 33 national parks, often called the 'crown jewels' of the National Park System for their superlative scenery, wildlife and wonders of nature. The largest area in the system is Glacier Bay National Monument, Alaska, which contains 2,803,840 acres. The smallest area is the House Where Lincoln Died which occupies one-twentieth of an acre opposite Ford's Theatre in Washington, D. C.

"More than 140 million visitors were recorded in National Park System areas in 1967. The annual attendance is expected to exceed 200 million in 1971 and 300 million by 1976.

"The national park idea, an American concept first expressed in the establishment of Yellowstone National Park, has been adopted by more than 90 nations. The National Park Service actively assists other countries throughout the world in establishing and expanding national park programs.

Allis-Chalmers' new 1970 model "Terra Tiger" with 18 horsepower engine. The new unit also features key electric starting as standard equipment, and streamlined body styling. The "Terra Tiger" with its watertight fiberglass body and big donut tires, is designed for hunters, fishermen, and campers. It also has numerous farm and commercial applications. Top speed on land is about 30 miles per hour, and from two to four miles per hour in the water.

ATV's - - -

W herever you want to go. Wherever you want to camp. Back in the deep woods, across the lake, over and beyond the mountain, through the swamp, anywhere in the roadless, trackless wilderness in rain, sleet, snow, summer or winter . . . an ATV will take you there.

ATV stands for All Terrain Vehicle and it also stands for an open door to the outdoors for many who couldn't, because of physical or age reasons, travel into the unspoiled forest, or up the side of a mountain or canyon.

Though it was developed for use by all outdoorsmen, hunters, fishermen, ranchers and sightseers, the ATV is an ideal means of travel for campers. It is perfect for two to four campers who want to get into a remote area and

Campers can get back into the deep woods through thick underbrush with Allis Chalmers Terra Tiger.

The Amphicat has super size balloon tires and drives with all six wheels for positive traction on ice and floats over snow. Can be winterized with windshield, canvas top and side curtains.

set up camp away from the usually crowded public campsites.

It is especially suitable for those who don't have enough time to get into peak physical condition, but would like to locate further "back in" without using up half of their vacation time hiking to and from camp.

Many Makes

Several makes of ATV's are now being offered. They are all of good quality, design and perform well. Each are made for special performance and vary in capacity. The following description will give an idea of what to expect from an ATV in the way of operation, loads, performance, what materials they are made of and how they are used:

1970 Eagle

The "Eagle" will climb 45-degree slopes, drive right through and over trees and brush, go through snow, sand and mud. The "Eagle" can also be driven right into streams and lakes since it is amphibious.

High 160 and 1 torque ratio gives "Eagle" the power to climb 45-degree slopes with full 1,000 pound payload. (Four adults and camping equipment). On level ground it is possible to cruise up to 20-mph in high gear.

The "Eagle" can be driven in either two or four wheel drive. It features low and high gear forward and reverse. Extra roomy interior allows two to sit in front and two in back. Storage is

open the door to all outdoors

Land a few tasty fish for a change in your camp fair. Drive to that hidden lake and right into it with the Terra Tiger. Giant tires and water tight body compartment give safe flotation and propulsion.

adequate and if necessary, it will pull optional trailer behind allowing the hauling of additional equipment.

12 H.P. Motor

Eagle's 12 h.p. power plant is mounted forward. There's no engine heating problem because the engine runs on low RPM and high torque. This also means minimum upkeep.

Centrifugal "V" belt and shaft drive and belts are self-adjusting. Electric rope pull start is featured, yet the engine can be hand-started with direct rope pull, if ever necessary.

Transporting is simple. Eagle can be hauled behind car on trailer or will fit in the back of any pick-up truck. Optional propeller will push Eagle up to 4-mph in water.

Specs

Specifications (standard) include: Articulated bodies with unobstructed undercarriage; all steel body with fiberglass upper body; 12 h.p. engine; 7½ gallon fuel capacity; electric rope pull start; hand operated disc brakes. Dimensions are 94" long, 50" high and 63" wide; 12 volt electrical system; 1,000 pound load capacity; 4-wheel positive traction drive and 2-wheel drive for cruising; also reverse. Steering system is automotive type; number of wheels is four; maximum gradeability is 45-degrees.

A wide range of optional convenience equipment is available for the Eagle. Vinyl top and side curtains, tire chains, dozer blade, carry-all trailer, lawn mower, wind-shield, pro-

Optional equipment with the Amphicat includes this trailer for transporting the unit on long trips to campgrounds, hunting areas or fishing trips.

This view of the Cushman "Trackster" show its capability of going through deep, loose sand. It is not designed to go over water without modification.

peller, roll bar, canoe carrier, winch and spark arrestor.

It is made by the Standard Engineering Company, Fort Dodge, Ia. 50501.

Most ATV's are equipped with wheels having balloon tires that aid in travel over rough ground, sand, mud and add to flotation capability. There are four to eight wheel models having heavy lugs or ridges on the tires to get better traction and to propel or aid propelling in water. A few models are equipped with caterpillar type tracks. Most bodies of these vehicles are made of high impact plastic and have a built-in flotation compartment.

The feature that makes travel over even the roughest terrain possible is the fact that the engines are geared to give maximum power without strain. This power factor reduces speed considerably and limits their road use. However, speed is not important as the primary use for ATV's is off road.

The Terra Tiger, made by Allis-Chalmers, has many features designed

The Cushman "Trackster" differs from most ATV's because it travels on tracks instead of tires. Actually it lays its own road and picks it up as it goes. This is a very safe type of vehicle and won't tip back or sideways when climbing steep hills.

to give better performance. Choice of two engines, one 10 hp and another with 18 hp.

Other features: Molded fiberglass hull is reinforced. Absorbs shocks. Can't rust or rot. Watertight integrity is maintained by the axle seals. 10 and 18 hp engines with plenty of power. Performance proven single cylinder, two-stroke, air-cooled design. Simple, no shift controls. Steering tiller, finger-tip throttle and brake give operator full, instant response. Positive 6 wheel drive transmits power to 6 super-soft flotation tires. Each steering clutch controls power to one side of the vehicle.

This is the "Eagle" all terrain vehicle. It is a 4-wheel type having a unique articulated body. The rear half is separated from the front allowing it to turn with contours and obstacles.

The Eagle is also amphibious. The rear seat arrangement makes it ideal for two duck hunters, or provides packing space for camp gear.

It can be used as either a two or four wheel drive and is available with options such as trailers, dozer blades and enclosures for rain or snow.

The Vesely Seirra Trail Boss with a 20 h.p. motor for all day operation. Is amphibious and has 6-wheel drive.

WEIGHT: 10 hp 400 lbs. 18 hp 600 lbs.

LOAD CAPACITY (Land): 600 lbs.

LOAD CAPACITY (Water): 600 lbs.

ENGINES: 10 and 18 hp. air cooled

TRANSMISSION: Torque Converter, Automatic Variable

SUSPENSION: Super Soft, Obstacle-absorbing tires

CONTROL: Single T-Bar Lever Control for Steering, Throttle and Brake

TIRES: Special High Flotation TERRA TIGER Tires with 2 lb. Air Pressure — 11x20" Tubeless

GRADEABILITY: Up to 45 degree inclines

DRIVE: Positive 6-wheel

SPEED: 10 hp 25 mph on land, 18 hp 30 mph on land, 4 mph on water

HEADLIGHT: Sealed beam, standard equipment

DIMENSIONS: 86" long; 54" wide; 37" high

WHEELBASE: 44"

TURNING RADIUS: Less than 4 feet

STARTING: Manual Recoil or electric

HULL: Waterproof with 11" to 18" freeboard

CAPACITY: Two passenger seating with 11 cubic feet of storage area for equipment

The "Trackster"

This is a new ATV manufactured by Cushman Motors. It represents a departure from the regular ATV's in as much as it travels on tracks, not on wheels. This track type provides a great degree of safety when moving sideways on steep grades. It will traverse snow, mud, sand and mountainous terrain. When equipped with a flotation modification and an outboard motor, it has limited use in the water.

The "go-anywhere" ATV has ample room for two passengers, plus a storage area. The fiberglass body is designed so that individual components can be quickly serviced. The air-cooled, two-cycle engine is coupled to hydrostatic transmissions. With its lightweight,

die-cast aluminum OMC 25-horsepower engine, the ATV reaches a speed of 16 m.p.h. Gasoline capacity is 10 gallons.

Belts Eliminated

Belts and chains have been eliminated by coupling the engine to the transmission by a drive shaft.

The operator controls speed by a T-handle. Also, there is a variable-speed governor. The driver increases speed by pushing the T-handle forward. When he twists the handle right or left, one track will go faster than the other, producing sensitive turning.

By slowly returning the handle to neutral, the driver slows down the tracks for braking. When the T-handle is neutral, both tracks are locked through the hydraulic system. Reverse is accomplished by releasing the neutral lockout lever and pulling the T-handle to the rear.

The vehicle "sping turns" within its own length by driving one track forward and the other in reverse. This allows the operator to wend his way through trees and up steep grades with ease.

The middle photo below shows another unique ATV . . . an eight wheeler. It is called the Pazzazz and gives a smooth ride into the most rugged areas. Bottom photo is the zippy Attex with six drive wheels. Has an exceptionally strong planetary gear transmission. Rear compartment is for third passenger or extra equipment.

Campers! Collect With a Camera

Be sure to bring a camera with you. Take home the mountains, rushing rivers, deep forests, wild flowers; the happy, sun tanned faces of your children. . . you can keep everything you cherish about camping and the outdoors with you throughout the year. . . on film.

Many campers add great interest and enjoyment by developing collecting hobbies. On their hikes through woods, over mountains and beside lakes and rivers they collect leaves, wild flowers, insects, rocks, semi-precious stones, edible roots, birds eggs and best of all many pleasant memories.

Some campers collect all the above and more, including bear, deer, moose, mountain sheep, fish, birds, people, mountains, lakes, rivers, deserts, valleys, forests and take everything home with them — on film.

There is no more rewarding phase of camping than that of recording the events and scenes of a memorable trip with either a still or movie camera, of capturing the carefree days of recreation on time-stopping film.

Simple or Complex

Taking photos on your camping trip can be about as simple or complicated as you want it to be. The primary concern should be for obtaining photos that will satisfy you and other family members.

The choice of cameras and accessories available today is almost unlimited as to performance and price. Easy to operate still cameras that produce excellent photos are offered at prices from 15 to 100 dollars. Those on the low end pricewise are basically "snapshot" types with fixed lenses and are adequate for taking snaps in bright sunlight within a range of eight to 15 feet in either color or black and white. They have flashbulb capability and drop-in loading ease, but nothing more.

As automatic features are added, the prices increase. In a range of prices from 25 to 75 dollars there will be such features as automatic focusing, electric light meter, automatic film advance and close-up taking to two feet included.

Quality Prints

Within their limitations, this group can be depended on for good quality prints and film slides that are clear and sharp. These cameras are well constructed, lightweight and can stand hard usage. They are not, however, as watertight and dustproof as is desirable, but with reasonable handling this should not present a problem.

Autoload

For a very fine camera in the medium price range a camper will find the recently introduced Bell & Howell Autoload series to be ideal. The most automatic model in the series is the Autoload 342 priced at $87.50 offered in an outfit that includes color film batteries and flashcube.

This model features automatic focusing accomplished with the touch of a button, cartridge film loading, automatic electric eye exposure control, and f/2.8 lens and a shutter that provides the right combination of lens opening and shutter speed from 1/30 to 1/500.

An electric film advance that positions the first frame upon loading, advances each frame after shooting and automatically winds up the film after the last exposure is included to prevent double exposures.

Electric Eye

The Bell & Howell Autoload 340 is an instant load outfit featuring a CdS electric eye that determines the correct lens opening and programs the shutter to the correct speed from 1/30 to 250, and provides zone focusing. Sells for $37.50.

The Autoload 341 outfit, also an instant-load type is the same as

Shown below are all three models of the Bell & Howell lower price series 240 and two models of the medium priced 35mm series.

The Model 342 above is a sturdy unit, simple to operate and lightweight. Shutter speeds from 1/30 to 1/500th.

Model 340 but has in addition the Focus-Matic feature for accuracy and indoor exposure control. It has an under exposure control in the bright-line viewfinder. Price $57.50.

Automatic 35mm

For a wider range of camping photos Bell & Howell offer two fully automatic 35mm cameras in different price ranges.

The Auto 35/2.8 camera is introduced at $69.50 and includes the exclusive Bell & Howell focusing system, Focus-Matic, a 40mm f/2.8 lens, a between-the-lens shutter with speeds that are programmed from 1/30 at f/2.8 to 1/250 at f/22, a bright-line viewfinder with shutter speed and flash-ready indicator, and an automatically rotating flash-cube socket.

SLR Model

For the camper who desires to obtain a fully automatic single-lens-reflex camera at a low price, the Bell & Howell Auto 35/Reflex (Model 237) is available at $159.50. This quality SLR camera offers a number of significant features:

Fully automatic CdS electric eye with manual exposure override for special lighting situations.

Thru-the-lens sensing and viewing.

Accepts ASA 25-400 film.

Precision Canon 50mm f/1.8 lens.

Interchangeable lens capability. Accepts new Canon 35mm f/3.5 wide-angle lens, offered at $49.50 with case and hood, the new Canon 95mm f/3.5 at $62.50 with case and hood, and the new Canon 125mm f/3.5 at $84.50 with case and hood.

Focal plane shutter from 1/8 to 1/500 plus B.

Has the Canon QL — Quick loading system.

Extremely bright viewfinder with special design micro-prism center for focusing.

Because there is so much activity connected with camping programs it lends itself especially well to movie taking. Costs are now within average budgets and technical know-how required to do a professional job is minimal. Even synchronized sound movies are possible with the new systems.

Movie Cameras

A line of high-quality compact super 8 movie cameras ideal for

Bell & Howell Model 372 super 8 movie camera.

Bell & Howell Model 375 Filmosound 8 movie camera.

New Bell & Howell Filmosound 8 projector, Model 468, and the new compact super 8 camera, Model 375, are used with the special cassette tape recorder to produce sound-synchronous home movies.

campers is available from Bell & Howell with prices starting at less than $50.

The new home-movie cameras offer the camper "super" compactness, all-new advanced styling, and a choice of models that have an unusually wide-range capability of movie-making options from macro-zoom photography to synchronized sound.

The Model 375 is a super 8 movie camera offered in the new compact style for less than $95. It will enable the user to obtain synchronized sound movies when used with the Filmosound 8 system. It can also be used for macro-zoom photography when used with an accessory wide-angle lens that will allow movie-making at less than 10" from the subject. There is also an accessory telephoto lens available. With these lenses, the camera is capable of a 4 to 1 range in focal lengths (8½mm to 34mm).

Auto focusing

The Model 375 super 8 cameras also feature the innovative automatic focusing system, called Focus-Matic. The system measures the distance between subject and camera lens when the user sights the camera at the feet of the person (or base of the object) being photographed. By pressing and releasing the control button located on the side of the camera, a reading of the distance in feet is recorded and the lens can be set accordingly. Focus-Matic uses principles of trigonometry to achieve its precise measurement.

Two ft. focus

Other features of the new Model 375 movie camera include: an f/2.8 lens; a 12.5 to 25mm zoom range; a normal lens that will focus down to two feet; automatic exposure control; large bright reflex viewing for accurate composition; under exposure signal visible in viewfinder when light level requires movie light; weighs just a shade over one pound and is compact, measuring only 3½" x 2¼" x 6⅞"; detachable chrome pistol grip included with the camera; and, it accepts accessory lenses. It is offered at a price of $94.95.

Two other super 8 movie cameras are available. The Model 374 has essentially all the features of the Model 375 with the exception that it has no synchronous-sound capability. It will, however, accept the wide-angle and telephoto lens accessories and is offered at a price $79.95.

The Model 372 camera is priced at $49.95. It offers an f/2.8 lens; an extremely large and bright viewfinder; automatic exposure control; under-exposure signal in viewfinder; detachable pistol grip; footage counter; and is the lightest and most compact of any of the three cameras introduced. It weighs only 13 ounces and measures just 3½" by 2¼" by 5¾".

Accessory lenses

The accessory lenses that can be used with either Models 374 or 375 include a wide-angle lens (8.5 to 17 mm) that focuses to less than 10" from the front of the lens and is offered at $19.95, and a telephoto (17 to 34mm) that also sells for $19.95. Lenses easily attach to the front of the camera lens.

Synchronous-sound movies can be obtained with the Bell & Howell Model 375 when used with the complete Filmosound 8 system which includes camera, cassette tape recorder and projector. It provides lip-synchronous-sound with movie equipment designed specifically for family use and family budgets.

Movie projectors

The Bell & Howell Model 468 home movie projector offers the unique capability of projecting either synchronous-sound movies or silent ones. This projector has all of the features currently available in other Bell & Howell Filmosound 8 projectors plus...

High-speed automatic rewind in seconds at the end of each reel of film. Movies can also be rejected and automatically rewound at any time during projection.

Bright f/1.2 lens with a 19-32 mm zoom range.

Advanced styling with a black cover and a pewter main frame.

Other significant features offered in the Filmosound 8 Model 468 projector include: variable speed control; accepts either super 8 or regular 8 film by a touch of a format selector lever; reel-to-reel threading; 400' film capacity; dial focusing; tilt control; and sturdy die-cast construction. The projector is offered at a price of $214.95. Bell & Howell Filmosound 8 projectors start at a price of $139.95.

With Filmosound 8, sound mov-

Bell and Howell Filmosound 8 projector, Model 468, with automatic rewind and super 8/regular film compatibility.

ies are obtained when the user has the complete Bell & Howell system. This includes a camera, sound synchronizing portable cassette tape recorder and the projector. The words and sounds of home movie subjects are recorded to match with every picture taken, and then, during projection, every word and sound played back on the tape recorder is matched with every movement on the screen.

STILL CAMERAS

Kodak offers five different models in the Instamatic series. They are primarily snapshot types and all have fixed focus lenses with the exception of Models 314 and 414 which can be set to take close-ups as near as two feet. In its normal setting the lens is in focus from six feet to infinity on these two models.

The Kodak Model 124 is the lowest price of all at $16.95. It takes flash, color and black and white snaps. Model 134 sells for $25.50. It features an electric eye exposure control, takes color, black and white and also uses flash cubes. Model 174 is priced at

$26.95. Main feature is an automatic film advance actuated by a spring motor. A single winding is enough for 12 pictures.

A Lumenized and color corrected Kodar f/8 lens is furnished with the Model 314 at $37.95. It has a close-up setting that is effective at two feet and snaps back to normal automatically. Signal in viewfinder indicates when flash is needed.

The Model 414 is the top of the Instamatic series and features a motorized film advance that permits taking pictures at the rate of one per second. It also has the two foot range adjustment and the automatic electric eye plus the viewfinder flash signal. Price is $47.95.

These types are limited in their scope of photo taking, mostly to close and medium distance snaps, but the quality of the prints and slides is very good. They are small and light in weight making them suitable for carrying in a backpack or duffle bag.

MOVIE CAMERAS

Kodak offers five models of easy to operate 8mm movie cameras. They range from a simple model with fixed lens to one having an electric eye, power zoom lens and reflex finder. All are compact, have the Instamatic loading feature, are battery driven and have a built in filter to allow using same film indoors or out.

Instamatic M22

Drop-in cartridge loading. Palm-size. Foldaway pistol grip. New slim design. New styling in satin-silver and textured black. Great movies with one setting. No need to focus. Illustrated exposure guide. Optical finder is bright, distortion-free. Built-in filter permits use of same film indoors or out. Battery driven—runs on only two AA-size batteries. *f*/2.7 lens, color-corrected and *Lumenized*.

Instamatic M24

CdS electric eye provides automatic exposure for movies indoors or outdoors. Viewfinder signal for insufficient light. Drop-in cartridge loading. Foldaway pistol grip. Optical finder is bright, distortion-free. Built-in filter permits use of same film indoors or out. Battery driven—runs on only two AA-size batteries. *f*/2.7 lens, color-corrected and *Lumenized*.

Instamatic M26

Faster lens gets brighter, sharper movies under broader range of lighting conditions. CdS electric eye provides automatic exposure control for indoor or outdoor movies. Viewfinder signal for insufficient light. Drop-in cartridge loading. Palm-size. Foldaway pistol grip. New slim design. New styling in satin-silver and textured black. Optical finder is bright, distortion-free. Built-in filter permits use of same film indoors or out. Battery driven—runs on only two AA-size batteries. *f*/1.8 lens is color-corrected and *Lumenized*.

Instamatic M28

Adds zoom at an eye-catching price. Focuses six feet to infinity. Zone focusing, too. Variable-power finder linked to zoom action. CdS electric eye provides automatic exposure indoors or out. Viewfinder signal is green while light is sufficient. Uses same film indoors or out. Runs on two AA-size batteries. Manual *f*/2.7 zoom lens (13-28mm) is color-corrected, *Lumenized*.

Instamatic M30

Extra-fast lens plus power zoom with fingertip control. Manual zoom, too! Reflex viewing shows what you're getting. No parallax worry. CdS electric eye provides automatic exposure for movies indoors or out. Viewfinder signal for insufficient light. Drop-in cartridge loading. Palm-size. Foldaway pistol grip. Scale focusing six feet to infinity. Zone-focusing, too! Built-in filter permits use of same film indoors or out. Runs on two AA-size batteries. *f*/1.9 power zoom lens (13-28mm) is color-corrected.

Instamatic M30

Instamatic M24

The Kodak Instamatic 134 is one of the low price models at about $25.

The Model 414 is the high price one in the Instamatic series. Has automatic features.

Single Lens Reflex

This type 35mm camera as offered by several importers and manufacturers is the ultimate in versatility. With a little experience a serious camper can get beautiful black and white prints, color prints and color slides of just about any phase of camping and outdoor life he desires.

These cameras are more expensive, but they are worth every dollar paid. One of the more important aspects of this type camera is that most of them will accept different type lenses. Bell & Howell's Canon, one of the best SLR's available, is offered with over 20 lenses ranging from a 19mm super wide angle to a 1000mm super telephoto.

The wide angle lenses are excellent for taking panoramas of breath-taking scenery and the telephoto's will let you get shots of wild animals from a distance without scaring them.

Model FT-QL of the Canon line is a fine choice for campers for several reasons. Although all cameras should be protected from dirt, moisture, jars and bumps, the Canon FT will withstand considerable rough handling and is dust and moisture proof.

A basic system which would provide leeway for the various camping conditions, scenery and background photos desired would be the FT Canon which comes with a 50mm f/1.4 lens. Add to this a 35mm wide angle lens and you would be able to get 90 per cent of the photos you wanted. For broadening the scope of photos, the ideal third lens would be a 200mm or 300mm zoom lens.

The Canon FT-QL also has many other featuses which make it a good camping companion. It has a behind the lens exposure meter which lets you determine the exact shutter and lens setting you need, in a matter of seconds. Shutter speeds are from 1 to 1/1000 second plus bulb. The QL in the name stands for quick load, a device permitting easy, fast loading and preventing threading failure. Film speed can be set to control the light meter.

Other suitable single lens reflex makes are the Mamiya/Sekor 1000 DTL and the Yashica TL-E and TL Electro X models. These are also 35mm models. They will accommodate various types of lenses with compatable mounting connections.

Yashica also offers a Model MAT 124, a twin lens reflex that takes 120 size film which is 2¼"x2¼". The second lens on this camera is the viewfinder. It projects the image on a ground glass and is viewed from the top.

Best feature is the electric exposure meter which consists of a pointer and forked needle. For the correct setting it is only necessary to adjust the shutter and lens opening unitl the needle rests between the fork. It is a good camera for camp, but a bit too bulky for backpacking. For detailed information and prices of any of these cameras check your local photographic dealer or write direct to the manufacturer.

This is the best selling FT SLR Canon 35mm. Top. Middle photo shows the FT and Pellix Canon models in new black professional finish.

Yashica TL-E

Yashica MAT 124

New Projector Holds More Slides in Less Space

All is not over when you arrive home from a refreshing camping trip in the great, clean outdoors. There's still a part of it to look forward to . . . the showing of the hundreds of slide photos you've taken.

One of the newest projectors available seems to have many desireable features especially for those who will build a large library of slides over the years.

A completely new system for the showing and storage of 2" x 2" color slides is being offered by Bell & Howell.

Key to this exclusive slide projection innovation is the utilization of a slide-containing cartridge termed Slide Cube instead of trays.

Each Bell & Howell Slide Cube cartridge holds up to 40 slides and is so compact that 16 cubes containing 640 slides can be stored in the same area that would be taken up by just one round tray holding 80 slides.

The cost of color slide storage has also been substantially reduced with the Slide Cube cartridges to approximately a penny per slide, as compared with an average of three cents per slide with a tray system.

The relative low cost of the Slide Cube cartridges will enable the user to keep all his slides cataloged and projector-ready in cartridges indexed by subject or category.

Four new Bell & Howell Slide Cube projectors are available in prices ranging from $112.50 to $184.50.

With all the new projectors, drop-in loading is a significant feature. Up to 40 color slides can be loaded into a Slide Cube cartridge in seconds, and the cartridge can then be easily and surely placed onto the projector. Everything else is accomplished with push-button ease.

Slides are gravity fed from the Slide Cube cartridge to a circular handling system which takes each individual slide past a preview/edit station, then moves it on to the projection station, and on back to gently drop the slides into a slide-collection chamber. At the end of a slide show, the user simply returns the slides to the empty cartridge by lifting the lever in the slide-collection chamber.

The preview/edit station on the new Slide Cube projector allows the user to preview each slide before projection and to edit slides for proper orientation or sequence: An exclusive scan/search feature is also incorporated into the new projectors.

When the user holds the cycle button down, the slides will continue to pass through the system without showing on the screen. The illuminated previewer and the search system enable the user to view and skip slides without the audience knowing it. The entire Slide Cube cartridge of 40 slides can be scanned in about 30 seconds.

A simple but highly effective feature common to all Bell & Howell Slide Cube projectors is the unique way the user is able to line up the first slide on the screen. A turn of the lens elevation knob is all that is needed to elevate the lens up to a full 20 degrees. No longer is there any need to use magazines or books to prop up a projector.

The Slide Cube projectors represent a sharp departure from the "hardware look" common with this type of equipment. They are handsomely styled in wood-grain, black and chrome and measure only 9"x9"x8". They are designed so that a projector can be left out in most any room setting and are compact enough to fit on a book shelf.

All four models utilize the innovative Slide Cube cartridges; feature drop-in loading; have the same exterior design; offer the exclusive scan and search feature; provide the unique 20 degree elevation control; use a 50-hour quartz-halogen lamp for brilliant, long-life projection; and have both slide and lamp ejectors.

The Model 977Q sells for $112.50 and additionally offers remote control, helical focusing and a 4" f/3.5 Luminar lens system. Model 978Q lists for $124.50 and offers automatic focusing. The Model 981Q also has automatic focusing and a remote control with a forward/recall provision. It sells for $159.50. The deluxe model offered at $184.50 is the Model 981Z, and it has a 3½" to 4½" f/3.5 zoom lens in addition to the automatic focusing and remote control.

As a slide projector system, there are a number of accessories that can be added to the Bell & Howell Slide Cube projectors. A deluxe storage top that replaces the standard one holds nine Slide Cube cartridges (360 slides). It has a detachable carrying handle and comes complete with the nine cartridges for $24.95.

Specialty Products for Camping

The new innovations in the camping products field are more than gimmicks or novelties. They are designed and produced to fill some actual need in the broad area of camping and its allied activities.

Products shown on these pages are the result of experience and the creative ability needed to manufacture a unit that would serve to overcome some problem or to make a camping journey easier and more pleasant.

Some items will catch on and become a standard in camping. Others though having much merit will not meet acceptance and will disappear from the market.

All are interesting and seem to have great possibilities. Look them over. Perhaps there's one that will be ideal for some purpose you have in mind. Write the manufacturer and get the details. Find out how you can put it to good use.

Visit any sporting goods store or leaf through an outfitter's catalog and you will see a galaxy of new tools for the camper. Some of these are tools that he can handily use at home as he makes preparation for a camping trip.

Whatever the camper's problem with gear or supplies, the problem doesn't last long. Observant manufacturers quickly find solutions.

A common problem with campers has to do with canvas. A rip in canvas can put an otherwise perfectly usable packbag or tent on the shelf for months — until one gets around to figuring out how to mend it. There are ways, and then there are ways. But one of the best ways to mend such a rip is with a new tool developed by United Shoe Machinery Corporation, Reading, Pennsylvania. Pictured here is a problem being corrected by USM's new Thermogrip electric glue gun.

A New Canvas

Repair Tool

A rip in canvas poses a repair problem.

Hot melting, quick drying glue is used through the electric glue gun, which needs only three minutes to heat up. It bonds canvas securely, giving waterproof protection.

The patch is also filmed with Thermogrip glue.

Immediately upon applying the glue to both the patch and areas surrounding the rip, the patch is placed over the rip and the bond is secured in less than 60 seconds. The hot tip of the electric glue gun may be run over the patch to further solidify the bond.

Unique amphibious camper trailer

Goes Anywhere in the Woods

Like to hit the trail for a few days of woodland adventure? Load up your family and pack up your NaviCamper. It'll carry a 500 pound load and go anywhere you can pull it.

Find your spot and set up in less than 10 minutes. Big, foam rubber cushioned seats turn into soft beds. Room for a family of six. Zippered entrance, screened windows with flaps and water proof sides and top. Can't beat that for camping comfort and convenience.

Navi Camper with pontoons lowered for water use is beached for a shore lunch. It is 18 feet long.

With plastic pontoons in traveling position. When sides and back are folded in and the top lowered unit is ready for road.

Does Anything on Water

From trailer to pontoon boat with an easy cranking action. NaviCamper takes to lakes, rivers or hunting sloughs. It skims across the water in a smooth plane hitting speeds over 26 mph with a 60 hp motor.

Pulls waterskiers with ease and takes sharp turns with quick, cat like maneuvers. Plenty of soft seating space for a party of fishermen or a boatload of party lovers. And if the weather takes a bad turn, roll down the canvas curtains for a snug, dry trip home.

Trailer has back porch for hauling

The Trans-Por-Teer has a 14 foot boat stowed on the "porch" in the upper photo. In the middle photo below an all terrain vehicle is shown in unloading position. Bottom photo illustrates how snowmobiles, equipped with front wheels for summer, can be carried.

The words "unique" and "innovative" are quite often over-used, but in the case of Trans-Por-Teer's new Camper-Hauler, these words are an understatement!

Not only does this Camper-Hauler haul — has a big cabin area, magnificent pulling ability — but is also superbly constructed.

You can have your 'something-to-do' when you get to 'where-you're-going' with this outfit. It will carry a Dune Buggy, a 14-foot boat, an ATV (All Terrain Vehicle). or two Snow-mobiles, or up-to six Trail·Bikes, and probably a thousand other things that haven't even thought of yet.

Until now, when you had another outdoor hobby in addition to camping, you had to buy a truck and truck-camper, plus a trailer to haul your gear. Or you could buy a truck for the gear then buy and pull a camper behind it for living.

With Trans-Por-Teer's Camper-Hauler, all you need is your gear and the family car.

The Camper-Hauler has an over-all length of 25 feet and features a fully insulated coach with above the floor plumbing to prevent freezing in winter — an 11,000 B.T.U. heater output — a 30 gallon water tank — and a six gallon gas water heater.

This Trans-Por-Teer also has a standard three cubic feet gas/electric refrigerator — a stool/shower combination — a combination 12v-110v electrical system — and sleeping accommodations for four with an optional bunk that will provide sleeping space for two additional people.

Portable Boats

**for cartop or in trunk storage
add great fun to any camping trip.**

• Sometime during almost every camping trip you'll be near water . . . a river, lake or pond. Many times there are no boat rental facilities available, but if you have your own on the top of the car or in the trunk you can fish or sail anywhere you wish.

There are many fine boats made today that are ideal for campers. Some fit on top of tent campers, other are car toppers. If you know in advance that you will be on or near a river one of the inflatable rubber boats would be ideal. These are better in rivers because they will go over rocks and snags without hanging, and if you get into extremely shallow water you can get out and pull them to deeper water with a minimum of effort. In any case you'll have a lot more fun if you take a boat of some kind.

Bombard inflatable boats stow in trunk of car. They are completely safe and comfortable. Seven models range in size from 8 ft. for four people, to 15 ft. that will accommodate 7 to 8 people. Prices are $265 up. From Gemico Corp.

This is a downriver kayak made by Old Town Canoe. It can be used in lakes or rivers, is lightweight and can be carried on top of car.

This is a new sailboard made by Gemico Corporation. It is 11 ft. long and weighs only 50 lbs. It is made of fiberglass and has a Dacron sail. A fine boat for sailing on a warm afternoon.

Equipment for fishing 'way back in.

fishing is usually a lot better in the deep woods but you have to travel light

Fishing is great sport by itself, but when it is used to supplement camp fare it is even more important. It isn't necessary to take along a giant tackle box filled with lures and other terminal tackle and a long rod. You can now buy pack rods and telescoping rods that are light and take only 12 to 18 inches of space. One of these plus a small reel and two or three lures and a couple of hooks are all you need. To go back in and get enough fish for the evening meal.

This telescoping spinning rod is called the "Handle Rod" made by the Baker Manufacturing Co.

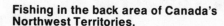

A baitcasting rod that telescopes to only 12"

Fishing in the back area of Canada's Northwest Territories.

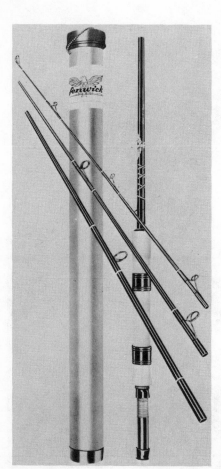

This is a Fenwick combination fly/spin pack rod. It comes in four pieces 22" long and weighs 14 ounces with tube. It is 7 ft. long when assembled and will mount a fly or spinning reel.

This vehicle is named Moto Brousse. It is a rugged 4 wheeler designed to get back into rough country with equipment and two passengers. It is perfect for getting to good fishing spots with ease.

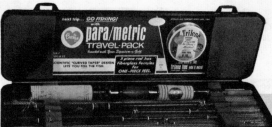

This five piece travel pack rod is one of several models offered by Berkley. Shown is a spinning rod with and lightweight case.

Here's a fine catch of big northern pike taken from Lac La Ronge in Saskatchewan, Canada.

A New Frontier

This Year
50 Million Campers
Will Invade the Outdoors!

Spruce knob, highest point in West Virginia.

Millions Camping:

Once upon a time the wild side was where the forests began. Wild life referred to the inhabitants there. And "wild, man, wild" was the way an intrepid woodsman might have described his face-to-face encounter with a bobcat or a she-bear searching for her lost cub.

It was always the restless ones who first stepped across to the wild side, who blazed the trails that others, a little less daring, would take. These were frontiersmen who knew the joy in probing beyond the frontier. They were men who held a strangely compelling empathy toward what they had never seen, but knew was out there.

Today's campers are a little like that. They are eager to explore, to follow the strange calls that emanate from forest and field and to touch the face of nature and feel the life there.

Daniel Boone was one of the restless ones whose senses were in tune with the siren calls of the wild — the thousand sounds of the night, the sudden quiet when a predator prowled, the shifting of the winds signaling a change in the weather, the smells of a campfire. It was said that Boone grew restless when duty required that he spend some time in the settlement, around people, and that his soul hungered for the primitive wilderness, for the tranquility and solitude it brought, the excitement and adventure it gave.

Separating fact from fiction in the lengend that has grown around the reputation of this backwoodsman is well nigh impossible. But it is fair to say that much of the fiction about Daniel Boone contains a lot of fact; and it is equally apparent that the historical facts have been enhanced for posterity by some delightful fictions. We do know for sure that he was a man who had a gnawing curiosity about what lay on the other side of the river, or just beyond the mountain. In that respect, he was like most of us.

50 Million Campers

This year, perhaps as many as 50 million Americans will take to the hills and mountains, the seashores and deserts, to live there for a time, to get as close to the heritage left by Boone and his kind as is possible in today's pressure-packed, fast-moving world. These adventure seekers are campers who have discovered a new frontier in this ages-old outdoor activity. They have a gnawing curiosity about what lies on the other side of the river, or just beyond the mountain.

In one sense, modern day camping is a phenomenal development. In Daniel Boone's time perhaps *four out of 100 Americans lived in towns,* and the towns themselves were quite primitive compared even with today's most isolated settlements. Nobody lived very far from the great outdoors. But now seven out of ten Americans live in the cities, a migration statistic largely accumulated in recent decades. It seems somewhat illogical, therefore, that so many millions would harbor a burning desire to get away from the comforts and conveniences for which, in most cases, they have worked and struggled to achieve.

New Appreciation

But the plushiest dwelling, the myriad comforts and the convenience of the push button — all identified with a modern, organized society — have not yet taken away man's affinity to the natural world into which he was born. And, in recent years, as more of his kind have clustered together in cities, becoming more and more removed from the wide open spaces, he has developed a new awareness of what he is missing, a new appreciation for the forests and mountains and streams that he seldom sees.

This accounts in part for the fact that most any night of the year will see more than one million Americans "camping out." Until recently this was considered a fair estimate only of the number camping on any given night of the "warm months" camping season. But now the camping season is every season. Indeed, winter camping is growing so fast in popularity that, in some areas, the more conventional types are being threatened in the ratings.

Family Affair

Camping today is a family affair, so much so that it has become the fastest growing family recreation — worldwide. There are no age restrictions. Campers come from every walk of life and their reasons for camping are innumerable.

Not too many years ago, campers, in the main, were rugged males whose leaky tents and improvised shelters, along with bad food and insect bites, were considered necessary evils to the main enjoyment of hunting and fishing. There was a time, too, in the early days of the automobile, when a tent shelter and cooking utensils were considered essential for long-distance drives of a hundred miles or more. But camping has changed and so have the campers. Today's camping is a relaxing and happy affair, and many have concluded that it is the finest kind of outdoor fun.

500,000 Improved Campsites

On the North American continent are roughly 500,000 improved campsites where family camping may be enjoyed in comfort and safety. Most of these cater to campers whose shelters may be anything from a two-man thent to an ultra-modern motor home costing $35,000 or more.

Some 60 percent of the improved campsites open to the public are privately owned. The others are in the national parks, national forests, state and provincial parks and on other government lands set aside, at least in part, for recreational purposes.

For the camper who finds these "improved" campgrounds a little too crowded there are the wilderness areas and the wilderness trails where he may enjoy unrolling his sleeping bag far removed from his fellow humans and their modern tents and trailers. Fortunately, there still is a choice, and all types of campers can find the locale and degree of solitude for which they are looking.

Both government and private enterprise in recent years have set in motion programs and plans to provide better camping facilities and more of them. The thousands of new campsites are only a partial result of this effort. Adding more improved facilities requires also that more protection be given to the primitive areas adjacent. It is to the credit of the various outdoor-oriented government agencies, private groups and camping-related businesses that a sizable degree of cooperation and understanding has been achieved in assuring this protection.

Comfortable Campgrounds

One result is a galaxy of new campgrounds with comfort and convenience facilities rivaling those at home. Another is the abundance of new and improved gear catering to every conceivable type of camping. Manufacturers have refined outdoor shelters — tents, trailers, pickups, motor homes — to the point of marvel.

No longer does camping have to be a drudgery, even in its most simple form. And through studied effort there has come about a kind of zoning — regulations and boundaries designed to keep the wild *wild* and the campground moderninity applicable to user preferences.

Many improved campgrounds offer hot showers, flush toilets, coin launderies, camp stores, movies for the kids and electrical outlets. National parks and state parks more and more are equipping their campgrounds with these conveniences. And usually they are well staffed with rangers, naturalists and others knowledgeable in what campers may have need of or may appreciate.

In a growing number of state parks are swimming pools, tennis courts, golf courses and playgrounds. These parks have been outfitted as resorts, admittedly to the disappointment of those campers preferring the outdoors left pretty much as nature made it. But such parks, outfitted primarily with families in mind, have retained the outdoor emphasis and do offer convenient and pleasant campsites.

Appeal to Women

All of these improvements naturally appeal to the wife and mother, who for years shunned camping because she saw her "dread" home chores being compounded by wilderness inconveniences. Now, thanks to campground luxuries and fingertip controls of the gadgets in camping trailers and such, Mom has taken to camping in a big way. So has the whole family.

Today a camper may travel to any part of the United States or Canada and find attractive, convenient and comfortable campsites awaiting him. In addition to the thousands of prepared facilities in the state, provincial and national parks and forests, there are many good campgrounds operated by cities and counties, and also by other federal agencies such as the Bureau of Reclamation and the Corps of Engineers.

Private enterprise likewise has done a remarkable job of increasing camping facilities by building thousands of campgrounds, a rapidly increasing number of which serve the traveling public in the manner of motels. Some belong to chains that issue printed directories and confirm reservations by teletype or telephone. Many provide such travel conveniences as grocery stores, heated swimming pools, equipped playgrounds for the youngsters, complete hookups for water, sewer and electricity, recreation rooms, hot meals and such other special services as the traffic demands in a given area.

Outdoor Ghetto

If the new commercial campgrounds for travelers and vacationers don't offer enough outdoor activities to suit the avid camper, they do satisfy many. Some are located near natural attractions and recreation areas.

Interestingly, a growing number of conservation-minded campers see the growth of private campgrounds as a partial answer to the threat of our most popular national parks and forests be-

This family is camped on the shores of Navajo Lake in a peaceful mountain area in Utah. Big advantage is that you can vary the camp menu with tasty fresh caught fish.

coming outdoor ghettos if too much of their territory is given over to camping.

It is argued that private enterprise may be able to better provide outdoor living facilities on the fringe areas beyond the park and forest boundaries, as indeed is being done in some places. Particularly is this seen as an answer to the needs of those whose camping shelters are on wheels.

Such are the problems brought about by the camping boom. But a boom also attracts solutions by new methods, new equipment and, in the case of camping, new outdoor facilities and areas to enjoy.

So fast has modern-day camping grown that more than $1 billion are spent each year on recreational vehicles alone. Additional millions are spent on towing them to and from the campgrounds, on overnight fees and on such necessities as food.

Tents Too

Of course, millions of campers use other shelters, consisting of every type from simple tents to deluxe motor homes. Interestingly, the tent is far from being on the decline. To the contrary, tent camping is more popular than ever, and many are the campers, including whole families, who would not consider any other type of shelter. "If you're not tenting, you're not camping," is their argument.

In this group are the wilderness campers, backpackers and the like who head for remote areas where vehicles ordinarily don't intrude. They get there, together with all their gear and supplies, usually on their own two feet.

Some travel by horseback, some by canoe. They must provide, through their own labor and ingenuity, certain basic necessities of camp. At the end of the trail they don't find prepared fireplaces, picnic tables and flush toilets. But they do find many challenges to their pioneer instincts.

The campsite must be carefully selected, cleared and laid out; a source of water must be located. There is wood to gather, a fire to build, water to boil for drinking, supper to prepare, clothing to wash and dry, sanitation to take care of and, finally, a little first aid for blisters, insect bites, scratches and similar irritations.

That's all part of the challenge, says the wilderness camper, who considers himself a completely separate breed from those he labels "pampered campers." But he will be quick to add that his lot also has changed rather dramatically in recent years.

He hikes in the best boots ever, wears the most comfortable (in any climate) clothing technology can produce, eats nourishing and tasty hot meals, pre-packaged dry and needing only water and heat in preparation, and he packs it all in light but sturdy gear scientifically designed and manufactured.

Light Sleeping Bag

This modern wilderness camper eas-ily carries a lightweight tent and a sleeping bag to assure both protection from the elements and complete comfort at night. His battery-powered light enables him to enjoy a bedtime chapter in the paperback he brought along; or, if he prefers, he can get the latest news and weather on his transistor radio. No pampered camper he, not quite.

Wilderness campers and others sticking to the more simple camping methods are better outfitted than ever for most any kind of outdoor adventure. In addition, many begin their wilderness sojourn at a base camp which in all likelihood is a vehicle camper parked at some improved campground.

In a very real sense, camping has provided a new frontier in human relations. As one camper put it, "If all the leaders of the world would gather around a campfire in the Rockies on a cool night and eat stew together, wars would be ended. Men cannot be angry under such soul-satisfying conditions."

Best of All

In one way or another, most campers will agree that the best thing about camping is that it is soul-satisfying. Those who camp will tell you that their fellow campers all seem to be interesting people, unselfish and relaxed and warm, and easy to know.

A GLOSSARY OF CAMPING TERMS

Backpacking
A type of camping, usually in the back country, which necessitates the camper's carrying all of his supplies and gear and reaching his destination under his own power.

Bottled gas
Butane or propane gas used for cooking and lighting and carried in cylinders or portable tanks.

Camper
A shorter term for pickup camper or truck camper.

Campground
A designated area comprising several to many permanent campsites.

Camp kitchen
A portable unit containing food, cooking utensils and all that is necessary for meal preparation.

Camp-out
A formally planned camping trip, usually by a club or organization.

Campsite
A designated site, usually in a campground, accommodating one family or one single-unit group.

Chuck box
Same as camp kitchen, but more often improvised from what is available.

Cooler
An insulated box or jug, designed to hold ice, in which food or drink may be preserved for later use.

Cottage tent
A popular family-style tent, an adaptation of the wall tent.

Coupling
The ball-and-socket connection for an automobile and trailer.

Ditching
Digging a trench at the campsite, usually to effect water run-off during heavy rain.

Down
Insulation plucked from geese or ducks and used in top-quality sleeping bags and winter outdoor clothing.

Drill
A comparatively inexpensive material used in tent making.

Duck
One of the more expensive and long lasting materials used in tent making.

Duluth
The name given to the most popular form of pack used by canoe campers. It is made of canvas, preferably waterproofed duck, and usually measures about 25 inches in length and 15 to 20 inches wide.

Dumping station
Facilities at larger campgrounds and some other places providing for the emptying of recreational vehicle holding tanks.

Dutch oven
A cooking container made of cast iron and designed for use over an open fire, considered by many outdoorsmen as the best single piece of cooking gear.

Fire starters
Inflammable materials, sometimes commercially prepared, for use in starting wood fires.

Fire trails
Roads and trails maintained on forest lands to enable fire fighters and equipment to quickly reach forest fires.

Freeze-dry
A method for processing and preserving foods to make them lightweight and easy to reconstitute in camp.

Generator
The vaporizing chamber on a gasoline stove or lantern, but not necessary on units using disposable fuel cylinders.

Grill
Any metal rack mounted over a fire on which are placed cooking utensils.

Ground cloth
A waterproofed cloth placed on the ground under a sleeping bag or a tent floor.

Guy line
An adjustable rope for maintaining tautness in a tent roof or wall.

Hard top
A designation used for travel trailers and, more recently, for tent trailers with hard tops.

Holding tank
A tank built into some recreational vehicles designed to hold refuse from the kitchen and bathroom areas until a dumping station is reached.

Hookup
Refers to electrical, water and sewer connections at improved campgrounds.

Improved campsite
A permanent site at a campground which provides such facilities as picnic table, fireplace or grill, running water and bathroom.

Insulation
Type and amount of material used in determining comfort ranges in sleeping bags and outdoor clothing.

Latrine
Basically a short ditch dug at a primitive campsite and used temporarily for bathroom purposes.

Minimotor home
A smaller and less luxurious motor home, with motor home basics nonetheless.

Motor home
A luxury type, self-contained living unit mounted on a truck chassis.

Mummy bag
A tapered sleeping bag.

Pack animals
Horses, mules or donkeys used to carry camping gear and supplies into wilderness areas.

Pack frame
Usually a lightweight metal frame with shoulder straps to which is attached a camper's pack. The frame keeps the pack from resting against the bearer's back.

Packsack
One of several designed canvas containers used by backpackers and hikers for carrying their necessities.

Pad
A thin, lightweight mattress usually made of foam rubber that many backpackers prefer to air mattresses.

Pickup camper
A camping unit mounted on the bed of a pickup truck.

Playground
An area designated for games and fun within the occupied campsite.

Poncho
A garment of many uses, the principal one being to protect from rain.

Poplin
A fabric used both for tent making and lightweight outdoor clothing.

Pop tent
An igloo-shaped tent that pops up like an umbrella.

Portage
Refers to the manual transporting of canoes and gear from one body of water to another. Also refers to a designated trail over which the canoeist carries his belongings from one body of water to another.

Prepared foods
Usually refers to freeze-dry or dehydrated foods that need only water and heat in campsite meal preparation.

Primitive
Areas where no comfort improvements have been provided.

Private campground
Usually refers to campgrounds privately owned but operated commercially for the general public. May also refer to campgrounds owned and operated by individuals or groups for their private use.

Reflector oven
An open oven with a baking shelf mounted between upper and lower slanted sides, all designed to reflect heat from the flames of a facing fire.

RVI
Recreational Vehicle Institute, the guardian of standards for the recreational vehicle industry.

Self-contained
Refers to recreational vehicles containing bathroom facilities, holding tanks, water supplies and power sources.

Site
A campsite

Slide
A tension adjuster on tent guy lines.

Slide-in camper
A removable truck camper

Tent trailer
A camping trailer whose walls, and sometimes the roof, are made of tent fabrics.

Trail tent
Another name for pack tents, mountain tents, backpacking tents. These tents are lightweight, compact and durable.

Travel trailer
An enclosed trailer, usually of metal, seldom measuring more than 30 feet in length and primarily for recreation.

Trenching
Same as ditching.

Truck camper
Same as pickup camper.

Tumpline
A simple band about 3 inches wide and about 18 inches long that is attached to two corners of a pack and looped around the front of the head, all designed to shift part of the pack weight to the head when the shoulders become weary.

Umbrella tent
Probably the most popular tent style because it is easy to transport and is easy to erect. The name comes from its umbrella shape.

Walk-in site
A campsite which is reached only by foot.

Wall tent
One of the oldest tent styles that is still popular. Its straight walls and high roof provide ample floor space and head room.

Water box
A wooden or metal box provided with openings and anchored in a stream or lake for use as a food cooler.

White water
A name for streams in which the water flows rapidly downward, creating foam and whitecaps. A favorite of experienced canoeists and raft adventurers.

Wilderness
Generally means those areas in national forests and national parks into which no motor vehicles or other "civilized" improvements may be taken. These areas are reached only by foot, canoe or horseback.

Windbreak
A natural or improvised barrier to prevailing winds, an important consideration in desert camping especially.

Wing tent
Basically a square tent with a wing-like fly extended beyond each corner, high at two corners, low at the other two.

WHERE TO WRITE FOR MORE INFORMATION

This Canadian campground is in Nova Scotia overlooking a bay on the Atlantic Ocean.

STATE PARKS

Alabama

Bureau of Publicity and Information, Montgomery 36104
Division of State Parks, Department of Conservation, Montgomery 36104

Alaska

State Division of Highways, P. O. Box 1841, Juneau 99801
Division of Lands, Department of Natural Resources, 334 Sixth Avenue, Anchorage 99503

Arizona

See listings in federal government sections.

Arkansas

Arkansas Publicity and Parks Commission, State Capitol Building, Little Rock 72201

California

Public Information Office, Department of Parks and Recreation, P. O. Box 2390, Sacramento 95811

Colorado

Colorado Game, Fish and Parks Department, 6060 Broadway, Denver 80216
Colorado Visitors Bureau, 225 West Colfax Avenue, Denver 80202
Colorado Department of Highways, 4201 East Arkansas Avenue, Denver 80222

Connecticut

State Park and Forest Commission, Hartford 06115

Delaware

Delaware State Development Department, Dover 19901

Florida

Florida Development Commission, 107 West Gaines Street, Tallahassee 32304
Florida Park Board, 101 West Gaines Street, Tallahassee 32304

Georgia

Department of State Parks, 7 Hunter Street, S. W., Atlanta 30334

Hawaii

State Parks Director, Department of Land and Natural Resources, 465 South King Street, Honolulu 96813

Idaho

Idaho State Department of Commerce and Development, Capitol Building, Boise 83701

Illinois

Illinois Department of Conservation, 102 State Office Building, Springfield 62706

Indiana

Tourist Division, Department of Commerce, Room 334, State House, Indianapolis 46204
Department of Natural Resources, 612 State Office Building, Indianapolis 46204

Iowa

State Conservation Commission, East Seventh and Court Avenue, Des Moines 50309

Kansas

Kansas Department of Economic Development, State Office Building, Topeka 66612
Kansas Park and Resources Authority, 801 Harrison Street, Topeka 66612
Forestry, Fish and Game Commission, Box 1028, Pratt 67124

Kentucky

Division of Tourist and Travel, Department of Public Information, Capitol Annex Building, Frankfort 40601

Louisiana

Louisiana Tourist Development Commission, Box 44291, Baton Rouge 70804
State Parks and Recreation Commission, Old State Capitol, P. O. Drawer 1111, Baton Rouge 70801

Maine

Maine Forest Service, Forest Recreation Development, Augusta 04330
Department of Economic Development, State House, Augusta 04330

Maryland

Department of Forests and Parks, State Office Building, Annapolis 21404

Massachusetts

Department of Natural Resources,

100 Cambridge Street, Boston 02202

Michigan

Department of Conservation, Stevens T. Mason Building, Lansing 48926

Minnesota

Minnesota Vacations, 57 West Seventh Street, St. Paul 55102

Director, Division of State Parks, Centennial Building, St. Paul 55101

Division of Lands and Forestry, Minnesota Department of Conservation, State Capitol, St. Paul 55101

Mississippi

Travel Department, Mississippi Agricultural and Industrial Board,

Parksville Lake seen from new road leading to Chilhowee Recreation area, Cherokee N.F., Tennessee.

1504 State Office Building, Jackson 39201

Mississippi Park System, 1104 Woolfolk, State Office Building, Jackson 39201

Missouri

Missouri Division of Commerce and Industrial Development, 803 Jefferson Building, Jefferson City 65101

Missouri State Conservation Commission, Farm Bureau Building, Highway 50 West, Jefferson City 65101

Missouri Department of Conservation, P. O. Box 180, Jefferson City 65101

Montana

State Highway Commission, Helena 59601

Nebraska

Nebraska Game, Forest Station and Parks Commission, State Capitol, Lincoln 68509

Nevada

Department of Economic Development, Carson City 89701

New Hampshire

Department of Economic Development, Concord 03301

New Jersey

Department of Conservation and Economic Development, 520 East State Street, Trenton 08609

New Mexico

State Park and Recreation Commission, P. O. Box 1147, Santa Fe 87501

New York

State Department of Commerce, 112 State Street, Albany 12207

North Carolina

Division of State Parks, Department of Conservation and Development, Raleigh 27602

Travel and Promotion Division, Department of Conservation and Development, Raleigh 27602

North Dakota

North Dakota Travel Department, State Capitol Building, Bismarck 58501

Ohio

Ohio Turnpike Commission, 681 Prospect Street, Berea 44017
Division of Parks and Recreation, Department of Natural Resources, 1500 Dublin Road, Columbus 43212
Development Department, 65 South Front Street, Columbus 43216

Oklahoma

Oklahoma Industrial Development and Park Department, 500 Will Rogers Memorial Building, Oklahoma City 73105

Oregon

Travel Information Division, Oregon State Highway Department, Salem 97310

Pennsylvania

Department of Forests and Waters, State Capitol Building, Harrisburg 17101

Rhode Island

Rhode Island Development Council, Roger Williams Building, Hayes Street, Providence 02908

South Carolina

Department of Parks, Recreation and Tourism, P.O. Box 1358, Columbia 29202

South Dakota

Department of Game, Fish and Parks, Pierre 57501

Tennessee

Division of State Parks, Tennessee Department of Conservation, 2611 West End Avenue, Nashville 37203
Public Relations Division, Tennessee Game and Fish Commission, Doctors Building, Nashville 37219

Texas

Texas Parks and Wildlife Department, Reagan Building, Austin 78701

Travel and Information Division, Texas Highway Department, P. O. Box 5064, Austin 78703

Utah

Division of Parks and Recreation, Department of Natural Resources, 132 South Second West, Salt Lake City 84101

Vermont

Vermont Department of Highways, Montpelier 05602

Virginia

Virginia Department of Conservation and Economic Development, 911 East Broad Street, Richmond 23219
Commission of Game and Inland Fisheries, P. O. Box 1642, Richmond 23213
Division of State Parks, 1108 East Main Street, Richmond 23219

Washington

State Parks and Recreation Commission, 522 South Franklin, Olympia 98501

West Virginia

Department of Commerce, State Capitol, Charleston 25305

Wisconsin

State Highway Commission, State Office Building, 1 West Wilson Street, Madison 53703
Wisconsin Conservation Department, Box 450, Madison 53701

Wyoming

Wyoming Travel Commission, 2320 Capitol Avenue, Cheyenne 82001

BUREAU OF LAND MANAGEMENT

Any regional office, or Bureau of Land Management, U. S. Department of the Interior, Washington, D. C. 20240

BUREAU OF RECLAMATION

Send 20 cents to Superintendent of Documents, U. S. Government Printing Office, Washington, D. C. 20402, and ask for a copy of *Reclamation's Recreation Opportunities.*

CORPS OF ENGINEERS

U. S. Army Corps of Engineers, U. S. Defense Department, Washington, D. C. 20315

NATIONAL FORESTS

Headquarters Office, Forest Service, Department of Agriculture, Washington, D. C. 20250
Or, contact the nearest local office of the Forest Service for state forestry departments. Regional Forest Service offices are located in Missoula, Montana; Denver, Colorado; Albuquerque, New Mexico; Ogden, Utah; San Francisco, California; Portland, Oregon; Atlanta, Georgia; Milwaukee, Wisconsin; and Juneau, Alaska.
For a free list of Forest Service publications, write to Superintendent of Documents, Washington, D. C. 20402. Ask for Price List 43.

NATIONAL MONUMENTS

U. S. Department of the Interior, National Park Service, Washington, D. C. 20240

NATIONAL PARKS

Write to the superintendent of any national park listed in that section of this book.
Or, write to Superintendent of Documents, Washington, D. C. 20402, and ask for Price List 35 of national parks publications.

NATIONAL PARKWAYS

U. S. Department of the Interior, National Park Service, Washington, D. C. 20240

NATIONAL RECREATION AREAS

U. S. Department of the Interior, National Park Service, Washington, D. C. 20240

NATIONAL SEASHORES

U. S. Department of the Interior, National Park Service, Washington, D. C. 20240

TENNESSEE VALLEY AUTHORITY

Information Office, Tennessee Valley Authority, Knoxville, Tennessee 37902

CANADA

The Canadian Government Travel Bureau, Ottawa, Ontario
Or, The Canadian Government Travel Bureau at any of the following U. S. offices:
263 Plaza, The Prudential Center, Boston, Massachusetts 02199
100 North LaSalle Street, Chicago, Illinois 60602
Room 1010, 617 Vine Street, Cincinnati, Ohio 45202
Inquirer Building, 250 Euclid Avenue, Cleveland, Ohio 44115
Book Building, 1257-1259 Washington Boulevard, Detroit, Michigan 48226

234 Constitution Plaza, Hartford, Connecticut 06103

Room 502, Merchants Bank Building, 11 South Meridian Street, Indianapolis, Indiana 46204

510 West Sixth Street, Los Angeles, California 90014

124 South Seventh Street, Northstar Center, Minneapolis, Minnesota 55402

680 Fifth Avenue, New York, New York 10019

Suite 305, Three Penn Center, Philadelphia, Pennsylvania 19102

1001-1003 Jenkins Arcade, Liberty and Fifth Avenues, Pittsburgh, Pennsylvania 15222

247 Midtown Plaza, Rochester, New York 14604

One Second Street, San Francisco, California 94105

304 Union Street, Seattle, Washington 98101

RCA Building, 1725 K Street, N. W., Washington, D. C. 20006

Provincial Travel Bureaus:

Newfoundland and Labrador Tourist Development Office, St. Johns, Newfoundland

Prince Edward Island Travel Bureau, Charlottetown, Prince Edward Island

Nova Scotia Travel Bureau, Department of Trade and Industry, Halifax, Nova Scotia

Tourist Development Branch, Department of Tourism and Recreation, Winnipeg, Manitoba

Tourist Development Branch, Department of Industry and Commerce, Regina, Saskatchewan

New Brunswick Travel Bureau, Fredericton, New Brunswick Tourist Branch, Department of Tourism, Fish and Game, Quebec, Province of Quebec

Department of Tourism and Information, Toronto, Ontario

Alberta Government Travel Bureau, Edmonton, Alberta

British Columbia Government Travel Bureau, Victoria, British Columbia

Department of Travel and Publicity, Whitehorse, Yukon Territory

Northwest Territories Tourist Office, 400 Laurier Avenue West, Ottawa, Ontario

Information on camping along the Trans-Canada Highway is available from any office of the Canadian Government Travel Bureau.

A SELECT BIBLIOGRAPHY OF CAMPING PUBLICATIONS

BOOKS

Advanced Camping Techniques. James Ralph Johnson. New York: David C. McKay Company, Inc.

A small volume of great value to the backpacker, whether he be traveling by foot or by canoe.

All About Camping. W. K. Merrill (U. S. Park Ranger). Harrisburg, Pennsylvania: The Stackpole Company.

The author bases the contents of this book on his 35 years of outdoor living. The book is not written to be read from cover to cover at one sitting; rather, it is a compact reference manual packed with useful information.

America Outdoors, a Newsbook Edwin A. Roberts, ed. Silver Spring, Maryland: *The National Observer.*

Written with the "nowness" of a news feature, this is a fascinating report on the nation's natural heritage.

The Ashley Book of Knots. Clifford W. Ashley. Garden City, New York: Doubleday & Company, Inc.

This book really covers knots, some 4,000 of them (including hitches, splices, etc.), and should be of interest to the camper, even though only a small number of the knots are of direct value to him.

Be Expert with Map and Compass. Bjorn Kjellstrom. La Porte, Indiana: American Orienteering Service.

A good discussion of the techniques for finding your way with map and compass.

Campground Atlas of the United States and Canada. Alpine Geographical Press, Box 2246, Station A, Champaign, Illinois 61820

Camping and Camp Cookery. Compiled by the editors of **The Hunter's Encyclopedia.** Collier Books, New York.

This is a paperback edition of a book published originally by The Stackpole Company. It deals primarily with camping and camp cookery peculiar to outdoor sportsmen.

Camping and Trailering, Eastern. American Automobile Association.

Camping and Trailering, Western. American Automobile Association.

An outstanding two-volume guide to campgrounds—both government and private—in the United States and Canada. Available only to members of AAA. For traveling campers, these two volumes are well worth the AAA membership dues.

Camping and Woodcraft. Horace Kephart. New York: The Macmillan Company.

Published originally in 1917, this is still a standard reference for many outdoorsmen. Contains information found in no other book.

Canoe Camping. Carle W. Handel. New York: Ronald Press.

This is a good guide to camping when the canoe is used as the basic means of transportation. Another, more recent book by the same author and publisher, **Canoeing,** deals more specifically with the techniques of canoeing.

Canoeing. Joseph L. Hasenfus. Washington, D. C.: American Red Cross.

An information-packed book on canoes and equipment, with primary emphasis on canoe safety.

The Complete Book of Nature Photography. Russ Kinne. New York: A. S. Barnes.

No book is really complete on the subject of nature photography, but this one comes as close as any. Clearly written, well illustrated and replete with excellent examples, this book is a must for the serious outdoor photographer.

The Complete Walker. Colin Fletcher. New York: Alfred Knopf.

This book very ably covers the subject of long-distance walking. The author knows the subject from experience. He has hiked the full length of the Pacific Crest Trail and the length of the Grand Canyon Park, among others. Several of his solo hikes have been the subjects of other readable books.

First Aid Textbook. American Red Cross. Philadelphia, Pennsylvania.

Free for the Eating. Bradford Angier. Harrisburg, Pennsylvania: Stackpole Books.

This book ably details methods of finding and preparing more than 100 wild edible plants. Wild fruits, wild greens, wild roots and tubers, wild nuts and wild plant sources for beverages are discussed in detail. This has been described as "a nature study cookbook."

Going Light with Backpack or Burro. David R. Brower, editor. San Francisco, California: Sierra Club. This is possibly the best book on the subject.

The Golden Book of Camping and Campcrafts. Gordon Lynn. New York: Golden Press.

This small, soft cover book is filled with information condensed for ready reference and quick reading. It is a good book to have along on any camping adventure.

Handbook of Knots. Raul Graumont. New York: Cornell Maritime Press.

Preparing a plastic tent for overnight use. Tent is about nine feet in circumference.

Aimed primarily toward the use of knots at sea, this book nonetheless is valuable to the person who will utilize ropes on any kind of outdoor undertaking.

Hikers' Handbook. Douglas Leechman. New York: W. W. Norton & Company.

A good reference on hiking.

Living Off the Country. Bradford Angier. Harrisburg, Pennsylvania: The Stackpole Company.

This is an excellent treatment of the subject implied by the title, with special emphasis on supplementing one's food supply or, if necessary, depending entirely on the land for natural food resources.

The Magic of Walking. Aaron Sussman and Ruth Goode. New York: Simon and Schuster.

The best book to date about walking. Every camper should read it. In two parts, the first practical and timely, the second "a peripatetic ramble through the literature of walking."

Nature's Heritage, Canada's National Parks. David M. Baird. Prentice-Hall of Canada, Ltd.

A quality book depicting, largely in outstanding photographs, the magnificent beauty of the Canadian national parks.

New Way of the Wilderness. Calvin Rutstrum. New York: The Macmillan Company.

This should be one of the first books read by any person or persons contemplating a first-time trip into the wilderness. Outfitting, methods of packing and transportation, wilderness cooking and survival are amply covered in the text.

Outdoors, USA, the Yearbook of Agriculture, 1967. United States Government Printing Office, Washington, D. C. $2.75.

The best presentation of outdoor subjects, including many of interest to campers—published to date by a department of the United States Government. Every camper should own a copy. It is a must for campers seeking outdoor enjoyment in the national forests.

Private Camp Grounds and Overnight Trailer Parks. Palos Verdes Peninsula, California.

Exclusive directory gives tent, tent-trailer, pickup camper, travel trailer, and motor home enthusiast information on location, sports and facilities available, where to write for reservations, charges, etc. Covers 5,000 private campgrounds and trailer parks. Camping Maps U.S.A., P. O. Box 2652, Palos Verdes Peninsula, California 90274.

Profitable Private Campground Construction and Operation. Rea Agnew. Palos Verdes Peninsula, California: Rajo Publications.

Rand-McNally Road Atlas. Skokie, Illinois: Rand-McNally & Company.

Rand-McNally Travel Trailer Guide. Skokie, Illinois: Rand-McNally & Company

Recreational Vehicle Park Guide. Chicago: Mobile Homes Manufacturing Association.

Scout Field Book. Boy Scouts of America. New Brunswick, New Jersey: Boy Scouts of America.

Contains an abundant amount of information of practical value to both old and young.

Sunset Western Campsite Directory. Menlo Park, California: Lane Publishing Company.

Texaco Touring Altas — United States, Canada and Mexico. Available from Texaco dealers.

Wilderness Cookery. Bradford Angier. Harrisburg, Pennsylvania: The Stackpole Company.
This book should be helpful to every wilderness camper, without exception.

Wildwood Wisdom. Ellsworth Jaeger. New York: The Macmillan Company.
A practical, comprehensive book of real value to both the experienced woodsman and the newcomer to camping.

Woodall's Trailering Parks & Campgrounds. Highland Park, Illinois: Woodall Publishing Company.

MAGAZINES

American Forests. Published monthly by American Forestry Association, 919-17th Street, N. W., Washington, D. C. 20006.

Audubon Magazine. Published monthly by National Audubon Society, 1130 Fifth Avenue, New York, New York 10028.

Better Camping. Published monthly by Kalmbach Publishing Company, 1027 North Seventh Street, Milwaukee, Wisconsin 53233

Camper Coachman. (Devoted exclusively to truck campers.) Published monthly by Griffin Publications, Inc., 10148 Riverside Drive, North Hollywood, California 91602.

Camping Guide. Published monthly by Rajo Publications, Inc., Second and Dickey Streets, Sparta, Illinois 62286.

Camping Industry, national business magazine of the camping trade. Published 6 times a year by Fishing Tackle Trade News, Inc., P. O. Box 70, Wilmette, Illinois 60091.

Camping Journal. Published monthly by Science & Mechanics Publishing Company, 229 Park Avenue South, New York, New York 10003.

Mobile Life (including **Outdoors Calling!**). Published monthly by Davis Publications, Inc., 229 Park Avenue South, New York, New York 10003.

Motor Camping. Published 7 times a year by Rajo Publications, Inc., Second and Dickey Streets, Sparta, Illinois 62286.

National Parks Magazine. Published monthly by National Park Association, 1300 New Hampshire Avenue, Washington, D. C. 20036.

Outdoor World. Published bimonthly by Preston Publications, Inc., 1645 Tullie Circle, N. E., Atlanta, Georgia 30329.

Wheels Afield. Published monthly by Petersen Publishing Company, 5916 Hollywood Boulevard, Los Angeles, California 90028.

Woodall's Trailer Travel, The Magazine of Family Camping. Published monthly by Woodall Publishing Company, 500 Hyacinth Place, Highland Park, Illinois 60035.

MISCELLANEOUS PUBLICATIONS

Campground Directories.
Available from any office of the Forest Service or from Headquarters Office, Forest Service, Department of Agriculture, Washington, D. C. 20250.

Campgrounds Along the Trans-Canada Highway. Canadian Government Travel Bureau, Ottawa, Canada.
This guidebook lists national and provincial facilities for camping and picnicking along or near the Trans-Canada Highway. Invaluable to any who plan to travel part or all of the 5000-mile transcontinental route.

Camping on the Public Lands (Information Bulletin #3).
Describes camping sites and facilities on public lands (not national forests or national parks) in the 10 western states and Alaska. Bureau of Land Management, Department of the Interior, Washington, D. C. 20240.

Canoeing on the Connecticut River.
Vermont State Board of Recreation and Water Resources Department, Montpelier, Vermont 05602.

How to Enjoy Backpacking. Gerry Cunningham. Colorado Outdoor Sports Corporation, Denver, Colorado 80217.

National Forest Ski Guide. Northern Region, U. S. Forest Service, Federal Building, Missoula, Montana 59801.

Off on the Right Foot, A Guide to Proper Wilderness Use. Distributed by The Wilderness Society, 729-15th Street, N. W., Washington, D. C. 20005.
Write for list of other publications and services.

Ontario Outdoorsman's Manual, The. Department of Lands and Forests, Toronto, Ontario. 25 cents.

Wilderness Traveler. Gerry Cunningham. Colorado Outdoor Sports Corporation, Denver, Colorado 80217.

U. S. Government publications. Available from Superintendent of Documents, U. S. Government Printing Office, Washington, D. C. 20402:

The Appalachian Trail.
A valuable leaflet. 5 cents.

Boating Regulations in the National Park System.
This U. S. Department of the Interior publication is necessary to any

camper utilizing the lakes and waterways of the national parks. 30 cents.

Camping in the National Park System.
This is a necessary publication for those who camp anywhere in the National Park System. It charts all of the camping facilities in the national parks and details their capacities, regulations, camping seasons, etc. 25 cents.

National Parks and Landmarks.
A descriptive list of areas administered by the National Park Service and related properties, some of which have been declared eligible for registration as National Historic and Natural Landmarks. 55 cents.

National Forest Wilderness and Primitive Areas.
A folder containing maps and data. 15 cents.

Official U. S. Coast Guard Recreational Boating Guide. 45 cents.

Wilderness.
Describes wilderness areas of national forests. 20 cents.

Quest for Quality.
U. S. Department of the Interior conservation yearbook, 1965. $1.

The Populations Challenge . . . What It Means to America.
U. S. Department of the Interior conservation yearbook #2. $1.25.

The Third Wave . . . America's New Conservation.
U. S. Department of the Interior conservation yearbook #3. $2.00.

Developing the Self-Guiding Trail in the National Forests. 20 cents.

Backpacking in the National Forest Wilderness . . . A Family Adventure. 15 cents.

Camping the National Forests. 20 cents.

Outdoor Recreation in the National Forests. 60 cents.

National Forest Vacations. 45 cents.

From Sea to Shining Sea, A Report on the American Environment by The President's Council on Recreation and Natural Beauty. $2.50.

The American Outdoors. 55 cents.

Reclamation's Recreational Opportunities. 15 cents.

Room to Roam.
Recreation guide to the public lands published by the Bureau of Land Management. $1.

CAMPING OUTFITTERS

Supplies and equipment for camping are available from many sources. Some campers prefer to shop both locally and through catalogs to secure the equipment and supplies best suited to their needs. Outfitting for the average camper may be done through sporting goods stores, the larger chain stores, and through large discount department stores that maintain outdoor recreation departments.

Outfitting for specialized camping often is handled by individual operators in a given area. Wilderness travel, hunting and fishing expeditions and such may call for special guides who usually serve as outfitters as well.

Following is a list of outfitters and suppliers who publish catalogs and other valuable information pieces. This listing is representative of reputable dealers who do business by mail.

Abercrombie & Fitch Company, 87-01 69th Avenue, Forest Hills, New York 11375

Alaska Sleeping Bag Company, 701 N. W. Dawson Way, Beaverton, Oregon 97005

Blacks Camping Equipment, 930 Ford Street, Ogdensburg, New York 13669

Bob Hinman, 1217 West Glen, Peoria, Illinois 61614 (hunting, fishing, shooting, camping equipment)

Camp & Trail Outfitters, 112 Chambers Street, New York, New York 10007 (lightweight camping equipment)

Camp Trails, 3920 West Clarendon Avenue, Phoenix, Arizona 85109

Colorado Outdoor Sports Corporation, P. O. Box 5544, Denver, Colorado 80217 (manufacturers and distributors of Gerry clothing, camping and outdoor equipment)

Don Gleason's Campers' Supply, 9 Pearl Street, Northampton, Massachusetts 01060

Eddue Bauer, Expedition Outfitter, 417 East Pine, Seattle, Washington 98122

Highland Outfitters, Inc., 3579 University Avenue (Eighth Street), Box 121, Riverside, California 92502

Holubar, Box 7, Boulder, Colorado 80302 (specialists in camping and mountaineering equipment)

I. Goldberg, 902 Chestnut Street, Philadelphia, Pennsylvania 19107

Kelty Pack, Incorporated, P. O. Box 3645, 1807 Victory Boulevard, Glendale, California 91201

L. L. Bean, Incorporated, Freeport, Maine 04032

Laacke & Joys, 1433 North Water Street, Milwaukee, Wisconsin 53202

Morsan, 8110 Route 17, Paramus, New Jersey 07652

Recreational Equipment, Incorporated, 1525 Eleventh Avenue, Seattle, Washington 98122

Smilie Company, 575 Howard Street, San Francisco, California 94105

the ski hut, 1615 University Avenue, Berkeley, California 94703

CAMPING ORGANIZATIONS

The National Campers and Hikers Association, 7172 Transit Road, Buffalo, New York 14221

Travel Trailer Clubs of America, 15904 Strathern, Van Nuys, California 91406

National Campground Owners Association of America, Bradford Woods, Martinsville, Indiana 46151

American Camping Association, Bradford Woods, Martinsville, Indiana 46151

Family Camping Federation, Bradford Woods, Martinsville, Indiana 46151

North American Family Campers Association, 76 State Street, Newburyport, Massachusetts 01950

Appalachian Mountain Club, 5 Joy Street, Boston, Massachusetts 02108

Appalachian Trail Conference, 1916 Sunderland Place, N. W., Washington, D. C. 20036

American Canoe Association, 15 Beacon Avenue, New Haven, Connecticut 06512

U. S. Snowmobile Association, 101 Snowmobile Drive, Eagle River, Wisconsin 54521

The Wilderness Society, 729 - 15th Street, N. W., Washington, D. C. 20005

Sierra Club, 1050 Mills Tower, San Francisco, California 90140

Outboard Boating Club of America, 307 North Michigan Avenue, Chicago, Illinois 60601

American White-Water Affiliation, 2019 Addison Street, Chicago, Illinois 60618

CAMPER'S DIGEST INDEX